DAMAGE NOTED

DATE _____

JAN 1 2 1999

Cambridge Middle East Library

Egyptian politics under Sadat

Cambridge Middle East Library

Editorial Board

EDMUND BURKE, M. D. C. GILSENAN, ALBERT HOURANI, WALID KAZZIHA, SERIF MERDIN, ROGER OWEN

Also in this series

Urban notables and Arab nationalism: the politics of Damascus, 1860–1920
PHILIP S. KHOURY

Egypt in the reign of Muhammad Ali
AFAF LUTFI AL-SAYYID MARSOT

Medicine and power in Tunisia, 1780–1900
NANCY ELIZABETH GALLAGHER

The Palestinian Liberation Organisation: people, power and politics
HELENA COBBAN

Women in nineteenth-century Egypt
JUDITH E. TUCKER

Egyptian politics under Sadat

The post-populist development of an
authoritarian–modernizing state

RAYMOND A. HINNEBUSCH Jr

ASSOCIATE PROFESSOR OF POLITICAL SCIENCE,
COLLEGE OF ST CATHERINE, ST PAUL, MINNESOTA

PROPERTY OF
CLACKAMAS COMMUNITY COLLEGE
LIBRARY
WITHDRAWN

The right of the
University of Cambridge
to print and sell
all manner of books
was granted by
Henry VIII in 1534.
The University has printed
and published continuously
since 1584.

CAMBRIDGE UNIVERSITY PRESS

CAMBRIDGE
LONDON   NEW YORK   NEW ROCHELLE
MELBOURNE   SYDNEY

Published by the Press Syndicate of the University of Cambridge
The Pitt Building, Trumpington Street, Cambridge CB2 1RP
32 East 57th Street, New York, NY 10022, USA
10 Stamford Road, Oakleigh, Melbourne 3166, Australia

© Cambridge University Press

First published 1985

Printed in Great Britain at the University Press, Cambridge

Library of Congress catalogue card number: 85-5768

British Library cataloguing in publication data

Hinnebusch, Raymond A.
Egyptian politics under Sadat: the post-populist
development of the authoritarian-modernizing
state. – (Cambridge Middle East Library)
1. Egypt – History – 1952–
1. Title
962'.054   DT107.85

ISBN 0 521 26726 9 hard covers

CE

Contents

Preface   *page* vii

1 The post-populist transformation of an authoritarian –
   modernizing state   1
2 Egypt under Nasir: authoritarian – populism   11
3 The making of Sadat's Egypt   40
4 The Presidency and the power elite   78
5 Politics among elites   122
6 The political infrastructure   158
7 Counter-elites and the pluralization of the political arena   186
8 The regime and the mass public   223
9 Public policy and the political economy of development   257
10 The post-populist reshaping of Egypt   289

Notes   304
Bibliography   309
Index   317

Preface

The idea of writing this book was first stimulated by the many profound questions raised by Anwar Sadat's 'de-Nasirization' of Egypt. Nasir's regime had long appeared to be the most successful, admired, and popularly based of the Arab world's modernizing states; yet a bare five years after his death, his successor was busily undoing much of his work. What explained this dramatic turnabout? Was it the work of a personality, internal social forces, or forced on Egypt by external constraints? How could the work of the adored charismatic leader be undone with so little popular opposition? Was the Sadat era a natural outgrowth of Nasirism or a 'counter-revolution?' As Sadat consolidated his new order, equally perplexing questions arose about the nature of the emerging system. There is little doubt that the Sadat era left a profound impact on Egypt, but there is little consensus about Sadat or his record: was he the great statesman admired in the West or the new Pharaoh who sold his nation to imperialism as his detractors in the Arab world believed? What real impact did his experiments with the structure of the state have: was 'democratization' a façade or a first step toward genuine pluralism? Was Sadat's *Infitah* a more or less suitable model of development for Egypt than Nasirite populism? Who benefited and who paid the costs of the change? A non-partisan assessment of the Sadat record seemed essential. This book resulted from the writer's effort to reach some plausible and coherent overall answer to questions like these which both made some theoretical sense and incorporated the wealth of evidence being made available in the 'political laboratory' into which Sadat's experiments turned post-October Egypt. Only the reader can judge if the effort succeeded.

I owe a debt of gratitude to the many persons and institutions that helped make this work possible. My understanding of Egyptian politics benefited immeasurably from the scholarly works of colleagues or from discussions with them about Egypt. Among those who most influenced me, I would like particularly to mention Anwar Abdel Malek, Galal Amin, Raymond Baker, Richard Dekmejian, Ali Dessouki, Fadwa al-Guindi, Heba Handoussa, Iliya Harik, Saad ad-Din Ibrahim, Robert Mabro, Clement Henry Moore, Donald Mead, Samir Radwan, Rifat Sa'id, Robert Springborg, John Waterbury and, above all, Nizeh Ayubi, whose sympathetic insight into and unfailing judgment about Egyptian politics I found the surest guide to understanding this great country. I am also indebted to Professor Ayubi, to Professor William Zartman, to Professor Richard Cottam and to Dr Roger Owen who read the manuscript and provided many suggestions invaluable for revising it. Professor Cottam first introduced me to Middle Eastern politics and from Professor Zartman I have learned much about it. Without the opportunity provided by the American University in Cairo to teach and do research in Egypt for four years, this book could not have been written. My understanding of Egypt owes much to the AUC students who participated, through research papers and class debates, in my seminars on Egypt. My thanks to the Egyptian leaders, of both government and opposition, who gave of their time to answer my many questions. The College of St Catherine, St Paul, and the Bush Foundation provided support for the writing of the book and typing of the manuscript. Many thanks are due to Virginia Pates, Harriet Kidder, Bev Amsden, Karen Philpot and Pat Traynor who did the typing. In Mrs Elizabeth Wetton of Cambridge University Press I was extremely fortunate to find a sympathetic and efficient editor to whom I am very grateful. Thanks, too, to Geraldine Stoneham, a very competent sub-editor.

The section on the NPUP in chapter 7 is a condensed version of a study originally published in *Arab Studies Quarterly*, Vol. 3, No. 4, Fall 1981. The section on elite composition in chapter 4 is an abridgment of a study in *The Journal of Middle East and South Asian Studies*, Vol. 7, No. 1, Fall, 1983, and that on the attitudes of the Egyptian bourgeoisie in chapter 8 of one in the *Middle East Journal*, Vol. 36, No. 4, Fall, 1982. The author thanks the publishers of these journals for permission to use these materials.

Last, but not least, I owe a debt of gratitude to my wife, Nancy, for her patience and encouragement in the long process of moving this study from research to publication.

St Paul, Minnesota
July 1984

Note on arabic transciption: Except where conventional usage dictates otherwise, Arabic names are rendered according to a simplified version of standard transliteration, omitting diacritical marks or notations for *alif* or for *ayn* at the beginning of a word.

Chapter 1

The post-populist transformation of an authoritarian–modernizing state

This book is a study of political change and state formation in an authoritarian–modernizing regime, post-1952 Egypt. Contemporary Egypt makes an excellent case study of the dynamics of change in such states. A group of radical army officers led by Gamal Abdul Nasir seized power 30 years ago and set out to forge an authoritarian state, impose an etatist–populist revolution from above, and challenge Western control of the Middle East. Under his successor, Anwar Sadat, this state underwent a remarkable transformation. Authoritarian rule adapted to growing pluralist pressures. Populist revolution from above gave way to social stabilization and economic liberalization. Egypt sought accommodation with and reintegration into the Western market and state system. Egypt remained an authoritarian–modernizing state, that is, a regime which used concentrated state power to direct socio-economic change and control the political arena. But it now sought modernization in concert with rather than in revolt against the dominant local and global forces. This 'post-populist' transformation was a function of more than a change in leadership or external constraints. Rather, it can best be seen as a natural evolution to which initially populist-oriented authoritarian–modernizing regimes seem vulnerable. This study is concerned, first, to explain why and how the state Nasir built was transformed under Sadat's post-populist rule. The book is also, however, a study of the consolidation of a post-colonial state, for, in spite of the discontinuities between the Nasir and Sadat eras, they can, together, also be seen as stages in a process of state formation which, by the end of the Sadat era, was probably relatively complete. From this perspective, Nasir can be seen as the founder of the modern Egyptian state who forged its master institutions, broadened its social base in a revolution from above, and carved out a place for it in the regional state system. Sadat, the second great innovator, consolidated the new state once the revolution ran out of steam by reconciling it to the dominant forces in its environment and adapting its institutions to the post-revolutionary era. Those who come after these two state-builders, including Mubarak, are likely to be mere managers of power, tinkering with, but basically concerned to preserve and defend the system. The second aim of this study is to describe and analyze this new political order in the relatively mature and stable form it had reached by the late Sadat period. In short, the book will examine both the forces and the outcome of Egypt's post-populist transformation.

Authoritarian–populism: the Nasirite starting point

Authoritarian–populism has been a characteristic phenomenon of the post-colonial world. Following the prototype pioneered by Ataturk, it came close to dominating the Middle East, reaching mature forms in Nasirite Egypt, Ba'thist Syria and Iraq, Libya, and Algeria. It was also a typical form of rule in Africa (Guinea, Tanzania) and Latin America (Mexico under Cardenas, Brazil under Vargas, Peru under Velasco). It appears to be a function of a specific stage of state formation and societal modernization. It is typically the product of nationalist reaction against imperialism, that is, of struggles for independence or against extroverted, dependent development; it is also chiefly a phenomenon of the early middle stages of development, the product of a challenge by a rising salaried middle class to traditional upper class dominance, prior to a large-scale mobilization of the masses. It may grow out of a nationalist movement, occasionally a revolution (Mexico, Algeria), frequently a military *coup* by middle-class officers. Formation of a strong independent state, free of imperialist control, is its first priority. In addition, state power is put in the service of economic modernization and a reformist redistribution of wealth and opportunity to the middle and lower classes. Public policy is highly interventionist, making frequent resort to state economic entrepreneurship and aiming to reshape and regulate the market in the interest of equity and development. But, essentially reformist, it stops short of the great transformations of communist societies. On the grounds that reform and development require strong leadership, an authoritarian regime is forged, concentrating power in the hands of politicians or military officers of middle- or lower-middle-class background, often headed by a personalistic or charismatic leader. They rule with the support of the army and through the bureaucracy and a single party/corporatist political structure. The regime seeks to forge a broad cross-class support coalition of all 'national' forces. But it typically lacks the penetrative and mobilizational capability of 'totalitarian' regimes. Overt opposition, usually strongest in the traditional and privileged sectors of society, is not tolerated, and the rudiments of liberal pluralistic politics usually repressed. Though the regime may be responsive and accessible to its constituency, its capacity to institutionalize participation is typically modest. As regards its authoritarian political structures and capabilities, the regime is distinguished from both liberal and communist states. In its middle–lower-class social base and nationalist–populist policies, it is distinguishable from traditional (e.g. Saudi Arabia) and post-populist authoritarian–conservative regimes (e.g. post-1964 Brazil).

2

The forces of post-populist transformation

Although a few authoritarian–populist regimes have proven quite durable, most seem exceptionally vulnerable to transformation. Such regimes may, as Apter argues, be essentially transitional formations, presiding over the early stages of state-building or 'the conversion from late modernization to early industrialization' (Apter 1965: 40, 379–90). Explanations for this vulnerability vary widely and every particular case is certain to have unique features, There are, however, three dominant approaches, each of which has been applied with some success to the Egyptian case. It seems most useful to review these arguments and their strengths and weaknesses through consideration of representative works on Egypt in each tradition.

Marxist approaches typically attribute change in authoritarian–populist systems to their special vulnerability to environmental forces, that is, the dominant social classes and global forces; the analyses of Nasirism by such Marxist writers as Abdel Malek (1968) and Hussein (1973) are entirely typical. Nasirism was seen as essentially a product of Egypt's national struggle against imperialism and dependency. The regime issued from a 'national democratic' revolution based on the national classes opposed to imperialist domination and to the local upper classes which collaborated with it. Etatism and populism were seen as responses to the impossibility of autonomous or equitable local capitalist development within the world capitalist system. The conditions for the brief success of the Nasirite revolt against the dominant world order were seen as the weakening of imperialism and the emergence of a competing socialist bloc. But, owing to its petit bourgeois leadership, the Nasir regime tried to stay above and balance between the bourgeoisie and the working classes, capitalism and socialism. Because it therefore lacked a definite social base and international alignment, it was inherently unstable. Unable or unwilling to pursue an authentic socialist course which would mobilize the masses and destroy the socio-economic dominance of the bourgeoisie, it was extremely vulnerable to an eventual shift in the balance of political power to the right. Under these conditions, to the extent it pushed development ahead, it created or strengthened the very forces which would be its undoing. Not only did the regime permit the persistence of a private sector, but it fostered the growth of a large bureaucratic 'state bourgeoisie.' Development advanced, but the corruption of the state sector and the high consumption of the bourgeoisie undermined etatist capital accumulation while permitting a covert private accumulation. In consequence, there was a growing contradiction between the interest of the bourgeoisie in a return to a capitalist model providing security and outlets for its wealth and the populist course favored by the leader and his mass constituency. A shift in the regional power of global forces tipped the internal balance of power toward the right. The 1967 Israeli strike at Egypt which threw the Nasirite

3

system into crisis, the impotence of the Soviet Union to resolve the crisis and the growing promise that only American power and petro-capitalism could, prepared the way once Nasir died for an embourgeoised ruling elite to shift course and seek accommodation with these forces.

The strength of Marxist analysis lies in its identification of the basic issues, forces and conflicts on which politics is ultimately based and change propelled: the big issues of class interest, the dominance of imperialism over the periphery, the conflict over the proper model of development. Its weakness is its tendency to consider political institutions, leadership and ideologies as epiphenomenal. Thus, it tends to neglect the fact that, at times, the state may be more than an instrument of class repression or an arena of conflict, and that it may achieve considerable autonomy of the socio-economic 'infrastructure.' In this capacity, the state may play a positive role, reconciling basic conflicts or mobilizing common action for shared interests, or, in bad times, making hard but necessary choices between equally undesirable alternatives. In consequence, Marxist theory pays little attention to the requisites of stability and effectiveness of a political system, to the institutional and leadership variables which determine whether it can master environmental forces and conflicts or is mastered by them. No understanding of why systems change can neglect the problem of systemic capabilities, and for this one must turn to other traditions of analysis.

Functionalist approaches attribute the instability of authoritarian–populist regimes to their failure to develop sufficiently differentiated, hence, effective, political institutions, particularly 'input infrastructures.' This makes them doubly vulnerable: on the one hand, they are susceptible to infection by traditional political culture which may abort the modernization effort; on the other hand, if modernization proceeds, they may be unable to absorb the participatory demands of new social forces they create. Several studies have applied essentially functionalist institutional analysis to Egypt, some stressing the first vulnerability, others the second.

Work published in the fifties and sixties by writers such as Vatikiotis (1961), Halpern (1963) and Berger (1962) typified a functionalist view which stressed the modernizing successes of the regime. The Nasirist commitment to state formation and modernization was accepted and seen as a function of the modernizing orientation of the salaried 'new middle class.' Authoritarian rule was seen as appropriate for a period of modernizing revolution from above. The army, modernizing and reformist in orientation, and the only truly national institution, provided the essential coercive base needed to maintain stability and override vested traditional interests. The bureaucracy, recruited on achievement grounds, carried out policy, imposing modernizing reforms, even at the traditional base of society. Yet authoritarian rule had certain costs which grew as modernization proceeded. Its stress on control tended to stifle independent

4

initiative and autonomy needed in a complex society, and it lacked political institutions to absorb the participatory demands of the modern social forces it was creating. As society became more complex, and participatory demands mounted, the regime would have to develop political institutions appropriate to the mobilization and pluralization of its social environment, or resort to costly repression certain to end in 'praetorianism.' Generally, these writers, with the Turkish precedent in mind, envisioned a gradual liberal transformation of the system as modernization advanced.

In the late sixties and seventies there appeared another breed of functionalist work by writers such as Springborg (1975), Moore (1974, 1980) and Akhavi (1975) which interpreted the Egyptian regime as having succumbed not to pluralization, but to retraditionalization. In these 'Neo-Patrimonial' interpretations, the elite was seen as chiefly engrossed in corruption and personal rivalries; national policy-making was stifled by personalistic authoritarian rule; institutions, paralyzed and fragmented by clientalism, were incapable of mobilizing the masses or implementing policy. The encroachment of this semi-traditional ineffective state on the 'autonomy' of the economic sphere, that is, its intervention in the market for political ends, only undermined economic rationality at the expense of development. The root cause of the reversion to traditionalism was seen as the failure to build political institutions, that is, either to share power in constitutional structures or develop the ideology and organization of totalitarian regimes. Lacking such institutions, the regime was vulnerable to traditional resurgence. It could not effectively mobilize the masses out of traditional culture; the lack of participatory rights and institutions fostered the resort to personalistic and clientalistic means of interest articulation and left the system without any check to patrimonialism at the top. The failure to build institutions was largely attributed to persistent traditional culture: the inherited authoritarianism and personalism of the top elite deterred it from building institutions and the lack of habits of autonomous political association of the populace gave it no incentive to. As such, there was no 'crisis of participation' in Egypt; political culture was an intervening variable which diluted the positive relation between social change and political pluralization anticipated by earlier functionalists. The authoritarian regime could thus persist indefinitely albeit at growing cost in system capabilities.

The strength of the functionalist approach is its institutional analysis of how political structures and culture shape the course of political conflict and the capacity of a regime to modernize. Despite their differences, functionalists agree on one major insight, namely that the Nasir regime lacked strong political institutions and hence was vulnerable to either praetorianism and instability or patrimonialism and stagnation. But functionalist analyses suffer from a major weakness in conceptualizing system change. They view it as chiefly the product of struggle between cultural forces of 'modernity' and 'tradition' to the neglect of the concrete conflicts of classes and global forces over Egypt's fate which provided the ultimate motor of change. Hence, they seem to miss much of what politics is about in contemporary Egypt. Typically, authoritarianism is viewed as an artifact of culture, to the neglect of its function as an instrument of class rule. The traditionalization of the regime is explained as a mere resurgence of inherited political culture rather than as an expression of conservative class interests. Functionalists generally do not distinguish between Nasir's populist authoritarianism and Sadat's post-populist variety because they fail to perceive the big differences between the social and global forces served by authoritarian power in the two regimes.

A third 'elitist' approach, inspired by writers such as Weber (1964), Mosca (1939) and Michels (1962), locates the forces of system change in changes in the composition and orientation of elites and the bases of their legitimacy. It has proven a congenial vehicle for the analysis of Egyptian politics in the hands of several writers. Dekmejian (1971) used Weber's notion of charismatic leadership in a convincing explanation of the rise and consolidation of Nasir's regime. But Weberian theory can also throw light on its post-populist transformation. Weber notes the special vulnerability of charismatic authority in its dependence on continued heroic performance by the leader. He also suggests that the charismatic legitimacy with which an authoritarian–populist regime is initially charged, must, as it encounters and adjusts to a recalcitrant reality, be either exhausted or 'routinized' in new institutions. Dekmejian argued that Nasir did embody his personal legitimacy in some parts of the political system, notably the Presidency, but less in others. But other writers (Entelis 1974) stress Nasir's failure to attach his legitimacy to participatory institutions or significantly to transform popular values. The 1967 defeat may, moreover, have partly reversed earlier levels of legitimation.

In the post–charismatic phase, in any case, elite orientation undergoes a major change: the earlier desire radically to transform society is replaced by efforts to stabilize the new socio-political order. This process seems to parallel the consolidation of a ruling class in Mosca and the elite 'embourgeoisement' observed by Michels, that is, the elite's use of power to acquire wealth, status and a stake in the status quo. But the political order in this phase of consolidation may, Weber suggests, take one of two forms. If a rationalizing ideology is sufficiently routinized, and if there is a balance between the ruler and other elites, legal–rational institutions may emerge; the lack of any routinization could easily result in system collapse, but a less intense or partial routinization and a lack of intra-elite balance would seem to open the way to a 'retraditionalization' of the regime, that is, a partial reversion to patrimonialism. Whether in the form of legal–rational development or reversion to 'traditional pluralism,' other elites will seek to curb the exceptional powers permitted the ruler in the period of charisma and radical change.

One strength of this approach is that it possesses the sensitivity to the *purposes* to which power is put which functionalism lacks, that is, change (charisma) or system-maintenance (legal–rational or traditional authority.) This is, of course, critical for distinguishing between regimes like Nasir's and Sadat's which, though structurally similar, are very different in orientation. It also provides a theory of system change at the elite level, that is, changes in elite ideology or in the balance of intra-elite power. But, like functionalist theory, it remains too abstract and devoid of social content to stand by itself. Changes in elite ideology and intra-elite power cannot be understood apart from social and global forces. Thus, a liberal transformation of an authoritarian regime could not be understood purely as a product of elite values and clearly depends on a certain development of class forces. Nor could the post-populist emergence of a conservative–authoritarian regime be understood as a mere reversion to traditional practices or a conservatization of ideology without consideration of the class and global forces it served.

The outcome of system transformation

As the preceding review suggests, the outcome of post-populist transformation is problematic. To be sure, except for rare totalitarian transformations (Cuba), the post-populist regime almost invariably presides over an end to the state's attempt radically to reshape society from above, a withdrawal from entrepreneurial and redistributory interventionism. Correspondingly, it permits a reassertion of the autonomy of society; economic liberalization, a revitalization of private capitalism, and, in consequence, a certain reintegration into the world capitalist system is typical. There may paradoxically also be a resurgence of traditional culture. But this retrenchment of the state is, nevertheless, compatible with several different kinds of socio-political formation. Extrapolating from the main approaches hitherto reviewed, it is possible to adumbrate three conceptual models which suggest possible alternative outcomes of the transformation process in Egypt. To the extent this process is still on-going, these models could be seen as representing simultaneously operative tendencies pulling the system in different directions.

1. *Authoritarian–conservatism*: In this model, the authoritarian state persists, but instead of seeking to propel social change, it uses its power to protect the status quo and the restoration of capitalism. In such an authoritarian–conservative state, the executive typically continues to dominate, but is transformed from charismatic leadership to Presidential Monarchy; bureaucratic rule is combined with limited pluralism for the regime's constituency and demobilization of the masses; policy is likely to be shaped by a conflict of technocratic rationalism and a resurgent patri-

7

monialism. Authoritarian–conservatism appears possible, however, in two quite distinct scenarios which make for rather different kinds of regimes.

(a) One scenario, which could be called *Neo-Patrimonial*, results when the charismatic-modernizing impulse is exhausted before it can be routinized or transform society and culture; hence, post-populist transformation comes prior to a significant mobilization and pluralization of mass society. In such an environment, the political system is inevitably retraditionalized. The legitimation of authority takes essentially traditional forms. As the concentrated energy at the center is dissipated, the ruler's control over the elite relaxes, producing a kind of uninstitutionalized traditional pluralism in which segments of the elite 'appropriate the means of administration.' State control over society contracts, allowing traditional elites to recover some of their old power. The mass public, passive and still encapsulated in traditional society, represents little challenge to the regime. Economic liberalization is likely to result in a 'dual' society, that is, islands of modern capitalism reintegrated into the world market in a persistent sea of pre-capitalist formations. This scenario is, of course, chiefly inspired by the 'Neo-Patrimonial' approach, but is also compatible with the post–charismatic retraditionalization of leadership in the Weberian system.

(b) The second scenario, which may be called *authoritarian–repressive* is chiefly Marxist in inspiration. In this case, it is assumed that modernization, class differentiation and mobilization are much more advanced. An expanding bourgeoisie, in control of the means of production and administration (whether private or public), long denied political power by the charismatic leader, finally recaptures state power. On the one hand, its representatives are incorporated into the ruling class; on the other, the ruling elite is itself embourgeoised. Once in a position to decide, the bourgeoisie imposes its preferred course, economic liberalization and a global Westward realignment. Growing class inequality, foreign cultural penetration and dependency mount, and with them class conflict between the bourgeoisie and the relatively highly mobilized opposition. While the bourgeoisie would prefer a liberal course, it accepts that the authoritarian state must be maintained to repress this challenge and exclude the masses from political power. Thus, in this case, authoritarianism, far from being an artifact of an unmobilized society, results from an increasingly mobilized and divided one.

2. The second possible major outcome is a movement of the political system in a liberal direction, that is, toward the limited state and pluralistic politics. In the Egyptian case, of course, it is clear that such movement is at best partial. Hence, the appropriate model, which might be called *pregnant pluralism*, conceptualizes a gradual covert liberal transformation of the system under rising pluralist pressures. This scenario assumes that modernization

advanced under populism and continues into the post-populist phase. As such, there is a proliferation of plural social forces and differentiated elites, whose desires for functional autonomy and power-sharing cannot readily be accommodated by authoritarianism. Economic liberalization, fueling the growth of societal power centers independent of the state, deepens the social base of pluralism. But class conflict must not be too intense to be contained by a liberal state. For this reason, the middle stages of development, when a middle class big enough to support liberalism has developed but before substantial mass mobilization, seem to provide the most favorable conditions for a liberal experiment. Where, as in Egypt, there is a long history of centralized bureaucratic and personal rule, institutional tradition is likely to be hostile to pluralization; but the high costs in repression, praetorianism and declining system capabilities as society becomes more mobilized and complex, force some institutional adaptation to a changing environment. The role of leadership in steering this adaptation is likely to be decisive. In Weber's view, the desire of other elites to check the arbitrary power permitted the ruler in the charismatic-revolutionary phase, produces, in the post-charismatic phase, either a covert traditional pluralism or movement toward a legal–rational state. The success of the liberal scenario assumes, therefore, that a strong legal–rational value orientation develops in the elite to ensure the institutionalization of pluralism and that the leadership enjoys the legitimacy needed to steer a liberal system transformation without fear of regime collapse. This scenario is inspired chiefly by classical functionalist theory at the environmental level, complemented by Weberian leadership concepts.

The strategy and sources of analysis

The various theoretical approaches hitherto considered are not necessarily incompatible. All agree that authoritarian–populist regimes are transitional formations vulnerable to collapse or transformation. They differ in the identification of the forces and outcome of change. But because each approach basically focuses on a different level of analysis – environment, political structure and elite orientation – they can, to an extent, be combined. The strategy of analysis followed in the study attempts to do this.

Following the Marxist lead, the study will take environmental pressures as the ultimate stimulus of system change, namely, the impact of global forces in Egypt, changes in the internal balance of class power and contradictions between class interests over Egypt's proper national and socio-economic course. Following the functionalist argument, however, the study will examine the effect of the political structures, that is, their capacity to cope with these pressures and conflicts and the way they distribute political power between

forces differing over ways to respond to them. But, also following the functionalist lead, the study will assess changes in the political system itself under
pressure of change in its environment or in the elite which presides over it.
Finally, following the suggestions of elite theorists, elites, those whose decisions
are the most immediate determinants of system change, will be studied. Their
changing value orientations and social composition will be critical for determining the strategies adopted for coping with environmental pressures. It is
assumed that elite change will itself be in part a result of environmental
pressures, but will nevertheless be shaped by a process of intra-elite conflict. In
a leader-dominant system such as Egypt, it is expected that the values and
personality of the ruler and the struggle between him and his rivals will be
decisive factors at the elite level.

The analysis will develop in the following order. The Nasir regime, its
vulnerabilities and the environmental pressures on it, the starting point of
system change, will be analyzed in chapter 2. Chapter 3 explains system change
as it unfolded under Sadat as an outcome of his effort to cope with environmental exigencies and defeat rivals. Subsequent chapters analyze the outcome
of system change, that is, the changes in the structure of power, elite composition and ideology, intra-elite politics, alterations in the political infrastructure, mass and counter-elite politics and the transformation of public
policy. The last chapter summarizes the argument in the light of the theoretical
framework.

The analysis relies on a combination of secondary and primary sources and
field research. It builds on the available scholarly literature on the Nasir regime
and the few secondary sources on the Sadat period. It makes extensive use of the
Egyptian and Western press. The writer's four years of teaching at the
American University in Cairo provided the opportunity for discussions with
Egyptian intellectuals, interviews with regime and opposition elites, some
semi-systematic surveys of public opinion and work with Egyptian students on
research projects relevant to political change in Egypt.

Chapter 2

Egypt under Nasir: authoritarian–populism

No understanding of Sadat's Egypt can dispense with an analysis of the rise and decline of the Nasir regime because Sadatism was both an out-growth of and a reaction against Nasirism. This chapter will examine both the enduring structures which Nasir created and passed on to his successor and the failures and liabilities which precipitated a successful reaction against his policies.

The rise of the Nasirite state

The roots of Nasirism: imperialism and underdevelopment

The Egyptian revolution of 1952 was a classic case of a Third World movement against imperialism and the delayed dependent development which resulted from it. In nearly 100 years of domination, Western imperialism shaped Egypt to suit its own needs, turning the country into a plantation for Western industry and its landed upper class into *compradors* with a stake in the extroverted economy. Egypt's agriculture developed but her peasants did not, and land concentration and population growth produced a growing and impoverished landless class. Industrial development was stunted and delayed while business and finance fell into the hands of foreigners. The introduction of Western education and bureaucracy generated an Egyptian 'new middle class,' but foreign control of the stunted modern sector limited its opportunities and frustrated its aspirations. A lumpenproletariat swelled a bloated and unproductive tertiary sector. As population growth, urbanization and education exceeded the absorptive capacity of a retarded economy, unemployment reached crisis proportions and was joined in the forties by a great inflation (Berque 1972; Hussein 1973: 15–61). While a tiny upper class lived a life of luxury, the mass standard of living fell continuously, per capita income dropping almost 50% in the first half of the twentieth century (Berque 1972: 620).

Simultaneously, a political crisis engulfed Egypt. The weak, narrow-based monarchy proved incapable of coping with the rising social discontent. A protracted nationalist struggle kept Egypt in ferment while the failure of established leaders to dislodge the imperialist presence gradually robbed them of legitimacy in the eyes of the masses. Middle class 'counter-elites' – the Muslim Brotherhood, radical nationalists, secular leftists – entered the political arena demanding greater nationalist militancy and a redistribution of wealth and power. The failure of the regime to respond gradually alienated the middle class, and it mobilized outside and against the political system; by the late forties anti-regime violence was making Egypt ungovernable. Yet counter-elites, divided among themselves, were unable to fill the growing political vacuum (Berque 1972: 652–74; Vatikiotis 1969: 315–73)

This combined social and national crisis precipitated the emergence of an anti-regime movement among middle-class army officers. Influenced by the middle-class opposition, some of them not far removed from the impoverished village or petty officialdom, and preoccupied with the humiliations of foreign control over Egypt, these officers soon developed into a force with the will and capacity to topple the *ancien régime* and break the impasse into which the country had fallen. The disaster of the Palestine war, which brutally exposed the bankruptcy of the establishment, made them determined to act, and on 23 July 1952, the Egyptian army overthrew the monarchy in a *coup d'etat*. The 'Free Officers' wanted to break the domination of imperialism, the foreign minorities and the landed upper class over the country, open up opportunities for the Egyptian middle class, do something for the peasants and create a strong modernized Egypt. They were convinced that they were the only untarnished or competent force in the political arena which could lead this project of national renaissance and social reform. The officers were led by a man who could fairly be considered the founder of the modern Egyptian state, Gamal Abdul Nasir (Stephens 1974: 30–108; Vatikiotis 1978: 47–124).

Establishment of an authoritarian regime: military rule, charismatic leadership

The collapse of the monarchy set off a power struggle in which various political forces bid for a share of power. The leaders of Egypt's veteran nationalist party, the Wafd, and those of various radical middle-class movements, by virtue of their links to the Free Officers and their blueprints for radical change, all made a claim. The Free Officers soon decided, however, not to share power and to establish an authoritarian regime. They clearly had a well-developed 'will to power.' The bureaucratic habits of command typical of the professional officer reinforced it, while the origins of the officer movement in a small personally knit 'in-group,' inhibited power sharing with 'outsiders.' Equally important, they feared that sharing power would jeopardize the radical but orderly reforms they envisioned. The right opposed any change and the left, in the officers' view, wanted too much. The Muslim Brothers' fundamentalism threatened their modernizing ambitions. The masses, they believed, were either too imbued with particularism, too deferent to traditional leaders, or too susceptible to extremist appeals to participate politically except under strong tutelage. To surrender their newly won power in the name of democracy threatened to return Egypt to the stalemate and disorder of the pre-*coup* period and sacrifice their dream of a strong new state. In their view, democracy was simply no important priority: the necessary national projects had long been delineated; what was needed was the discipline and will to carry them out and this they intended to supply.

Military rule was not, however, established without a struggle, first in the streets and, when several Free Officers joined the civilian opposition, inside the army as well. The decisive factor in the conflict was Nasir's forceful leadership inside Free Officer councils, his ability to keep the core of the officer movement together and through it control of the army. Step by step all dissident political forces were repressed: bourgeois political parties disbanded, leftwing workers smashed and, finally, the Muslim Brotherhood crippled. Freedom of expression and activity was curbed, overt opposition driven underground. Officers who had put their connections to political forces above loyalty to the victorious Free Officers were purged and cohesion among the new leadership re-established. But this was achieved at the cost of alienating much of the politically active population; if the new regime was to survive it had to break out of this political isolation and forge a base of popular support (Baker 1978: 25–84; Stephens 1974: 109–39).

In fact, the Free Officers were remarkably successful in doing this. The decisive factor in this achievement was Nasir's growing stature as a charismatic leader, that is, his success in forging a psychological bond with the masses, who came to accept him as a national and popular hero who could do great things and be trusted with their confidence. The objective conditions were right for the emergence of a charismatic nationalist leader; Egypt was in a time of troubles, traditional identities breaking down, the people yearning for a hero–savior and increasingly susceptible to nationalist mobilization. The weakened grip of Western imperialism over the Middle East was vulnerable to nationalist challenge. Nasir seemed to be the right man at the right time. He was the first authentic Egyptian to rule Egypt in a thousand years; a son of the village, he spoke the language and lived the life style of the common people. His populist policies, notably the 1952 land reform, seemed to show that, in contrast to his predecessors, he cared for them. Above all, however, in the string of nationalist victories he won over the hitherto all-powerful foreigner, he transformed Egypt from a despised dependency into a major international actor, courted by East and West. The expulsion of the British presence after almost a century of occupation, the thwarting of the Western security pacts and arms embargo, the nationalization of the Suez Canal and the successful defiance of the joint British–French–Israeli attack, the growing acclaim for Nasir throughout the Arab world, crowned by the union with Syria in 1958, all helped awaken a nationalist revival in the people and restored to Egypt a sense of worth and dignity so long lacking. To Nasir went all the legitimacy which traditionally accrues to leaders victorious over the foreign enemy. Joined to the traditional submission of a people conditioned by hydraulic culture,[1] this was enough to rally the nation behind the regime. Traditional elites, long discredited, and middle-class rivals, still too narrowly based or divided, offered no credible alternative and lost much of their followings to Nasir. By contrast, the Free Officers formed a cohesive team entrenched at the levers of a growing security apparatus and a state machine habituated to obey whoever occupied its command posts. Charisma and coercion combined to consolidate a remarkably stable regime possessing a tremendous fund of political capital. Thus Nasir won a free hand to transform Egypt from above (Dekmejian 1971: 2–54). But this achievement had its hidden costs. The mistrust engendered in the struggle with civilian rivals, the ease of the officers' victory, and the popular mandate they rightfully believed they had been given, reinforced their authoritarian biases and led them to neglect the problem of creating political institutions.

Regime ideology

The Free Officers lacked a fixed ideological doctrine, but they did possess a set of shared beliefs, goals and methods and a serious commitment to fundamental change in Egypt which shaped their policies. The core of the Nasirist program was, above all, nationalism; the new leaders sought to create a strong, modernized Egyptian state. Nationalism in foreign policy translated into a drive to end Egypt's political and economic subordination to the West, to restore its Arab–Islamic identity diluted by a century of Westernization and to replace Western imperialism with Egyptian leadership of a non-aligned Arab world. Because strength and independence were impossible while Egypt remained backward, nationalism translated internally into a crash modernization drive.

The Nasirist modernization strategy was essentially a populist form of etatism. Etatism assumed a powerful state was needed to lead modernization and sought to fashion a mixed economy under state tutelage. As opposed to communism, a private sector entitled to a fair profit was to be preserved, provided it served national development. As opposed to capitalism, the state would plan, stimulate and direct development; in time it directly assumed functions of investment and production through a large public sector. On the political level, etatism translated into authoritarian–corporatism. All 'national' classes and groups, from workers and peasants to national capitalists, excluding only reactionary and foreign-linked elements, were embraced through a single political organization in an 'alliance of popular working forces.' The state, of and for the whole people, defined, on the basis of impartial expertise, a rational public interest to which all lesser interests were expected to defer. Policy would be shaped and directed from above and the state would peacefully arbitrate differences between classes and groups to the exclusion of class conflict or pluralistic group competition. This orientation expressed a strong technocratic elitism, but it was balanced by an equally strong populism. Because a united national community was impossible in a society divided by great inequalities of wealth and opportunity, Nasirism believed the state had to ensure that the fruits and burdens of development were equitably distributed and that the haves did not exploit the have-nots. Classes and differential remuneration could not be eliminated but state intervention attempted to narrow such social gaps.

This national etatism was an entirely natural expression of the origins and situation of the new regime. Its nationalism expressed the preoccupations of a movement born of the crisis of decolonization and nation-building. Its search for a third way, avoiding alignment with communism or capitalism, expressed the world-view of middle-class nationalists determined on independence in the global arena and national unity internally (Abdel Malek 1968: 190–371; Dekmejian 1971: 133–43; Heaphy 1965; Vatikiotis 1978: 52–64).

An authoritarian–bureaucratic state

Nasir's Egypt rested on more than coercion and charismatic legitimacy; between leader and mass the new regime shaped a huge authoritarian–bureaucratic state. At its apex was a powerful Presidency which was, by virtue of the personal stature of its incumbent and the nearly unlimited authority with which he endowed it, not only the steering mechanism, but, to a great extent, the motor of the new state. Nasir both dominated and energized the system. A man of great intensity, drive, endurance and no small intellectual capacity, he made the Presidency an activist, interventionist, innovating force in the service of his vision of the common good. Uncorruptible, with a strong sense of personal honor and integrity, and a powerful identification with the common people, and ever watchful of those around and below him, he made it the main source of accountability in the system, too. Initiative and responsibility were thus highly concentrated in the Presidency at the expense of other political institutions.

Around Nasir was a core elite whose members served as vice presidents, premiers or in strategic ministerial or party posts. Except for a handful of outstanding civilians, this group was exclusively military, recruited and replenished from the Free Officer movement. An outer circle of the elite was made up of relatively apolitical civilian professionals and technocrats who held less politically crucial ministries and another stratum of officers appointed as sub-ministers and to the governorships, crucial political-security links between center and periphery. The military, scattered across the heights of the state apparatus, functioned as a relatively cohesive political cadre which decided and enforced the regime's policies; the civilian experts provided them with the

technical competence needed to do the job. This new team at the top represented a major social transformation in the composition of the elite from the
upper-class King's men and landlord-lawyers of the old regime. The Free
Officers were of modest social background, chiefly from a salaried middle class
not far removed from the village and, in their nativist and populist outlook,
linked to the masses. Many developed leadership and organizational skills, and
some, notably the military engineers, technical competence. For a while at
least, they possessed the discipline, determination and coercive resources to
impart new movement to a stalemated society, to impose reform against
resistance from vested interests and to establish a new order out of socio-political breakdown. The civilian technocrats and professionals were recruited
chiefly from upper- and middle-class families, but rose to the top not, as before,
through wealth and family name, but through the bureaucracy and the universities on the basis of education, skills, experience or the patronage of a Free
Officer. They made up a new technocratic breed skilled in the tasks of
modernization. This military–technocratic team was neither unsuited for or
atypical of a country undergoing a phase of state-building and forced modernization from above. But, habituated to an administrative style and preoccupied
with control, it proved better at the concentration of power than the motivation
and mobilization of men needed to set development going from below as well as
above (Ayubi 1980: 343–60; Berger 1962: 377–88; Binder 1965; Dekmejian
1971: 167–224; Dekmejian 1975: 185–212).

Participation in the policy process was, in this authoritarian–bureaucratic
state, barely institutionalized, largely taking the form of intra-elite bureaucratic
and personal rivalries. Nasir dominated the process. His office, dynamism and
popular stature raised him above other elites; convinced by his successes that he
alone had the answers to Egypt's problems, and distrustful of those around him,
he found it hard to delegate or share power. To be sure, until the mid-sixties, the
Free Officer core functioned as a collegial leadership. Nasir had to mobilize
majority support to purge opponents and could be defied. Although he was not
formally accountable to them, the Free Officers remained indispensable to his
rule and he could not, without great risk, go beyond the group consensus when
one existed. But the elite was often divided on both personal and ideological
grounds. Some officers were identified with conservative Islamic orientations
(Kemal ad-Din Hussein), some with more technocratic stances (Abd al-Latif
Baghdadi), others with a leftwing populist view (Ali Sabri, Kemal ad-Din
Rifa'at). There were differences between Egypt-first and Pan-Arab orientations. There were conflicts over bureaucratic jurisdictions such as the attempt of
the other senior Free Officers to contain Marshal Amer's efforts to turn the
army into a personal fiefdom and expand his influence into civilian domains. At
the level of the cabinet and its committees, 'bureaucratic politics' went on
between factions over budgets, jurisdictions and programs. Proposals were

sponsored or solicited by segments of the military leadership or pushed by bureaucratic 'entrepreneurs' on the basis of expertise. Because of military in-groupism and a certain ideological distrust on the part of the Free Officers of higher-class civilian technocrats, a latent civil–military cleavage was characteristic of the whole era; frequently, this took the form of conflict between a statist or populist initiative by military-politicians and the more conservative or cautious recommendations of technocrats. In all these conflicts Nasir usually had the last and frequently the first word. He often took the initiative in policy innovation and if he wanted his way badly enough it was unlikely an elite consensus would form against him. He might use or stimulate elite rivalries to impose his view, steer a centrist course between divergent orientations, or tip the balance between them. And the steady attrition of senior Free Officers who opposed his or the majority view in favour of less senior ones, gradually increased Nasir's relative stature. Policy-making typically took place in small intra-elite arenas such as the Free Officers' inner councils or the cabinet, though occasionally parliament, the press, or interest groups were permitted some input. When the decision unit so widened, middle or sub-elite interests might be considered in policy-making. But generally elites neither possessed nor spoke for wider popular constituencies, and institutional mechanisms for aggregating the views of the broader public upward were lacking. The sole input from the mass public seems to have been an informal, indirect one through the person of the President who kept his finger on the pulse of public opinion. Through inclination or the desire to protect his legitimacy, or to mobilize mass support against elite resistance to his policies, Nasir periodically intervened in the intra-elite political process in the name of popular interests. Both the centralization and personalization of power in Nasir's hands were system assets in carrying out major, rapid change. But once the stabilization and fine-tuning of a new order became the first priority, they proved costly. Because decisions often turned on informal power struggles at the top or access to the President, both technical rationality and the views of affected interests were sometimes ignored, resulting in policies ill-conceived or difficult to implement in the face of resistance (Ayubi 1980: 391–5, 469–72, Dekmejian 1975: 180–4; Moore 1980; Vatikiotis 1978: 190–4, 266–309).

The top elite rested on a vast bureaucratic sub-structure made up of the ministerial bureaucracy, the armed forces, and a huge public sector. The men who managed these organizations – top bureaucrats, state managers, army commanders – can be considered a 'middle elite.' Part of this middle elite carried over from the old regime, but the new rulers also cultivated a new breed of upper-middle-class technocrats in an effort to infuse their base with a more modernizing, dynamic leadership. Moreover, educational and bureaucratic expansion opened new paths of opportunity for the middle and even lower middle class to move upward, somewhat democratizing recruitment (Ayubi

1980: 360–5). The new regime aimed to enhance the efficiency and expand the functions of its bureaucracy. It tried to sweep out the nepotism, corruption and lethargy typical of the old regime. It also forged a multitude of functional ministries and public organizations entrusted with the growing new tasks the state was assuming: new Ministries of Planning, Land Reform, Industry, High Dam, etc., sprang up beside their traditional counterparts. Bureaucratic penetration of the peripheries proceeded as a multitude of new local officials spearheaded the spread of public services and the 'bureaucratic mobilization' of the countryside.

The expansion of the bureaucracy, however, ran well ahead of its rationalization and it soon became as much an obstacle to development as an instrument of it. Many segments of the state machine proved highly susceptible to all the typical bureaucratic pathologies – inefficiency, ineffectiveness and an unresponsiveness to constituents. Many officials lacked a work ethic or a sense of duty. Many sought a government job only for lack of an alternative in an underdeveloped society or to escape manual labor or the backwardness of the village. The low salaries in the public service did nothing to substitute for their lack of motivation, especially as the bureaucracy was used to absorb excess labor, and pay levels stagnated. Some officials, possessing some literacy and authority, became, in dealing with an illiterate, powerless public, overbearing or exploitative. The bureaucracy also suffered from overcentralization and excessive red tape which undermined efficiency and adaptability at lower levels. The political elite could not assume subordinates shared regime goals since the class interests of senior bureaucrats were sometimes at odds with them, and because the particularist demands of traditional culture or the personal interests of underpaid officials often clashed with bureaucratic rationality and the public interest; hence elites were loath to thrust authority on those below them and those below were unaccustomed to accept responsibility. Finally, bureaucrats, suited at their best to carrying out technical tasks and administering rules, proved far less capable of generating the motivation and changing attitudes which were required to carry out the social change they were entrusted with. Yet, in the implementation of many regime programs, from land reform to the extension of social services into mass society, there was no substitute for the bureaucracy. And in some, at least, of these tasks, such as land reform, the management of the Suez Canal, and the building of the High Dam, it proved relatively effective and efficient (Ayubi 1980: 175–327; Baker 1978: 70–87; Harik 1972).

Though the Nasir regime was essentially personalistic and bureaucratic it could not wholly dispense with a political infrastructure if it was to control opposition, maintain a popular base, and provide some channel of elite–mass linkage. Several such structures were created, but they never achieved much autonomy of the government, or, given its ability to change the rules of political participation at will, a significant level of institutionalization.

Parliament was clearly overshadowed by the executive. The cabinet was responsible to the President, not parliament. He could legislate by decree, dissolve parliament at will and screen all candidates for election to it. Thus parliament could not function as an elite-accountability mechanism. Nor was it developed into a channel of elite recruitment or interest aggregation. It was little more than an access channel and a sounding board maintained, at regime sufferance, for the more active parts of its constituency. Judging by the backgrounds of deputies, this was basically the professional and middle land-owning classes, although in the sixties democratization measures added worker and peasant contingents to parliament (Binder 1978: 55; Dekmejian 1971: 154–5; Wheelock 1975: 62–9).

The regime built a single party, named after 1962 the Arab Socialist Union (ASU), tying it to society through a pyramid of soviet-like assemblies and committees. But, like parliament, the party never developed much autonomy or assumed many real functions. It never became an elite recruitment mechanism; indeed, deficient in voluntary activists, nominally enrolling virtually the whole population regardless of ideological commitment and hence infiltrated by many elements unsympathetic to the regime, it could hardly have been allowed to serve as a recruitment pool. On the contrary, its leaders were largely imposed from above: at the top, Free Officers dominated, 'bureaucrats on loan' were appointed to middle-rank positions, while at the base the existent local power structure was coopted, that is, local officials or notables who, in return for support, were allowed to retain local power. Given the imposition of leaders from above, the party was crippled as a mechanism of elite accountability. It was not even effective as a channel for the aggregation of established interests; the various groups incorporated into it were not allowed to organize as separate factions advocating alternative policies or as entrepreneurs mobilizing constituencies around issues. Lacking ideological solidarity and organizational muscle, it failed even to serve as an effective instrument of mass mobilization and policy implementation. To be sure, in a mid-sixties 'radicalization experiment', the regime, convinced of the need for a mechanism to control the ballooning bureaucracy and the covert sabotage of its reforms by local elites, tried to build a more ideologically disciplined and organizationally coherent party. Marxist intellectuals were appointed to many middle-level positions and working-class, peasant and youth cadres were recruited, indoctrinated, and appointed to local leadership in place of suspect local notables. But this experiment was pursued half-heartedly and shortly abandoned. Thus the regime failed to develop the means of replenishing the elite from and mobilizing the activism of the mass social forces with the greatest receptivity to and stake in Nasir's reforms. Nasirism, in brief, failed to institutionalize itself in an ideological party which could ensure its long-term durability. As an instrument for the downward transmission of government communications, the cooptation of local influentials and the control of opposition, the party played a useful role as a 'collaboration movement.' But it never took on much political life as either a 'vanguard' or 'patronage' party (Binder 1978: 35–64, 309–71; Harik 1973).

Interest groups were turned into corporatist instruments of government control. Professional and worker syndicates were subordinated to the regime, and peasants, through the cooperative structure, were brought in a similar way under government tutelage. Syndicate elections were typically manipulated to produce a compliant leadership: militant trade union leaders were replaced by cooperative ones and regime candidates were often imposed on the professions. In the sixties, as upper- and middle-class opposition to regime policy increased, the ASU and the syndicate leaderships were used to police the professions. Trade unions were expected to enforce a ban on strikes. In short, all interest groups were supposed to subordinate their special claims to the common interest which the government claimed to represent. Within these bounds, they were permitted some scope to articulate interests and were sometimes success-ful in winning benefits or deflecting threats to their constituents. Some acquired a kind of 'representation' in elite ranks: the Ministers of Justice and Health were picked from appropriate professional syndicates, and the Minister of Labor was normally a senior trade unionist. For politically ambitious individuals, syndi-cate politics could give access to the elite. But interest groups could overtly challenge neither the rulers nor their policies.

Finally, the mass media acquired a growing political significance in Nasir's Egypt as a pervasive instrument for shaping public opinion. It was through radio and television that Nasir forged his personal link with the masses. The press was used to transmit government views, and though, within limits, some debate and criticism was permitted, overt opposition to the regime's main policy line was not (Harik 1971; Springborg 1978; Wheelock 1975: 23, 63–4, 127–9).

Generally, the scope of political rights and freedoms was strictly limited by the authoritarian powers of the regime. The judiciary was of modest effectiveness in a continuing regime of martial law. Overt anti-regime activity or expression enjoyed no protection. The unchecked coercive powers of the regime, combined with a multitude of structural controls and the great personal legitimacy of the leader put a virtual end to pluralistic politics from 1954 onward. Indeed, given the domination of the executive and the bureaucracy (output channels) over the ineffectual and poorly institutionalized political infrastructure (input channels), political participation of any kind in Nasir's Egypt was of limited scope. In such a bureaucratized polity, the heart of politics was reduced to competition for the high office from which one acquired the authority to make decisions and dispose of resources. For those with connec-tions, participation often took the form of clientalism: the search for adminis-trative exceptions, special concessions, or privileges through corruption or personal patronage. For those without them, it occasionally took the 'anomic' form of anti-regime conspiracies, for example, among the old bourgeoisie in 1961 and the Ikhwan (Muslim Brotherhood) in 1965. As long as Nasir's charismatic legitimacy was untarnished, most Egyptians were content to leave the business of governing to him; only after the 1967 defeat did growing numbers of them question and seek to influence political outcomes.

The failure to institutionalize participation was partly a failure of leadership. It was due in part to the dominance of charisma, in part to the bureaucratic habits of military rulers, in part to Nasir's domineering personality which made him reluctant to share power with those around him. Nasir's commitment to an orderly centrist model of development also deterred him from widening participation; if given a share of power, the political right was sure to attempt a restoration of the old order, the left to unleash social strife. But these factors were reinforced by the inherited cultural expectations of rulers and ruled alike as to how government was conducted: the Pharaonic and Sultanic traditions of autocratic personal rule, the great discretion allowed the ruler in traditional Islam, the dependence of a hydraulic society on government, reinforced by the growth of etatism, and the absence of an entrenched pluralist tradition, all gave historical roots to authoritarianism (Ayubi 1980: 77–136; Baker 1978: 27–34; Moore 1974; Vatikiotis 1978: 153–72, 268–99).

The achievements and limits of revolution from above

The achievements of the Nasir regime in the pursuit of its basic goal of building a strong, independent, modernized Egypt appeared, until the mid-sixties, to mark a significant break with the dependency and stagnation of the pre-1952 period. Even in retrospect, the Nasirite experiment still appears to have been one of the more coherent and vigorous efforts of a modernizing elite to reshape the state and its environment.

The regime embarked, firstly, on a radical-nationalist foreign policy. That a strong, intensely nationalist leadership at the helm of the Arab world's largest and most pivotal state should have embarked on an activist foreign policy seeking to substitute Egyptian leadership for Western domination of the Arab world was perhaps inevitable; again and again strong rulers in Egypt have sought to project their power into the Arab world. Nasir's effort to reshape Egypt's international environment seemed, until 1967, a qualified success. Adeptly exploiting several changes in the external balance of power, namely, the local weakening of Western imperialism, the Soviet challenge to Western world dominance and the national awakening of the Arab peoples, Nasir won a series of significant nationalist victories. The British withdrawal, the successful seizure of the Suez Canal, and the defeat of the Western security pacts, put Egypt at the head of an aroused Arab nationalist movement and resulted in a substantial retreat of Western influence and control from the Middle East. This policy also won political and economic benefits internally. The Arab adulation of Nasir was a major component of the regime's charismatic legitimacy. It was as leader of the Arab world that Egypt won substantial foreign assistance from both East and West and though she remained economically dependent, this dependence was diversified enough to protect her political independence. Nasir's success was, of course, only relative to the failure of previous Arab leaders, and his policies were not without costs. The other Arab regimes were unwilling to accept Egyptian hegemony and ultimately thwarted Nasir's attempt to impose even a foreign policy consensus on the Arab world. The effort to project Egyptian influence was a drain on Egypt's slim resources; the Yemen intervention proved particularly costly. Pan-Arab leadership carried heavy responsibilities, above all the defense of the Arab world and the championing of Arab and Palestinian grievances against Israel, and this entailed grave security risks and onerous military and financial burdens. Nasir's Egypt failed to become the Prussia of the Arab world, but it played a decisive role in the emergence of a state system in the Arab world relatively independent of overt Western control (Kerr 1971; Stephens 1974: 140–343).

The regime's effort to fashion a strategy capable of coping with Egypt's socio-economic problems was also vigorous and innovative. Its goal of economic modernization faced formidable obstacles. There were no easy advances possible in Egypt's land-scarce, labor-surplus economy without large investments. If her falling standard of living was to be stabilized and raised, a 'big push' seemed essential. The Free Officers were convinced that the most rational strategy was to complete the development of Egypt's hydraulic agriculture through the building of a High Dam at Aswan and to launch a crash industrialization drive aimed at diversifying Egypt's productive base and maximizing her self-sufficiency (Mabro 1974: 228–9). Yet, with per capita income already very low and under pressure from continuing population growth, the mobilizable surplus for such a program appeared slim. Moreover, because they did not want to become dependent on either East or West, align with either capital or labor against the other, or pay the political costs of pushing down consumption in an already impoverished society, the Free Officers eschewed the vigorous but repressive capitalist and communist models which elsewhere proved able to extract a surplus. Their search for a middle course which could win aid from both East and West, distribute the unavoidable burdens of development between capital and labor and mobilize resources at acceptable cost, accounts for the evolution of the regime's socio-economic policy after 1952.

In the first decade, regime policy was a kind of regulated capitalism which stressed growth over equality. Redistributive measures were largely limited to land reform. Private entrepreneurs were considered partners in the development effort. The state largely confined itself to regulating and guiding the private sector effort and to investment in the Dam and an iron and steel industry. Egypt sought foreign aid in the West for its major projects and even welcomed foreign investment in certain areas. The regime's resource problem was muted because it had inherited foreign exchange reserves accumulated during the war. Gradually, however, a growing crisis of resource mobilization pushed the regime onto an ever more statist path. Its reserves were soon exhausted. Foreign policy conflicts with the West and Egypt's rejection of World Bank conditions resulted in Western refusal to finance the High Dam and kept foreign investment away. This, in turn, sparked Nasir's seizure of the Suez Canal and the Suez invasion, subsequent to which the government nationalized foreign assets in the country.

The regime's acquisition of major segments of the economy encouraged its first effort to plan economic development, but this exercise soon brought home the deficiency of the state's control over the economy for this task. It also led to a widening cleavage between the regime and Egyptian private capital which caused Nasir to question and then move to reduce his dependence on the private sector. Private capital, in part because of a lack of confidence in a regime unwilling to share power with it or guarantee the inviolability of property, in part because of its high propensity to consume and its preference for quick profit investments in the tertiary sector, could not be brought to direct the levels of investment Nasir wanted into priority productive sectors. He was thus driven to look for ways to increase the state's command over the domestic economic surplus. On social grounds, too, Nasir was dissatisfied with his reliance on the private sector. Inequality was growing. Entrepreneurs, frequently enjoying monopolies, earned large profits and lived a life of consumption comparable to those in advanced societies. Yet the masses gained little from economic development; a labor surplus economy run for private profit kept wages low and unemployment among both workers and the salaried middle class, high. Thus, Egypt seemed to be paying many of the social costs of a capitalist road, without getting the developmental benefits. Whether out of sympathy for the common man from whose ranks he came or a realization that he could not long retain mass support under these conditions, Nasir became convinced that a major wave of populist redistributory measures was needed. The spread of radicalism throughout the Middle East fed by national conflict with the West and the rising prestige of socialist models, probably also influenced him. There were also political reasons for Nasir's change of course. He had become increasingly impatient with the latent opposition of the bourgeoisie to his developmental and reformist policies. The success of the Syrian bourgeoisie in engineering the breakup of the United Arab Republic and the half-hearted attempt of its Egyptian counterparts to use this crisis to curb Nasir's arbitrary power, suggested that this powerful, independent social force could even challenge the political power of the rulers. It appears Nasir finally decided that if the bourgeoisie would not invest, the state would seize its economic assets and invest the profits itself in the sectors it considered crucial. This would allow it to determine a more equitable distribution of the burdens and benefits of development, to eradicate the last centers of independent power resistant to it, and make itself eligible for increased assistance from the Soviet bloc (Abdel Malek 1968: 97–165; Mabro 1974: 124–40). At base, a largely capitalist strategy of development seemed to prove incompatible with the nationalist foreign policy, populist orientation and authoritarian rule to which the regime was committed. Rather than abandon its basic orientation, it chose to alter its development strategy in a more leftist-statist direction.

Thus, Egypt embarked on a series of policy and structural changes which went under the name of 'Arab Socialism.' The heights of the modern economy were nationalized, namely, banking, foreign trade, parts of internal trade, large and medium industry. A multitude of egalitarian measures aimed to broaden opportunities and narrow class gaps were implemented: open university education, guaranteed state employment for graduates, maximization of employment in state firms, rent reductions and price controls, subsidization of popularly consumed commodities, ceilings on incomes and a steeply progressive income tax, and arrangements for worker 'profit-sharing' and participation in management. In the village, further land reform halved the ceilings on land ownership and tightened enforcement of tenancy and rent limitation laws. The property of the wealthiest families was confiscated. The private sector, however, was still considered to be a legitimate participant in the new order and small industry, agriculture and much of the trade and construction sectors remained under its control. These changes, resulting from pragmatic considerations rather than ideological conversion, promulgated by Presidential decree from above and unaccompanied by popular struggle, represented an intensification of the etatist–populist character of the regime rather than a choice of socialism over capitalism (Abdel Malek 1968: 155–7; Dekmejian 1971: 124–32; Mabro 1974: 105–63). The regime remained unwilling to go all the way toward a radical-socialist model: such a course would result in dependency on the East, totally alienate the bourgeoisie on which the regime was dependent, commit it to a Stalinist-like capital accumulation which would not spare the rich peasants and middle classes and carry high costs for national unity and regime support.

These policy initiatives resulted in a major structural transformation which decisively entrenched state dominance of the heights of the economy. This greatly enhanced the regime's capacity to reshape the socio-economic system according to its objectives, namely, to redress growing inequalities and to channel the economic surplus into priority investment sectors. But because the state's displacement of private enterprise and growing intervention in the market was not accompanied by the development of effective instruments of a command economy, its mobilization and allocation of resources remained inefficient. The absence of an ideological party at the center deprived the state-run economy of a consistent source of dynamism to substitute for the profit motive. The economic planning apparatus remained rudimentary. The first plan was little more than a list of investment projects lacking a serious mapping of linkages between sectors and thereafter economic decisions were made without benefit of any plan at all. Thus, investment choices were made as much on the basis of bargaining between bureaucratic interests as a rational weighing of alternatives for optimizing resources. Planners also lacked the authority and the developed fiscal, monetary and regulatory mechanisms to enforce a coherent and efficient management of the economy. The management of the public industrial sector suffered from an overcentralization of decision-making which permitted managers little of the autonomy or initiative needed to maximize efficiency. Nor did they have a clear incentive to do so: few were ideologically committed to making 'socialism' work and the heavy use of subsidies and administered prices and clientalist practices undermined the evaluation and control of managerial performance. Labor redundancy and the difficulty of dismissing workers undermined the discipline and motivation of the work force. Inefficient state foreign trade bodies were responsible for delays in the import of parts and materials which multiplied bottlenecks in the economy and lacked the entrepreneurial experience to develop export markets needed for a healthy balance of payments. The private sector retained a role in the economy, but high tax rates, bureaucratic red tape and the anti-capitalist climate of the sixties discouraged productive investment; although the private sector still controlled half the GNP, it accounted for only a tenth of total investment. The state proved largely unable to either mobilize or extract accumulated private wealth for development. The cumulative effect of barely planned administrative intervention in the market, whether in the form of price fixing, subsidies, or taxation, often diluted incentives for both public and private producers and led to a misallocation of resources. In short, the regime's economic management system remained a rather *ad hoc* combination of bureaucratic and market mechanisms which resulted in serious inefficiencies and bottlenecks.

The growing government control over the economy steadily pushed up the state's rate of extraction (proportion of revenues to GNP) whether from taxation, control of foreign trade, or public sector surpluses. But the inefficiencies of the system cost Egypt a part of its potentially mobilizable economic surplus. Moreover, some of it was diverted to salaries for surplus government employees or subsidies on popular consumption goods as a matter of policy and some of it was dissipated through corrupt practices. A large proportion of public expenditure financed a burgeoning bureaucratic and military establishment. All this added up to a growth in public consumption which ate up potential savings. Investment was nevertheless pushed ahead, as much as five percentage points in the mid-sixties. There was thus a shortfall in savings which had to be made up by growing dependence on foreign assistance. In short, the statized economy seemed little more effective than the private sector at mobilizing the domestic savings needed for Egypt's modernization. What it did do was shift the priorities for which resources were used: in effect, it took the surplus which would otherwise have gone to the private bourgeoisie and have been consumed in high living, funneled abroad or invested in the tertiary, agricultural or light industrial sectors, and used it to support a large army, a big salaried bureaucratic class, increased popular employment and welfare and significant investment in intensified industrial, agricultural and infrastructural development. (Ayubi 1980: 226–34; Mabro 1974: 110–40, 176–85; Mead 1979).

These policies did result in durable advances in economic modernization, although not without high costs and enduring negative side-effects. Industrialization advanced at an average annual rate (1952–70) of 5.7% and was diversified and shifted away from purely light industry (Mabro 1974: 146). Some industrial investments were economically unsound by the standards of capitalist cost accounting, but the overall return on investment in the public sector proved reasonable in the long run (Handoussa 1979: 106). Industry's share of the GDP increased from 15.3% to 23.2% between 1952 and 1970 while that of the tertiary sector remained relatively constant (Mabro 1974: 189). The industrial advance also provided employment, popular consumption goods at fixed prices and social security for workers. The regime also pushed ahead the development of education and modernizing skills. Education expanded at about 8% per year, roughly equally at all levels. Illiteracy dropped from 75% to 65% (1950–70) and there was a nearly 100% expansion between 1947 and 1966 in the population employed in the 'modern' sector, that is, professional, technical, commercial and clerical positions, raising its percentage of the labor force from 12% to almost 20% (Ibrahim 1982b: 389–99). Unfortunately, the supply of manpower was not well-tailored to the needs of the economy. Despite efforts to shift education toward scientific and technical fields, the guarantee of employment to graduates channeled an excess of students into traditional fields resulting in a scarcity of middle-level technicians and too many college graduates who had to be absorbed by the bloated bureaucracy.

In agriculture there was a significant rationalization drive. Land reform replaced an agrarian economy dominated by big private estates with one of medium sized farms and small peasant holdings embraced by a state-controlled cooperative network. The cooperative system, at least initially, appeared a successful compromise model which preserved small ownership, yet promoted land consolidation, a common crop rotation, economies of scale, technical innovation and an improved flow of credit and inputs. The state also substituted for private middlemen in supply and marketing operations and, given that the state extracted until the late sixties only about 5% to 8% of agricultural income, it probably did so to the benefit of peasants as well as itself. At the same time, the state, through cooperatives, local party and government structures, increasingly penetrated the village, raising the delivery of services and attempting a 'bureaucratic mobilization' of the population for development. The result was neither a village revolution against the traditional power structure nor a transformation of traditional culture. But there was a modest pluralization of power in the village and an enhanced receptivity to modernization. Finally, land reclamation and the High Dam project advanced the intensive and extensive development of Egypt's slim agricultural base. The costs of land reclamation were high and the Dam had negative side effects; but the Dam proved to be a relatively cheap and natural culmination of Egypt's hydraulic agriculture which paid for itself in increased output in a few years. Altogether, these efforts arrested and slightly reversed until the late sixties the steady pre-revolutionary decline in Egypt's agricultural production per man and per *feddan* (1 *feddan* = 1.038 acres); and while the average 3% yearly growth of agriculture over the period was no agricultural revolution, it was, by comparison to the preceding and successive period, no small achievement (Harik 1974; Mabro 1974: 56–106, 171; Radwan 1977: 60–77). Overall, the total growth rate of the economy, estimated at around 4% per year over the Nasir period, fell well below expectations. Given that population growth continued high, per capita income probably increased less than 2% per year, hardly a significant rise in the standard of living. But in checking and partly reversing a half-century of decline before 1951, the Nasir era represented for Egypt a period of relatively high performance.

Nasir's policies also resulted in a palpably although not radically more equitable distribution of Egypt's limited resources. In the village, agrarian reform legislation narrowed class gaps. Land reform transferred about 15% of the surface to 11% of the agrarian population, destroyed the giant estates and helped reduce the landless population from 59% to 43% (1950–70). Together with accompanying tenancy laws and rent reductions, the reforms doubled the share of small peasants (< 5 *feddans*) and wage earners in agricultural income. Arresting the previous tendency to dispossession and concentration, they added significantly to the security of the rural poor (Mabro 1974: 71–4; Radwan 1977: 16–23). But land reform only marginally affected middle landowners who, taking a disproportionate share of subsidized agricultural inputs, maintained or advanced their positions. In the non-agricultural sector, reform also had a modest equalizing effect. Nationalizations leveled high concentrations of private wealth. The positions of workers and minor governmental employees improved. Real wages for industrial workers rose 44% (1952–67) exclusive of increased benefits. In the bureaucracy, large wage differentials persisted (perhaps around 33 to 1); but from 1952 to 1967 the income of top bureaucrats fell 10–20% while that of minor governmental employees increased 85% (Ayubi 1980: 377–9; Mabro 1974: 223–4). Expansion in education and government

27

employment opened opportunities for the middle and lower classes; as a result the sixties were a period of expanding social mobility (Ibrahim 1982b). Welfare benefits, including fixed low prices for popular consumption commodities such as bread and textiles, made life bearable for the masses who would otherwise have been subject to a Malthusian solution to Egypt's overpopulation. But the middle and upper classes also got their share of subsidies; for example, engineers and army officers received subsidized housing. The tax system, progressive in principle, was in practice defeated by evasion. Overall, the proportion of wages as opposed to income from property in the GNP seems to have increased from 44.8% in 1958 to 50% in 1970; and the share of the national income received by the top 10% of society declined by 10% while that of the bottom 60% increased by 12% (Issawy 1982: 100). But because of persisting private control of the means of production, the economy continued to generate new inequalities even as the state moved to reduce old ones. In short, Nasirism did not carry out a thorough social revolution. But without the redistributive interventions it did undertake, the distribution of the burdens and benefits of development would certainly have been much more inegalitarian. That this containment of inequality was paralleled by economic growth was no small achievement.

The populist social base of the state

The accumulated achievements of the Nasir regime resulted in a shift in the balance of socio-political power in Egypt. The dominance of the Turko-Egyptian landed upper class and the *haute bourgeoisie* of largely Levantine or European origin over land, business and political power was shattered, although for the most part they survived with reduced assets. This opened the way for the Egyptian upper-middle and middle classes to move upward, some to political positions through the state, some into spaces vacated in the private economy by the old upper class. The authoritarian state permitted the bourgeoisie as a class little autonomous power. But the technocratic elite, largely recruited from the urban upper-middle class, enjoyed influence at the top and was beholden to the regime for career advancement (Moore 1980: 109–30). The rural middle class was allowed to retain substantial land, to fill the lower and middle ranks of the bureaucracy with its offspring, and, except for the brief radicalization of the mid-sixties, to dominate the village branches of the state party (Binder 1965, 1978). Charisma and populist policies also helped mobilize and absorb into the regime's base social forces toward the bottom of society. The growing class of minor governmental employees, broadened and increasingly recruited from the lower classes, was dependent on and favored by regime policies. The working class, which nearly doubled under Nasir, was a relatively class-conscious force receptive to the appeals of socialism. Those in the public sector, incorporated into government controlled trade unions, and favored by higher salaries and security than other workers, had a special stake in Nasirite policies. Small merchants, artisans and the urban masses below them lay outside regime corporatist structures, benefited less, and were traditionally susceptible to oppositionist Islam; but the leader's charismatic–nationalist appeal won over much of the urban mass. The peasantry, linked to the regime through agrarian reform, the cooperatives, the mass media, and, briefly, an energized government party, were brought, if only passively, into the political arena on the regime's side (Abdel Malek 1968: 368; Binder 1965: 405–7: Harik 1974). Through charisma, nationalism, expanded opportunity and equality, and its all-embracing corporatist political structures, the regime incorporated into its base a broad cross-class 'populist coalition' embracing both the rising new bourgeoisie and the newly mobilizing masses. With the exception of hostile elements of the old elite, and residues of opposition on the extreme left and Islamic right, it encompassed a great majority of Egyptians. This widened social base imparted an impressive stability to the state. Through the balancing of the heterogeneous forces inside his coalition and repression of the minority outside it, Nasir achieved the personal power to pursue the policies he thought best.

The decline of the Nasirite state: the seeds of Sadatism

Even as the Nasir regime assumed, in the mid-sixties, its fully developed form as a seemingly successful modernizing state, the seeds of a decline never to be reversed had taken root. The very strengths and virtues on which it had risen – powerful charismatic leadership, a development strategy avoiding the worst costs of capitalism and communism, Pan Arabism – had their negative sides and accumulating costs. The regime's efforts to forcefully reshape its domestic and international environments produced forces which boomeranged against it. Its political institutions proved too feeble to counter these challenges. Taken separately, Nasir may have been able to cope with these forces, but they converged with an impact which, though unable to topple his regime, exhausted and brought his revolution to a halt. The decline of Nasirism spawned the forces which would give rise to Sadatism.

Widening contradictions between the radical populist policies pursued by Nasir and the dominant bourgeois segments of the regime's social base, was perhaps the ultimate factor in the undermining of Nasirism. The regime's development strategy permitted a 'national capitalist' class to retain substantial assets in construction, agriculture and trade; indeed the 'foreign economic evacuation' opened new opportunities for Egyptian entrepreneurs in these fields. They quickly found new ways of generating wealth in a statized economy and prospered on the economic expansion. Entrepreneurs were enriched on monopolies in wholesale trade, by dealing in blackmarket goods, as subcontractors to the state or middlemen between it and the market. In the countryside, middle landowners who inherited local power after the land reform, joined with the remnants of big magnates who retained substantial holdings, to turn the regime's agrarian development policies to their own benefit. Yet, though the private middle bourgeoisie advanced, the regime's 'socialist' ideology and policies threatened, in some ways constrained, and ultimately alienated it, and its actions in turn tended to undermine regime policies. Merchants and contractors exploited the state and hoarded rather than invested their capital. Middle landowners, alienated by the intensification of the land reform and the attack on their local political power in the sixties, tried to evade and sabotage the regime's rural reform drive. The private bourgeoisie became a latent interest group in the system seeking to defend or widen the scope of the market. And it had strong ties of family or mutual class interest and ideology with elements inside the state itself (Shukri 1978: 41–48; Waterbury 1976c: 309–10, 324).

A greater contradiction yet was the consolidation of a new 'state bourgeoisie' at the very heart of the regime, combining in its hands state power and control over the production of national wealth, and, at best, ideologically ambivalent toward the radicalized form of Nasirism which developed in the sixties. Etatist expansion did enhance the power and career opportunities of this social force. But much of it was recruited from families whose ideology, economic interests, opportunities and life style were incompatible with 'socialism' and often actually curbed by the 'socialist' measures. Many of the economists asked to plan and manage the 'socialist' economy were Western-educated liberals with little sympathy for 'socialism.' Most of the engineers who ran the public sector and staffed the technical ministries were recruited from the top of the social structure and sometimes former owners were actually entrusted with the management of nationalized firms; for example, the huge Arab Contracting Company, though partly nationalized, continued to be run almost as a family firm (Moore 1980). Generally, these high status families, still able to acquire disproportionate access to higher education, were able to perpetuate their control of elite positions even in socialist Egypt. There were, of course, many middle-class elements for whom socialism opened otherwise closed doors to the top, but, in time, as they acquired the income of the upper stratum, many of these newcomers adopted corresponding attitudes. Many, in fact, were recruited from the rural middle class antagonized by the intensification of land reform. Even the Free Officers themselves were gradually 'embourgeoised': many married into families of the old elite, lost touch with their modest backgrounds, adopted the life style of the rich, and struck political alliances with factions of the state and private bourgeoisie. They lost interest in pushing the revolution ahead, became engrossed in the pursuit of personal interests, and began to see mass discontent rather than the privileged classes as the main threat to the regime. Marshal Amer, for example, living in the grand style of an 'old pasha,' seemed chiefly concerned to turn the military into a personal fiefdom. He and others emerged in the sixties as spokesmen for anti-socialist interests.

Reliance on non- or even anti-socialist elements to implement 'socialism' predictably undermined the whole effort. Because they were not ideologically motivated and expected to live a Western life style, they had to be paid what were by Egyptian and socialist standards, high salaries at the expense of equality and the treasury. Indeed the ranks of highly paid bureaucrats and managers swelled following the 'socialist transformation.' In spite of this, few were happy with the income ceilings, austerity measures, and import restrictions which cramped their life style. Hence, though there were many who performed their duties with integrity and distinction, there were also many who engaged in corrupt practices, enriching themselves at the expense of the state's economic surplus. Many adopted 'elitist' attitudes toward the masses, reluctant to cooperate in efforts to engage popular participation in the factories or villages. Many of their policy decisions, for example, the stress on consumer durables rather than simple farm implements, or on higher over mass education, reflected class biases incompatible with the regime's socialist ideology. The official ideology was socialist, collectivist, and anti-imperialist, but the 'state bourgeoisie' kept a covert 'counter-ideology,' liberal, pro-Western, and consumption-oriented, alive at the very heart of the state.

Thus, even as the leader steered the ideology and policy of the regime left, a new state bourgeoisie created by but ultimately incompatible with this course was emerging as the dominant social force in Egypt. It, in effect, controlled the means of administration and production, was chiefly recruited from and retained its links and sympathies with the upper and middle strata, used its power to protect or advance itself and was in a good position to pass its privileges on to its children. It differed from a private bourgeoisie in that, not owning the means of production and unable to constrain the arbitrary power of the ruler (as in a liberal–capitalist state), it remained insecure. To this extent, it therefore had an interest at odds with both Nasir's personal rule and the 'socialist' ideology which prevented it from translating its control of the means of production into actual ownership. Once the initial etatist expansion ended and career and enrichment opportunities stagnated, it lost whatever stake it had had in Nasir's policies (Ayubi 1980: 182–4, 404–20, 477–86; Hussein 1973: 160–83; Shukri 1978: 37–80, 206–11).

Simultaneously, the political muscle of the formerly 'hard' Nasirite state was visibly slackening. At the apex, there was a loss of cohesion and drive by the military elite core which had made and sustained the revolution. It was increasingly divided, in part by power rivalries such as that between Nasir and Amer over the latter's stranglehold on the armed forces. More fundamental was the widening gap between Nasir, who until 1967 moved toward an ever more radical form of populism, and more conservative Free Officers; by the mid-sixties, senior Free Officers Abd al-Latif Baghdadi and Kemal ad-Din Hussein had broken with him over the nationalizations and the intervention in Yemen. They were replaced by more leftwing officers, but other conservatives, such as Sadat, remained at the top. The result was a growing ideological heterogeneity and a dissipation of dynamism among the elite. A team committed to the unified implementation of a common program ceased to exist (Dekmejian 1971: 217–24).

Elite fragmentation fueled a growing patrimonialization of the state establishment as rival leaders tried to turn the institutions over which they presided into personal 'fiefdoms.' This intensified conflicts over programs and resources, undermining the implementation of coherent policy, whether it was the design of an education strategy or a birth-control program. Networks of mutual protection and advancement sprang up between elites and their subordinates, infecting the bureaucracy with patron–clientalism; this undermined the chain of command and accountability to the top because, at its extreme, clients put loyalty to their patron over the duties of office and legal authority, and because the upward flow of information was distorted. Perhaps the two most damaging examples of this phenomenon were the cases of the military and the political police. Marshal Amer's ability to turn the army into a personal fiefdom immune to Presidential authority in which his often incompetent cronies and clients were promoted and rewarded at the expense of dedicated and competent officers, had disastrous results in the 1967 war. The political police also became nearly a law unto itself at the expense of the security and rights of citizens. As the cohesion and accountability of the establishment declined, it struck alliances with private sector elements which sought to colonize the state and turn it to the service of particular interests. The result was an expansion in corruption, that is, embezzlement, black marketeering in public property, nepotism, and kickbacks in public contracts, which dissipated part of the state's economic surplus. Although these tendencies were never legitimized, or their perpetrators secure, they amounted to a certain appropriation of the means of administration by officials typical of patrimonial regimes. Patrimonialism at the top naturally accentuated bureaucratic pathologies, such as neglect or abuse of constituents, inertia and inefficiency. Since, at this very time, the state machine was being burdened with an ever-growing number of new tasks, the consequences rippled through society; inevitably many of the new social institutions bureaucratically created and controlled were, once the drive from the top slackened, corrupted or paralyzed.

Patrimonialization partly resulted from the imposition of modern organization in a semi-traditional, resource-scarce society, but the weakness of its political institutions made the regime especially susceptible to it. In the absence of political channels of interest aggregation, individuals naturally sought privileges and exceptions through bureaucratic channels, corrupting and fueling clientalism inside the state machine at the expense of policy implementation. In the absence of strong checks – an effective party or parliament, social forces independent of the government – officialdom was accountable at best only to the political elite at the top and no countervailing forces from below existed to keep it responsible. As long as the political elite retained its cohesion and drive, it kept the bureaucracy at least to a degree animated and accountable, but by the mid-sixties it was itself becoming part of the problem. Nasir, alone, could not control these various pathologies and, indeed, as former colleagues began to turn into dangerous rivals, he took to encouraging or tolerating elite corruption and fragmentation as a means of control (Ayubi, 1980; 204–87; Baker 1978: 70–87; Waterbury 1976a).

By the mid-sixties, the twin ills of embourgeoisement and patrimonialization were undermining Nasir's policies and shifting the balance of social forces against them. These threats could probably have been contained; but ultimately they were not, chiefly because Nasir failed to create the political instruments to mobilize and organize those social forces which favored or benefited from Nasirism. At the top, a core of leftist Free Officers around Nasir and at the levers of the ASU and the security apparatus, Marxist intellectuals clustered in the media, some technocrats and most trade union leaders were still pro-Nasirist. But they were increasingly a minority in a vast establishment and, without an ideological party capable of replacing the moribund Free Officers' organization, they could not be replenished and reinforced by committed new elements from below. Nor was any effort made to recruit a core of 'socialist' technocrats and managers to run the economy. Nasir did indeed, as his critics argued, try to 'build socialism without socialists' (Ayubi 1980: 439–51; Binder 1978: 326–71). Large segments of the masses supported and benefited from Nasirism, but without an effective party, they remained, except for brief spurts of activism during the middle sixties radicalization experiment, politically passive. Worker participation in the factories remained nominal; common soldiers were insulated from politicization. In the villages and *baladi* (traditional non-Westernized) urban neighborhoods, the ASU remained dependent on local notables whose power would have been threatened by mass mobilization or local officials too readily corrupted by the local power structure and habituated to bureaucratic methods. Thus, large segments of Nasir's potential mass constituency were left with minimal political consciousness, encapsulated in webs of clientalism, deferent to the notability, and powerless. Their energies could not be mobilized for development; an organized popular force which could give social roots to new institutions and sustain them once the impetus from the top declined, never took form. For example, as soon as the drive for cooperatization from the government center disappeared, agricultural cooperatives rapidly deteriorated: elections were not held, corruption went unchecked, local notables and officials exploited poorer peasants and diverted benefits to themselves (Baker 1978: 205–12; Mayfield 1971). Thus, as the Nasirist thrust came under covert attack, there existed neither a unified leadership nor organized political force committed to it nor political institutions through which those with a stake in it could defend it. Ironically, the institutional weakness of Nasirism was but the other side of its main political strength, the leader's mass charisma, which in enabling Nasir to overshadow other elites and institutions and retain mass support, deprived him of the incentive to create a viable party system. Authoritarian by instinct, and apparently unaware of the extent of hostility to his policies inside a deferent elite, Nasir chose instead to maintain his freedom of action by playing off various factions inside the regime.

Finally, Nasirism was weakened by a mounting imbalance between commitments and resources which climaxed in the mid-sixties. The capacity of the regime to mobilize resources was constrained by Egypt's poverty and the inefficiency and corruption of its economic apparatus; yet its commitments – to an ambitious development program, a large army, salaries for a technocratic elite and a substantial welfare state – had enormously expanded. The result was a gap between savings and investment which the regime was increasingly dependent on foreign assistance to fill. Aggravating this imbalance was a short-run crisis growing out of its import-substitution industrialization strategy: it required massive imports of technology, parts, materials, even whole factories, but because of the inevitable lag between such imports and the start-up time of new projects (especially long-gestating ones like the High Dam), growing internal consumption, and the regime's poor export entrepreneurship, Egypt's imports surged ahead of exports. This, combined with shortfalls in foreign assistance, aggravated by a cut-off of US food aid over the Yemen crisis, led to a widening balance of payments deficit and a foreign exchange crisis which pinched the inflow of needed production materials. Inflation was fueled by big investments and increasing domestic income combined with supply inelasticity, especially for food. These pressures were enough, by the mid-sixties, to force the regime into an austerity program which brought the development effort to a halt (Mabro 1974: 175–85, 228–34). Ultimately, the imbalances between resources and commitments, supply and demand, were, to a large extent, a consequence of the leader's attempt to maintain his broad nationalist–populist coalition. He could not sacrifice an activist foreign policy or the large army needed to support it without risking the nationalist legitimacy on which the regime and his own stature rested. He could not further squeeze the bourgeoisie, extract too much from the peasants, or allow the urban mass to go without bread and work if he wished to retain their support. Without abandoning some part of his coalition in a sharp turn to the right or left, Nasir could not impose the primitive capital accumulation of the kind pioneered by communist and capitalist regimes (Waterbury 1976c). And this he was unwilling to do, whether from his nationalist–centrist ideology or his compulsion to meet the expectations of the broad constituency on which his charisma and hence his power depended. His regime was, therefore, rendered vulnerable to periodic resource crises and external dependency. This is not to say that, in the long run, Nasir could not have sustained his strategy, given a little more austerity, discipline, and the continued foreign assistance for which Egypt's geo-political importance made her eligible; but because of the 1967 war, he was never given this chance.

The last and most immediately decisive factor in the decline of Nasirism was the 1967 defeat by Israel. Ironically it was the well-spring of the regime's power, its non-aligned, anti-imperialist Pan-Arab foreign policy which brought on this disaster. Nasir's challenge to Western interests and allies in the region had earned him accumulated resentment in the West; by the mid-sixties, Washington had come to perceive him as a Soviet client and was prepared to support an Israeli strike which might bring him down. Yet, because Nasir was never willing to commit himself to the Eastern bloc he could not expect Soviet protection. At the same time, a rising Syrian–Palestinian challenge to Israel was peaking; despite an unfavorable military balance, Nasir could not, except at risk to his charismatic legitimacy, do less than extend it political support. Thus, he gave the expansionist party in Israel a chance to attack him. The rapid collapse of the Egyptian army in the war showed how far Nasir's foreign policy ambitions had exceeded his capabilities. Israel occupied Egypt's Sinai Peninsula. The same charisma which Nasir's expulsion of one foreign power had won for him led him into a trap which entrenched a new one on Egyptian soil (Kerr 1971: 106–56; Stephens 1974: 435–92).

The twilight of Nasirism

The 1967 defeat, coming at a time when the Egyptian political system was already weakening, threw the regime into a profound crisis. Its energies and resources diverted to coping with the consequences of the defeat, the system proved incapable of self reform; instead the defeat accelerated the forces undermining it. Although there remained formidable barriers to them, pressures for major system change which would later mature under Sadat were already accumulating in the three post-war years before Nasir died.

The regime's central preoccupation was necessarily the military and diplomatic struggle to roll back the Israeli occupation of Sinai. Convinced that Sinai could not be liberated without force of arms, Nasir personally supervised the reconstruction of the armed forces with Soviet assistance; patronage networks were uprooted, competent commanders appointed and professionalism restored. Egypt's new army challenged the Israelis in the War of Attrition, but this took a fearful toll of Egyptian lives and the United States seemed determined to keep Israel strong enough to prevent an Egyptian advance. Nasir tried to further commit the USSR to Egypt's cause, but though the Soviets improved Egypt's defenses, they seemed reluctant to provide her with sufficient means to break the Israeli occupation. Hence, in 1969 Nasir accepted the Rogers Plan for a diplomatic settlement though he had little confidence that American mediation could substitute for the military struggle. In fact, the Americans failed to follow through, but the fighting was stopped until 1973 (Haykel 1975: 50; Stephens 1974: 517–20, 545).

The war and these subsequent developments had enormous consequences for the regional and internal balances of power and prestige which paved the way for the undoing of Nasirism as a foreign policy. The defeat of the major radical nationalist states, Egypt and Syria, shattered the credibility of radical Pan-Arabism; the conservative pro-Western oil states, headed by Saudi Arabia, enhanced their legitimacy by paying for the rebuilding of the Arab armies and, in return, Nasir had to end his nationalist challenge to them. Inside Egypt the war and its aftermath brought home the costs of Pan-Arab activism, and though in the short-run the Israeli occupation further embroiled Egypt in the Arab–Israeli conflict, in the long-run the costs of the struggle led her to look to her own identity and interests. The success of American over Soviet arms in the war and the failure of the USSR to protect its local allies strengthened forces hostile to Moscow and favoring accommodation with the West. Post-war developments convinced a growing part of the Egyptian elite that America held the cards to a solution and that Egypt would have to come to terms with her. Nasir's acceptance of the Rogers Plan represented a tacit acceptance of the US as a major arbiter in the Arab world and of the irreversibility of Israel which made it easier for his successor to take decisive strides toward a Western alignment and an Israeli peace. Thus, the way was paved for Sadat (Ahmad 1975; Stephens 1974: 511–20; Waterbury 1976c: 317, 340–1).

The defeat also engendered an almost permanent economic crisis which sapped the strength of the Nasirite system from within. It deprived Egypt of major revenue sources such as the Suez Canal, the Sinai oil fields, and tourism, only part of which was covered by Arab subsidies. At the same time, it greatly increased the financial burden on the state. There was an enormous diversion of resources into the reconstruction of the army, but also to provide for those displaced from the destroyed canal cities. The resource gap, a problem before the war, widened alarmingly. Something had to give, and it was chiefly the development effort. Investment plummeted (to around 11%) and factories were made idle for want of scarce foreign exchange. The result was economic stagnation and a shrinking surplus which made it impossible to relaunch the stalled development effort (Mabro 1974: 176; Waterbury 1976c: 317–18). The perception spread that the Nasirite model had failed and that Egypt would have to look outward for resources if her economy was to recover; thus, the road to Sadat's *Infitah* (economic opening) was being prepared.

A major crisis in the political system was also helping shift the balance of power against Nasirism. The populist coalition through which the regime had dominated the political arena since the fifties was badly weakened. One symptom of this was a mini-crisis of participation; unprecedented mass demonstrations in 1968 signaled that the attentive public had lost confidence, if not in Nasir, then in the regime, and now wanted a say in its future. Nasir's response, the '30 March Manifesto,' was primarily a pacifying measure. There was a modest relaxation of controls over political expression, but Nasir had no intention of sharing power in a time of war crisis and faltering authority. Another symptom was a profound demoralization which swept over Egyptians in the post-war years. It was partly a loss of confidence in the ability of Egypt to determine her own fate, partly the frustration of the high expectations stimulated in the sixties and now cut short by war and economic decline. It took the form of rising *incivisme*, privatism and a search for new loyalties; if the nation–state had failed, Egyptians could turn to family, self-enrichment or religion. Slowly the high hopes that had sustained Nasirism gave way to a despair and passivity which could offer no resistance to those wishing to undo the work of the leader. Finally, there were signs that the regime's coalition was breaking up into opposing factions tacitly advocating contrary solutions to Egypt's crisis. The left, though weakened, remained in the field arguing for an intensification of the revolution, the arming and mobilization of the masses for a popular war, a regime of austerity to level the privileges of the bourgeoisie. The right, feeling vindicated in its view that military rule, socialism, and the Soviet connection were bankrupt, wanted political and economic liberalization and a turn to the West. Thus, the seeds of pluralization, even polarization, were taking root, forces which would eventually put rising pressure on the monolithic authoritarian structures of the state. For the time being, however, Nasir continued to balance these forces. He had no patience with leftist prescriptions for class struggle in time of war, and the social composition of the establishment on which he depended was incompatible with a turn to the radical left. A radical opening to the right, a turn to capitalism and the West, was impossible as long as America backed the Israeli occupation and, in any case, Nasir had no desire to undo all the work of his career (Dekmejian 1971: 252–4, 309; Stephens 1974: 511, 533–7). But he did make certain modest concessions to the right. The brief radical mobilization effort of the sixties was abandoned: the 'Socialist Youth Organization' dissolved, efforts to organize lower strata in the village ended, the peasant cooperatives neglected; thus there was a resurgence of the local power of landlords and rich peasants and a contraction in the penetrative capacity of the state. Liberalized elections to the party and parliament permitted the haves to recover the places some had lost in these institutions in the sixties. A modest liberalization of the economy was begun. Foreign exchange was diverted from the starved public sector to private sector industry in hopes of expanding export revenue and an influx of luxury imports was permitted to appease the bourgeoisie. Yet there were also increases in taxes on workers' salaries, necessities and peasant crop deliveries to the state. This increasing inability of the regime to distribute burdens equitably prepared the climate of opinion for further attacks on populism after the succession of Sadat. These developments signaled a weakening of the etatist and popular forces with the greatest stake in Nasirism and a strengthening of conservative forces which wished to undo it (Dekmejian 1971: 253–309; Harik 1974: 222–41; Hussein 1975: 4–34; Shukri 1978: 39–40).

Finally, there were changes at the very top which signaled the exhaustion of Nasirism. The credibility of rule by the Free Officer core still committed to Nasirism was greatly weakened by its partial responsibility for the defeat. Correspondingly, the presence and prestige of more pragmatic and Westernized civilian elites increased. The rebuilding of the army strengthened professional military officers, too, many of whom secretly blamed Nasir for defeat by Israel and the subsequent scapegoating of the army. Thus, two groups on which Sadat would rely for support were already poised to play crucial roles in system change. Nasir himself was not overtly challenged. The elite needed him to contain popular anger, and the last remaining leaders with the stature to threaten him, Amer and Zakaria Muhi ad-Din, fell in the aftermath of the war. Of the original senior Free Officers, only the ineffectual Hussein Shafa'i, and Anwar Sadat, a man who had long bided his time, remained; these were the finishing touches on the system of one-man-rule Sadat would inherit. But in elite, and to a lesser extent popular circles Nasir's personal charisma was weakened and faith in Nasirism shattered. Except in defense and foreign policy, Nasir, overburdened and in declining health, was no longer a source of system drive and accountability. He was forced to make concessions to the right and to tolerate growing corruption and indiscipline in the establishment. Nasir retained the capacity to neutralize forces wanting radical system change. But his declining ability to make things happen paralyzed the regime. When he died, there was little to hold it to the course he had set. (Haykel 1975: 50; Hussein 1975: 17–18; Stephens 1974: 542–3; Waterbury 1976c: 322).

Nasir passed to his successor, Anwar Sadat, a seemingly intractable system crisis, a demoralized people, a divided elite. The mass grief displayed at his funeral showed how lost Egyptians felt at the passing of the leader they had come to depend on. But sobered by the grim years after 1967, many were prepared for the lowering of sights the new leader would preside over. And, Nasir left his successor with means to cope; his charismatic legitimacy had infused the regime with enough authority to give it staying power in the face of crisis. Its Presidential command post was well established, the habits of compliance of the state machine largely intact. Time would show that Sadat was up to using these formidable levers of power not only to contain threats to regime survival but to harness the pent up forces of change in pursuit of a new vision of Egypt's future. The very tools Nasir forged to carry out his works would serve equally well their undoing.

Chapter 3

The making of Sadat's Egypt

This chapter analyzes the forces behind the transformation of Egypt under Sadat. It will be argued that this transformation resulted from a convergence of three basic forces: (1) the preferences of Sadat and much of the power elite for a break with Nasir's policies because of their belief that they had failed and an anticipation that their interests would be served by change; (2) Sadat's effort to defeat opposition to his policies and consolidate a new political base for the regime rooted in forces with a stake in them; and (3) 'environmental' constraints and opportunities which pushed and pulled Sadat along the path of change. The development of this struggle over policy and power fell roughly into three phases. From 1970 to 1973, Sadat struggled to consolidate his position against rivals while coping with intractable foreign policy and economic crises inherited from his predecessor. In 1973–6, Sadat, responding to new opportunities, used the political capital won in the October 1973 war to steer a major redirection in Egypt's foreign and domestic policies. The last phase, 1977–81, saw both the consolidation of Sadat's new course and spreading opposition to its consequences.

Sadat's struggle to survive (1970–3)

The succession crisis

Sadat's Egypt was born of a major leadership crisis. On Nasir's death, the political elite which inherited power was deeply divided. Nasir had failed to groom an obvious successor (Shazli 1980: 91; Shukri 1978: 31–2) and the succession process was weakly institutionalized. Thus, a power struggle broke out between two major factions in the power elite which was to determine the direction of Egypt's post-Nasir course. On one side was a small but well-placed faction composed of leftwing Free Officers and their civilian allies who held high positions and influence in the sixties. Ali Sabri, a Free Officer, senior party (ASU) chieftain and newly appointed Vice President, was the informal leader of this group. It also included a formidable number of the very top political elite, most of whom were also Free Officers: Interior Minister and party boss,

40

Sha'rawi Guma; Information Minister, Muhammed Fa'iq; party *apparatchek*, Abd al-Muhsin Abu al-Nur; Minister of Presidential Affairs, Sami Sharif; chief of the political police, Ahmad Kamel; War Minister, General Muhammed Fawzi; several other ministers and the Speaker of Parliament. The leftist faction enjoyed a majority on the executive committee of the state party, the ASU, a collective leadership organ which had assumed increasing authority in the sixties. A larger but more diffuse conservative faction was led by the new President, Anwar Sadat, who assumed that office by virtue of his position as Vice-President on Nasir's death and was confirmed in it by the ASU and a popular plebiscite. Sadat's main asset was the superior legal legitimacy of his office. He had not been close to the center of power in the late Nasir years and did not possess an organized power base; in fact his rivals consented to his assumption of the Presidency partly because they thought he represented no threat to them and could readily be controlled. But Sadat did enjoy political seniority as one of the two remaining senior Free Officers and he had extensive contacts and diffuse support in the political elite.[1] Prominent conservative personalities aligned with him from the outset were Hussein Shafa'i, the second surviving senior Free Officer, Sayyid Marei, a veteran minister–politician and Mahmud Fawzi, a senior statesman–diplomat. Once he assumed office, Sadat became the natural leader of all those opposed to the Sabri group. Civilian centrists such as Muhammed Hassanein Haykel and Aziz Sidqi joined him chiefly to prevent the Sabri faction from dominating the post-Nasir state. Some other important figures such as the prominent Free Officers, Mahmud Riad and Abd al-Qadir Hatim, simply accepted Sadat's legal authority.

At issue between the two factions was the distribution of power, particularly Presidential power. Sabri's group wanted a collective leadership in which the President would be held closely accountable to the rest of the power elite, specifically to the Supreme Executive Committee of the ASU (where it held a majority). Seeing themselves as Nasir's true heirs, they could not permit Sadat, who had failed to keep up with the revolution's leftward evolution in the sixties, to assume the tremendous powers Nasir had acquired for the Presidency. Sadat, however, who considered himself to have been unfairly pushed from the center of power by upstarts like Sabri, had other ideas. He promised to consult the party bodies over the main lines of policy. But within these lines he fully intended to exercise the broad discretion Nasir enjoyed and would accept no tutelage over the power to decide for Egypt which the people had 'deposited' with him. Nor would he allow himself to become a front for rule by the Sabri clique or tolerate factional struggles against his authority (Sadat speeches, 14 May, 22 June 1971). Sadat and his rivals clashed from the outset over what the latter considered unilateral actions taken by the President without consulting or against the wishes of the executive committee. But for Sadat and his allies who were long-time members of the elite and, in their view, underrepresented in the executive committee because of Sabri's electoral manipulations, its incumbents enjoyed no special authority, and by the weight of Nasirite tradition, the committee was subordinate to the President. Thus, the institutionalization of authority remained uncertain, and each faction asserted the superior legitimacy of the constitutional body it controlled. At base, the struggle was over who shall rule.

But issues were far from separated from this power struggle and from the outset it was apparent that Sadat and Sabri stood for different conceptions of the course Egypt should follow. Sabri's group was identified with the turn Nasirism had taken in the sixties: internally, heavy industrialization, state socialism, efforts to make the party superior to other power centers such as the military and the cabinet, strong governmental controls over society, and, to many, the police repression which marred Nasir's rule. In foreign policy, they stood for militancy toward Israel and a close alliance with the USSR. Sadat was known, by contrast, to have had strong reservations about all these policies. Prominent Sadat supporters like Fawzi and Haykel argued for a diplomatic opening to the West on the grounds that Egypt's isolation from the West reduced her foreign policy options. The Sabri group retorted that expectations of American diplomatic help were an illusion unless Egypt was prepared to return to capitalism. In fact, many of those around Sadat were identified with conservative socioeconomic policies; Marei, for example, had clashed with leftists in the sixties over his solicitude for the rights of landlords. One of Sadat's first acts as President, the return of certain property seized from wealthy families, showed his sympathies lay in the same direction.

There were several watersheds in the conflict. Sadat's appointment of Mahmud Fawzi as Prime Minister in defiance of the left's desire to put one of their own in this post, was the opening shot; immediately the cabinet split into pro- and anti-Fawzi factions. Sadat rejected the Sabri group's demand to reopen the War of Attrition and extended the ceasefire with Israel. He also proposed to reopen the Suez Canal in return for an Israeli withdrawal from the Canal bank and sought US mediation in dealing with Israel. In Sabri's view, these were moves toward a separate peace in violation of Egypt's policy of refusal to concede Arab rights. The showdown came over Sadat's commitment to join with Syria and Libya in forming the so-called 'Federation of Arab Republics,' which Sabri opposed because Sadat took this decision without consulting the ASU executive committee. In a meeting of the committee, the Sabri majority voted the project down, but Sadat took his case to the central committee and, after a bitter personal altercation with Sabri failed to resolve the issue there, to parliament where his opponents finally conceded. By this time, both sides had about decided they could no longer co-exist and each began to try to widen their support in preparation for a confrontation.

Sabri's group ostensibly enjoyed an advantage since its members headed many of the key power institutions, including the coercive, political and information apparatuses. In these capacities, they presumably combined authority of office with clientage ties to institutional bases and organizational links to mass society. Sadat, in contrast, controlled only the office of the Presidency and the presidential guard, and while the Presidency had constitutional authority over the army, police and party, the positioning of his rivals at the apex of these institutions made the reliability of the chain of command problematic. Sadat did not, however, leave the matter to chance; rather he set out to forge alliances with the second-ranking officials in these institutions in order to cut his rivals off from their structural bases.

The struggle for control of the army was critical. Sadat met several times with top-ranking army officers to put his case and, in spite of the leftist sympathies of War Minister Muhammed Fawzi, won over the bulk of them, including Chief of Staff Muhammed Sadiq. The professional military, disliking political disunity on the home front in wartime, was disposed to support 'legitimate' authority. Sabri's Soviet connection, far from making him indispensable, focused military resentment over the Soviet advisory mission and lagging weapons deliveries on him. The military also blamed him for the scapegoating of the military brass after the 1967 defeat and leftwing challenges to military autonomy and privileges. Sadat promised to restore the military's prestige and autonomy and perhaps to rid it of the Soviet advisors. And Sadat's conservatism was far more congenial than leftwing Nasirism to the class interests of the military elite. Sadat pursued parallel efforts to win support in other state institutions. He linked up with second-rank officials in Guma's Interior Ministry and in the intelligence services; indeed a lower-ranking intelligence officer brought Sadat tapes of plotting by his superiors against the President. Technocrats were easily won over. They resented leftwing attacks on their privileges and class interests. Having struggled for a share of power against military-politicians like Sabri throughout the Nasir years, they could only welcome the chances to reach the top which a Sadat victory promised. In general, Sadat profited from the career ambitions of those who saw their prospects blocked by the Sabri group or anticipated advancement to their places after their fall. Parliament, an old stomping ground for Sadat and his ally, Marei, and a bastion of the more conservative wing of the regime's base, was readily won over to Sadat in spite of the leftwing sympathies of the Speaker. Generally, the establishment resented the Sabri group for its police abuses and relative social radicalism and welcomed Sadat as a champion who would relieve it of both.

Sadat must have believed he had secured his alliances because he struck first, dismissing Ali Sabri as Vice President. The superior legal authority by which Sadat could dismiss other office-holders allowed him to make a decisive first strike. The Sabri faction, too divided by internal rivalries (as for example, those between Sabri and Guma), lacking the legal authority for a political move against the President and too unsure how the use of force against him would be received, thus missed its chance. They could respond with nothing better than *en masse* resignations, hoping to cause a paralysis of the regime and force Sadat to compromise; but this only removed them from their already precarious bases of power. As they resigned they tried in vain to rally their institutional bases. General Fawzi assembled the military high command and accused Sadat of preparing a surrender to Israel and America; but Chief of Staff Sadiq, speaking for the military, declared it would stay out of politics. In the Interior Ministry, Mamduh Salim, a Sadat ally, quickly took over the levers of police power. The Sabri group tried to use the ASU apparatus to mobilize mass demonstrations on its behalf; but here too, its chain of command was weakened by the defection of *apparatcheki* who stayed loyal to Sadat. The ASU and the organized labor hierarchy which was, in the main, pro-Sabri, did bring some supporters into the streets for the left; but on the whole the links of Sabri's political machine to popular forces proved very brittle. Thus there was nothing to prevent Sadat from moving quickly to arrest his rivals. In the upshot, the President turned out to be the only one with reliable coercive force at his command. A key factor in this outcome was the loyalty of the presidential guard commander, General Muhammed Leithy Nassif, who carried out the arrests. The Sabri group may have thought this officer was with it because he was a personal friend of Sami Sharif, but in the crunch he put official duty to his superior ahead of personal connections (Binder 1978: 372–406; Haykel 1975: 122–38; Marei 1978a: 607–57; Rubinstein 1972; Sadat 1978: 204–24; Shukri 1978: 48–53; Waterbury 1976b: 238).

Sadat's victory had important consequences. His main opponents, the men who constituted the only serious and immediate threat to his authority he was ever to face, were removed and their places taken by his allies and clients; this was the first decisive step in the consolidation of Sadat's rule. The Free Officers were destroyed as a cohesive political force dominating the apex of power. The elites most committed to Nasirism as it had matured in the sixties were decimated and Sadat left free to steer Egypt to the right. And the purge had foreign policy implications: the removal of the men seen by the USSR as its partisans turned Moscow against Sadat and represented a signal to the US that Egypt, far from being a Soviet client state, was now governed by an elite ready to turn her Westward.

The crisis laid bare the nature of the Egyptian state without Nasir: a semi-institutionalized authoritarian-bureaucratic polity. The limits of institutionalization were manifest in the conflict over the authority of the Presidency; a consensus on the rules of intra-elite politics without Nasir did not yet exist. Hence the outcome was shaped as much by informal jockeying for political support in which personal rivalries, connections and clientage played a role, as by accepted rules. In this conflict Sadat's opponents were handicapped by their own personal rivalries and resentment among the rest of the elite at their monopoly of top positions; Sadat, who had made far fewer enemies, was an attractive patron for ambitious politicians who would profit should he sweep his rivals out of power, and he proved very skillful at the use of intra-elite rivalries in coalition-building. Nevertheless the conflict was partly shaped by impersonal rules and institutions. Wide intra-elite acceptance of the traditional legal authority of the Presidency proved decisive. It gave a man of previously modest political stature exceptional power, including the critical right to dismiss his rivals; in the crunch, loyalty to the legal supremacy of the Presidency overrode both personal links and the clientage ties of the Sabri group to its institutional bases, an outcome hard to square with pure 'bureaucratic feudalism' models of Egyptian politics.[2] Another indicator of partial institutionalization was the minor role of the military and of coercive politics in the conflict. Neither side wholly refrained from the threat or use of force and Sadat's better command of the coercive levers was critical; but this command rested on legal authority and the military, partly in deference to this authority, chose to refrain from king-making and to allow the force of legality and the competing political skills of the rivals to decide the outcome. This depoliticization of the military was a watershed in Egypt's evolution away from 'praetorianism.' Nasir had, it appears, substantially, if partially, routinized his charismatic authority in a legal institution. Sadat's victory in the succession crisis certainly reinforced this authority, an indication of which was the smooth succession on his own death.

The authority so institutionalized was, however, a bureaucratic one, incompatible with broad political participation. The mass public played little role in the succession dispute. Sadat's assumption of the Presidency was presented to the public as a *fait accompli*. Sabri's abortive attempt to mobilize mass support in the conflict demonstrated how little the party was an effective elite–mass linkage; had it been shaped into an ideological party committed to Nasirism, his power position might have been very different. That the modicum of mass political action in the crisis took the form of protest demonstrations is a manifestation of the absence of alternative means of registering mass opinion – whether through competitive elections or the mobilization party which so serve elsewhere. In the absence of the system's only elite–mass link, Nasir's charismatic bond, the decisive conflict over Egypt's future was played out largely isolated from mass demands or supports. The conflict was, however, by no means a mere elite rivalry isolated from class ideologies or interests. Sadat was greatly advantaged by his ability to appeal to the class interests represented by the elite and by the incompatibility of the Sabri group's leftwing ideology with the class interests of the power bases it was trying to mobilize against him. The Sabri group's subordinates chose Sadat over their own immediate superiors less from personal preference than as a vote against leftwing radicalism and the Soviet alignment. The outcome of the conflict would have profound consequences for the fortunes of broad social forces in Egypt and the participants understood this. But while various wings of the bourgeoisie were well represented in the struggle the masses were not. The partial institutionalization of Presidential authority cannot be separated from the rallying of the bourgeoisie as a class to Sadat.

The crisis of Israeli occupation

The first priority of Egypt's new President was necessarily to find a way of putting an end to the Israeli occupation of the Sinai. The occupation was a festering national humiliation on the resolution of which the President's legitimacy as a national leader was riding. The closure of the Suez Canal and the costs of maintaining a huge mobilized army in the desert was becoming an impossible burden on the economy. Without a solution to the occupation, Egypt had no prospects for political or economic revitalization. The creeping Israeli annexation of the territory made a solution doubly urgent. 'No war – no peace' was rapidly becoming more intolerable to Egypt than the risks of war.

Nasir's policy, resting on the assumption that the Arabs would have to recover their territory largely by force of arms, had concentrated on developing Egypt's military capability and hence the Soviet alliance. He did accept the Rogers Plan for tactical reasons, but never put much confidence in the prospect of an American peace compatible with Egypt's national honor and obligations, and consistently refused a 'separate' Egyptian–Israeli peace leaving out the other Arab states (Haykel 1975: 53–7, 97; Riad 1982: 39–50, 75, 90–1, 141–6, 168). Sadat, from the outset, showed more affinity for a negotiated compromise – even partial – settlement. His proposal to open the Suez Canal in return for a partial Israeli withdrawal was step-by-step diplomacy before Kissinger, a ploy thought by many diplomats to intimate his readiness for an interim separate peace (Riad 1982: 184–211). Moreover, for more than two years Sadat concentrated on trying to convince the Americans to sponsor a peace requiring Israeli withdrawal on the view that those who provided the Israelis with the means to maintain the occupation could alone end it. Once it was clear that diplomacy wasn't enough and that until Egypt showed she could fight her interests would be ignored, Sadat turned to his war option. But rather than planning for a war to recapture the Sinai, he decided on a strictly limited one to establish a bridgehead on the East Bank of the Canal as a way of breaking the Israeli grip on the area and opening the way to negotiations. Limited war would unite the Arab world behind Egypt, forcing use of the oil weapon; would shatter the myth of Israel's invincibility and hence her belief in security through territorial expansion and, above all, pave the way for an American-sponsored peace. This strategy meant shrinking from the total war effort needed to eliminate the Israeli occupation without negotiations in which Arab rights would have to be sacrificed and hence was a big step toward a separate peace. Sadat must also have known that the price of an American peace would be an end to Egypt's anti-imperialist Pan-Arab role.

This redirection of Egypt's post-Nasir policy was partly a function of the change in leadership. Nasir's personal pride and view of Egyptian Pan-Arab obligations had limited his flexibility, and his history of conflict with Israel and the US made them little interested in accommodating him. Sadat, more 'Egypt-centric', less capable of Pan-Arab leadership and unhandicapped by a history of personal frictions with the US, had less to lose and a greater chance of success in seeking an American-sponsored peace; he was also personally more inclined to a policy of accommodation. Many of the Westernized civilian elites Sadat brought into his inner circle and much of the bourgeoisie on whom he sought to rest his regime had lost all stomach for continuing conflict and yearned for a Western diplomatic solution (Ahmad 1975; Haykel 1975: 114–20, 146–67, 198–206; McLaurin *et al.*, 1977: 60, 70–4).

External pressures and opportunities were, however, decisive in consolidating Sadat's orientation. The views of Saudi Arabia acquired growing weight in Egyptian decision-making as Egypt's financial dependency on her increased and a more conservative elite was consolidated in Cairo. The Saudis advocated a break with the Russians and reliance on American mediation, and passed on to Egypt Washington's intimations that the first would bring the second. The Saudi's eventual commitment to use the oil weapon, if needed, to bring the US around to the Arab view, gave more credibility to a strategy of negotiations. Sadat could, as some Egyptian elites advised, have turned to Qaddafi's Libya for financial support. But Qaddafi's disdain for Sadat as an unworthy successor to Nasir, his radicalism, which found echoes among Egyptian Nasirites and Islamic militants, his insistence on unity with Egypt and the dislike of the Egyptian bourgeoisie for him, made him a political threat and liability for Sadat. Moreover, he carried no diplomatic weight in Washington (Haykel 1975: 184–98; Marei 1978a: 695–6; McLaurin *et al.* 1977: 60, 120).

More important yet were the positions of the great powers. The US seemed determined to keep Israel strong enough to render a military solution to the occupation impossible while holding out the promise, tempting to Sadat, of a diplomatic solution under its auspices. The Soviets, though unable to deliver a diplomatic solution, seemed unprepared to give Egypt the offensive military equipment which might give her a chance for a wholly military one. The Russians were skeptical of Egypt's seriousness in preparing for war, and feared a new round might end in a 1967-type disaster in which they would be asked to save Egypt and risk detente and confrontation with the US (Riad 1982: 215–17). To the Soviets, such risks seemed ever less worth while for a regime which had purged pro-Soviet leaders, was increasingly infected with anti-Soviet sentiment, and seemed prepared to chuck them for American help. They therefore alternated between advocating further pursuit of a negotiated solution and a more radical mobilization of Egyptian society in preparation for war. Sadat and those around him became convinced that Moscow either wanted to freeze the situation for the sake of detente or to bring about a leftwing revolution in Egypt. Whether to keep Egypt on a leash or believing that punishing Sadat would halt his rightward course or bring on a more pro-Soviet leadership, the Soviets procrastinated on arms deliveries to the point that Sadat took it as a calculated snub. In 1972 Sadat expelled Soviet military advisors. This was a major watershed in the evolution of his course away from the USSR and toward a search for an American peace; it resulted from both accumulated resentments against Moscow and American intimations that this step would bring the diplomatic pressure on Israel that Sadat wanted. In the most immediate sense it was the deterioration of Egyptian–Soviet relations which shaped Sadat's strategy of limited war; while the idea was in his head from the outset, limited Soviet military support foreclosed on any option other than a limited war (Haykel 1975: 165–79; Marei 1978a: 679–85; Riad 1982: 201, 230–1; Sadat 1978: 225–33; Shazli 1980: 100–2). Sadat's policy carried grave risks and costs, but he probably had no other realistic option. In theory, a radical move to the left, making Egypt eligible for greatly increased Soviet assistance and involving a total mobilization of Egyptian society for protracted war, might have allowed the liberation of the Sinai without political concessions; but, in practice, such a course was compatible with neither Sadat's orientation nor his bourgeois support base.

Relative to his search for a political settlement, Sadat's pre-war strategy was in many ways quite adept. He shrewdly maneuvered between the super-powers. A friendship treaty with the USSR signed shortly after Sabri's removal, aimed to appease and hold the Soviets to their commitments to Egypt. The expulsion of the advisors was a warning to Moscow that its Egyptian alliance could not survive disregard of Egypt's most vital national interest, the liberation of its land, and a demonstration to the US that Egypt would reverse its alignments if it suited this interest. But Sadat did not wholly burn his bridges to the Soviet Union and he finally received major quantities of weapons which were to make possible the crossing of the Canal. Simultaneously, Egyptian diplomacy exhausted in Washington and elsewhere every possibility of a settlement without resort to war. Although Sadat's warnings and overtures were ignored by the US, his diplomacy convinced the world that Israeli intransigence was the cause of the war and that Egypt sincerely wanted peace. It also paved the way for a more even-handed American mediatory role once Egypt upset the military status quo. Sadat's Arab policy, no less astute, forged the two Arab alliances critical to his strategy: military partnership with Syria made possible limited war; alliance with Saudi Arabia delivered the oil weapon and Saudi good offices with Washington. Sadat's repudiation of the 'Cold War' Nasir had carried on with the other Arab states in favor of all-Arab unity, was critical to this success

(Haykel 1975: 114–20, 198–203; Marei 1978a: 679–747; McLaurin *et al*. 1977: 71–3; Sadat 1978: 210–44; 276–89; Waterbury 1976b: 3–40).

A precarious consolidation of power

In the wake of his victory over the Sabri faction, Sadat was in a position to constitute a loyal team at the top and to extend his sway over the establishment. The new leadership was made up of veterans from the Nasir period, but, purged of the military left which held power in the sixties, it was distinctly more civilian and centrist. It was nevertheless a coalition of diverse elements united chiefly by loyalty to Sadat and opposition to his rivals. Close to the President, pro-Western and conservative, were Mahmud Fawzi, who served as Prime Minister for about a year, and Sayyid Marei, Agriculture Minister and later ASU chief. Closer to the Nasirite center were Aziz Sidqi, Industry Minister and later, Prime Minister, and Muhammed Hassanein Haykel, the influential editor of *al-Ahram*. Around these personalities was a crop of lesser technocrat–ministers. Mamduh Salim, a career police officer, politically distinguished chiefly by his loyalty to Sadat in the conflict with Sabri, assumed the critical Ministry of Interior. The military was well represented by a number of Free Officers who had sided with Sadat in the succession crisis and served either as key officials, such as Vice President Hussein Shafa'i, Foreign Minister Mahmud Riad, and Deputy Premier Abd al-Qadir Hatim, or as Presidential advisors or troubleshooters such as Hassan Tuhami and Hassan Sabri Khuli. Sadat's chief military ally, Sadiq, became War Minister. But the entrusting of the Premiership and the ASU to civilians and Sadat's close personal links to top civilians signaled the emergence of a rough power balance in the regime between military and civilian elements. Sadat's ability to balance and mediate rivalries between the civil and military, conservative and centrist wings of his team enhanced his predominance.

His new team in place at the center, Sadat extended his control over the structural bases of the regime. Pro-Sabri elements were replaced with trusted Sadat stalwarts in the ASU. Its political teeth were also drawn, for Sadat could tolerate neither the previous accumulation of power by its executive nor its pretensions to a revolutionary legitimacy potentially at odds with his own legal authority. Its legitimacy as an expression of the popular will was tarnished by accusations that it had been a mere mechanism of control, and gradually it was supplanted by parliament as the arena of intra-elite consultation. Sadat also struck at leftist elements in the trade unions, replacing them with his own men. New elections produced a more conservative parliament.

Faced with the formidable challenges inherited from Nasir, Sadat could not be content to merely assume control of the levers of state. He also had to build a base of support and generate some popular legitimacy. In this effort his strategy

49

was multi-sided. Before the mass public, he donned the mantle of Nasirism, for identification with Nasir and the Revolution was a legitimacy asset for which he had as yet no substitute. Those loyal to the Nasirite heritage were assured that its principles still governed Egypt's policy. In spite of Egypt's economic crunch, he tried to appease government employees with increases in wages and pensions. In a shrewd sally into the politics of divide and rule, he freed leaders of the Ikhwan imprisoned under Nasir and covertly encouraged a revival of Islamic groups in order to contain the left. But he did not wholly burn his bridges to the left and kept a number of token leftists in ministerial positions until *Infitah*.

Yet, Sadat lacked Nasir's charismatic stature with the masses and even had he wished to rule in the style of Nasirite populism, he could never hope to be accepted by Nasir's constituency on the same basis as the *Rais*; lacking such unchallengeable legitimacy, he could not hope to play a balancing act above the various groups and classes quite as Nasir had done. Sadat needed, therefore, to build a solid constituency among some element of Nasir's coalition which would lend him strong and consistent support and accept him as a leader, not an inferior Nasir. His choice of the bourgeoisie – in both its state and private wings – as this constituency was natural: the bourgeoisie was the most strategic social force in Egypt; it dominated the state establishment, and after 20 years of modernization, would be a much stronger base than the small upper crust so easily swept aside by the Free Officers in 1952; moreover, it was prepared to respond to Sadat's conservative ideological proclivities. Sadat's intention to court the bourgeoisie was apparent from the outset. His fight with the Sabri group was in the name of a 'correction of the revolution,' which in its assault on the personal property and rights of the bourgeoisie in the sixties, he held to have gone awry. This correction was manifested in a whole series of concrete measures pleasing to the bourgeoisie: the return of sequestered property, the lifting of 'political isolation' which allowed rich families to return to political activity, the closing of detention camps, the reining-in of the police, the reinstatement of judges fired by Nasir for their defense of property and personal rights, the repudiation of government power to seize private property. Sadat's famous public burning of the tape recordings kept by the intelligence service on the eve of his victory over Sabri was a signal that henceforth rule of law would be respected in Egypt. Some limited economic liberalization measures encouraged the investment of Arab capital in Egypt. On the foreign policy level, Sadat's overtures to the West and his growing wariness of the Soviet Union pleased bourgeois opinion (Lachine 1978: 15; Marei 1978a: 653–4; Sadat 1978: 206–10).

Nevertheless, Sadat's position could not really be secured without solutions to the acute economic and military crises faced by Egypt. Economic growth had virtually halted, sparking rising struggle over distribution and resentment among those – such as new graduates – whose aspirations could find no outlet. The army could not be satisfied until its lost honor was recovered. Sadat was expected to do something about the humiliating Israeli presence, but he appeared indecisive and unwilling to take on Israeli power. His right to rule alone in the authoritarian style of Nasir was certainly not accepted by all. A collapse of the whole regime could not be ruled out, for after Nasir's death, much of the charismatic legitimacy that had sustained it in troubled times rapidly eroded. Sadat faced a grave crisis of authority.

The most overt manifestation of this crisis was the 'student movement' which spilled over from the campuses in massive demonstrations and unrest in Egypt's cities in early 1972. The catalyst was Sadat's failure to deliver on a promise that 1971 would be the 'year of decision,' that is, of war with Israel. Sadat's apparent lack of stomach for the fight was openly ridiculed by students for whom the continuation of 'no war – no peace' was intolerable both on nationalist grounds and because being subjected to the prospect of interminable military service made it impossible to plan a normal life or career. Virtually the whole student body was united by these grievances. But students, cutting across the political spectrum, also expressed a diversity of other demands. Leftists, on the ascendency, demanded Egypt go on a serious war footing; they wanted an end to the import of luxury goods and conspicuous consumption by the bourgeoisie, demanded the rich bear their fair share of austerity and ridiculed plans to stimulate tourism in a country supposedly at war. In an attack on the conservatism of the new leadership they singled out Sayyid Marei as a 'feudalist and capitalist.' They demanded workers jailed for strikes be released. They rejected negotiations with Israel and called for firm support of the Palestinian cause and, above all, for action against the Middle East interests of the US whose feared Phantom bombers were being used for Israeli raids on Egyptian cities and factories. The right voiced Egypt's growing anti-Sovietism. Right and left converged in demands for an end to the police presence on campus, abolition of censorship and for freedom of expression. Far from being a mere campus revolt, the students, recruited from all classes, expressed in a more intense form the discontent of broad sectors of the attentive public, and indeed they were soon joined by other strategic groups. The Engineers' and Lawyers' Syndicates joined in the call for greater political freedom, while journalists pressed for an end to censorship; this open defiance by formerly docile elements of the regime's constituency was a sign of a dangerous withering of the controls long used to keep it in line. Also dangerous were efforts by students to link up with discontented workers, and the strikes and protests by workers which punctuated this whole period. The participation of junior officers in the demonstrations indicated the potential for the spread of unrest into the military where thousands of students and graduates had been conscripted into the lower ranks of the officer corps. The demand for action against Israel was sure to set off vibrations inside the military; a symptom of this was an incident in which a junior officer led a column of armored cars on the Hussein Mosque where he harangued the crowd on the need for a war of liberation. Disaffection in the streets even seeped up into parliament where the government was criticized for lack of military action and for its resort to censorship and decree law. Sadat's response was, in view of the broad base of disaffection, prudently conciliatory. While police were used to contain the protests, Sadat reserved most of his ire for student leftwingers, whom he had jailed. In a gesture of appeasement, he appointed a new government of 'austerity and confrontation' under Aziz Sidqi which promised to prepare seriously for war and raise taxes on luxury consumption. The disturbances reached a high point in January 1972 and then subsided, but sporadic worker and student protests continued into 1973 (Baker 1978: 129–30; Marei 1978a: 662–8; Sadat, speech 31 Jan. 1973; Shukri 1978: 118–29).

No sooner had Sadat weathered these popular disturbances than he was faced by a challenge from the very heart of the regime, an anti-Soviet movement exploited by ambitious elites for political ends. Anti-Soviet sentiment had become widespread in the officer corps after the 1967 defeat, fueled by resentment at the Soviet advisors and the Soviet failure to provide the arms Egypt wanted. In 1972 War Minister Muhammed Sadiq put himself at the head of disaffected officers. They were joined by three senior ex-Free Officers, Abd al-Latif Baghdadi, Kemal ad-Din Hussein, and Zakaria Muhi ad-Din, who led a petition movement within the elite calling on Sadat to limit Soviet influence as a threat to Egypt's independence. Others, including Vice President Shafa'i and prominent civilians such as Mustafa Khalil and Ismail Fahmi jumped on the bandwagon. At *al-Ahram*, Haykel opined that the Soviet failure to help Egypt justified her approaches to the United States. The Muslim right proclaimed that the Holy City could never be liberated with atheistic weapons.

This movement was a challenge to Sadat's authority because he had, up to this point, insisted that Egypt could not dispense with Soviet military help and had personally signed the Soviet friendship treaty. In addition, the ex-Free Officers accompanied their anti-Soviet demands with a call for Sadat to purge remaining leftists and share power with them in a government of national unity; their initiative seemed to enjoy wide backing among the very center–right groups Sadat counted as his own constituency. Sadat also had special reason to fear the ambitions of War Minister Sadiq, who seemed to regard himself as a king-maker for his role in the succession crisis, and was trying to use anti-Sovietism to build a military power base. He also opposed Sadat's notion of limited war. Sadat's first response was to threaten to strike at his opponents; he had no intention, he warned, of compromising Presidential authority. But then, in a bid to coopt anti-Sovietism, he followed with the wholesale expulsion of the Soviet advisors. His hand so strengthened, and the opposition from the right appeased, Sadat quickly sacked Sadiq as War Minister (Haykel 1975: 180–1; McLaurin *et al.* 1977: 65–8; Sadat 1978: 234–7).

Having removed the threat from the 'right,' Sadat moved to demolish the persisting threat from the left. In early 1973 university campuses were closed in a bid to stop a resurgence of the student movement. A wave of purges swept remaining leftwingers out of the ASU, the media establishment and university faculties. This was a retribution against the 'adventurous left' which had sought to push Sadat into struggles with Israel and the US of a kind and at a time not to his liking. Sadat then dismissed Aziz Sidqi as Premier and assumed the portfolio himself, thereby removing an ambitious and independent personality on the center–left of the political spectrum. Sidqi was identified with mainstream Nasirite policies such as public sector industrialization with Soviet aid. He had supported Sadat against Sabri, but his ambition and his apparent bid as premier to build a popular base independent of the President made him suspect. He clashed with conservative landlords in parliament, who resented his effort to shift the tax burden to the rich and his support of statist industrial interests, and with Sayyid Marei who encouraged anti-statist elements in the ASU to criticize the cabinet and fanned Sadat's suspicions of the Prime Minister. Sidqi did not hide his doubts about American mediation or his contempt for the 'defeatism' he saw growing in conservative circles. Sadat removed him both because he found his independence and orientation uncongenial and as a concession to the right. Sidqi was out of step with the brand of conservative liberalism spreading with Sadat's blessing in elite circles (Fahmi 1983: 13, Marei 1978a: 674–8, 689–92; 708).

These challenges to Sadat and his responses reveal something about the nature of Egyptian politics. The widespread activism of this period, largely on issue and ideological grounds, is hardly compatible with the view that traditional passivity and patron–clientalism dominated the political arena. The eruption of political activism at this time can be explained by the precarious legitimacy of the leader, the failure of policies, and the relaxation of police controls, just as the quiescence of the Nasir period is better explained by the opposite than by any political-cultural immunity of Egyptians to political activism. But because the system provided no effective institutional channels for activism it took the form of the petition, strike, or demonstration and though parliament did mirror what was happening in the streets, it was little more than a sounding board. The President was not immune to such outbursts from below and had to bend with the political wind. But because political demands were contradictory, Sadat had some choice as to which he would respond. His opponents, divided, could not come together against him, while he could strike at them one by one. To survive in the long-run however, Sadat would have to legitimize his regime.

Sadat redirects Egypt (1974–6)

The October 1973 War was a major watershed in the development of the Egyptian political system under Sadat. Sadat's ability to take credit for the war, and portray himself as the 'Hero of the Crossing,' greatly enhanced his personal legitimacy and made him a leader in his own right. For a decisive two to three years, he was virtually free from challenges; the beleaguered, insecure Sadat of the pre-war period was transformed into a President radiating confidence and determined to get his way. The whole political establishment was strengthened by the war; there was a 'rekindling of political will' which, for a while, recharged the political elite with new hopes and energies (Baker 1978: 132). Sadat used the political capital won in the war and the opportunities created by it to transform Egypt's foreign policy and economic strategy. In the *October Paper*, the document setting forth his intended post-war course, he stressed continuity as much as change. In practice, his subsequent reversal of Nasir's priorities was of the magnitude of a 'counter-revolution' from above. Global forces played the most immediate role in the shaping of Sadat's course after October. His attempt to manipulate them produced a foreign policy opening to the West and a corresponding economic *Infitah* which altered the balance of power in state and society, permitting a virtual 'restoration' of the bourgeoisie.

Sadat's new foreign and economic policies: the forces of transformation

Sadat insisted that his new course was a mere adaptation of Nasir's nationalist foreign policy to new conditions. There would be an opening to the West, but Egypt would remain non-aligned. The struggle to regain lost Arab land would continue. Arabism remained a policy cornerstone, though in place of revolutionary Pan-Arabism, he envisioned a network of economic and diplomatic cooperation linking Egypt to the wealthy Arab oil states. In fact, by the end of 1976, a major foreign policy transformation was well on its way to consummation. Egypt's relations with the Soviet Union, hitherto its main political and military backer, were close to the breaking point; instead Sadat unabashedly pursued the patronage of the United States, the country he had shortly before recognized as the main backer of Egypt's Israeli tormentor. Equally remarkable, in two major post-war troop disengagement agreements, Sinai I (1974) and Sinai II (1975), Sadat accepted partial and separate accords with Israel which came close to withdrawing Egypt from the military conflict, and decisively weakened the Arabs' ability to force a total Israeli withdrawal from all Arab lands. Not just Egypt's traditional leadership of Arab nationalism was destroyed by this go-it-alone policy, but access to the new Arab wealth she needed was jeopardized. What explains this dramatic reversal of Egypt's traditional foreign policy?

The predisposition for this course had been established by elite disillusion-ment with the costs and failures of Nasir's Pan-Arabism and by the post-1967 friction with the USSR. Only the failure of the US to respond to Sadat's overtures prevented a policy transformation prior to the October War. Paradoxically, Egypt's relative success in the war actually strengthened this tendency, for the vindication of her humiliated pride was a psychological watershed permitting Egyptians to consider a withdrawal from Nasir's Pan-Arab visions and ambitions without damage to their self-image. The military–political power balance at the close of the October War was, however, the most immediate determinant of Egypt's course. Sadat's strategy of seizing a foothold on the East Bank of the Canal succeeded so well that he decided to push further into the Sinai but this campaign, too late and poorly conceived, ended in a retreat. The Israelis regained the initiative and carved out a 'salient' on the West Bank of the Canal which put Sadat's armies to the east in jeopardy. Forced to accept a ceasefire under these conditions, Sadat found that his bargaining hand, insofar as it depended on the military balance, was weak (Haykel 1975: 214–16; Shazli: 1980: 270). His political leverage, by contrast, was much stronger. American policy was now conscious, in the wake of the oil embargo, of the need to placate the Arabs if US Middle East interests were to survive. Israel was put on the defensive; its military superiority had been challenged with some success and its American patron now expected it to cooperate in efforts to defuse the Middle East crisis. The US perceived that Egypt was ready for a peace settlement and that a successful American mediation effort might both protect its interests and 'roll back' Soviet influence in the area.

When Kissinger arrived to mediate a disengagement of forces, Sadat responded with alacrity. In part, he feared a resumption of the fighting might go against him. The Soviets' failure, in the face of American intimidation, to enforce the ceasefire against Israeli violations convinced him he could not depend on their help. His whole position as 'Hero of the Crossing' was at risk if he lost his Sinai foothold. In any case, American mediation was what he had wanted all along. Anxious to demonstrate to the Americans his statesmanship and readiness for peace, Sadat underplayed his hand in the negotiations.[3] The resulting agreement removed the Israeli salient and entrenched and legitimized an Egyptian presence in the Sinai, thus rescuing Sadat from his military predicament. It committed the US to continuing the mediatory role he wanted. But, by defusing the war crisis and ending the oil boycott, the disengagement destroyed the conditions which might have forced rapid super-power imposition of a comprehensive settlement; and by accepting a withdrawal of his missiles on the West Bank of the Canal and a mere token force in the east, Sadat seriously weakened the war option needed to play a credible hand in subsequent negotiations. Sinai I was perhaps the major watershed in the transformation of Egypt's foreign policy (Brown 1980: 37–50; Fahmi 1983: 45–51, 69–81; Golan 1976: 146–64; Sheehan 1976).

The next step was Sinai II, a second disengagement agreement which significantly deepened Egypt's disengagement from the Arab–Israeli conflict and her realignment with the US but at the expense of a more comprehensive settlement. Sinai I set the stage for it by reducing Sadat's military option, staking his prestige on American mediation, and making him grateful to and trustful of Kissinger. The worsening of Soviet–Egyptian relations, further narrowing Sadat's options, also helped push him into Sinai II. In spite of the bad blood between Sadat and the Kremlin, the Russians had provided the weaponry which made the Canal crossing possible and they thought they were entitled to some gratitude. To Sadat, however, they had again demonstrated, in the ceasefire affair, their unreliability. When he opted to put his eggs in the American basket, the Soviets either decided to punish him or to cut their losses in Egypt. They refused to replace much of the weaponry Egypt had lost in the war or help him out of his economic difficulties (Fahmi 1983: 170–5, 186–7). Cut off from Soviet support, Egypt's military capability deteriorated; its bargaining leverage with Israel declined and its dependency on American diplomacy increased. Sinai II had risks and costs, but if Sadat wished to keep American patronage, he could hardly refuse an American sponsored agreement. Post-war economic constraints and opportunities pulled in the same direction. Egypt's options were sharply constrained by her economic problems; on the other hand, the war had opened up new sources of economic help, surplus Arab petro-dollars and Western aid and investment. Both the West and the conservative oil Arabs began to provide Egypt with enough aid to stay afloat, consolidating a growing economic dependency which had direct bearing on foreign policy: continuing aid and investment could only be expected in the context of a diplomatic and economic opening to the capitalist world. Ultimately, this depended on ending the conflict with Israel. By the middle of 1975, the obstacles to a comprehensive settlement seemed to have convinced Sadat that Sinai II was the only viable road to this end. Negotiations for a comprehensive settlement seemed bogged down. The Arabs withdrew from Jordan and gave the PLO (Palestine Liberation Organization), with whom the Israelis refused to deal, the right to bargain for the Jordan's West Bank. Israel seemed determined to avoid an overall settlement in exchange for conquered territory and the Americans appeared unwilling to force her into one. Thus, Sadat was faced with the choice of holding out in an effort to increase pressure on the US and Israel to move toward a general settlement, or taking the easier path toward a separate one. In the Sinai II agreement he took a decisive step along the latter road.

In essence, the accord exchanged a limited Israeli withdrawal in the Sinai for a mere token Egyptian military presence there and American 'observers' between the two armies. Thus it nearly put an end to the Egyptian war option and came close to taking Egypt out of the Arab–Israeli power balance. Since Israel won, as the price of her withdrawal, a massive delivery of advanced weaponry from the US, it came out of the agreement with enhanced military superiority over the Arabs and a much-reduced incentive to make further concessions for the sake of peace. Israel also won an American promise to refrain from pressing it into dealings with the PLO or concessions to Syria. Indeed, the Americans, satisfied that the Arab–Israeli conflict had been defused for the immediate future, lost the sense of urgency which had driven their post-war diplomacy. By relying exclusively on the Americans and agreeing to a separate second disengagement Sadat decisively undermined the prospects of a general Arab–Israeli settlement. The agreement was also a first step in Egypt's withdrawal from the Arab world: it caused a decrease in Arab financial support to which Egypt was entitled as a front line state and it was a big step in alienating her from Arab nationalist opinion which had long-sustained Egyptian leadership in the Arab world. As against these longer-range costs, Sadat finally had concrete benefits to show for his war and diplomacy: the Suez Canal and Sinai oil fields won back, a significant withdrawal of the Israeli army, ending its threat to the Egyptian heartland, the promise of a massive infusion of Western aid into the economy. Before long, however, Sadat would again be faced with the choice of sticking with the Arab world in pursuit of a comprehensive settlement made much less likely by his own actions, or taking the ultimate steps toward a separate peace. Just as his war strategy ended in Sinai I, and the latter led to Sinai II, so the last would push Sadat along the road to Jerusalem (Baker 1978: 136–48; Brown 1980: 148–53, 208–20; Fahmi 1983: 164–5).

Simultaneously, Egypt's economic policy was undergoing an equally radical transformation. A creeping liberalization had since 1968 been gnawing at Nasir's socialist edifice, setting the stage for this (Cooper 1979). But the announcement of the *Infitah*, marked an entirely new direction in economic policy. Sadat insisted that the new policy intended no retreat from 'socialism,' but an adaptation to new conditions. Egypt's economy, he argued, sapped by military spending and bureaucratic inertia could not alone mobilize sufficient resources for an economic recovery. Post-1973 conditions, were, however, right for attracting a major influx of Arab and foreign capital; hence an economic open door was required. Moreover, recovery required that the private sector be revitalized and allowed to play a role in the economy (Ministry of Information 1974: 60–5). In practice, however, *Infitah* spelled a major reversal of Nasirist economics: through an unrestricted opening of the economy to foreign imports and investment, a recession of etatist and populist intervention in it and a downgrading of the public sector, Egypt was gradually reintegrated into the world capitalist system.

A multitude of forces converged to produce this policy transformation. Egypt's economic crisis in the early seventies was certainly one powerful factor behind it. The economy was stagnant, growth having fallen to perhaps 1% by 1974 while, in good part because of defense burdens, average private consumption was actually around 7% lower than a decade earlier. The country labored under a staggering debt load, estimated at from $4 billion to $10 billion, and 1974 debt service absorbed 40% of export earnings. Rapid population growth continued. The prospects of extracting much of a surplus from an already impoverished society appeared dim: to squeeze either the masses, taught under Nasir that they were entitled to a minimum of economic rights or the bourgeoisie which expected a rising standard of living in return for the support the regime needed, carried grave political risks. Much of the elite had lost faith in a public sector burdened by bureaucratic inefficiency, corruption, and populism as a viable engine of development. This was especially so in the absence of the Soviet technical and financial support on which it depended, and, in any case, much of the elite believed more and better such support was available in the West. Last, but not least, as population growth surged ahead of a stagnant agriculture, Egypt steadily lost the ability to feed herself and the West alone possessed the food surplus needed to make up the gap; to buy it required hard currency obtainable only in the West and to get it as aid required a Westward reorientation. On many counts, therefore, a convincing case could be made that Nasirism had failed and that Egypt could not survive without an economic bailout which only the rich Arabs and the West could provide (Waterbury 1976b: 201–15; 1976c: 322–5).

Fortuitously, Egypt's grave need was matched by new opportunities. The post-war Western concern to safeguard its Middle Eastern interests, combined with Egypt's Westward diplomatic opening, made Egypt eligible as never before for Western capital and technology. The post-war boom in oil prices produced a massive transfer of global wealth to the Arab oil producers which Egypt had a chance – and having helped produce it, perhaps a right – to share. To continue a policy of socialist austerity amidst such capitalist riches must have seemed foolish if not impossible; rather, Egyptian elites perceived a unique opportunity to spark a new economic takeoff combining Western technology, Arab capital and Egyptian manpower. The opening to the international capitalist market was tailored to make this possible. To attract capital and to compete on this market, in turn, required the internal introduction of capitalist economic norms. Once Egypt began to get a share of the new wealth, she rapidly became ever more dependent on it; an enormous increase in imports after the war quadrupled her balance of payments deficit in 1975–6 and thereafter a huge deficit covered by Western or Arab aid became a permanent fixture of the economy. This dependency made the new course increasingly irreversible. The country also became more vulnerable to constraints on her policy options issuing from external donors and investors who were undivided in urging, as a condition of continued assistance, a more thorough and rapid dismantling of

Nasirite policies in favor of the capitalist market. Once these forces had joined to local interests, they acquired a foothold in the political process which further increased their clout.

While 'objective' economic factors set the context for Egypt's economic policy changes, the actual decisions resulted from a political process in which the balance of power was rapidly shifting toward indigenous social forces with an interest in these changes. The private bourgeoisie was recovering its economic power and political influence. Small and medium capitalists encouraged by the modest liberalization after 1967 were joined by the return to Egypt of those who had made fortunes in the Arabian Gulf. Segments of the state bourgeoisie recruited from private sector families or enriched in office were friendly to private enterprise and little enthused about 'socialism.' Both these elements wanted the security and opportunities to increase their wealth, and the access to Western goods which the Nasirite system failed to provide. They were aware that a free market system which rewarded those with scarce capital and skills was far more favorable to them than one which tried to minimize these effects by administrative means. They knew that economic liberalization would open up enormous new opportunities as traders, agents and partners with foreign firms for those with Western connections, education and business experience. Those in official positions were aware of the opportunities for commissions, or higher paying jobs in foreign firms. They were therefore easily convinced that Nasirism had failed, though their own opposition explained, in part, its failure. The bourgeoisie pressed vigorously for many of the changes which became a part of *Infitah*, and once *Infitah* was adopted bourgeois pressure groups scrambled to take advantage of and extend it (Ahmad 1975: 53; Shukri 1978: 39–51; Waterbury 1976c: 305–13).

Finally Sadat's own preferences and political needs played a critical role in the new policy. He shared the view of the bourgeoisie that Nasir's 'socialism' had outlived its usefulness. A new course was needed to consolidate his support among the bourgeoisie, and indeed, his commitment to *Infitah* soon brought much of this class to regard him as virtually indispensable. Most decisive, Sadat viewed *Infitah* as inseparable from his foreign policy: he believed that the kind of American commitment needed to recover the Sinai from Israel was contingent on Egypt's reintegration into the world capitalist system, and that the greater the economic opportunities opened to American investors, the more sympathetic the American government was likely to be (Baker 1978: 137). Thus, Sadat had multiple reasons to initiate *Infitah* and though he did so under pressure of domestic demands and foreign constraints, he did not do so reluctantly.

The intimate linkage between foreign policy alliances and economic strategies in weak vulnerable states such as Egypt is clearly manifest in the dynamics of policy change in Egypt. Just as Nasir's conflicts with the West and friendly Soviet overtures were associated with moves away from capitalism and conflicts with the local bourgeoisie, so the collapse of Egypt's Soviet alliance and the growing responsiveness of the US to Sadat's needs, were associated with the opposite. It was not that external forces determined internal events; rather, the two were related in a process of mutually reinforcing positive feedback. Thus, Sadat's purge of the Sabri group diluted Soviet support; this paved the way for post-war American responsiveness which in turn reinforced Sadat's liberalization of internal policy and his alliance with the bourgeoisie.

The politics of policy transformation

While the transformation of Egyptian policy was shaped by a convergence of external and internal forces, it was, in most immediate terms, the result of leadership by a revitalized Presidency. To impose his new course, Sadat had to defeat persistent opposition inside the political elite, mobilize potential support and neutralize potential opposition among the wider public. The character of the political system was decisive in determining the outcome of this struggle.

The first challenge to Sadat's new course was from elements inside the elite opposed to his reliance on American diplomacy to achieve an Israeli withdrawal. In relatively short order Sadat disposed of these dissidents. The first major casualty was the Chief of Staff, Saad ad-Din Shazli, who was dismissed in December 1973 because of differences with Sadat over the conduct of the war and the subordination of the military option to American mediation. In spite of Shazli's popularity in the officer corps, the support of most of the top brass for Sadat neutralized him. The next to go was Muhammed Hassanein Haykel, the influential editor of *al-Ahram*, who used his newspaper to question the wisdom of relying exclusively on Kissinger in the negotiations process. Haykel believed that if the Arabs combined a continuing war option and the oil weapon, they had the leverage to force a favorable overall peace settlement. A disciple of Nasir's policy of balancing the great powers, Haykel had advocated a diplomatic opening to the US to match Egypt's dependence on the USSR, but Sadat's American alignment seemed to be replacing one dependency for another. Haykel was also an advocate of Egyptian ties with Qaddafi, as a way of reducing Egyptian dependence on the conservative oil princes, and had criticized Sadat's coolness toward Libya. And he had openly described the outcome of the war portrayed by Sadat as a great victory as 'no victory – no defeat.' Sadat could not tolerate an establishment voice so at variance with his policies; moreover, he must have believed that such voices casting doubt on American motives jeopardized his chances of convincing Washington that Egypt's opening to the West was more than a mere tactical maneuver. The replacement of Haykel by Ali Amin, a rightwing journalist known for his American ties, was intended as a signal of reassurance to Washington. Despite his great prestige as a long-time confidant of Nasir and his wide-ranging contacts in the establishment, Haykel was also dismissed with ease. In the following months, other leftovers from the Nasir era were also edged out of the establishment either because of more muted disagreements with Sadat or because the President wanted his own men in their places. Vice President Shafa'i, a senior Free Officer and former RCC member was replaced by the commander of the Air Force, Husni Mubarak, in April 1975; thus Sadat sought to consolidate his support in the professional military, reward the 'Heroes of October' and dispose of a last prominent symbol of the Nasir era possessing revolutionary credentials equal to his own. A number of other Free Officers were also quietly retired. Thus, Sadat disposed of most of the remaining old revolutionaries with some claim to be consulted on policy and with a stake in the past. Even Hafiz Ismail, Sadat's national security advisor, and once described as his 'Kissinger,' was removed over foreign policy differences. Sadat now placed in power his own men, many beholden to him for their rise and almost exclusively from the center and right of the political spectrum. In 1974 a new cabinet was formed under Abd al-Aziz Higazi, a liberal economist with good connections to Western financial circles. Sadat's personal confidant, Sayyid Marei, a staunch advocate of liberalization, was made Speaker of the parliament, charged with revitalizing it as the regime's main link to its bourgeois constituency (Aulus 1976). Thus Sadat strengthened the personal power needed to pursue his policies.

In 1974–5, Sadat initiated a public debate over Nasir's heritage and Egypt's future course which, developing into a growing attack on the policies of his predecessor, came to be known as the 'de-Nasirization campaign.' Sadat portrayed himself as standing above this debate as a neutral arbiter, unwilling to see the ideals of the Egyptian revolution disparaged, but prepared to listen to those advocating changes in the methods of realizing them. In fact, Sadat was giving the 'green light' to the right wing to launch an open attack on Nasirism, as a way of broadening support for a new course. It responded with alacrity, sparing almost no part of this heritage. Nasir was accused of having replaced a British occupation with an Israeli one, of having stifled all initiative in a tide of bureaucratization, of ruining the economy by his socialist policies, and, of favoring loyalty over merit at the top. The major attack on Nasirism concentrated on its biggest vulnerability, 'dictatorship.' Attacks on the loss of political freedom, abuses of human rights by the police, mass arrests of opponents, seizure of private property and violations of the judiciary were themes calculated to appeal to all across the political spectrum who had suffered for their dissent under Nasir. At the same time, the right was allowed to press for a reversal of Nasirist policies. It pushed for a widening of political freedoms, rule of law, and an end to the political role of the police. It vigorously advocated the translation of the principle of *Infitah* into a wide range of concrete liberalization measures: the liberalization of trade, an end to punitive taxation of high incomes, and to limits on land ownership, permission for foreign banks to come into Egypt and a reduction of the public sector in favor of private enterprise. A growing boldness in its demands on government in the assembly reflected the feeling of the bourgeoisie that power was flowing its way. On the other hand, while voices in defense of Nasirism or opposed to liberalization were not absent, they were muted and ambivalent. The left argued that, for all its faults, the public sector was superior to private and foreign investment as a motor of development and predicted that *Infitah* would result in growing corruption and a loss of national independence. But leftists acknowledged the repression under Nasir from which, indeed, some of them had suffered. Some even argued that Nasirism had merely produced a corrupt 'state bourgeoisie,' or admitted that in an era of surplus petro-dollars an economic open door made some sense. Those wishing to defend even parts of the Nasirite heritage were put on the defensive by the undeniable failures and costs of Nasir's rule (Ajami 1981: 95–7; Waterbury 1976b: 235–55).

The de-Nasirization campaign accomplished its objective, a considerable strengthening in Sadat's personal power position. By activating the right wing of the bourgeoisie Sadat had widened the scope of conflict, bringing in forces which favored his rightward course and diluting the resistance of elements inside the state establishment who were dubious of it. By encouraging overt divisions in elite opinion, yet refraining from taking sides, Sadat was able to bring the competing opinion groups to accept him as an arbiter above the fray and hence immune from attack. Tarnishing the image of Nasirism made it easier for Sadat to reverse Nasir's policies; cutting Nasir down to size enabled Sadat to escape being measured by fidelity to his ways and made room for a new hero to emerge on the Egyptian stage. Thus de-Nasirization was paralleled by an official cult of personality portraying Sadat as the 'Hero of the Crossing.' Sadat's willingness to risk de-Nasirization suggested that, in his calculations, his own legitimacy was now secure, no longer dependent on his status as Nasir's successor.

The mass political arena was not wholly devoid of protest or reaction against de-Nasirization, *Infitah*, or continuing economic difficulties. For those at the bottom, there was little improvement in the first years after the war. The higher growth rate, about 4% per year in 1974–6, was, given a 2.2% population growth, insufficient to make much immediate difference. Not only were major financial infusions not yet forthcoming, but the government labored under a severe liquidity crisis, in no small part due to skyrocketing prices of imported food. There were food shortages, public services were allowed to deteriorate and an inflationary spiral reaching perhaps 30% per year allowed to go unabated. A worsening unemployment problem was indicated by the decline of the absorption rate of new entrants into the job market from 80% before 1967 to 50% by 1974. At the same time there was an explosion in luxury imports and conspicuous consumption by the bourgeoisie; for example, the importation of cars jumped from about 5000 per year before 1967 to 25,000 in 1973–4 alone (Kanovsky 1978: 230; Kanovsky 1981: 360–1). Popular discontent with policy changes and continuing economic troubles did sporadically take a political form. Bus drivers went on strike for higher wages, an illegal and rare form of protest in Egypt, and there were riots over the breakdown of public transport; in 1975–6 there were strikes and marches on parliament and disturbances by industrial workers (Shukri 1978: 256–60). Their chants – 'Where is our breakfast, Oh Hero of the Crossing?' 'Nasir, where are you?' 'Out with Higazi' – showed that some workers were making a connection between the new policies and their personal distress. Groups of students supported the worker protests, defended Nasirism and denounced the 'selling of the country to the imperialists' and the *Infitah*. The communist party, which under Nasir had merged with the ASU, reconstituted itself as a clandestine organization. And there was a first sign that Islamic fundamentalism, regarded by the regime as an ally against the left, could take a hostile form: young militants of the 'Islamic Liberation Party' attempted an abortive *coup d'etat* against Sadat in the name of Arab unity and Islamic government and against accommodation with Israel and the West.

Yet what was more remarkable was the very limited scale and effectiveness of mass protest against what was, after all, the dismantling of much of the work of the adored hero, Nasir, to the apparent benefit of the 'haves'. Active opposition was sporadic, uncoordinated and, in most cases, confined to relatively small segments of workers and students; occasional larger-scale disturbances resulted as much from specific grievances as opposition in principle to government policy. And the peasantry, under the influence of pro-regime notables, remained largely inert through it all. In fact, the years of de-Nasirization were, as compared to the pre-war and late-seventies periods, the most free of opposition for Sadat. This was due in part to the authoritarian–bureaucratic nature of the political system. The absence of an organized political force committed to Nasirism and of rights and channels of political participation made it easy for Sadat's men to capture the state and hard for Nasirites to mobilize support from above or below. Equally important, however, was the erosion of the myth of Nasir and the contrasting rise in the personal legitimacy of Sadat. While Nasir appeared, to many, to have left Egypt in very difficult circumstances, Sadat appeared to be extricating her from them. His immense prestige as an apparently successful war leader put him temporarily beyond criticism; symptomatic of the new mood was an article in a leftwing journal which supported worker protests but felt obliged to hail the government 'which could fight Israel.' Having broken the Israeli hold on Egypt's territory, Sadat's promises to lead her into a new age of peace and prosperity enjoyed after October all the credibility they lacked before and which, in time, they would lose. Some Egyptians, believing that Egypt's sacrifices were over and that she would reap the benefits of the war – an honorable peace and Arab money – were prepared to leave the details to Sadat; most were at least willing to give his new policies a chance. And many were not even aware that the new order meant a repudiation of Nasir's heritage, for it unfolded only gradually, accompanied in the beginning by protestations of loyalty to the revolution. Thus, it appears that when the leader's legitimacy is high by virtue of success against the foreigner, or an improvement in conditions of life, Egyptians are prepared to grant him respect, obedience and exceedingly broad discretion to decide for the country as he thinks best. That legitimacy and political structure, rather than an unchanging political culture, best account for mass quiescence in this period is indicated by the contrast with the opposition Sadat faced before 1973 when his legitimacy was low and after 1976 when hitherto non-existent channels of political activism emerged.

In 1975–6 several cracks appeared in the *Infitah* team, but the outcome of the episode only further consolidated the new economic policy. In 1975 Prime Minister Higazi resigned, apparently a victim of resistance to *Infitah*. He was a scapegoat for the emerging twin ills of the economic open door, inflation and corruption. 'If we are not capable of putting an end to corruption' or controlling 'unbearable increases' in prices, declared Sadat, 'we are in trouble.' Higazi's replacement was Interior Minister Mamduh Salim who announced that his mission was to push on with *Infitah* against those in the state apparatus who were obstructing it. Sadat wanted a stronger hand at the tiller to protect *Infitah* from both those who opposed it and those who abused it. Then in 1976 there was a turnover in Egypt's top economic managers following their resistance to IMF demands, backed by Egypt's international donors, for further economic rationalization in exchange for continued aid, including cuts in subsidies to popular consumption goods. Sadat, in bad need of a new infusion of funds and convinced of the need to show he could take the hard decisions needed to establish a sound fiscal and investment climate, overruled his ministers and brought in a new more-liberal team headed by Abd al-Munim Qaysuni to implement the IMF demands. Thus, outside intervention in the policy process pushed Egypt a further step along the road of *Infitah* (Aulus 1976: 86–9; Dessouki 1981: 414–15).

The middle years of Sadat's rule seemed to end not only in the consolidation of a new policy course but also a restoration of the personalistic and authoritarian–bureaucratic nature of the state which in the pre-war period had seemed jeopardized by the decline in the power of the ruler and the control of the regime over society. Personalism was most marked at the top, in the greatly enhanced personal power and legitimacy of the President, the cult of personality, the ease with which Sadat swept aside the objections of other elites to his policies. The fate of those who opposed Sadat manifested the bureaucratic side of politics: men who were counted powerful while in office, lost all power as soon as they lost their office. The ease of removal of men like Shazli and Haykel, who enjoyed extensive clientage ties and prestige, and their apparent inability or unwillingness to mobilize clients and allies as a check on Presidential authority suggested how little such resources could stand up to a revitalized Presidential chain of command. Nor could these elites, basically officials rather than politicians with popular constituencies, overtly appeal for public support in intra-elite conflicts. As such, the big policy conflicts which decided Egypt's post-populist redirection took place in a limited bureaucratic arena. The Egyptian state appeared in this period almost a mere complex of offices filled and emptied at the whim of the President, as if it were his personal patrimony.

Yet wider political forces were not in fact irrelevant to the intra-elite political struggle. Sadat's consolidation of power was due in part to his success in mobilizing the right wing of the bourgeoisie to his side on the basis of class interest. Conversely, his ability, based on a new-found legitimacy and authoritarian controls, to contain the mobilization of counter-forces from other parts of the political spectrum neutralized a variety of potential constraints on his actions. Finally, the impact of external forces on the decision-making process was especially marked in this period. The identification of an actor in the power struggle with the global forces on which Egypt was becoming dependent was an asset, resistance to them a liability; thus, most of the elites purged by Sadat fell in opposition to Western pressures on Egypt which Sadat chose to accommodate – whether the Kissinger-engineered deals with Israel or IMF demands – while those brought in to replace them were on friendly terms with the West. The relative passivity of the political arena, excepting the pro-Western bourgeoisie, and the intolerance of the authoritarian system for opposition, probably made Egypt more vulnerable to foreign demands, because in the absence of countervailing internal pressures on decision-makers, they could afford to be especially accommodative to the outside.

The crystallization of post-populist Egypt (1977–81)

This final period (1977–81) was marked by two major developments: (1) Sadat's foreign and economic policies climaxed in a new order; (2) there was a resurgence of opposition to this order which, together with Sadat's efforts to accommodate and contain it, gave a new more pluralized, less patrimonial shape to the political system.

A revolution in foreign policy alignments

Sadat's foreign policies culminated in the late seventies in a remarkable revolution in Egypt's international alignments which sacrificed its place in the Arab world for a separate peace with Israel and exchanged non-alignment for overt American clientage. This outcome was prefigured by Sinai II, but, publicly, Sadat remained committed to Egypt's traditional foreign policy for nearly two years afterwards. He held to the common Arab position on a comprehensive peace with Israel. Egypt sought an all-party Geneva conference with a role for the PLO, rejected formal peace with Israel as long as she occupied Arab land, and considered that normalization of relations would be a very long-term process. Sadat insisted that if negotiations failed, Egypt still had a military option. How, then, did this foreign policy transformation come about? By late 1977, peace negotiations were stalled and Sadat was becoming impatient. Egypt and her leaders badly needed peace and the return of the Sinai. Sadat's prestige would dissipate in the absence of new movement toward the goals for which the October War was fought. The Arab aid on which he was counting to redeem his promise of prosperity, was declining as Egypt withdrew from the conflict with Israel. The Arabs seemed prepared to give Egypt less than a fifth of the $12 billion Sadat considered essential. The parsimony of the Arab oil states toward Egypt, their readiness to join Western creditors in pressuring her for austerity and the humiliation of having to beg for what Egypt thought her war sacrifices had entitled her, disposed Egyptian leaders to look to Egypt's own interests regardless of the Arab consensus. But the most immediate factor pushing Sadat toward a change in policy was his growing perception of an all-party Geneva conference as an intolerably protracted if not dead-end road to peace. Israel was determined to keep her hold on the Palestinian West Bank and the Golan Heights. Sadat's inability, owing to his fight with the USSR, to rebuild Egyptian military capability, together with the outcome of Sinai II, gave the Arabs little military leverage over Israel. Thus, only pressure the American president was extremely reluctant to exert would budge her from these territories. If Egypt stuck with the Arab position, she might get nothing more in the Sinai (Sadat 1978: 302–4). But Sadat knew Israel would be willing to relinquish the Sinai for a separate peace which put Egypt out of the Arab–Israeli power balance and relieved pressure on her for a wider settlement. These factors, added to Sadat's personal impulsiveness and, as Fahmi (1983: 283) put it, 'weakness for the *grande geste*' led him to decide on his historic trip to Jerusalem. He calculated that the 'electric shock' effect of the trip would mobilize American opinion on Egypt's side, revitalize the sagging US commitment to a Middle East peace, and make it harder for Israeli hardliners to obstruct one. It might not only push Israel back from the Sinai but unjam the whole peace process. In fact, the trip did dramatically underline Egypt's desire for peace and revitalize the American mediatory role. But it was also a tacit recognition of Israel and her control of Jerusalem without a *quid pro quo*. Because the other parties to the conflict, Syria and the PLO, distrusted Sadat and refused to follow his lead, and because Israel realized he was prepared to proceed without them (Fahmi 1983: 289), the trip in practice both increased Sadat's leverage in bargaining for Egypt and further undermined the prospects for a comprehensive settlement (Fahmi 1983: 188–251; Lachine 1978: 23).

The trip marked a final break in Egypt's already poor relations with the radical Arab states. The mini-war between Egypt and Libya expressed the conflict between a classical Arab nationalist policy and Sadat's movement in the opposite direction. Relations with Syria, Sadat's necessary partner in any military action, were broken. After Palestinians assassinated Sadat's confidant, Yusuf Sabai, and killed Egyptian commandoes at Larnaka Airport, Sadat, in major breaks with precedent, denounced *fedayeen* raids on Israel and repudiated the claim of the PLO to be the legitimate representative of Palestinians. Sadat was rapidly burning his bridges to Arab nationalism.

Subsequent to the Jerusalem trip, Sadat worked to translate Egypt's new stature in American eyes and Washington's verbal commitment to Israeli withdrawal into concrete pressures on Begin. At Camp David he found out just how much his new diplomatic currency would purchase and in the absence of a credible military threat, it was far less than he hoped. The Sinai would be returned to Egypt, but the most Israel could be brought to concede on the West Bank was an undefined 'autonomy' and Begin ruled out a Sinai-like settlement with Syria. Thus Sadat was faced with the choice of conceding failure or accepting a separate peace and trying to translate 'autonomy' into some real dilution of Israeli control on the West Bank. While a part of the Egyptian elite argued against Camp David, Sadat's enormous personal stake in the 'peace process' probably made a retreat impossible. The new popularity he had won as 'Hero of Peace' would be forfeited and the initiative conceded to his radical opponents. Sadat's sense of his personal mission to bring peace to Egypt had been heightened by internal and external acclaim. Egyptians expected him to deliver peace. He savored his image in the West as a courageous and far-sighted statesman who alone had defied conventional opinion in pursuit of it, and would not tarnish it by a return to the 'fear and hatred,' the transcendence of which set him apart from the Syrian and Palestinian 'dwarves.' He may have believed American assurances that Camp David would ultimately lead to new Israeli concessions.

In the post-Camp David negotiations, Egypt tried to link a peace treaty and normalization of relations with Israel to a timetable for self-government for West Bank Palestinians, a reduction in Israeli control, and the principle that ultimately they be allowed to determine their own future. To avoid the appearance of a separate peace, Egypt resisted giving a treaty with Israel precedence over her mutual defense obligations with the Arab states. Israel, however, denied any linkage between Egyptian–Israeli relations and West Bank arrangements, insisted that 'autonomy' implied no reduction in her presence or powers over the West Bank and continued to 'thicken' Jewish settlements there, and insisted a peace treaty that did not take precedence over Egypt's Arab obligations was no treaty at all. Because the American position was initially closer to Egypt's, Egypt seemed to have a strong hand. But West Bank Palestinians rejected the concept of 'autonomy.' Then an impatient Sadat undermined the hand of his own negotiators by making it known he would proceed with the treaty regardless of progress on the autonomy issue. Relieved of the need to do so, the US proved unwilling to extract concessions from Israel. This was decisive and in the end Egypt abandoned almost all her earlier demands. The peace treaty was signed and normalization proceeded despite the absence of West Bank autonomy. The provisions of the treaty implied that it took precedence over Egypt's Arab obligations. The Sinai was to be returned to Egypt within two years. But security arrangements there, prohibiting all but token Egyptian forces and inserting an international force between Egypt and Israel, diluted Egyptian sovereignty and virtually removed Egypt from the Arab–Israel power equation. For Sadat, peace and land seemed more important than these concessions and an American West Bank initiative might yet, he hoped, materialize (Fahmi 1983: 292–308; Shamir and Gamma 1981).

Sadat believed the other Arabs had no choice but to acquiesce in Egypt's course since without her they were militarily and diplomatically incapable of pursuing war or a different kind of peace. At the first Baghdad Conference after Camp David, however, virtually the whole Arab world, including Sadat's conservative allies, closed ranks in a warning that Egypt could not have both a separate peace with Israel and normal relations with the Arab world. Sadat was not, however, deterred and, indeed, the all-Arab opposition to his policy only aggravated Egyptian alienation from the Arab world. Egypt had spilled blood and treasure for the Arab cause; what right had the rich and ungrateful Arabs, who had been so niggardly in sharing the exorbitant wealth they won from Egypt's fight, to dictate her foreign policy? American promises of boundless largesse to which peace would entitle Egypt did much to bolster Sadat's defiance. Once Egypt signed the treaty, Arab sanctions were imposed: diplomatic relations were severed, the Arab League transferred from Egypt, aid payments and several joint enterprises suspended. The Arabs stopped short of prohibiting remittances by Egyptian workers, a move which would have really hurt, and American aid made up at least in the short-run for the lost Arab aid. But Egypt's isolation from the Arab economy threatened not only the loss of Arab petro-dollars and markets but also of Western investors for whom an isolated Egypt was far less attractive as a base for Middle East operations. Sadat, however, was convinced that the anti-Egyptian consensus would soon collapse.

Egypt's movement toward peace was paralleled by a decisive movement into a close American alliance. After Sinai II Sadat was convinced he no longer needed the USSR (Fahmi 1983: 170–3). Soviet–Egyptian relations deteriorated beyond the point of repair as Sadat cancelled the friendship treaty and debt repayment to the USSR, pursued a bitter propaganda war with them and in 1981 expelled the Soviet ambassador. As his last Soviet links snapped, Sadat's dependence on

American aid and diplomacy increased, and thus his need to demonstrate Egypt's value to the US. Sadat seemingly reasoned that since US support for Israel resulted from her role in protecting Western interests in the region, if Egypt could play this role Israel's value to the US would decline while American willingness to mediate in Egypt's favor and Egyptian eligibility for the arms and aid she no longer got from the USSR would increase. Sadat's feud with the Soviets and his claims of Soviet internal subversion and encirclement of Egypt via Libya and Ethiopia, were meant to bolster his requests for more aid; his border war with Libya and his dispatch of military aid to Sudan and Zaire, were to show Egypt's value as a bulwark against Soviet penetration. As Egypt's Arab relations turned sour, the US connection was even more vital to replace lost economic aid. Since he could no longer offer America the door to the Arab world, he openly offered to take the place of the fallen Shah of Iran as its guardian of order in the region. American forces were granted 'facilities' on Egyptian territory and Soviet, Libyan and Iranian threats eclipsed Israel as Egypt's major security preoccupation. The Americans were slow to provide Egypt with arms but in time, some, insufficient to threaten Israel, were forthcoming. American economic aid, however, reached a billion dollars a year, making Egypt the second largest recipient of US aid after Israel. The holding of joint American-Egyptian military maneuvers on Sadat's death to deter a presumed threat to Egypt from her Arab neighbors symbolized Egypt's new role. The Egypt which had led the fight to expel Western influence from the Arab world, now welcomed it back and turned herself into a major American client state isolated from her Arab environment; it appeared as if a new American–Israeli–Egyptian concert was emerging in the Middle East, a veritable revolution in international alignments (Abdel Malek 1979). But Egypt was finally at peace after 30 years and the long Israeli occupation of her territory terminated.

Sadat and the Opposition

Sadat's policies began, in the second half of the decade, to alter the bases and parameters of politics. De-Nasirization, sparking a resurgence of the right and a reaction on the left, sowed the seeds of political polarization. *Infitah* and the Western alignment, both deepened and yet contained this process. They produced a massive infusion of economic resources which filled the treasury, and sparked rising investment, growth (5–8% per year) and consumption. The new prosperity widened and solidified the regime's support among those who got the lion's share of the benefits, the bourgeoisie. Revitalization of the private sector created powerful interests with a stake in the regime. Contractors, real-estate speculators, and merchants flourished on the economic boom; importers, partners and agents of foreign firms, tourist operators, lawyers and middlemen who helped investors negotiate bureaucratic tangles, thrived on the cuts they took from the resource inflow. As demand rose, the agrarian bourgeoisie prospered on fruit and vegetable cultivation, chicken and cattle raising. The state bourgeoisie did no less well because much of the foreign aid and investment was channeled into the public sector or joint ventures. Officials reaped commissions on state contracts and engaged in widespread corrupt practices. Together, these groups were forming a 'parasitic bourgeoisie' living off *Infitah*. On the other hand, the lower-middle and lower classes bore the main costs of *Infitah* while reaping the fewest benefits. Inflation eroded the incomes of petty employees and industrial workers and the peasantry remained socio-economically depressed. The economy could not absorb the graduates of an ever-expanding higher education system. The explosion of conspicuous consumption at the top fed a growing perception that class gaps were widening, the rich getting richer and the poor poorer. Thus social cleavages widened, expanding the bases of political opposition and pluralization (Baker 1981). Yet, the availability of new resources enabled the regime to contain rising social conflict. Increased revenues allowed it to avoid or cushion unpopular extractive or rationalization measures which might otherwise have been required. A part of the new consumption could be diverted to wage increases and food subsidies as an investment in social peace and political stability. Egypt's massive export of labor to the Arab world was a safety valve permitting the ambitious, discontented or unemployed to 'exit' rather than 'rebel.' Some common folk, such as taxi drivers, tourist guides and skilled labor, benefited from the increase in demand *Infitah* unleashed. Finally, economic growth enabled Sadat to make a plausible case that his policies were working and that Egypt, once through the 'bottleneck' of transition, would (sometime after 1980) enter a period of prosperity long denied her. Thus the regime faced growing dangers but also acquired new means to cope with them.

Sadat, had, in this period, two basic political objectives. He sought to maintain the power needed to complete and sustain the changes in Egypt's global role and economic structure he had initiated. But he also sought to accommodate, without jeopardizing this power, the growing pressures for political freedoms issuing from a more polarized, pluralized society. He needed a way of satisfying the participatory expectations of his bourgeois constituency in particular. He also wanted to provide a safety valve for elements on the left which had parted company with the regime over de-Nasirization and ones on the right which, repressed under Nasir, were now being permitted to re-emerge to balance the left. In a word, Sadat sought to adapt the authoritarian state to the growing social and ideological pluralization of the political arena. His initial effort crystallized in the so-called 'multi-party experiment' which replaced the ASU with a party of the right, a government party of the center and a party of the left. These parties were permitted to compete in parliamentary elections and to advocate 'constructive' policy alternatives. But, the President, standing above the competing parties, retained his full powers. When, in the 1976 elections, the government party won an overwhelming number of parliamentary seats and the right and left parties appeared content to play the game with a handful, Sadat's experiment appeared to have paid off. But the experiment, encouraging political organization on both the right and the left, soon resulted in an overt pluralization of the political arena troublesome to the regime. In fact, after 1976 Sadat was faced with a growing reaction against his policies from both ends of the political spectrum. His effort to contain these threats, yet avoid resorting to full-scale repression, took the form of an alternate tightening and relaxation of controls and constant policy innovations by which the President sought to stay a step ahead of his opponents (Rubinstein 1977).

The first and most significant challenge to Sadat's policies was the 'food riots' of January, 1977. The dimensions and violence of these disturbances were unprecedented since the 1952 revolution. Beginning as demonstrations by workers in Helwan and students in Cairo, the protests were soon joined by the slum poor and spread to Alexandria and provincial towns from one end of Egypt to the other. For the first time in decades, the army had to be called out to support the police; 79 protestors were killed, 800–1000 wounded and 1500 jailed. While the riots were sparked by the steep rise in prices of popular commodities resulting from the IMF-imposed cuts in government subsidies, many participants were protesting the government's whole course, in particular an economic policy which translated into austerity and cuts in consumption for those at the bottom and growing consumption and enrichment at the top. Protests came from both sides of the political spectrum. Elements on the left tried to turn the disturbances into protests against de-Nasirization and capitalism. The chants of the crowd for Nasir suggested a growing nostalgia for the old populist days. Islamic elements, protesting Western cultural penetration and imported 'immorality,' burned down nightclubs and attacked luxury shops. Government offices and the homes of the elite were attacked. Neither Sadat nor his wife were spared: the slogans 'Down with Sadat's Palaces,' and 'Jihan, Jihan, the People are Hungry,' identified the President with the rich and privileged for the first time (Shukri 1978: 345–58).

The regime never appears to have been in serious danger of falling; the rioters had neither the will nor leadership to overthrow it and the security forces held firm. The riots nevertheless had major political consequences. First, the government backed down on the price increases and never again attempted any radical cuts in this social 'safety net' for the poor; fear of popular reaction henceforth became a deterrent to further major capitalist economic reforms. Secondly, the riots were a severe blow to the authority and prestige Sadat had accumulated after 1973. Thirdly, they inflamed Sadat's hostility toward the left, including the newly formed National Progressive Unionist Party (NPUP), a coalition of Nasirites and Marxists which he chose to blame for the disturbances. The bulk of post-riot punitive measures were aimed at leftists and Sadat moved perceptibly to the right in his political discourse. He was increasingly critical of Nasirites and, for the first time, Nasir himself, who he now blamed for Egyptian dependence on the USSR, the 1967 defeat, abuses of power and the lack of democracy in Egypt. 'Those calling themselves Nasirites' were trying to 'bring back detention camps and a socialism of poverty for everyone.' Thus, Sadat made an open break between himself and the heritage of his predecessor which widened the polarization between the regime and the nationalist-left. Finally, there was a retightening of controls over the political arena: new laws provided harsh punishments for all forms of public protest. Sadat's limited political liberalization suffered a temporary reversal.

In the summer of 1977 another major challenge to the regime came from Islamic fundamentalists whose role in the 'food riots' Sadat had chosen to ignore. A militant group called *al-Takfir wa'l-Hijra* abducted and murdered the Minister of *Waqfs* (religious endowments), a moderate establishment cleric. Paramilitary in character and viewing the regime as an 'infidel' one outside the bounds of Islamic morality, this group had adopted a strategy of violence against the government. The regime quickly smashed it, but it could no longer ignore that the Islamic fundamentalism it formerly encouraged, was turning against it as Sadat became identified with the West and Westernization. Sadat tried to contain the threat by enlisting the orthodox religious establishment against it, adopting a pious and conservative public deportment and giving lip-service to Islamic 'legislation.'

In September of 1977 Sadat's famous 'trip to Jerusalem' gave a sudden major boost to his sagging popularity and authority. Although some Egyptians had private reservations about the appropriateness or efficacy of the trip, the majority rallied around the President and his initiative. Impressive numbers of common Egyptians were mobilized in the streets to acclaim him with apparent enthusiasm. The bourgeoisie was happy. Defense Minister Gamasi gave the initiative the blessing of the military and the Shaikh al-Azhar that of Islam. Even some followers of the NPUP ignored their leaders and supported the President. Criticism from the Arab world only enhanced Sadat's standing at home, stimulating an 'Egypt-first' sentiment and resentment of 'rich and ungrateful Arabs' who expected Egypt to fight while they lived a life of ease. The Sabai and Larnaka Airport incidents touched off a wave of anti-Palestinian sentiment. Egypt, in short, closed ranks around her leader against the rest of the Arabs. The enthusiastic response to the trip reflected the profound yearning of Egyptians for peace and the prosperity the regime led them to believe would accompany it. Sadat profited from this to recover the political initiative.

Support for the trip was not totally unanimous. Besides the left opposition, there was a break in the consensus within the political elite itself and in a most strategic spot: the Foreign Minister, Ismail Fahmi and his deputy resigned in protest. Fahmi had been an advocate of a negotiated settlement under American auspices and had a reputation for anti-Soviet views. But he had reservations over Sadat's exclusive reliance on the US, advocated an improvement in relations with the USSR on grounds that Egypt's negotiating hand required a military option, and had urged a rejection of Sinai II. Fahmi was more anti-Israeli than Sadat and, as an advocate of close relations with the conservative Arab states, could not support an overt break with the common Arab position. Fed up with Sadat's disregard for his views, he refused to take responsibility for a decision in which he had had no part (Fahmi 1983). Although Fahmi had no wide personal following, his opposition was a reflection of the private views of some foreign policy professionals and a segment of the articulate public who understood the risks and costs of the 'Peace Initiative.'

In the months after the trip to Jerusalem, Sadat, feeling more confident, again relaxed his grip over the political arena. He tolerated the publication of independent (and critical) newspapers by both the official rightwing opposition Ahrar and by the NPUP. In a brief but major new departure, he also permitted the resurrection of the Wafd Party, Egypt's veteran liberal-nationalist movement repressed after 1952. It reappeared with a barely changed name (New Wafd) and much of its old leadership and liberal program intact. The new party, based on the private wing of the bourgeoisie, and chiefly anti-statist in orientation, called for a more thorough economic liberalization and a political one to match it. Although careful to applaud Sadat's de-Nasirization, it gave vent to not a little of the hostility felt by remnants of the *ancien régime* against the 1952 revolution. Sadat tolerated its revival chiefly with the aim of pleasing the liberal bourgeoisie. The revival of a pro-Western force on the liberal right could also help contain the leftwing and Islamic opposition to his policies. The new party turned out, however, to be a potent rival of the government party for the loyalties of the bourgeoisie and a magnet for diverse elements seeking an alternative to the regime but sympathetic neither to Islamic fundamentalism nor the left. From the beginning it challenged the regime.

By early 1978 there was a surge in opposition criticism from both the right and left, focused largely on economic troubles and corruption, which again put the regime on the defensive. An Islamic populist preacher, Shaikh Ashur Nasr, known for his constant criticisms of governmental neglect of the poor, was expelled from parliament for denouncing Sadat. Both the liberal and leftist press mobilized public outrage over government plans to sell land around the Pyramids to a Western developer at cheap prices and in disregard of dangers to the archeological treasures and of Egyptian law; although Sadat's personal associates were involved in the deal, his own bourgeois constituency was so aroused against it that he was forced to cancel it. In an unprecedented public speech, Sadat felt obliged to defend himself against criticisms of his lavish

73

lifestyle and rumors of the corrupt activities of his associates, above all, Osman Ahmad Osman. The lack of progress in negotiations with Israel after the trip to Jerusalem opened Sadat's foreign policy to criticism. The New Wafd challenged the President's hold on his bourgeois constituency and the National Progressives (NPUP), if allowed to operate unchecked, threatened to mobilize mass social discontent. These two parties, at opposite ends of the political spectrum, joined forces in parliament to bring government policies under an unprecedented critical scrutiny. In May 1978 Sadat cracked down. Denouncing the Progressives as Soviet agents intent on stirring up class strife, and the Wafdists as corrupt old regime figures who wanted to 'turn the clock back' to the pre-revolutionary period, he staged a referendum which banned all 'atheists' and pre-1952 politicians from politics. The Wafd disbanded and a blockade was imposed on the NPUP's access to the public. Sadat then reshaped the party system. He took personal control of the government party (renamed the National Democratic Party) and announced a new official ideology, 'Democratic Socialism,' which advocated a centrist course equally opposed to the radical left and the Wafd's *laissez-faire* doctrines. A new left of center 'opposition' party, the Socialist Labor Party (SLP), led by moderate reformists and meant to coopt the constituency of the NPUP, was also unveiled; Sadat hoped this opposition would prove more 'constructive' than its predecessors.

In September 1978 Sadat signed the Camp David accords. They were greeted with far less enthusiasm than the trip to Jerusalem; the manifest retreat from the minimum Arab position to which Egypt had been committed, the disapproval of Egypt's closest ally, Saudi Arabia, and the warnings of the Baghdad conference disturbed Egyptians far more than the earlier break with Arab nationalists. The regime, however, was able to mobilize support for the accords: it again fanned the smouldering Egyptian resentment of the Arabs; but it also insisted the accords were a mere first step toward a comprehensive settlement rather than a separate peace and made an effort to give serious substance to the West Bank 'autonomy' plan. Whatever their qualms about the agreement, most Egyptians were prepared to give the government the benefit of the doubt. Like previous major stepping stones in Sadat's course away from traditional Egyptian postures, Camp David was marked by a significant turnover in elite ranks. The foreign minister who replaced Fahmi, Muhammed Ibrahim Kamil, although a close personal friend of Sadat, could not support it and along with the members of his delegation, resigned. Defense Minister Gamasi, one of Sadat's closest supporters since 1974 and the Chief of Staff, Muhammed Ali Fahmi, were dismissed. Neither of these generals had overtly challenged Sadat, but the President wanted men at the critical command posts of the military establishment untarnished by reservations about his course; the officers who succeeded to these positions were unquestioning loyalists. In a major cabinet turnover, the veteran Salim government gave way to a 'peace cabinet' under

Mustafa Khalil and 22 new ministers charged with reorienting Egypt's government from one of war to one of 'democracy, peace and social welfare.' Sayyid Marei quietly resigned as Speaker of parliament. The passing of many of Sadat's closest post-October stalwarts from the forefront of the political stage paved the way for the emergence of the Vice President, Husni Mubarak, as the most senior of Sadat's lieutenants (Rubinstein 1979).

After six months of negotiations the Camp David 'process' culminated in an Israeli–Egyptian peace treaty and 'normalization' of relations with Israel, that is, an Israeli ambassador, Israeli tourists and Israeli beer on the streets of Cairo. Regime denials could not disguise that this was, indeed, a separate peace, especially after the Arab states went ahead with their sanctions. The government stressed that Egypt had finally recovered her lost territory and promised that peace would bring prosperity. The anti-Arab campaign was stepped up. The Arabs, Sadat declared, could neither buy Egypt nor isolate the intellectual center of the Arab world; the fight with Israel, not even Egypt's own fight, had caused her economic woes, but now she would look to her own interests. The orthodox religious establishment was prevailed upon to legitimize the treaty. Some Egyptians genuinely welcomed it. Much of the bourgeoisie cared little about the Arab cause and knew that neither business prosperity nor the good life were secure without peace, although a few businessmen worried about the loss of opportunities in the Arab world. The majority, though uneasy over a flawed treaty which isolated Egypt from the Arabs, acquiesced in the belief that there was no real alternative save war. An articulate minority which believed Sadat had played his cards very badly opposed the treaty.

In the aftermath of the treaty, Sadat, seeking to present an image of internal unity behind it, launched an offensive against the opposition. Parliament, from which the opposition had agitated against his foreign policy and in which even government deputies sometimes seemed on the verge of revolt against it, was dismissed; in the subsequent elections the government made sure no deputy which had opposed the treaty was returned. Sadat also attacked the press, proposing to abolish the journalists' syndicate which he considered a bulwark of those engaged in 'irresponsible criticism.' He proposed a political 'code of ethics' to ensure that criticism remained 'responsible' and outlawed transgressions against traditional family values such as disrespect for the head of the big Egyptian family, that is, the President (Cantori 1980).

Yet far from declining, opposition widened significantly in the post-treaty period. Much of it grew out of discontent with the treaty. Virtually no progress was achieved in the 'autonomy' talks, yet normalization was allowed to proceed. Israel's aggression against Lebanon, Syria and Iraq, made possible, according to the opposition, by Egypt's separate peace, embarrassed the government; it could only lamely assert that it would not allow Israel's 'foolish' actions to undermine peace. Opposition was inflamed by rumors of plans to divert Nile water to help irrigate the Israeli Negav, the rewriting of school textbooks to change the negative image of Israelis and efforts to push Egyptian professionals into relations with Israeli counterparts. The silencing of critics of 'normalization' appeared to be repression for the sake of Israel. As time passed, the negative psychological effect of isolation from the Arab world and disillusionment that peace would bring prosperity, increased. Sadat's overt abandonment of non-alignment for American patronage grated on the sensibilities of the opposition. Accumulated grievances over unabated economic distress and official corruption, soured many on *Infitah*. Sadat himself publicly acknowledged that *Infitah* would have to be altered to help those – workers, peasants, government employees – who had not benefited from it. The 'lack of democracy' and Sadat's personalistic rule were also part of the brew of discontent. Sadat had faced opposition all along, of course; what made the post-treaty period different was that previously acquiescent parts of the political spectrum – the mainstream Islamic and even the secular center – were now joining it, and disparate opposition forces were coalescing against the regime. Dissidence was taking on wider and deeper dimensions than at any time since 1973.

A startling rise in the breadth and intensity of the Islamic movement had been apparent since 1977 when Islamic forces swept the student union elections, then spilled over into the mosques, *baladi* quarters and small towns. But it was only after the Iranian revolution and the peace treaty that the mainstream of the movement took a clear anti-government direction. Sadat's asylum to the Shah, his support for a liberalized law of personal status and, above all, his separate peace treaty turned Islamic militants against him. Islamic opposition was manifested in student demonstrations, criticism of the treaty in the Ikhwan press, and a growth in violent attacks on security forces. In the end, Sadat, breaking with his former allies, denounced the Islamic movement as a state within a state that he would no longer tolerate.

The secular opposition also significantly widened as the left and liberal-right (pro-Wafd) were increasingly joined by centrist elements. The initially 'tame' SLP turned into an authentic opposition, bitterly critical of the regime. It took issue with normalization of relations with Israel in the absence of any Israeli concessions to Palestinian rights and followed a populist line in criticism of the government's socio-economic policies. Like its predecessors, this government-created opposition party was taking itself seriously; as Sadat shut off one channel of dissidence, it only seemed to find new ones through which to express itself. Growing centrist opposition was also expressed in petitions signed by nearly 80 prominent Egyptians grouped in a 'National Coalition.' They called for a freeze in relations with Israel, a return of Egypt to its role in defense of the Arab cause, and an end to American bases and dependency; they also criticized the personalistic character of Sadat's rule, his failure to share power within the elite or observe democratic rights and the independence of the press and judiciary. The petitioners were mostly moderate liberals and Nasirites, including ex-Free Officers, former Vice Presidents and many ex-establishment figures who had served and been shunted aside by Sadat. Sadat's personal support within his own constituency was fraying, as his foreign policy started to go beyond even the establishment consensus of what was acceptable.

Sadat initially tried to appease the dissidents. In 1980 he personally assumed the Premiership and brought in a new economic management team, promising to stamp out corruption and favoritism and reform *Infitah*. A reversion to populist measures, such as slashes in prices of popular goods, and increased price controls, was meant to assuage mass discontent. To divert dissidence over his Western and Israeli relations, he tried to portray communism as the chief enemy of Islam and made much of the Soviet invasion of Afghanistan. Finally, alarmed at the breadth and growing boldness of the opposition, Sadat resorted to repression. In 1981 a wave of arrests swept up at least 1500 opposition leaders from across the political spectrum including Islamic militants and even leaders of the SLP. Scores of mosques were seized from militant preachers and government controls over thousands of others tightened; the recalcitrant Pope of the Coptic church was fired; and seven publications, including the SLP organ, closed down (Merriam 1982).

In October 1981 the Sadat era came to an abrupt end after the President was gunned down by Islamic militants in apparent retaliation for the crackdown. The lack of public grief in any way comparable to that which greeted Nasir's death suggested that there was little sorrow among the mass public at Sadat's passing. Paradoxically, however, Sadat's work may last far longer than Nasir's did, for, in contrast to his predecessor, he had institutionalized his course in a political establishment whose interests were compatible, indeed served, by the main lines of his policies. The following chapters will examine the structures and performance of this new order.

Chapter 4

The Presidency and the power elite

At the close of the Sadat era, the huge authoritarian–bureaucratic state which Nasir built remained largely intact. Under Sadat, it was increasingly used for purposes other than those for which Nasir intended it, and forces both inside and outside of it were working to alter it. But the regime, adapting to and containing these forces, largely resisted structural transformation, continued to set the framework for elite politics and to dominate the political arena. The core of the political system, the center of all important decisions, was the powerful authoritarian Presidency shaped by Nasir for himself and inherited by Sadat. The ministerial bureaucracy and military establishment through which the President exercised his power remained the major institutions of state power, towering over society. The political infrastructure – party system, parliament, interest groups, press – acquired greater autonomy and capacity as channels of interest articulation and aggregation, but originally designed as instruments of control from above, they remained subordinate to the state apparatus. As such an understanding of politics in Sadat's Egypt must depart from a study of the Presidency, the power elite around it and the ideology that shaped their decisions and Egypt's fate.

Sadat's rule: Presidential monarchy

The Presidency remained, no less under Sadat than Nasir, the command post of the political system, a seat of enormous concentrated and personalized political power. Sadat's power grew out of the office he inherited, giving a man of initially limited stature a great advantage over all his rivals. His successful defense of its powers against the efforts of Ali Sabri to 'hamstring' his right to make Presidential decisions as Nasir had done and to make the Presidency accountable to a collective leadership ensconced in other power centers of the bureaucratic state, ensured it would continue to overshadow all other institutions. But if Sadat's power was comparable to Nasir's, he used it for different ends and in different ways and domains.

The office: the bases of Presidential power

The power of the President stemmed, in great part, from the enormous constitutional authority and customary prerogatives of his office. Perhaps the foremost key to the President's power in Egypt is his wide powers of appointment and dismissal; most important was the right to appoint the Prime Minister, the cabinet and the chiefs of the armed forces, but in a highly bureaucratic society, Presidential patronage extended over a much wider scope of positions including public sector managers, newspaper editors, judges and party leaders. Sadat's right to appoint loyal followers to the strategic levers of state power and to dismiss those who incurred his displeasure was a main source of elite deference to the President. As chief executive the President also stood at the top of a legal chain of command which entitled him to obedience from the civil and military bureaucracies. The Prime Minister was merely the President's chief assistant and the cabinet a 'staff' expected to turn his general policy into detailed legislation and executive action. While covert evasion or administrative incompetence may often have frustrated the implementation of the President's intentions, the bureaucratic machine had no history of overt resistance to him and he could, in fact, usually depend on at least passive compliance. In the exercise of his executive prerogative, the President acted largely unconstrained by legal or administrative restraints. The President was also by tradition undisputed chief legislator and the dominant source of major policy or ideological innovation. Although such innovation may often have been a Presidential response to pressures from below and although party and parliament were permitted greater scope as arenas of interest articulation under Sadat, such upward flow of influence was exercised at the President's sufferance and on condition that his ultimate prerogative to decide was acknowledged. Formally, parliament and party organs were elected from below, but in practice the President picked or could veto their incumbents, and he could dissolve them at will. While formally the cabinet held power at the confidence of parliament and the latter approved and could reject legislation and the budget, in practice, Presidential control of the dominant majority party, and the modest sense of institutional solidarity enjoyed by parliament, resulted in a legislative deference to the President permitting him to appoint governments at will and secure the passage of any piece of legislation he really wanted. He could also legislate by decree when parliament was not in session (although it could but never did nullify such decrees) and by-pass it through popular plebiscites which invariably ratified Presidential proposals. Finally, the President not infrequently made use of the plebiscite to change the constitution or to alter the rules of the political game – as, for example, in 1978 when he rewrote the rules of the party system and in 1980 when he changed the constitution to permit himself an unlimited number of six-year terms in office. Given the President's ability to so reshape the institutions and conditions of political participation from above, the political infrastructure could not function as an effective accountability mechanism or check on executive power.

Sadat the political man: the orientation of Presidential power

Sadat the political man determined the ends for which the formidable powers of the Presidency were employed. Sadat's personality and attitudes do not explain everything that happened in Egyptian politics after 1970, for at every step he faced powerful constraints with limited resources. Yet he took pride in trying to lead and shape events and faced few legal limits or organized interests which could check him in doing so. As he steered Egypt he always had a range of options and consistently he chose a 'rightist' course, conservative, stabilizing, adaptive, pro-Western, while imparting to the Presidency a strongly traditionalist character – all in almost exact contrast to Nasir. Explaining the direction Sadat's Presidency gave to Egypt, requires some understanding of how his life experiences shaped his worldview, personality and style.

The village culture in which he was raised left an early and enduring imprint on Sadat's orientation. His traditionalism was, in part, a product of village culture. His view of Egypt as 'one big family' in which political strife was out of place and his nostalgic image of the village as a place of harmony where men were content with their lot, were artifacts of his village upbringing which in time gave to his outlook a conservative impatience with dissent and insensitivity to inequality. His patriarchal style of rule seemed an extension of village headmanship to the national level. Sadat's personalization of political relations may owe something to village culture. At the very center of the state, he constructed a personal entourage cemented by kinship ties. He also seemed to personalize inter-state relations, shaping Egypt's foreign policy in no small part according to his personal relations with other leaders. His confidence in his 'friend Henry' went a long way to setting Egypt on a pro-American course, perhaps deluding him that this relationship could overcome the vested interests which shape American Middle East policy; conversely, he let personal friction with Soviet leaders result in a greater deterioration of Egyptian–Soviet relations than a pure calculus of national interest would have advised. Sadat's shrewd adaptability is a trait often attributed to the Egyptian peasant. Historically, in the face of superior power, the peasant will submit; but he will also try to deflect harm and win its favor through flattery and deference (Mayfield 1971: 67–72). This adaptability runs through Sadat's career. An 'expert at political survival,' he was one of the few Free Officers to come through the post-1952 elite conflicts unscathed largely due to his deference to Nasir. In his later adaptation to the realities of Israeli and American power there is a parallel to the Egyptian peasant's adaptation to foreign conquerers. Unable to beat them, Sadat decided to embrace them. His fawning attitude toward American leaders, the backers of Egypt's main enemy, as he sought to manipulate them into providing diplomatic and financial aid, had something in it of the clever *fahlawi*. Sadat's malleability was all the more striking by contrast with Nasir, the proud *Saidi* whose sense of honor would never let him surrender to the American–Israeli *combinazione*.[1] The exaggerated self-importance which led Sadat to dismiss the opinions of many of those around him, is also a typical *fahlawi* trait.

A second layer of experience relevant to Sadat's political formation was his reaction to Egypt's struggle with imperialism. From childhood, Sadat was marked by the hatred of the foreign presence typical of most Egyptians; he was brought up on stories of the heroes of Egyptian nationalism such as Mustafa Kamil and imagined himself in the place of 'Zahran,' the legendary peasant leader martyred at Denshawy. In school, he participated in the nationalist demonstrations which made up part of the political socialization of his generation. Ataturk, the soldier who rid his country of the foreigners, became his model and he sought entry to the military academy. Immediately he received his commission, Sadat began to agitate among his colleagues. He led the formation of one of the earliest segments of the Free Officers' organization. Involved in numerous anti-British conspiracies, including the assassination of the anglophile, Amin Osman, Sadat risked life and career for the cause and was eventually cashiered and imprisoned (Sadat 1978: 5–22, 59–69). In short, his credentials as an Egyptian nationalist were impeccable. It is significant, however, that his nationalism took a rightwing form hostile to the left, manifested in his association with the Muslim Brothers and his flirtation with the Axis powers. Sadat's nationalism does not appear to have diminished in later years. His anguish at the 1967 defeat and the personal humiliation he felt at the claims of foreigners that Egyptians could not fight, is entirely convincing (Sadat 1978: 175).

Yet Sadat's nationalism, like that of many of his contemporaries, was ambivalent. Revolt against the foreigner was diluted by admiration for, a sense of inferiority to and desire for acceptance by the rich, powerful and 'civilized' West. Early in his career rebellion and resentment dominated Sadat's attitude; in *Revolt on the Nile* (1957) he denounces the West for sucking the blood of the East and complains that Westerners would not accept Egyptians as equal. The sense of inferiority to the West seems to have surfaced after the 1967 defeat which seemed to show what was in store for those who rebelled against the dominant world order. Sadat's speeches before the October War are filled with a mixture of defiance of the US, bewilderment at American support for Israeli occupation of Egyptian land, and pleas for a change of heart toward Egypt. Once, after 1973, Sadat sensed a willingness on the part of the West to accord Egypt – and its President – proper respect, resentment rapidly gave way to a seemingly uncritical embrace of all things Western. It was as if, having finally won verbal acceptance by the West, all the claims of nationalism were satisfied and the wrongs suffered by Egypt forgiven. As Ajami (1981) observed, in spite of the emotional nationalism which moved Egyptians like Sadat, a thorough cultural revolution which could liberate Egypt from the imprint of colonialism and cultural dependency, had never been carried through. This residue of the colonialized mentality left Sadat very vulnerable to the flattery heaped on him by the West as he moved toward accommodation with Israel, and deaf to the objections of his advisors and other Arab rulers who appeared to him less 'civilized' than the Western statesmen with whom he was hobnobbing. Sadat soon seemed, in his deprecation of the Arab rulers who opposed him, to adopt what Ajami called 'second-hand colonial imagery.' They were now 'dwarves' rather than brothers, the Arab world a place of barbarism and disorder over which Egypt would play the role of sentry on behalf of the 'civilized' world. Ajami describes the lure of the West for Sadat: 'The world's mightiest power – and a civilized one as well – becomes Egypt's full partner. Libya, Syria, Iraq fade into cosmic insignificance. Egypt and her President break out in grand style' (Ajami 1981: 102, 109–16). The question was, could Egypt's national identity be so sharply divorced from its Arab–Islamic context and remain authentic? Yet there can be little doubt that Sadat saw himself as delivering his country from the evils of war, bringing her the peace and prosperity she had longed for. In his own mind, he was no less a nationalist because the good of his country required adaptation to, rather than rebellion against the realities of world power.

A third level of experience which helped shape Sadat was his involvement in the post-1952 revolutionary regime with Nasir and the other Free Officers. The evidence suggests that Sadat's political outlook was shaped by his relative inability to win respect and build close personal relations with the other senior Free Officers. His relations with Nasir were never close, marred, according to his own testimony, by the latter's deep suspiciousness and aloofness from others. While overtly Sadat was the loyalist of Nasir's comrades he could not have been pleased by Nasir's assumption of leadership, while Sadat was imprisoned, of the movement Sadat had helped found. Sadat saw himself as having taken personal risks and won popular acclaim as a result of his role in the Amin Osman affair, and believed the other Free Officers suspected his ambitions and were jealous of him on this account. Whether from jealousy or disdain, some of his colleagues, at least, treated him with little respect, and after suffering several rebuffs when he tried to take the initiative, Sadat withdrew to the peripheries of the ruling group (Sadat 1978: 119–23). In consequence, his closest friendships and personal ties came to be less with fellow revolutionaries than with the likes of Sayyid Marei, scions of old families among whom he acquired a reputation as a sympathetic figure (Marei 1978a: 621). These friendships certainly had some effect in biasing Sadat against the policies followed by Nasir in the sixties at the expense of the wealthy.

Contrary to early appearances, Sadat was not without political ambition or ideas and in 1970 when he assumed the Presidency he felt 'full of challenge' to put an end to the many mistakes and wrongs of the Nasir era. His reversal of

Nasir's policies was at least partly motivated by an element of personal resentment against Nasir, a desire to undo the injustices inflicted on his wealthy friends, and to leave his own mark on Egypt, for if his Presidency was to be more than a mere pale imitation of Nasir's he would have to do things quite differently. Once in the seat of power Sadat proved very different from the obsequious 'yes-man' lacking a taste for politics. Almost as if he sought to erase the humiliations of the Nasir period, he set out to show himself a man of action and decisiveness, unconcerned for the fears and opinions of the lesser men around him (Sadat 1978: 206–14).

Finally, Sadat was shaped politically by his class background. Sadat was from a well-off peasant family; his father owned a plot of land and was employed as a petty civil servant. This background is compatible both with Sadat's anti-feudalism and his respect for private property. Sadat never wholly lost a certain populist identification with the common man from whose ranks he rose. His populism, however, never possessed the keen edge of indignation against injustice or the dislike of the wealthy which characterized Nasir. Even as a poor youth in the city he never felt, he tells us, 'jealous or spiteful' toward the rich (Sadat 1978: 8). His brief experience as a petty entrepreneur probably disposed him to those with the enterprise to do well with money. Sadat's rapid upward mobility soon distanced him from his modest origins. His divorce of his first wife, a village girl, in favor of the educated and sophisticated Jihan was a milestone in his ascent. So was his friendship, after 1952, with old families like the Mareis. Sadat was soon made over from an impulsive firebrand conspiring against the establishment into a man of moderation and urbanity with a taste for the good things in life. In contrast to Nasir who maintained a modest life style and refused to move in the fancy circles of the Egyptian or international social elite, Sadat gradually assimilated their life style and worldview. He acquired an overlay of cosmopolitanism which pulled him away from his own modest social and cultural roots, and made him vulnerable to the blandishments of the rich and powerful inside and outside of Egypt.

These layers of experience shaped a set of values that helped distinguish the direction the Sadat Presidency gave to policy from Nasir's. Both men sought the good of their country. But Nasir remained to the end little removed from his modest background and a rebel against the rich and powerful inside and outside Egypt. Sadat was fundamentally disposed in a conservative direction, and was a realist adaptable to the domestic and international power structures in which he would have to operate and where he sought acceptance.

The style of Presidential power

Precisely because of the enormous powers of the Presidency in Egypt, the man who holds the office acquires exceptional latitude to rule the way he wants.

83

Sadat's particular personality and goal orientation translated into a particular style of rule which helped distinguish his Presidency from Nasir's and left an imprint on the whole political system. The office made the man, but the man remade the office.

The traditionalization of the Presidency was perhaps the major change in the style of rule from Nasir's time. Sadat's conception of authority was habitually expressed in patriarchal terms. He seemed to see Egypt as the authoritarian patriarchal family writ large, with himself as the 'father' entitled to respect and obedience. In contrast to Nasir who addressed Egyptians as 'brothers,' Sadat regularly spoke of them as 'My children' (Sadat Speeches 5, 20, 25 May 1971). The 'Law of Shame' (*Aib*), a new version of provisions in force under the monarchy, institutionalized the ruler's right to respect and deference and provided legal penalties for disrespect; nothing angered Sadat more than criticism of his person (or family and friends) which he took as a violation of traditional codes of conduct. There was a patrimonial quality, too, in Sadat's rule. He habitually spoke as if the Egyptian political system were his personal property, referring to 'my constitution,' 'my political parties,' even 'my opposition' and seemingly regarding political rights as favors he might grant or withdraw on good behavior; in his effusive use of the word 'I' he spoke as though nothing happened in Egypt which was not his doing (Dimbleby 1977: 204–6). In contrast to Nasir's austere simplicity, there was much of the style of royalty in Sadat's deportment: his pompous uniforms, the entourage, barber, masseur, valet that accompanied him, the numerous luxurious Presidential residences, the repossession of Farouk's Abdin palace. Finally, in Sadat's informal adoption of the title *al-Rais al-mu'min*, reminiscent of the caliphate, in his use of religious authority against opposition and in his displays of public piety there was a fusing of religious and political authority typical of the historic Islamic monarchy.

Yet, far from seeing himself as a traditionalizer, Sadat viewed himself as a heroic man of action, with the 'mission' to bring peace and prosperity to his country. He liked to think that he was able to shape events, rather than merely react to them. He was a 'master of decision' who sought to jolt the status quo, who was prepared to override conventional opinion, and who was always two steps ahead of his rivals, keeping them off balance with 'electric shock diplomacy' and constant innovations in policy (Shukri 1978: 36). Each year of his Presidency, Sadat told Egyptians in 1980, had witnessed a 'remarkable achievement.' 'I am only speaking as a peasant from the Nile Valley,' he was fond of boasting, but 'I ordered 17,000 Soviet advisors out in one week and went to the US Congress to tell them I was a friend.' He had launched the great October War and then made the trip to Jerusalem, an initiative on which 'none of the Arab leaders would have dared to embark.' In contrast to these 'dwarves' he thought of himself as a farsighted and magnanimous statesman. A massive cult of personality was created around him: 'Hero of the Crossing, Hero of Peace.' In fact, this style often translated into an impulsiveness and lack of careful calculation in decision-making, and a disregard for the views of his advisors. But Sadat did seem to enjoy a self-confidence which was at times an asset in governance. He apparently kept a cool nerve in the showdown with Ali Sabri. His decision to go to war in 1973 was taken against the fears of top generals that Egypt was not prepared. The trip to Jerusalem, taken in the face of the opposition and incredulity of advisors and allies alike showed that, for better or worse, he had the inner certitude to take risks (Fahmi 1983: 14, 282–3; Marei 1978a: 703; Sadat 1978: 248).

Nevertheless, Sadat's role as President–Hero was of a very different order than Nasir's. The Sadat Presidency was a much less activist, interventionist one requiring less leadership of and less domination of those around and below him. In part, this stemmed from differences in personality. Nasir was hard driving, dynamic, domineering and suspicious; he was personally a source of enormous energy at the top of the regime, pushing the elite into motion, keeping tight control and a close watch over it. Sadat was a much more relaxed and tolerant person. Far from riding herd on the elite, he rose late, took extended vacations and, as Marei wrote, 'did not believe in trying to catch his assistants in mistakes' (Marei 1978a: 621). Sadat was more magnanimous toward opponents too; he had a genuine abhorrence of police repression and, unlike Nasir, kept his rule relatively free of the executions, mass imprisonments and torture common in many authoritarian regimes. This relaxed control over opponents and reduced demands on his subordinates gave Sadat's rule a benevolence which accurately reflected his personality. But these distinctions also resulted from the very different uses to which Nasir and Sadat put Presidential power. Nasir wanted to transform Egypt even if it meant running roughshod over vested elite interests; and much of his interventionism and reluctance to share power was a response to the tendency of elites to evade his demands. Sadat's goals, peace through negotiation and economic prosperity through private enterprise, required far less application of political power in society, and, far from threatening elite interests, advanced them.

Finally, Sadat's view of himself as a ruler who, in contrast to his autocratic predecessor, was bringing democracy to his people, had some effect on his style. It was reflected chiefly in his relaxation of control over the elite and the political arena. Sadat's more relaxed personality and less ambitious goals were certainly more compatible with a less unlimited exercise of personal power than Nasir's. But Sadat's role as democratic law-giver was sharply circumscribed by other dimensions of his role conception. Neither his 'mission' nor his patrimonial style allowed for strong limitations on Presidential prerogatives or much room for overt legitimate opposition. In fact, Sadat's conception of democracy was of a system on the model of Islamic *shura* (consultation) in which the ruler would engage in 'constructive' consultation with the citizenry, but would retain full power to make the ultimate decisions and would brook no overt 'destructive' opposition to them. It is true Sadat held that the will of the people was 'sovereign' and that the leadership was accountable to it; but he claimed that as President he expressed the true wishes of the people who had deposited their trust in him at his election. He insisted that the people were overwhelmingly behind him and spoke as if he believed the 99.9% outcomes of his frequent plebiscites were accurate representations of public opinion and dissidents a mere handful of troublemakers. He wanted Egypt's political institutions – the cabinet, parliament, courts – to function freely, but if they deviated from the public interest for which he spoke, it was his prerogative to intervene and set them right (Sadat speeches, 20 May, 9 Sept. 1971). Sadat, it appears, wanted to have democracy and yet keep his power and policy free from challenges; when he was forced to choose he invariably opted for authority over democracy.

Sadat and the intra-elite political environment: the techniques and limits of Presidential power

Sadat's rule was also shaped by the intra-elite political environment in which he had to operate, and by his efforts to manipulate it. Sadat's Presidency was different from Nasir's in part because both the environment and his strategy for coping with it were different. In decisive respects it is clear this environment allowed Sadat to exercise greater personal power than Nasir. Nasir was, to a degree, constrained by the core elite, men who could not readily be purged without mobilization of a majority coalition; they could sometimes defy him and several 'centers of power' not always responsive to the Presidential will existed. By contrast, once the Sabri faction was purged, Sadat emerged far above any other member of the political elite in stature. He was able to take many major and controversial decisions without consultation with and even in disdain for the opinions of the elite who he treated as mere staff rather than colleagues (Ya'ari 1980: 111–12). This was especially so in the foreign policy sphere, Sadat's main concern, where it is clear he led – even defied – rather than followed elite opinion. Thus, in the Sinai II negotiations Sadat excluded his top military and foreign policy elites from key bargaining sessions with Kissinger and then overrode their objections to many details of the agreement. He decided on his own to go to Jerusalem without even trying to create an elite consensus behind him. He allowed his top generals little say at Camp David and so often overrode and undermined the hand of his foreign policy professionals in the peace treaty negotiations that they sought to keep the Israelis away from him (Golan 1976: 160–4; Sadat 1978: 306–8, 331). To an only slightly lesser degree Sadat seemed free to turn the political liberalization experiment on and off at will. Occasionally a member of the elite opposed him, but no one who did so was able to keep his position. No 'centers of power' remotely autonomous of the President ever emerged. Thus, in the foreign policy and, to a lesser degree, the political sphere, Sadat seemed to operate virtually without intra-elite constraints. What made this all the more remarkable was the fact that Sadat ruled without the tight political controls and the appeal to popular support Nasir used to control the elite. What conditions, methods and resources enabled Sadat to so readily control the elite, squelch opposition in its ranks and keep himself far above the rest of it?

One underlying factor without which Sadat's unchallenged supremacy probably would not have been possible was the inherited elite political culture. After 20 years of the Nasir Presidency the elite was habituated to and accepted the rules and customs of an authoritarian Presidency; the deference of the elite to the office gave the President a great advantage, decisive in coping with the only major threat he faced, that from the Sabri faction. No doubt reinforcing the habits learned under Nasir was the age-old tradition of autocracy rooted in Egypt's riverine, hydraulic society. Yet custom, in itself, is an insufficient explanation: it was by no means self-evident when Sadat became President that he would even survive, much less become a new Pharaoh.

The considerable measure of personal legitimacy Sadat was able to achieve made a big difference. His status as a senior Free Officer was an indispensable credential in a regime which grew out of an officers' revolution. The credit he won from the October War gave him a tremendous boost in elite eyes. His apparent indispensability to the diplomatic process which followed, the concessions Egypt appeared to win from his friendship with 'Dr Henry' and the promise that he would win both land and peace for Egypt, gave Sadat a stature no rival could equal. War and foreign policy crises are everywhere the crucible of power concentration and Egypt was no exception.

Sadat's accumulation of power benefited enormously from the post-1967 decline of the Free Officers' movement and the accompanying de-politicization of the military. Nasir had to deal with a core elite which, having helped make the revolution, had a claim to a relatively permanent share of power and which had connections, some direct, in the military. Sadat, once he disposed of the Sabri group, was free to create his own elite, largely of technocrats or professionals who lacked coercive bases or special political credentials and who, being his creatures, were beholden to him, and could be freely dismissed. The top generals he coopted into power were largely de-politicized professionals with no mind to challenge his authority.

But this should not disguise that Sadat's emergence as undisputed leader owed much to his own skill as a politician.[2] He was a master of the politics of divide and rule. Initially, when the main danger to him was from the military-left, Sadat profited from the animosity of the military brass and of prestigious centrist Nasirite civilians like Sidqi and Haykel toward this grouping, to build the support needed to dispose of it. This done, Sadat gradually edged mainstream Free Officers and centrist Nasirites out of power, while bringing into the circles of power rightwing civilians and professional officers happy to rise at the expense of the Nasirite establishment. Sadat subsequently profited from continuing intra-elite rivalries; for example, that between Gamasi and Mubarak certainly helped Sadat control his two top generals, the men who potentially represented the most credible alternatives to him in the late seventies (Ya'ari 1980: 116).

Sadat's success in the game of divide and rule was due in great part to the inability of rival elites to construct independent bases of power. They were, of course, hampered in any such effort because overt organization of such a base, whether institutional or popular, was not a legitimate part of the intra-elite game. Elites generally refrained from and usually lacked the means to appeal for mass support in intra-elite conflicts. Institutional bases typically displayed little solidarity, whether based on personal loyalty or shared policy preferences. Thus, when Sadat moved against a powerful opponent he usually had little trouble soliciting support among the target's subordinates or clients, frequently by promising them their superior's position. Nevertheless, Sadat took care, through periodic shakeups to pre-empt the development of any personal power base from which the Presidency could be challenged. While, in Nasir's 18 years, 131 persons (7.2 per year) held ministerial posts for an average tenure of 44 months, between 1970 and 1979, 186 so served Sadat (20.6 per year) for an average of 21 months. Some of the elite simply dropped out of power; not a single minister from Sadat's first post-Sabri government was still around at the end of the decade. Others were rotated into different positions, for example from minister to governor or public corporation chairman, a practice which mitigated the resentment such rapid turnover would otherwise have created. Finally, the ubiquitous security apparatus deterred elite efforts to organize against the President. No less than three separate intelligence services were at the command of Sadat and his team: the National Intelligence Service under the direct command of the President; the Defense Intelligence Service under the War Minister; and the Secret Investigations Department under the Minister of Interior; each watched the elite, above all the army, and each watched and checked the other (Shazli 1980: 120).

Sadat supplemented these practices with other rather traditionalistic methods of ensuring the loyalty of the elite. Increasingly, as the opportunity arose, he installed close personal and family relations into strategic positions; thus, the Osmans presided over key segments of the public sector. Sayyid Marei was entrusted with the Speakership of parliament; both headed key professional syndicates and had sons chairing key parliamentary committees. Mahmud Abu Wafia was first encouraged to lead the government party and later the official opposition. Sadat's tolerance of elite self-enrichment and corruption was also a control mechanism; those in favor could expect exceptional access to privileges as long as they remained deferent; once sullied, elites had a stake in maintaining the power structure, since a change at the top could well bring the day of reckoning. Even those pushed out of power were frequently kept on the public payroll or given generous pensions, on condition they refrain from opposition. To be sure, Nasir also employed some of these practices, but they took on a new order of magnitude under Sadat.

Sadat's ability to stay on top also owed much to the fact that when leading the elite in new policy directions, he did so step by step. Whether from calculation or because his course evolved gradually, Sadat was never so far in front of elite opinion as to precipitate a broad elite consensus against him. To take only the most important case, had Sadat announced early an intention to conclude a separate peace with Israel and enter a close American alliance, such a hostile coalition would probably have formed; on the other hand, his first steps along this path, the decision to seek a negotiated solution and to balance the Soviet alliance with a diplomatic opening to the US were acceptable to all but the left wing of the elite. Many accepted the concessions made in the first and second disengagements in the belief that the diplomatic process would issue in a comprehensive settlement, and if it did not, that Egypt could always resort to a more militant strategy. At each step along this course, however, Sadat presented the elite with a *fait accompli* which enmeshed Egypt in a web of commitments from which she could not easily extract herself and which further narrowed her options. Two steps ahead of the elite, he kept them off balance. By the time the process was completed, those who objected were powerless to stop it, and, indeed, as along this road Sadat coopted new persons supportive of his course into power, they found the balance of elite opinion shifted against them (Rondot 1981: 77).

The final – and perhaps decisive – key to Sadat's consolidation and maintenance of power was the solid base given to his rule by his alliance with the bourgeoisie, both its state and private wings. Unlike Nasir, who continually threatened its interests and had, therefore, to keep its members under control through a mix of coercion and mass political support, Sadat quickly won the support of a majority of this social class through policies favourable to it. Elites desirous of challenging Sadat must always have known that to do so would jeopardize the interests of their class and that, as such, they could not hope to carry the establishment with them; whatever their reservations regarding Sadat, the bulk of the bourgeoisie had no reason to expect a better deal from any other ruler.

However, it is precisely in this very strength that the limitations on Sadat's power lay. Much of the support Sadat won from this constituency was a product of resentment of the interventionist, domineering style of Nasir and the leftwing Free Officers around him, and the expectation that Sadat would maintain a lower Presidential profile in state and society. Sadat had to meet this expectation. He relaxed control over elites, permitting them more autonomy in their own domains. Outside questions of foreign policy and the rules of the political game, Sadat was more likely than Nasir to avoid taking a position on an issue, allowing it to be decided in a process of intra-elite interest aggregation involving a broader range of actors than under Nasir. As long as they did not challenge Presidential prerogatives, elites acquired new freedom to incrementally advance and protect their interests and views in domestic economic and social fields. The majority of Sadat's unilaterally imposed decisions were in foreign policy; in domestic fields where elite interests were more directly at stake, he reserved the right to intervene in the smallest matters and occasionally did so. But in practice his initiatives were much more circumspect, and when he acted, it was much more likely to have followed a process of intra-elite consultations in which he was prepared to take advice. When he did take an initiative threatening to established interests – such as his so-called 'administrative revolution' – it frequently petered out without much visible effect. Or, as in the case of the Pyramid Plateau incident which aroused bourgeoisie opinion or the Law of *Aib* which sparked a defensive reaction among the judiciary, journalists and lawyers, Sadat retreated or compromised. He did so not because his opponents could legally or politically block his measures, but because in the face of informal but broad and intense opposition among strategic sectors of bourgeois opinion, he thought it prudent to marshal rather than expend his political capital. Unlike Nasir, he refrained from coercive measures or the mobilization of mass opinion against established interests. Thus, although Sadat was generally more immune from elite challenge than Nasir and enjoyed wide personal prerogatives in certain fields like foreign policy, this enormous personal power was tolerated precisely because its 'scope' had been considerably narrowed. The domain of Presidential power had shrunk from Nasir's time, but within this domain Sadat exercised more unlimited power than Nasir had. While this narrowing of the scope of his power was acceptable to Sadat because he had no desire to ride roughshod over the elite and since social stabilization and economic liberalization required more deference to specialized elites and less unfettered state intervention, it was also the outcome of a kind of tacit 'social contract' between the ruler and the ruling class.

From charismatic leadership to Presidential monarchy

Under Sadat, the Presidency remained a concentration of great personalized power, but the bases and orientation of that power had changed greatly: Nasir's charismatic leadership was 'routinized' in 'Presidential Monarchy' (Apter 1965: 214–15). This could be seen in the more traditional role conception adopted by the President, in his tendency to treat the state as if it were his private property, and the citizens his political dependents. There was also the increased use of traditional techniques of rule, 'divide and rule,' the tolerance of corruption, the creation of a familial network in strategic positions. The bases of legitimacy shifted: while Nasir's authority was rooted in revolutionary charisma, Sadat's, in spite of his cult of the hero, increasingly rested on traditional religious and patriarchal symbols of rule. The ends for which power was used were also very different: while Nasir sought to use power to impose a revolution on Egypt, Sadat used it to conserve and stabilize an emergent post-revolutionary order. Finally, it can be seen in the success of the elite, the 'staff,' in narrowing the scope of arbitrary power of the ruler, shrinking the very large political domain typical of charismatic rule. It was not so much that effective legal-constitutional limits now constrained the President, for his prerogatives remained enormous and their sway still ambiguous; rather an informal understanding akin to custom and the changing intra-elite balance of power limited him. While the development of such constraints may be the first step toward legal-rational authority, under Sadat they more closely resembled traditional limits on the arbitrary will of the ruler; hence, intra-elite relations more closely approximated patrimonial than constitutional practices. In the absence of strong political institutions, the enormous personalized power typical of charismatic rule seems inevitably to evolve, once the charismatic impulse is exhausted, in a patrimonial direction.

A changing power elite

There was substantial continuity in the Egyptian political elite from the Nasir to Sadat eras. Many of the very top leaders, including the President himself, were men of power under Nasir. Most of those who presided over Sadat's Egypt rose through recruitment channels established under Nasir, and exercised power in ways similar to Nasir's days. Nevertheless, an accumulation of gradual changes begun under Nasir and accelerated under Sadat produced an emergent transformation in the political elite which helps account for and was reinforced by the accompanying alterations in political structure and policy under Sadat. This section will examine changes in the structure, the channels and bases of power, and the composition of the elite under Sadat.

The pyramid of power under Sadat

The Egyptian political elite below the Presidency can usefully be viewed as stratified into four basic layers. The *top* or *power elite* was made up of vice presidents, ministers, top generals and party executives and the provincial governors. From the broader top elite, a smaller *core elite* can be distinguished which held the most strategic positions for an extended time, was closest to the

President, the fount of power, and exercised substantial influence over him and broad public policy. The rest of the top elite – most cabinet ministers and provincial governors – were chiefly non-political technicians or administrators subject to rapid turnover. They exercised considerable discretion in their own domains and had some input into policy-making in specialized areas requiring expertise or experience. The top elite, even the core elite, were dependent on the President for tenure, lacked independent bases or constituencies and, in most cases, strong ideological commitments. Most therefore habitually deferred to the President, and the few who took issue with him or displayed too much independence were quickly removed. But over those below them and the fate of Egypt they exercised exceptional sway.

The *middle elite* embraced high civil servants, senior military commanders, public sector managers, most newspaper editors, top religious and academic leaders, heads of syndicates and chambers of commerce and chairmen of parliamentary committees. The *sub-elite* was made up of middle level officials and local notables, that is *umad* (village headmen), leaders of the local branches of the state party and most members of parliament. The middle and bottom layers of the pyramid of power were quite large: in the early seventies, grades two and three of the civil service alone made up more than 20,000 officials and members of basic level party committees amounted to more than 30,000 persons (Akhavi 1982: 227). In a highly centralized bureaucratic state most of these elites enjoyed little autonomous authority and had strictly limited influence over national policy. But they could articulate interests upward at the sufferance of higher authorities and, if they had expertise, help shape policy alternatives in limited issue areas. Within their own constricted local or institutional domains they necessarily enjoyed some sway.

The top elite: the channels and bases of power

Access to the top elite in Egypt was determined by a recruitment system largely established under Nasir, but significantly altered under Sadat. In the aftermath of the 1952 *coup*, which established the leading Free Officers at the very apex of the system, cooptation from above, chiefly by the President from four or five basic channels was established as virtually the only pathway into the elite; under Sadat the system of cooptation remained unchanged, but there were important shifts in the channels and bases of recruitment. (1) Under Nasir the Free Officers' organization was a privileged recruitment pool for top elite posts, Nasir promoting, as need arose, second- and third-ranking Free Officers to high office on the basis of participation in the revolution, ideological commitment, political or administrative talents and occasionally technical skills (notably military engineers). Their prior claim on strategic regime posts excluded all but a few civilians from the core elite. The most important change in recruitment under Sadat was the atrophy and disappearance of the Free Officers' organization which he formally disbanded in the late seventies. Revolutionary credentials thus disappeared as a recruitment criterion; perhaps as a kind of substitute indicator of political loyalty, close friendship or kinship connections to the President took on an enhanced role, especially for recruitment to the core elite. (2) Nasir also recruited from civilian channels although these seldom gave access to the core elite. Ministers were picked from the state bureaucracy, on the basis of seniority or a technical specialty (engineering, agronomy) and senior judges from the judiciary. Senior professors and administrators especially from the economics and professional faculties were recruited from academia to fill posts requiring expertise. Nasir also recruited from the ranks of private professionals, notably lawyers and doctors, but as his statist course matured this channel dwindled. Besides education and skills, political reliability or an apolitical stance were also required of civilians and those enjoying patronage or kinship connections to a political officer enjoyed an advantage over other candidates. Under Sadat, as the Free Officer monopoly was ended, access to the top elite, including the core elite, from civilian channels widened significantly. Bureaucrats and academics with technical qualifications and the right political orientation were recruited in large numbers. Moreover Sadat deliberately reopened recruitment paths from the private sector – business and the free professions – coopting some to the very top. (3) Under Nasir, representation or support of constituencies, institutional or territorial, played little overt role in recruitment: victory in party or parliamentary elections counted for little and, as a rule, neither the bureaucracy nor the military were able to force self-selected representatives on the President (although for a time Marshal Amer's military clients were able to use him to advance themselves). Under Sadat, societal groups or governmental institutions were even less able to force their representatives on the leader or elites to use support from below in competition for office, although some officers and politicians made abortive efforts to do so. But a growing incidence of party or parliamentary apprenticeships among those reaching the top suggested that the cultivation of constituencies below and acquisition of some 'representative' status had acquired greater weight as a criterion of Presidential cooptation.

The power elite: an empirical study

This section analyzes data on the occupational and educational composition, recruitment paths and class background of the top elite. The core elite is first identified and profiled, then the ministerial elite as a whole is analyzed and, finally, data on the party elite and provincial governors is examined. The analysis attempts to identify changes in the elite from the Nasir to Sadat eras, and as between the pre- and post-*Infitah* periods of Sadat's Presidency. It then

Table 1★ Core political elite under Sadat by occupation (1970–81)

Ex military or ex-police	Military or police	Engineer***	Academic	Lawyer	Diplomat	Businessman	Medicine	Journalist
**Anwar Sadat (President)	Nabawi Ismail (Min. of Interior)	Ahmad Izz ad-Din Hilal (Min. of Oil)	Mustafa Kamal Hilmi (Min. of Education)	Fikri Makram Ubayd (Deputy Premier, Party chief)	Mahmud Fawzi (Premier)	Mansur Hassan (Min. at Presidency, Information, party leader)	Fuad Muhi ad-Din (Deputy Premier, party leader, Min. of Health)	Muhammed Hassanein Haykel (Editor of al-Ahram)
**Hassan Tuhami (Presidential advisor)	**Ahmad Ismail Ali (Min. of Defense)	Mustafa Khalil (Premier, party chief)	Abd al-Aziz Higazi (Premier, Min. of Finance)	Mahmud Abu Wafa (Party leader)	Ismail Fahmi (Min. Foreign Affairs)			
**Kamal Henry Abadir (Presidential advisor, party parliamentary leader)	Kamal Hassan Ali (Min. of Defense, Foreign Affairs)	Aziz Sidqi (Premier, Min. of Industry)	Hafiz Ghanim (Party Chief, Min. of Education)	Albert Barsoum Salama (Party leader, Min. of parliament)				
**Hamdi Ashur (Presidential Advisor, Min. Local Admin.)	Abd al-Ghani Gamasi (Min. of Defense)	Osman Ahmad Osman (Min. of Reconstruction)	Hamid Sayyih (Min. of Economy)	Muhammed Hamid Mahmud (Party leader, Min. Local Admin.)				

**Abd al-Qadir Hatim (Deputy Premier, Min. of Information)	**Muhammad Sadiq (Min. of Defense)	Ahmad Sultan (Deputy Premier, Min. of Power)	Abd al-Razzak Abd al-Majid (Economy, Min. of Planning)					
Husni Mubarak (Vice President)		Sayyid Marei (Party chief, Speaker of Parliament, Presidential advisor)	Muhammad Abdullah Marzaban (Economy)					
Mamduh Salim (Premier, Min. of Interior)			Abd al Munim Qaysuni (Deputy Premier for Econ.)					
**Zakaria Tawfiq Abd al-Fattah (Min. of Supply)								
No.: 8 22.8%	No.: 5 14.3%	No.: 6 17.1%	No.: 7 20.0%	No.: 4 11.4%	No.: 2 5.7%	No.: 1 2.9%	No.: 1 2.9%	No.: 1 2.9%

*Sources: al-Ahram files, Egyptian informants

**Senior ex-Free Officers

***Includes agronomy and architecture

seeks to explain changes in the kinds of men recruited to power in terms of change in the environment and policies of the regime.

The core elite   Given the well-known difficulties of measuring power, no more than a rough portrait of the core elite can be attempted. Nevertheless, even such an approximation is adequate to reveal a major transformation in the core from Nasir to Sadat periods.

Identifying the core elite under Nasir is relatively easy. The 11-member Free Officer Revolutionary Command Council initially embodied it; in time, about half of the 34 or so second- and third-rank Free Officers made it to the inner core, serving either as key ministers, party leaders or in the Presidential bureaucracy. Several prominent civilians who were close to Nasir and exercised major influence over key policy areas or institutions can also legitimately be included in the inner core, notably press magnate Muhammed Hassanein Haykel, Agrarian reform administrator Sayyid Marei, veteran diplomat Mahmud Fawzi, industry czar Aziz Sidqi and top economist Abd al-Munim Qaysuni; indeed these men outlasted most of the Free Officers in positions of authority. Nevertheless, under Nasir the officer movement served as the main recruitment pool to the core elite and the bulk of the civilian elite remained technicians confined to the outer rim of the top elite.

There was a steady attrition in the ranks of the Free Officer core from 1952 onward, but after Nasir's death it was rapidly decimated. Of the first-rank Free Officers identified by Dekmejian (1975: 177–8), only Sadat and Hussein Shafa'i survived Nasir's death and Sadat had pushed Shafa'i out of power by 1975. Of the ten second-rank Free Officers in high office on Nasir's death, two were quickly retired, four were purged in the 1971 succession conflict, three voluntarily broke with Sadat thereafter, and only one remained on his team to the end. Of the 14 third-rank officers in power on Nasir's death, four were purged with Ali Sabri, four were subsequently purged or resigned, four stayed as part of the elite core around Sadat and two served him in lesser positions. Thus, of 26 Free Officers active in 1970, only about eight were really absorbed into the 'Sadatist elite.' And, by the end of the seventies, four senior and three lesser Free Officers had re-entered the political arena in overt opposition to Sadat, either as part of the nationalist left NPUP (Khalid Muhi ad-Din, Kemal ad-Din Rifaʻat, Lutfi Wakid) or the centrist 'National Coalition' (Zakaria Muhi ad-Din, Abd al-Latif Bagdadi, Kemal ad-Din Hussein, Sidqi Sulaiman).

Table 1 identifies the persons who for more than a brief period could probably be considered to have been in the core elite under Sadat. Persons were included in the core on the basis of four criteria. (1) High strategic office is a basis of very real power in Egypt; hence, all prime ministers and most defense and foreign ministers and holders of key economic, political, and security portfolios (except for those with very short tenures) are included. (2) Persons who appeared to be personally very close to the President and hence to enjoy exceptional access and possibly influence over him. (3) Ex-Free Officers who remained active and prominent members of Sadat's team for a significant period seemed to enjoy a special status. (4) Ministers enjoying exceptional longevity in a rapidly changing ministerial elite (specifically, serving in eight cabinets or more, a convenient breaking point discovered in ministerial tenure patterns) are included on the assumption that they enjoyed the special trust of the President and exceptional influence in their domains. All those in the table were not in the elite throughout the Sadat era: some, prominent early, fell into obscurity by the end of the period while others only emerged at the top later. A look at their careers and power bases gives some insight into the kinds of persons who exercised exceptional power in Sadat's Egypt.

Even among this blue-ribbon group, several men stood out for the extent and durability of their power. Osman Ahmad Osman was, for much of the seventies, perhaps the second most powerful man in Sadat's Egypt. A multi-millionaire capitalist, Osman and his family presided over a huge business empire embracing both the public, private and joint venture sectors. Osman openly used his wealth to buy prestige and favor in elite circles. He also held several public offices, including Minister of Reconstruction, presided over the grandiose project to rebuild the Suez Canal cities, was made czar of the state's 'food sufficiency' projects and served as head of the Engineers' Syndicate. After he was subjected to public criticism for alleged corrupt activities, he withdrew from high office, contenting himself, at the end of the decade with the role of chief of the Ismailia parliamentary delegation; but his sons and nephews, cousins and sons-in-law were in and out of public office as deputy ministers, heads of public firms, prosecutors, and parliamentary committee chairmen (Ajami 1982:495–6). In brief, Osman headed a formidable clientage network. But what most set him apart from the rest of the elite was his extremely close personal relations with the President, and through the marriage of a son to one of Sadat's daughters, his virtual incorporation into the Presidential family. By all accounts his influence with the President was unrivaled. He appears to have been an early and effective advocate of economic liberalization and an extremely well-placed informal 'representative' of the business wing of the Egyptian bourgeoisie at the center of power. He also, of course, used his influence with the President to serve his family and his private fortune with spectacular effect (Ajami 1982: 495–6; Moore 1980: 123–6).

A second man who enjoyed exceptional and durable influence was Sayyid Marei. Marei had a long and distinguished public career. From a wealthy and prestigious land-owning family, he was a deputy of the conservative Saadist Party under the old regime. An agronomist, he was picked by Nasir to carry out the first agrarian reform and later served as Minister of Agriculture. His cautious technocratic approach to agricultural issues (in particular his skepticism toward land reclamation and state farms) and his defense of landowners' property rights brought him into collision with leftist military-politicians in the sixties, but his influence revived after the 1967 war. Under Sadat, Marei exchanged his technocratic role for a political one. He presided over the early attempt to liberalize the ASU and purge it of leftist influence, and was then made Speaker of parliament with a similar mission. As chairman of the Committee on the Future of Political Life, he was a major force behind the multi-party experiment. He also served as head of the Agronomists' Syndicate and had a son made chairman of the Agricultural Committee of parliament; through these roles he seemed to act as an informal representative of the agrarian bourgeoisie at the top. Like Osman, Marei stood out for his very close personal relations to the President; he was a long-time close confidant from the fifties, was Sadat's deputy when the latter was Speaker of parliament under Nasir, and like Osman, married a son to one of Sadat's daughters. He also seems to have carried major influence with the President as an advocate of both economic and political liberalization, and of loosening the Soviet connection (Marei 1978a; Springborg 1979b).

Appointed in 1975, Vice President Husni Mubarak was, by the end of the seventies, the equal of these two men in the power elite. As a successful Air Force commander, Mubarak enjoyed prestige and a following in the armed forces and was regarded as an informal 'representative' of the military at the top. He also appeared to enjoy the close trust of and regular access to Sadat. The 1978 removal of General Gamasi, who apparently tried to prevent Mubarak from extending his influence in the army, and Mubarak's 1980 appointment as Secretary General of the ruling party – in effect as the President's chief political troubleshooter – signaled the consolidation of his stature and his emergence as the number-two man in the regime. By virtue of his personal stature, military support and, above all, his office, he was the natural unrivaled choice to succeed Sadat as President.

The backgrounds and resources of several other members of the core elite, probably less influential and usually less durable, can be indicated more briefly. Prime Ministers, by virtue of their office, the access to and trust of the President which they enjoyed, and the wide scope of matters over which they could influence his decisions, ranked high in the core elite. As chief implementers of Presidential policy, they made a host of lesser 'who gets what' decisions. They also enjoyed patronage prerogatives over some cabinet and many lesser government appointments. Aziz Sidqi, a powerful statist-oriented industry minister from the Nasir era, was probably the most independent-minded of Sadat's Prime Ministers and the only one to attempt to build a personal political base; however, precisely for this reason and because his views were out of step with Sadat's liberalization, he was soon removed. Mamduh Salim enjoyed exceptional tenure as Chief of Government; having won the President's trust in the succession crisis, and enjoying extensive ties in the state bureaucracy, he was of great value to Sadat at the rudder during the *Infitah* transition. Mustafa Khalil, another successful minister–technocrat from the Nasir era, was at the center of power under Sadat for an extended period, serving as party boss, Prime Minister, and again as a party leader. Despite differences with the President over Sadat's concessions to Israel during the peace negotiations, he remained in favor to the end. Mahmud Fawzi and Abd al-Aziz Higazi were of lesser stature and tenure.

Defense Ministers, especially Sadat's two most durable and trusted military chiefs, Marshal Ahmad Ismail Ali and General Abd al-Ghani Gamasi, carried political weight as advisers on defense matters and as at least tacit 'representatives' of military interests. A remnant of the Free Officers with close personal relations to Sadat (e.g. Hassan Tuhami and Abd al-Qadir Hatim) continued to serve in high positions, often as political troubleshooters. The rest of the core elite fell into basically four categories. One foreign minister, Ismail Fahmi, enjoyed sufficient tenure to leave a significant impact on his policy domain. There were, secondly, the minister–technocrats, men such as Qaysuni, Higazi, Marzaban, Sayyih, and Abd al-Majid who, as deputy prime ministers for economic affairs, or ministers of the economy or of finance, participated in policy-making in crucial economic issue areas and were more than mere administrators. Minister–technicians like Hilal and Sultan presided for long periods over important functional domains. Thirdly, there were police professionals, for example, the very durable Interior Minister Nabawi Ismail who enjoyed broad political–security responsibilities. A fourth group was made up of partially private-sector figures who usually acted as political organizers, linking the regime to its extra-state constituency. Mansur Hassan, an *Infitah* millionaire, Muhammed Hamid Mahmud, a big landlord with long-time personal links to Sadat, and prestigious professionals like Fikri Makram Ubayd and Fuad Muhi ad-Din all filled key party or political–administrative roles (e.g., Minister of Local Administration, Information, etc.) Mahmud Abu Wafia was a landowner–politician who married into Sadat's family. He was a leader in the organization of the ruling party in parliament and apparently a force behind political liberalization; in parliament he was also vocal in the encouragement of local and foreign private capital (defending or advocating tax exemptions for it and the limitation of the public sector).

It is thus clear that there was a significant transformation in the composition of the core elite from the Nasir to Sadat periods. Civilianization was substantial. To be sure, the military remained well represented. The President and Vice President were ex-officers. But prime ministers, always officers under Nasir, were exclusively civilians under Sadat. Only a few ex-Free Officers remained at the apex. The active duty officers serving in the core elite were professional soldiers who Sadat confined to the role of staff subordinates, a very different breed from the officer-politicians of Nasir's day who, having helped make the revolution, could claim the broad diffuse authority of a revolutionary elite. In place of the military, technocrats recruited from the state bureaucracy and economic notables from the private sector emerged in force. The emergence of many figures who had at least one foot in the private sector represented a substantial dilution of the nearly exclusively statist character of the core elite under Nasir. Under Sadat, in short, the inner core changed from a body of relatively like-minded 'revolutionary comrades' of similar background into a much more occupationally differentiated and heterogeneous collection of personal confidants, technicians, bureaucrats, politicians and economic notables.

The ministerial elite   Tables 2–4 compare the ministerial elite as a whole between the Nasir period, the whole Sadat period and the post-*Infitah* sub-period of the Sadat Presidency. Because the columns on the whole Sadat period include members of the transitional governments following Nasir's death, many of whom were Sadat's rivals rather than his own men, they reflect the continuity in the elite from the Nasir to Sadat eras. By contrast, the post-*Infitah* columns count only those ministers, purely Sadat's men, *first recruited* after the initiation of *Infitah* (beginning with the April 1974 government); hence they are indicators of the changes Sadat effected in the elite to make it compatible with this major redirection of the Egyptian polity. Because of the possibilities of error and problems of incomplete or incomparable data (especially where, as in the recruitment path breakdowns, the numbers are small), the tables are not intended to represent a definitive mapping of the elite. But the data are adequate as a rough indicator of the typical elite backgrounds and pathways and of the major changes in them over the period.

Table 2, comparing elite educational specialties over the three periods, provides evidence that the specialties expected of ministers shifted significantly under Sadat. Under Nasir, those with exclusively military training made up the biggest single ministerial contingent (20.8%), many of whom filled purely political roles; under Sadat they rapidly dwindled and by the *Infitah* period only 6.6% of new recruits had such training, namely, the military and police professionals heading the Ministries of War and the Interior. The role of military officers who also held technical degrees, and even more so those with non-technical degrees, similarly shrank. Simultaneously, the proportion of those trained in engineering or agronomy rose from 21.5% of the elite under Nasir to 26.5% under Sadat and after *Infitah* about one-third of all new recruits had such training. There was also a significant increase in ministers trained in economics or business, rising from 9.2% under Nasir to 13.2% under Sadat and after *Infitah* to 21% of new recruits. At the same time, there was a dramatic fall in those trained in social science, from a substantial 11.5% under Nasir to a

Table 2* *Educational specializations of ministers*

Educational specializations	Nasir period		Period Sadat period		Post-*Infitah* recruits only	
	No.	%	No.	%	No.	%
Military or police	27	20.8	22	12.6	5	6.6
Military–Technocrat**	10	7.7	13	7.5	4	5.3
Military – other***	7	5.4	8	4.6	1	1.3
Engineering	19	14.6	33	19.0	17	22.4
Agronomy	9	6.9	13	7.5	7	9.2
Medicine	3	2.3	9	5.1	3	4.0
Law	19	14.6	35	20.1	14	18.4
Economics/business	12	9.2	23	13.2	16	21.0
Humanities	1	0.8	4	2.3	2	2.6
Social science	15	11.5	3	1.7	1	1.3
Pure science	4	3.1	5	2.9	3	4.0
Religion	3	2.3	5	2.9	3	4.0
None	1	0.8	1	0.6	0	0.0
Totals	130	100.0	174	100.0	76	100.1%

*Sources: Nasir elite: Dekmejian (1971); Sadat elite: *al-Ahram* files
**Denotes persons combining military education with a technical degree such as engineering
***Denotes persons combining military education with a non-technical degree, such as in law, the social sciences or humanities; data are missing on 17 Sadat ministers and one under Nasir

miniscule 1.7% under Sadat. There was a perceptible advance in those trained in law, from 14.6% under Nasir to 20.1% under Sadat. Finally, there was a modest rise in recruitment of those with religious training.

Table 3 tries to identify the career paths, that is, typical combinations of occupations and institutional channels, followed by those who reached ministerial positions.[3] Several significant changes under Sadat can again be identified.

The decline of the military career route is the most salient change. Under Nasir it supplied one-third of the elite and filled 40% of all ministerial positions; but by the *Infitah* period only 10.2% of new recruits were from military backgrounds. The decline in the military role was, of course, gradual. Several military–bureaucrats (path 2) were inherited from the Nasir period; and a

Table 3* *Recruitment paths of the ministerial elite*

Recruitment paths	Nasir period No.	%	Sadat period No.	%	Post-*Infitah* recruits only No.	%
A. *Military*	44	33.5	40	22.7	8	10.2
1. Military only	16	12.2	7	3.9	3	3.8
2. Military–bureaucratic	20	15.2	20	11.4	5	6.4
3. Military–political	8	6.1	13	7.4	0	0.0
B. *Academic*	31	23.7	30	17.0	19	24.4
4. Academic only	16	12.2	12	6.8	7	9.0
5. Academic–bureaucratic	14	10.7	13	7.4	10	12.8
6. Academic–political	1	0.8	2	1.1	1	1.3
7. Academic–bureaucratic–political	0	0.0	3	1.7	1	1.3
C. *Engineer or agronomist***	19	14.5	46	26.1	24	30.8
8. Engineer only	0	0.0	1	0.6	1	1.3
9. Engineer–academic	5	3.8	7	3.9	1	1.3
10. Engineer–academic–bureaucratic	4	3.1	4	2.3	3	3.8
11. Engineer–bureaucratic	10	7.6	22	12.5	13	16.7
12. Engineer–bureaucratic–political	0	0.0	8	4.6	3	3.8
13. Engineer–bureaucratic–business	0	0.0	3	1.7	3	3.8
14. Engineer–political	0	0.0	1	0.6	0	0.0
D. *Bureaucrat*	9	6.9	6	3.4	4	5.1
15. Bureaucrat only	8	6.1	3	1.7	3	3.8
16. Bureaucratic–political	1	0.8	3	1.7	1	1.3
E. *Law*	15	11.5	29	16.5	11	14.1
17. Law only	0	0.0	2	1.1	2	2.6
18. Law–academic	3	2.3	3	1.7	1	1.3
19. Law–bureaucratic	1	0.8	6	3.4	1	1.3
20. Law–judiciary	7	5.3	5	2.8	2	2.6
21. Law–political	3	2.3	5	2.8	2	2.6
22. Law–academic–political	0	0.0	4	2.3	1	1.3
23. Law–bureaucratic–political	1	0.8	4	2.3	2	2.6
F. *Other professional or business*	7	5.3	11	6.3	7	9.0
24. Business–political			2	1.1	2	2.6
25. Professional only			1	0.6	1	1.3
26. Professional-bureaucratic–political			4	2.3	2	2.6
27. Professional–academic			4	2.3	2	2.6
G. *Diplomat*	4	3.1	10	5.7	3	3.8
28. Diplomat only	3	2.3	8	4.6	3	3.8
29. Diplomat–political	1	0.8	2	1.1	0	0.0
30. Police	2	1.5	3	1.7	2	2.6
31. Syndicalist	0	0.0	1	0.6	0	0.0
Total	131	100.0%	176	100.0%	78	100.0%

*Source: Nasir elite: Dekmejian (1971); Sadat elite: *al-Ahram* files; data are missing on 15 Sadat ministers
**Excludes agronomy under Nasir

sprinkling of them continued to be picked to head the Transport, Communication and Aviation Ministries where their qualifications were suitable. Until *Infitah*, a handful of Sadat's old military cronies having some political experience were entrusted with political portfolios such as Minister of Cabinet Affairs or Minister at the Presidency; but after 1974 the military–political career (path 3) ceased to channel new faces to the top. An exclusively military career (path 1) offered ministerial access only to the professional officers appointed Ministers of War (except for General Kamal Hassan Ali who moved laterally from this position to foreign minister).

Academia remained a relatively stable channel of recruitment, making up about one-fifth to one-fourth of the ministerial elite. Academics may have dipped in the early Sadat ministries, but under *Infitah* they showed a strong recovery, with one of every four new ministers rising from academia. Table 3, in fact, understates the presence of those with academic experience, for if engineers, lawyers and doctors (paths 9, 10, 18, 22, 27) who spent part of their careers in university faculties (if only part-time) are classified as academics, their proportion rises to 34.7% of post-*Infitah* recruits. The most important academic recruits were the economists picked to head the crucial Ministries of Economy, Finance and Planning, and as Deputy Prime Ministers for Economic Affairs. Some academics were coopted directly from the university (path 4), but more spent some apprenticeship in state or political roles (paths 5–7), indicative of the overlap between academia and government service in Egypt.

Engineering appeared to become the dominant professional springboard to power under Sadat. Engineers made up 21.4% of the elite under Nasir when agronomists are included in the category (see note 3); under Sadat they reached 26.1% of the elite and, after *Infitah*, almost every third new ministerial recruit was an engineer. Most engineers clearly rose through the bureaucracy and public sector (paths 11–13), and, in fact, the dominance of this career path actually increased under *Infitah* when one-fourth of all new ministers reached office along it. Most of these engineer-bureaucrats were entrusted with technical tasks, that is, the Ministries of Agriculture, Irrigation, Power, Industry, Transportation, Housing, etc. But some of the more senior, talented, or ambitious of them, having branched out into politics and/or business (paths 12–13), ranked among the most influential of the political elite and played roles of far broader scope than mere technicians. Given the rise of the technocrats, 'classical' bureaucrats lacking professional, technical or academic specialties had slim chances under both Nasir and Sadat to reach the ministerial elite. Finally, diplomacy (the foreign policy bureaucracy) became an important subsidiary route into the elite under Sadat, increasing from 3.1% under Nasir to 5.7%.

The free professions and business were revitalized under Sadat as bases for political careers. Lawyers made up a bigger part of the elite under Sadat (16.5%) than Nasir (11.5%). Many of these rose through careers in the judiciary or bureaucracy (paths 19, 20, 23). Lawyers rising directly, through politics or academia (paths 17, 18, 21, 22), did, however, increase from 4.6% under Nasir to 7.9% under Sadat. Those reaching the cabinet from other professional (e.g. medicine) or business careers (paths 24–7) increased from 5.3% under Nasir to about 9% of new recruits under *Infitah*. Although those following legal, professional and business careers into the elite (paths 17–27) made up 16.8% of the elite under Nasir, their access to the cabinet dwindled in the late Nasir period (1961–70) to a mere 9.6% of the portfolios (Dekmejian 1975: 206); under Sadat, they recovered, reaching 22.8% of the elite and 19.8% of ministerial portfolios. If bureaucrats also having business careers are added to this group (path 13), it made up about 27% of all new recruits under *Infitah*; about one in four new recruits therefore had at least one foot in the 'private sector.' This signified a real dilution under Sadat in the overwhelmingly statist character of the Nasirite elite. It is also clear, however, that *some* service in state institutions was hardly less important as a criterion of recruitment than under Nasir; while under Nasir 75.6% of those reaching ministerial positions had done some service in the military, bureaucracy or judiciary, this was still true of 74.5% under Sadat. The lawyer, doctor or businessman who goes into politics (as opposed to civil service) and rises to the top (paths 17, 21, 24, 25), so common in more liberal political systems, increased in incidence from 3.9% under Nasir to 9.1% during *Infitah* but remained a relative rarity in Egypt.

Table 4 shifts the focus from occupational starting points to the channels of elite recruitment. It records the incidence of use of six basic channels (as coded in table 3) into the elite. It confirms the previous findings. The military has declined as an institutional channel to the top while the civilian bureaucracy has greatly expanded, becoming the major beneficiary of the de-politicization of the military under Sadat. Academia has held its own. One major change is the increasing incidence of political service as part of an elite career, up from 9.3% under Nasir to 20.1% under Sadat. Thus under Sadat parliamentary notables and party managers began to use parliament as a springboard to the cabinet; among the most notable of such cases were the careers of Ahmad Abu Ismail who rose from chairman of the parliamentary budget committee to be Minister of Finance and Fikri Makram Ubayd whose parliamentary career helped him reach a deputy prime ministership. Indicative of the growing importance of political channels to the top is the fact that the incidence of political credentials among civilians reaching the ministerial elite grew from 4.9% under Nasir to 15.1% under Sadat. Finally, it appears that direct cooptation from a private professional career remained as rare under Sadat as Nasir.

By way of conclusion, the following differences and similarities between the paths to power under Nasir and Sadat seem apparent. Under Nasir the best way to get to the top was to combine military with bureaucratic or political service (paths 1–3) or to come to official notice through academic achievement or

Table 4* *Incidence of use of institutional channels by ministers*

Institutional channels	Nasir period No.	%	Sadat period No.	%	Post-*Infitah* recruits only No.	%
1. Military	44	24.0	40	15.4	8	7.4
2. Academia	45	24.6	52	20.1	27	25.0
3. Bureaucratic	68	37.2	106	40.9	52	48.1
4. Political**	17	9.3	52	20.1	15	13.9
4a. (Political civilian only)***	(9)	(4.9)	(39)	(15.1)	(15)	(13.9)
5. Judiciary	7	3.8	5	1.9	2	1.9
6. Private profession or business only	2	1.1	4	1.5	4	3.7
Total incidence	183	100.0	259	99.9	108	100.0

*Source: Table 3, plus data on institutional incidence taken from Dekmejian on the "other professional or business" category.

**Denotes service in the party, parliament or as a political advisor/troubleshooter in the Presidential bureaucracy.

***A subdivision of the political category excluding the military.

technocratic skill. Under Sadat an engineering career was the surest bet, but those with professional or academic degrees who spent some time in the bureaucracy and dabbled in politics on the side also stood good chances. While political channels for persons outside the state started to open up, the elite under Sadat remained highly bureaucratized.

Party elites   There was a significant change in the leadership composition of the ruling party from the Nasir to Sadat eras. The most important change was the end to Free Officer control of the top positions. Under Nasir, a Free Officer invariably held the top party executive post, and officers a majority in the central leadership committees. In 1962–4, typical years, Nasir was chairman of the executive committee and 66% of its members were officers, while 62% of the leading *apparatchek* in the general-secretariat were officers. Under Sadat, in contrast, the head of the party was usually a civilian until he and his Vice President assumed the top party positions in 1978; but even then persons of military background made up only 22% of the Politburo of the NDP (Dekmejian 1971: 148–52; Akhavi 1982: 232). The demilitarization of the party resulted in an increased heterogeneity in the backgrounds of the party elite. Table 5 summarizes basic data on the most important of Sadat's top party

Table 5 *Party elite under Sadat*

	Previous political career	Occupational background	Post-party post
Sayyid Marei (1st Secretary, ASU*)	Minister	Technocrat–Landowner	Speaker of National Assembly
Hafiz Ghanim (1st Secretary, ASU)	Minister	Educator	–
Mustafa Khalil (ASU Secretary General)	Minister	Technocrat	Prime Minister
Mamduh Salim (ASPE* President)	Minister	Police–Bureaucrat	–
Mahmud Abu Wafia (ASPE Secretary General)	Deputy	Professional–Landowner	–
Fuad Muhi ad-Din (ASPE Secretary General)	Minister	Professional	Prime Minister
Muhammed Hamid Mahmud (ASPE Secretary General)	Minister	Professional–Landowner	–
Fikri Makram Ubayd (NDP* Secretary General)	Deputy	Professional	Deputy Prime Minister
Nabawi Ismail (Deputy Secretary General, NDP)	Minister	Police–Bureaucrat	–
Husni Mubarak (Secretary General, NDP)	Vice President	Military	President
Mansur Hassan (Deputy Secretary General, NDP)	Deputy	Businessman	Minister of Culture & Information

*ASU: Arab Socialist Union
 ASPE: Arab Socialist Party of Egypt
 NDP: National Democratic Party

managers since 1971. By occupation, three groups, technocrats, 'free' professionals and military or police elements are fairly evenly represented.

The party continues, it is clear, to be dominated, as under Nasir, by government leaders. Most party chiefs served at the ministerial level before becoming party leaders, and some powerful ministers whose power derived from their government posts, simultaneously held top party posts; thus Prime Minister Mamduh Salim was made leader of the government party over the heads of party notables in 1976, while in 1980 Vice President Mubarak and the powerful Interior Minister, Nabawi Ismail were inserted as Secretary General and Assistant Secretary General of the NDP. Yet, a majority of party leaders can

Table 6* *Educational specializations and career routes of Egyptian governors,*
1978

1. *Educational specializations*	
Military	8
Humanities/social science	2
Engineering	2
Medicine	2
Law	2
Agronomy	6
Commerce	1
No data	3
2. *Career routes*	
Military or Police Only	4
Bureaucratic Only	5
Military and Bureaucracy	2
Military or Bureaucracy plus Party or Parliamentary Service	7
Free Professional, Academic or Farmer, plus Party or Parliamentary Service	5
No Data	3
Totals	26

Source: al-Ahram files, informants.

be considered to have had a foot in the private sector as well as government, that is, in the professions, landownership or business. Moreover, some followed careers quite outside the state bureaucracy: Mansur Hassan, Fikri Makram Ubayd, Mahmud Abu Wafia and Muhammed Hamid Mahmud were all essentially parliamentary notables who had followed professional careers and had interests in land or business. Their rise signals a significant opening of the government party to persons lacking extensive governmental career experience, and is symptomatic of Sadat's effort to make the party a channel of recruitment for persons in the private bourgeoisie.

Finally, a sign that party leadership may be taking on increased importance as a political credential, is the assumption of the Prime Ministership by two men, Mustafa Khalil and Fuad Muhy ad-Din, following extended tenure as party chiefs. The party may have started to become a genuine recruitment channel under Sadat.

Provincial governors A process of occupational differentiation parallel to that in the ministerial elite seems to have taken place at the gubernatorial level. Under Nasir, these posts were almost a military monopoly. Data on governors under Sadat are available only for 1978 (see table 6), but it appears representative of a tendency which matured after *Infitah*. The military, to be sure, remains well represented, holding about 35% of these positions. Of the 23 governors on whom data are available, 18 were recruited from the state establishment. But the majority now have either professional or technocratic training. After those with military education, agronomists seem particularly favored for appointment. Most strikingly, five of the 1978 governors were academics, professionals – and even a private farmer – who apparently reached their positions through party or parliamentary service rather than a bureaucratic career.

The class composition of the elite There is little quantitative evidence, but considerable consensus in the literature on the changing class composition of the post–1952 Egyptian political elite. It is widely recognized that the officers who carried out the 1952 coup were largely from rural middle-class families and in occupation ranked with the salaried new middle class (Beeri 1966; Binder 1965; Dekmejian 1971: 212). Their assumption of power at the expense of the landed aristocracy and the *haute bourgeoisie* created a gap between political and social power which had inevitably to be bridged. From the outset the bridging process began. Part of the new officer elite itself underwent rapid embourgeoisement; it changed its style of life, increased its income and married into high-class families (Springborg 1975). The civilian elites – in particular the engineers – who the officers recruited to help them run the new regime were largely from the upper and upper middle classes since both academia and the professions were largely monopolized by these classes. The nationalizations gave these new elites control of the modern means of production, and through generous salaries, corrupt practices and business on the side, they assured themselves a relatively high income, life style and status. Thus was born the 'new state bourgeoisie,' a development largely recognized as nearly complete by the time of Nasir's death (Binder 1965; Hussein 1973).

Under Sadat the embourgeoisement of the political elite further matured. First, the disappearance of most of the Free Officers at the top removed the one element of the elite which was, at least in origins, middle class; the failure to replace the defunct Free Officer organization with some other recruitment channel which reached down in the stratification system spelled a social contraction of the recruitment pool. At the same time, the rise of the engineers to the very top, a profession which Moore (1980: 109–30) has shown to be recruited from the highest social strata, enhanced the high social status of the elite; the same could probably be said for the prestigious academics and lawyers which were now recruited in place of the military. Secondly, *Infitah* opened up lucrative opportunities hardly existent under Nasir for the political elite to further enrich itself, largely through commissions from foreign investors; it also

opened up new opportunities to invest this and other wealth in business
ventures with private Egyptian or foreign capital and thus to acquire a growing
stake in the private sector. Although the precise scale of the movement of the
political elite into private business has not been measured, few doubt that it has
been a major phenomenon of the *Infitah* era (Ajami 1982: 486–502; Mursi 1976:
136–7, 250–5). Ayubi (1982) reports on numerous cases in the files of the
Administrative Control Authority of officials who have gone into business on
the side, making use of their public connections and facilities for private gain.
Mokhtar's (1980) study of 30 prominent businessmen showed that five had
recently emerged from public sector careers. In short, the 'state bourgeoisie'
was increasingly becoming a private-property-owning bourgeoisie.[4] Finally,
the growing recruitment of landowners and businessmen, unquestionably of
the highest-class status, not only consolidated the upper-class character of the
political elite, but helped to bridge the divisions of the Nasir era between the old
private bourgeoisie and the new state bourgeoisie. Under Sadat, the acceler-
ating movement of state elites into the private sector, and private sector elites
into the state, and a growing web of marriage, political and business alliances
between these social forces seemed to produce a new more unified and
uniformly upper-class political elite.

The forces and consequences of elite transformation

The transformation of the political elite from Nasir to Sadat resulted from a
complex cumulative interplay of environmental change and political struggle.
In 1952 a small group of middle-class military politicians imposed themselves
on a largely agrarian society, excluded traditional private-based elites from
power, and set out to impose a statist modernizing revolution from above. Their
policies required the recruitment of a new breed of technocrats – economists,
agronomists, engineers – who steadily made their way up the ladder of power.
Gradually, the military elite and its technocratic staff was embourgeoised, that
is, transformed into a 'state bourgeoisie.' This represented the first major
change in the elite.

After 1967, external defeat and internal exhaustion began to shift the balance
of social power away from the military-politicians, setting the stage for a second
major change in the elite in the first half decade of Sadat's rule, namely
'de-militarization.' The 1967 defeat weakened the legitimacy of military rule
and shifted sentiment in the officer corps in favor of professionalization. Sadat's
successful defeat of military rivals in 1971 and his subsequent removal of other
officers who showed political ambitions in favor of professional soldiers,
established the principle of a de-politicized military. His purge of the military
was basic to Sadat's consolidation of power: civilianization not only allowed him
to broaden his base of support in the civil bureaucracy and extend it to private

sector elites, but replaced ambitious and dangerous rivals with more deferential and less politicized figures. Moreover, the skills and attitudes of the military politicians were irrelevant to Sadat's new course. The coercive skills appropriate to a period of forced revolution from above were of diluted utility in an era of social stabilization; the end to the effort to make Egypt the political–military center of the Arab world and the lessening preoccupation with external conflicts reduced the need for specialists in the projection of national power.

A third dimension of change which matured in the second half of Sadat's rule, namely, an occupational differentiation and social pluralization of the elite, resulted from a combination of de-militarization, shifts in the 'needs' of the system and changes in the relative power of social groups precipitated by Sadat's new policies. His foreign policy of accommodation shifted the premium from the skills and attitudes of revolutionary officers to those of the professional diplomats and professional soldiers devoid of ideological ambitions. The new stress on economic growth and the economic liberalization, which produced a more complex mixed economy, called for new skills and experience in elite roles. The rise of the engineer–bureaucrats had its roots in Nasir's statist technocratic revolution, that is, the creation of a massive public sector and the expansion of engineering education; but it was only with the departure of the military and the enhanced stress on purely technical competence over ideological commitment that they reached the top *en masse*. They were now the natural choice to run Egypt's array of functional ministries. Although their dominance may seem incongruent with the threat to the public sector implicit in *Infitah*, it is a sign that the big role of the state bourgeoisie and the state sector in the economy may be diluted but is unlikely to soon disappear. The growth in appointments of agronomists, experts in the management of agrarian society, to governorships seemed to reflect a growing preoccupation with economics over political–security matters in an era of social stabilization. The growing recruitment of economists at the top was certainly a concession to the needs of *Infitah*: not only were their skills in great demand in an era of renewed market economics, but the presence in power of men with links to and attitudes congenial to the Western financial and business worlds was essential to the economic open door. Similarly, the recruitment and high visibility of a businessman like Mansur Hassan could not have been unrelated to a desire to give investors confidence that the new economic course was deeply rooted in the power structure. The enhanced role of lawyers, specialists in legality, contract, the defense of property rights and skilled in the manipulation of the complex inter-relations of interest typical of the market society, was certainly appropriate in an area of *Infitah*. Conversely, the decline in the social scientist contingent in the elite may reflect an end to the period of planned social engineering. Even the greater recruitment of those with religious training is a symptom of liberalization; reflective of the end to appointment of non-religious

persons to the religious ministries, it signaled the increased functional autonomy allowed elites in this era. Finally, the change in the composition of party
elites reflected the changing needs and social base of the regime. Under Nasir
the party was chiefly an instrument for the imposition of the military regime's
revolution from above on Egypt's social elite: hence its domination by military
politicians. Under Sadat, as this social elite began to reconquer power, the party
began to turn into a recruitment channel for it (especially needed, given the
disappearance of the Free Officers' organization as the dominant recruitment
channel). The party became a channel of political apprenticeship in which
bureaucrats could prove their political loyalty; more important, it emerged as a
channel of mobility open to those outside the state machine, that is, the private
sector. The opening of this channel to private elites reflected their growing
social power under *Infitah*, Sadat's need to reduce his dependence on statist
elites necessarily ambivalent toward *Infitah* and to give his regime stronger roots
in the social force with the greatest stake in the economic course and on whom
its success ultimately depended.

A final dimension of elite transformation, also maturing in the post-*Infitah*
era, was the completed embourgeoisement of the elite following on the closure
of the military career route from below and the growing recruitment from the
private bourgeoisie and privatization of the state bourgeoisie, which merged
these two forces into an elite of a much more homogeneous bourgeois character.
By the end of the Sadat era, the class which then – in its various state and private
wings – had come to control the means of production had finally reasserted its
control of political power after an extended period of rapid change and social
instability under Nasir in which the two were partly separated.

Elite change resulted from a confluence of two forces. On the one hand,
environmental changes engendered a kind of push upward from the societal
base of new elements into the elite. Global pressures and growing modernization and pluralization engendered more complex social and economic
structures requiring new specialized *skills* at the top. Environmental changes
also resulted in shifts in *social power*, for example away from the military and
toward the private bourgeoisie; the state, responding to these changes, sought
to absorb the strategic social forces which dominated its master institutions.

On the other hand, the changing 'needs' of the system and the shifts in social
power which determined opportunities to acquire resources usable in the rise to
the top, were in great part determined by changes in the political 'superstructure': the leader's struggle to defeat opponents and broaden his base, and
the policies which favored the skills and influence of some groups over others.
Moreover, the state determined the channels of political mobility and ultimately
arrival in the ranks of the top elite required a 'pull' from above. In short,
recruitment was determined as much by the character and policies of the state as
by environmental change, and it remained under Sadat as under Nasir,

essentially state-centered. What had changed was that under Nasir power flowed from a mix of revolutionary credentials, charisma, and bureaucratic office. Under Sadat, it shifted to the bureaucratic–patrimonial mix typical of post-revolutionary regimes. Thus, most aspirant elites climbed upward along bureaucratic ladders on the basis of seniority and performance, and exercised authority only as long as they stayed in office. But strategic personal connections were decisive in determining which of them would reach the top elite. And the emergence at the very top of a group of men resembling a kind of royal family who, regardless of office and on the basis of personal links to the President, exercised extensive power immune to the turnover which affected most ministers and generals, was a clear symptom of the emerging patrimonial cap at the top of the Sadat elite.

Elite ideological transformation

The ideology of the Egyptian power elite underwent, during Sadat's rule, a thorough transformation which nearly effaced the 'Nasirism' of the previous period. Nasirism proved so vulnerable because much of the elite, regarding it as an imposition by the leader, was never intensely committed to it and Nasir never bothered to recruit a new elite which was. Even for Nasir it was less a doctrine than a general outlook altered by pragmatic responses to changing circumstances and experiences. For a period, it seemed to embody a successful nation-building formula, but after 1967 its credibility was shattered and a new set of experiences and circumstances gradually reshaped elite ideology. On the one hand, the very high costs incurred by Egypt in its nationalist effort to challenge the dominant world order in the Middle East, and the perceived weakness of the etatist economy in the late sixties undermined elite confidence in Nasirist solutions; on the other, the opportunities for Egypt to cut her losses and exploit post-1973 diplomatic and economic opportunities strengthened the hand of those led by Sadat who sought an ideological revision. Ideological change was also a function of the social transformation of the core elite from a band of petty bourgeois outsiders challenging a dominant local and imperial order to a privileged establishment with interests to protect and frequently much to gain from an end to Nasirism.

Ideological transformation can be partly traced through official doctrine. The *October Paper* was the first major landmark in the evolution of post-Nasirist ideology. Insisting that the basic principles of the Nasirite revolution, including socialism and Arabism, still held, it avoided a clean break with the past. But their mode of application, it argued, had to be adapted to a new era; the revolution would be institutionalized in a constitutional order, which preserved its 'achievements' but rectified the 'deviations' of the sixties, and an 'opening' (*Infitah*) would be effected to the new international diplomatic and economic environment. Gradually, as actual policy departed from traditional postures and Sadat ever more consciously viewed himself as shaping a distinctive new order, he needed new doctrinal formulations to distinguish it from Nasirism and fill the vacuum left by the latter's disappearance as the official credo. In 1978 a new doctrine, 'democratic socialism,' purportedly a new middle way between the excesses of liberal-capitalism and totalitarianism, was unveiled, which was supposed to embody the principles of the new emergent order (Abu Talib 1978). In 1980 Sadat issued a White Paper which defined Egypt's new Arab role in the post-peace-treaty era. Because official ideology was more an instrument of legitimation than a guide to action, however, a study is also needed of the implicit operative ideology of the elite, as distilled from its accumulated words and actions,[5] to understand the world-view which shaped policy and political action in Sadat's Egypt. The following analysis attempts to synthesize both explicit and implicit ideology. It views the transformation of elite ideology as taking place along four dimensions, namely, the conception of community, the preferred socio-economic model, Egypt's national identity and place in the world, and the conception of authority.

Community: from revolutionary to re-traditionalized society

Nasirist ideology viewed Egypt as a revolutionary community of equal citizens engaged in a struggle to transform itself and its place in the world. By the Sadat era, the symbolism of revolution, hitherto so pervasive had virtually disappeared. To be sure, the 1952 revolution itself was never disowned; but its radicalization in the sixties when leftist views were absorbed into regime ideology, was now repudiated. Marxism was vigorously attacked in official discourse as an alien idea employed by 'haters' who tried to create envy in the poor and stir up class strife; the failed socialism of the sixties, Sadat asserted, had been a 'nasty' experience, little more than concentration camps, secret police, and the confiscation of property. As an alternative to and bulwark against these alien ideas, Sadat advocated a traditional organic conception of community based on family and religion and supposedly more compatible with indigenous values. The patriarchal family and the village community were held up as the ideal models for Egypt which Sadat liked to describe as one big family or village. They were supposedly characterized by deference to the authority of elders, 'shame' as a deterrent to improper conduct, harmony between rich and the poor, freedom from class envy, extremism or hate, and the 'traditional Egyptian virtues' of endurance, will, tolerance and solidarity; all this contrasted with the negativism, hatred and discontent of 'those trying to stir up class strife.' In contrast to the relative secularism of the Nasir period, Islam also played a growing role in this conception of community: faith was now seen as Egypt's main source of energy. Thus, the October War achievements were attributed to the religious zeal of the soldiers. Islamic law was designated the basic source of legislation and its scope increased at the expense of secular law. Islam ('free of fanaticism,' that is militant fundamentalism) was a bulwark against alien ideas, shielding youth against Marxist atheism and the individualistic materialism which undermined the traditional heritage of love and loyalty. This change in the symbolism of community was in part an effort to anesthetize social conflict and held little appeal for more modernized segments of the elite. But for some at the top, like conservative landlords and religious figures coopted into the regime, and above all Sadat himself, a product of village culture, it represented an authentic return to supposedly indigenous traditional values.

Socio-economic model: From populist–etatism toward capitalism

Under Nasir, the dominant ideology put heavy stress on the role of the state in society. State entrepreneurship and the public sector were the leading forces of economic development. The state was responsible for ensuring the basic needs of the people, achieving a more equitable distribution of wealth than the market could, and maximizing national self-sufficiency. State goals and public duties, in turn, took precedence over private interests and individual rights.

The *October Paper* took the first step away from this view. Egypt's economy, impoverished by war, could only advance, it claimed, through an *Infitah* permitting an influx of new Arab and foreign private capital and technology. The private sector had also to be revived and given a widened role in development. The public sector, streamlined, and pushed back from areas better left to private initiative, would persist as a tool of economic management and to undertake big projects, such as infrastructure, needed to make private and foreign investment attractive. But now it was seen not as the cutting edge of development, but as a mere support for private capitalism. In the succeeding years, elite reaction against etatism accelerated. The state, it was held, had taken on far more responsibilities than it could competently discharge. People expected it to do everything for them, to the detriment of individual initiative. Individual rights had been sacrificed to the state. Populist redistribution was also held to be increasingly inappropriate now that the great inequalities of feudalism and colonialism had been eradicated. Indeed, while few advocated reversal of important measures like the land reform, many in the elite believed redistribution under Nasir had gone too far at the expense of growth and private enterprise; Sadat himself declared that socialism, believing justice required impoverishing the rich, had merely increased the number of poor. Populist intervention in the market, such as subsidization of mass consumption, employment maximization, and limits on prices and incomes, distorted market efficiency and sacrificed growth. Now, the dominant elite view held, priority had to go to economic growth, the key to which was capitalism. Great faith was placed in the ability of foreign capital and Western technology to spark an economic takeoff and in the ability of *Infitah* to bring these things to Egypt. The age of 'absolute dependence on the state' Sadat declared, had given way to that of individual initiative in which Egyptians should imitate the pioneering spirit of American capitalism. The pursuit of individual self-interest, castigated under Nasir, was now legitimized, and 'socialism' replaced as the ideological watchword by 'freedom.' The success of this new course depended on the 'liberation' of private initiative from stultifying state controls, and the emergence of a market in which the keys to development – capital, advanced technology and skilled personnel – could be obtained and kept at internationally accepted standards of reward. Thus, if the problem was lack of investment, the solution was to increase tax incentives for investors; if it was the brain drain, the indifferent motivation or even corruption of officials, the solution was to abolish the limits on salaries imposed under Nasir. As one writer put it, the old idea that justice requires 'leveling' must change and the mediocre accept that those who distinguish themselves should be rewarded. Individuals with capital, Sadat affirmed, could now 'earn freely without limits.' On the other hand, Egypt's chief attraction to foreign capital, the cheapness of its labor, had to be maintained if *Infitah* was to work. Progressive taxation, not nationalizations or sequestrations, was now the only legitimate tool of social redistribution. But once Egypt successfully passed through the 'bottleneck' of transition to capitalism, everyone would benefit from the trickle down of the new prosperity.

Yet neither etatism nor populism wholly disappeared from the establishment under Sadat. A large minority of the elite, socialized into the bureaucratic culture of a hydraulic society, was unconvinced that the economy could do without state regulation or that *laissez-faire* was the cure of all evils. Nor, whether for fear of the political consequences or from the persistence of older concepts of justice, were the inegalitarian implications of the new way wholly embraced. Sadat himself, toward the end of the seventies, in his calls for state controls on profiteering, and his acknowledgment that more attention had to be given to those who hadn't benefited from *Infitah*, displayed an ambivalence typical of the elite. 'Our society,' he declared, 'is not spiteful toward profit that is the fruit of honest work and it encourages initiative, but none should escape taxes and they must be progressive; otherwise social peace will be destroyed and we will ... return to the one-per-cent society' (Sadat speech 18 Sept. 1977). Sadat's ideal economic order seemed to be a society of petty capitalists: 'I want every Egyptian to own a part of Egypt, be it a lorry, a taxi, a piece of land or a house'; nor should the worker in his Egypt be subject to arbitrary dismissal by his wealthy employer (Sadat speeches 16 July 1977, 24 May 1978). The official 'democratic socialist' ideology also captured some of the ambivalence of the elite. It legitimized private property and free enterprise, but also affirmed the need for state regulation of the economy, progressive taxation, and welfare services to ensure social justice. Such a 'balanced society,' avoiding the anarchic individualism of unregulated capitalism and the class hatred and repression typical of Marxist socialism, was said to reconcile individual and society (Abu Talib, 1978). Despite these cracks in the elite's commitment to market capitalism, however, the Nasirite belief in the use of state power in the service of development and equality had decisively dissipated.

National identity: from Arab–Islamic nationalism to cosmopolitanism

Under Nasir, the dominant ideology combined an Arab–Islamic identity for Egypt with nationalist anti-imperialism, Pan-Arabism and non-alignment. The 1967 defeat, shattering the self-confidence Egypt had hitherto built up, and Egypt's post-1973 need for Western diplomatic and economic help to extricate her from the crisis, decisively undermined this orientation. These developments shifted influence toward the more Westernized wing of the elite and fanned the pre-1952 cosmopolitanism of Egypt's ruling class which though repressed under Nasir had never been extinguished.

The first major alterations in Nasirist ideology appeared in the aftermath of the 1973 war. Egypt unambiguously committed herself to peace with Israel, and though Sadat insisted that this must be a comprehensive peace which returned Israel to her 1967 borders and realized Palestinian rights, he was now prepared to accept partial and separate steps under American auspices toward the ultimate goal. Egypt's Arab role, according to the *October Paper*, would be undiminished, but Nasir's activist Pan-Arabist challenge to 'reactionary' Arab regimes would be replaced by a policy of cooperation with all Arab states. Egypt would remain non-aligned, but would no longer challenge Western influence in the Middle East. Before long, however, Egypt's inexorable march toward a separate peace with Israel and Western alignment and away from her Arab commitments rendered this early orientation obsolete. By the late seventies a radical cosmopolitanism and an unprecedented anti-Arabism dominated elite circles. Egypt's close foreign policy alliance with the US was one expression of the new mood. In its most extreme aspects – the open bid to play the role of local American surrogate in place of the Shah, the offer of 'facilities' to American forces operating against an Islamic regime – it spelled the end not just of Egypt's anti-imperialist role in the Middle East but of her traditional non-alignment as well. The alacrity with which segments of the elite adopted the Western view of the Arab–Israeli conflict in place of the Arab one – namely, that it was a mere psychological problem rather than a struggle against a residue of Western imperialism – was another symptom of change. So was the pride taken by many in the elite at Western approval of Egypt's peace initiatives which were proving, as Sadat himself declared, that – in contrast to the other Arabs – Egyptians were civilized. Most striking was the view of Tawfiq al-Hakim, Egypt's foremost playwright, that Egypt and Israel were linked as islands of civilization in a sea of barbarism. Democracy was adopted in part so that, as Sadat put it, Egyptians could raise their heads with Britain and the US, and distinguish themselves from the instability and repression characteristic of the rest of the Arab world. The pre-Nasirite Pharaonic conception of an Egyptian identity separate from the Arabs was resurrected. By the end of the decade, a virulent anti-Arabism radiated from many elite circles. The Arabs became the scapegoats for all of Egypt's ills: she had spent her blood and ruined her economy fighting for them, but they had never shown any gratitude; even the inflation from which Egypt suffered was the work of the oil shaikhs. The signing of the separate peace with Israel was, of course, the most decisive and concrete manifestation of the low priority given by the elite to Egypt's role in the Arab world.

Despite the ascendency of cosmopolitan tendencies, there remained a strong current in the elite which did not believe Egypt could or should extricate herself from an Arab role or identity. It was partly to reconcile the realities of his foreign policy with these sentiments that Sadat issued the 1980 White Paper redefining Egypt's role in the Arab world. In it, Egypt's central role in the Arab world was reaffirmed. Pharaonic conceptions of her identity could, it was acknowledged, be no substitute for Arabism. In spite of the ingratitude shown by the Arab rulers for the heavy burden carried by Egypt in the struggle against colonialism and Zionism, and their attempts to ostracize her, Egypt remained the heart of the Arab world. The major innovative theme in the document was the claim that Egypt's new role was to lead the Arab world to peace. The treaty with Israel was neither a separate peace nor an obstacle to a comprehensive one but a first step toward an overall just peace for which Egypt continued to work (Sadat 1980). The break with the Arab states was viewed as transitory since the other Arab leaders had no practical alternative to the course set by Egypt and because, while Egypt could do without them, the Arab world could not do without its heart.

Authority: from charismatic dictatorship to limited liberalization

Under Nasir, both liberal democracy and single party totalitarianism were rejected as proper bases of authority in favor of a kind of Bonapartism, that is, charismatic authoritarian rule of a leader speaking for and based on the support of the masses. Under Sadat a strong strain of authoritarianism persisted, most notably in the acceptance of a dominant Presidency and the patrimonial conceptions of rule advocated by the President. Yet, the elite also insisted that Egypt was moving under Sadat from revolutionary to constitutional legitimacy, toward democracy and a state of laws and institutions rather than men. Thus, it remained highly ambivalent in its conception of authority.

Constitutionalism and democracy were seen in two major changes from the

Nasir period. First, the rule of law had replaced arbitrary personal rule and Egyptians now enjoyed security of person and property; there were, Sadat claimed, 'no concentration camps, no confiscation of property, no arrests without legal grounds' in his Egypt. Secondly, the single official party and the political uniformity implicit in the notion of the 'Alliance of Popular Working Forces' was replaced with a multi-party system. There can be no democracy, Sadat argued, without ample opportunity for the voicing of different opinions and without a 'constructive and free opposition.'

Yet democratization was also considered to hold dangers which must be carefully guarded against. Because the masses were used to dictatorship, if too much freedom was permitted too quickly, it would result in chaos and revolt; Sadat was fond of citing the Portuguese case where a too rapid transition from one-man-rule to democracy had led to such results. Even an advocate of political liberalization such as Sayyid Marei cautioned that full-blown liberalism was, for Third World countries like Egypt, characterized by many cleavages and big gaps between rich and poor, inappropriate; if political parties were allowed to form freely along class, sectarian or ideological lines, the country would be torn apart. Some in the elite expressed confidence that the masses, religious, adverse to extremism and 'infinitely patient,' were not susceptible to anti-system appeals, but there was an equally strong and definite fear of the masses in the elite outlook. Some believed the masses lacked the sense of responsibility which had to accompany political rights (thus one ruling party official and public sector manager told the writer that if given the right to strike, Egyptian workers would strike every day). As such, any disrespect for authority, even verbal, had to be punished lest it set an example others would quickly follow. One official expressed the fear that the tiny opposition in parliament was merely the 'tip of the iceberg.' The fear that youth were susceptible to 'alien ideas' or 'fanatical religious trends which misunderstand Islam' ran through elite discourse. Some inside the elite, a group Sadat referred to as 'those who favor emergency measures' appear, in fact, to have had very grave doubts as to the wisdom of the whole liberalization experiment.

For these reasons, it was generally accepted that definite limits on liberalization were needed, that the exercise of political freedoms had to be disciplined by a 'code of ethics' ensuring that it did not threaten national unity or social peace. Only certain defined methods and channels of participation were permissible. Opposition could be expressed only through the established parties or through petition of parliament or the President; use of arenas such as the mosque or the campuses – where there was 'no room for politics' – much less the streets, was considered illegitimate. Above all, overt attempts to mobilize mass support against government policy was impermissible. A conflictual political style was also unacceptable; criticism was permissible if 'constructive'; 'attacks,' the 'inciting of one group of people against another,' 'throwing doubt on everything' was not. Neither was the false notion that the role of the opposition was to 'obstruct the government's policy, irrespective of its worth to the people.' Those political forces which refused to accept the regime's basic policies – that is, *Infitah*, peace with Israel – thereby lost their political rights. The opposition and government parties had a right, Sadat declared, to differ on ways of achieving the people's goals, but it was clear he would determine what those goals were. Anyone who attacked them was viewed as attacking Egypt, as almost guilty of treason: 'Egypt is above everyone, every interest, every leader.' As a result, a wide spectrum of opponents were progressively excluded from participation: 'The centers of power,' 'those who exploit religion,' 'those brought up on the teaching of the Soviet Union,' 'those who corrupted political life before 1952,' 'communists wearing Islamic dress,' 'those who wear the shirt of Abdul Nasir.' What they wanted, claimed Sadat, was political power above all else and this they could not have. The right to set basic policy would remain the prerogative of the President. When this was challenged, or participants transgressed on the rules of the political game, the President would intervene, as 'supreme arbiter' in the name of the higher national interest and the popular will, to set things aright.

It is clear that the elite wanted enough political liberalization to protect itself from the arbitrary power of the ruler and allow it greater freedom of political expression, and that Sadat sought to accommodate it; but both feared that excessive liberalization might result in the erosion of authority or the mobilization by counter-elites of a mass challenge to the policies they favored. Hence they wanted a strictly limited liberalization confined to elite levels which would not result in the pluralization of the mass political arena.

Ideological variation and a new conservative consensus

The Egyptian political elite under Sadat was not a political monolith. The changes charted here emerged only as a result of an extended period of intra-elite conflict. Even at the end of the seventies, differences persisted inside the elite. Ideological change was neither uniform nor complete and residues of earlier views persisted. Etatism, not surprisingly, remained much stronger and liberalization, and to a lesser degree cosmopolitanism, weaker inside the bureaucratic establishment than among elites recruited from the private sector. There were also contradictions between various ideological tendencies: traditionalism potentially clashed with liberalization and cosmopolitanism; in a sense, the elite seemed to display two contrary faces: 'modern' liberal and cosmopolitan in their relation to the outside world, more 'traditional' and 'authoritarian' toward the masses, symbolized, in Shukri's words, by 'the nightclub and the mosque' (1978: 324). There was ambivalence and conflict within the elite over the degree of political liberalization, the proper scope of the market and Egypt's relations to the Western and Arab worlds. At the risk of oversimplification, it appears possible to identify four general ideological tendencies inside the elite defined by differing conceptions of authority, that is, regime type preference, and differing 'populist' or 'conservative' policy orientations.

		Regime type preference	
		Authoritarian	Liberal
Policy orientation	Conservative	Authoritarian–conservative	Liberal–conservative
	Populist	Authoritarian–populist	Liberal–populist

The strongest tendency was probably authoritarian–conservatism, a position represented by big landowners such as Muhammed Hamid Mahmud and police bureaucrats like Nabawi Ismail. It leaned toward the retention of authoritarianism and a traditional model of social relations internally, mixed with an advocacy of capitalism and a pro-Western cosmopolitanism in global relations. Liberal–conservatism, perhaps best represented by Sayyid Marei was probably the next strongest orientation. It was identical to the first, except that it advocated the liberalization (at the elite level) of the political system. Liberal–populism was a far weaker trend, perhaps best represented by the leader of the official opposition, Ibrahim Shukri. It advocated a thorough liberalization of the political system. It was more Arab–Islamic nativist than the dominant elite tendencies, and advocated a more statist and populist socio-economic model. Authoritarian–populism, that is, mainstream Nasirism, was clearly a recessive tendency; well represented by men like Aziz Sidqi at the beginning of the Sadat period, it had no prominent overt spokesman at the end. But Nasirite sentiment seemed to linger among technocrats in the heavy industrial sector. It, of course, combined authoritarianism with an etatist–populist socio-economic orientation and Arab–Islamic nativism. Sadat, of course, held the balance between these tendencies, wavering chiefly between authoritarian and liberal conservatism, but ultimately most comfortable with the former.

These variations should not be taken to signify sharp divisions within the elite. Most members of the elite did not fall clearly into one category or the other. Most, pragmatic and flexible rather than ideological, were close to the center. Most deferred to the President on issues and those who did take strong stands on principles in conflict with the dominant orientation were gradually expelled from elite ranks. And, intra-elite opinion differences were contained by a growing sense of a shared stake in the regime and, as differences in elite origins and interests were muted, of common class interest. By the second half of the Sadat decade, indeed, the political elite displayed a remarkable cohesion expressed in a growing, ever more conservative ideological consensus.

Chapter 5

Politics among elites

Politics is the business of elites even more in an authoritarian–bureaucratic state like Egypt than elsewhere. This chapter will analyze the intra-elite political process by examining the evidence as to the 'rules' by which the game is played, the stakes, and the resources which shape outcomes.

The decision-making process

In the highly centralized Egyptian state, the executive branch dominated decision-making. It was the focus of all policy proposals whether they originated in the bureaucracy, with influential personalities, or with interest groups, and it was the arena in which all major political decisions were made, relatively free of pressures or constraints from the rest of the political system. This decision-making arena was structured by the relation between its two major components, the Presidency and the cabinet, led by the Prime Minister. The Presidency embraced, in addition to the President, his secretariat (headed by a minister at the Presidency) and an entourage of personal confidants and 'presidential advisors.' The cabinet functioned as the President's specialized staff, responsible for advising him on policy and implementing his decisions. Sadat did not encourage its development as a collegial decision-making body, tending, instead, to make key decisions in *ad hoc* consultations with the ministers and advisors concerned with a given issue area. Nor did he provide strong leadership in the cabinet; unlike Nasir, he did not regularly preside over it (even when Prime Minister, he usually left this to a deputy), and was content to leave the day-to-day business of government to his ministers, intervening only when something went wrong or to give general instructions. This sometimes left a leadership gap since the Prime Minister often lacked the power to lead the cabinet: many senior ministers, Presidential rather than Prime Ministerial appointments, were often his political equals.

Policy-making was typically mediated by a process of intra-elite bargaining and rivalry inside the executive between factions varying in their goals and political ties. Small personalistic factions bound by family or friendship ties (called *shillas*) and patronage networks competed to advance and defend their control of office and influence, frequently in pursuit of mutual personal and often venal benefits (Springborg 1975). Sadat's own entourage was the most outstanding example of such a clique in the seventies; bound by both friendship and kinship ties, this group of clients helped buttress Sadat's power, while using their influence with him to aggrandize themselves and their own clients, through the accumulation of offices and wealth. Sometimes factions were broader, institutionally based in branches of the bureaucratic state, competing over programs, jurisdictions and budgets (Dekmejian and Dahry 1976). Many of the proposals which were the grist of the policy mill were developed in individual ministries by the minister and his senior civil servants and the budget process in which resources were allocated was largely a process of aggregating and reconciling the rival requests of these ministries. Finally, particularly at watersheds in the making of high policy, 'opinion groups' crystallized, committed to opposing policy preferences; these preferences usually had implications for the fortunes of broad social forces, but only in the most informal way could these factions be said to 'represent' such forces in the policy process. In many cases, personal, bureaucratic and ideological interests were inextricably intertwined in the composition and orientation of factions.

In the most important of all factional conflicts after Nasir, that between Sabri and Sadat, all three factional dimensions were operative: differing policy orientations (radical vs moderate), rival bureaucratic bases (Presidency, professional military vs ASU, security police) and conflicting personal alliances. The post-succession Fawzi cabinet was paralyzed by conflict between Aziz Sidqi and Sayyid Marei reflecting not only the intense personal rivalry of the two most prominent civilian politicians to survive the Nasir era, but also the rather different constituencies and hence ideologies they informally spoke for, that is, statist industrialization vs agrarian capitalism (Marei 1978a: 632–7). In the mid-seventies, there were intrigues between members of Sadat's 'family circle' and Prime Minister Mamduh Salim, largely revolving around the former's jealousy of Salim's power and position. There was also a certain split within the Salim cabinet between a *shilla* made up of Abd al-Munim Qaysuni and his protégés, Hamid Sayyih and Salah Hamid and other figures in the cabinet including the Prime Minister; this conflict however was not over venal benefits, but policy preferences, namely, the clash between economic rationality and political caution. Divisions in the Khalil cabinet between supporters of the Prime Minister and those who sided with Vice President Mubarak were chiefly over personal power and patronage. (Ya'ari 1980: 120). An example of a salient institutional rivalry which surfaced in the late seventies was that between the Ministry of Industry, speaking for public sector interests, and the Investment Authority of the Ministry of Economy where careers and ideologies were bound up with private foreign investment. Noticeably absent under Sadat was the most pervasive rivalry of the Nasir period, that between military politicians and civilian technocrats, unless the Mubarak–Khalil rivalry can be considered a pale shadow of it.

The personalistic–bureaucratic character of the Sadat regime defined the resources which carried the greatest weight in intra-elite conflicts, namely 'strategic personal connections' (Springborg 1975: 88), and authority of office. In the succession crisis, both were operative, notably the authority of Presidential office and the competitive use of personal connections to mobilize intra-elite support. Once Presidential authority was consolidated, the bureaucratic chain of command running downward limited and defined the ways in which personal connections counted: those to the President became the most important single resource in the political game, but all others counted for much less. Thus those, especially in his entourage, who enjoyed the confidence of the President, were not only in an unmatched position to influence his decisions, but also to act as power brokers; these men were powerful irrespective of office. For other elite actors, however, high office was a crucial resource. Official incumbents had some decision-making power in their own domains, and individual ministers had considerable decree power within the bounds of very loosely drafted parliamentary legislation. High officials enjoyed some discretion over funds and appointments, had privileged access to the President and benefited from the habitual compliance of those below them in the bureaucracy. They acquired all this with office, and lost it when they lost office. Another resource, possessed by most office holders, technocrats or professionals, was functional expertise or experience on the basis of which they could argue the merits of the policies they supported. Revolutionary credentials, that is, Free Officer status, often weighty enough under Nasir to override authority of office or functional expertise in the political process, was radically devalued under Sadat; nonetheless, it retained a residual prestige in elite circles which sometimes counted for something. Distinctive of the authoritarian–bureaucratic state was the very modest extent to which demands and supports from constituencies, institutional or territorial, played an overt role in political conflicts. On only two occasions after the 1954 consolidation of the regime was an overt attempt made to mobilize clients and support from below in a challenge to the Presidential-dominated political process, namely by Amer's faction after his 1967 dismissal and during the succession crisis, and in both cases it failed; the low legitimacy of such actions and the precarious solidarity of constituencies simply made it too risky to be attempted except by the most powerful factions and over very high stakes. More covert efforts to exercise influence by speaking in the name of constituencies enjoyed greater tolerance under Sadat than before as long as they did not challenge Presidential authority; thus ministers sometimes articulated the interests of their bureaucratic domains, interest group leaders and parliamentary deputies the interests of their constituents, provincial governors those of their provinces, the press the ideas of amorphous opinion groups, and, at least on lesser matters, they were sometimes heeded. But there was no institutionalized mechanism such as an effective party system for aggregating from below or mobilizing from above such demands and supports into the elite policy process. And compared to authority of office and strategic personal connections, constituency support remained a secondary currency in the game of power.

Finally, except for the brief succession crisis the policy process ran in fairly well-defined institutionalized channels. It might be set in motion by the proposals of individual ministries often generated by high civil servants or interests associated with a particular policy domain. If such proposals generated intra-elite conflict which could not be settled in the cabinet, Sadat typically intervened on one side or another; if the issue was serious enough, this could result in the dismissal of the losing side and the formation of a new cabinet better able to work together toward the direction thus defined by Presidential intervention. Policy innovation might also be launched by Presidential initiative, perhaps under the influence of close personal advisors or the pressure of a major problem or crisis and after consultation with ministerial experts. Details and implementation of the initiative were typically left to the responsible ministers and could themselves become issues of intra-elite conflict inviting a new Presidential intervention. The following sections will examine intra-elite politics in specific policy domains and among particular segments of the elite.

The military elite and defense policy

The military elite remained a critical force in the Egyptian political system under Sadat. Without its support, his rule would have been vulnerable to challenge; in the absence of a mechanism for regular replacement of the ruler, it was the only force with the potential to impose such a change at the top. Yet, without losing control of the military establishment, Sadat presided over a successful transformation of its role in the state. It was turned from a dominant political actor into a professional force subordinate to legal authority, its role in policy-making, even in defense matters, radically curtailed. This was paralleled by a de-radicalization which ended the role the army had assumed since 1952 as 'defender of the revolution' and of the Arab nation against imperialism and Zionism. An analysis of this transformation provides a useful vantage point for an understanding of 'military politics' in Sadat's Egypt.

Long-term developments which were maturing even before Sadat took power established favorable conditions for these changes. From the sixties, de-radicalization steadily advanced as the army leadership underwent an embourgeoisement which turned it from a populist 'tribune of the people' into an advocate of established interests. Many officers, including top Free Officers, opposed the nationalization measures and the second land reform, which in some cases touched the interests of their own families; they also stood against the opening of political office to leftists. The 1967 war accelerated the trend; many officers blamed the defeat on Nasir's anti-imperialist Arab nationalist activism, on lack of Soviet support, or even on the socialist measures. Believing themselves to have been made scapegoats for the failures of the political leadership, many were permanently disaffected by Nasirism (Baker 1978: 92–3; Mortegy 1975: 23; Shazli 1980: 84).[1] The 1967 defeat also marked the beginning of de-politicization. Not only was the military's claim to political leadership discredited, but many both inside and outside the army blamed the defeat on its involvement in politics. Nasir's removal of Marshal Amer's clique from control of the army, and the full backing he gave to the non-political professionals put in Amer's place to rebuild it on strictly professional lines, was a watershed in this development (Haykel 1975: 47–51). Moreover, the great expansion in the size of the army after 1967 made it difficult for the officer corps to act as a cohesive political force and, in particular, to plan and execute overt intervention in the political sphere. The defense of the front line, and the absorption of increasingly sophisticated weaponry preoccupied it and increased the weight of 'military technicians' who prided themselves on professional competence and were impatient of anything which could distract the military from its professional mission. The vastly better performance of the officer corps in the 1973 war reinforced the prestige and ethic of political neutrality represented by these professionals.

While the tide of military intervention in politics was thus receding when Sadat came to power, military-politicians remained at the center of power, often prepared to challenge his policies. His ability to stay on top and complete the de-politicization of the military elite depended in no small part on his skills as a political tactician, able to manipulate rewards and punishments, and on his success in establishing legitimacy in military eyes. The most critical watershed in this struggle was, of course, Sadat's defeat of the leftist Free Officer faction at the outset of his Presidency. The decisive factor in Sadat's victory was his ability to win the support or neutrality of the professional military in spite of the alignment of War Minister Muhammed Fawzi with the Sabri camp. The superior legitimacy of the Presidency helped determine the military's choice; preoccupied with the Israeli challenge at the front, it was impatient of any threat to internal stability and was as such biased toward legal authority. But its choice was also political since Sadat was perceived as sympathetic to its class and professional interests and Sabri as a threat to them. Sabri was identified with the leftwing course it disliked, the increasingly unpopular Soviet connection and ASU attacks on military privileges and autonomy. Sadat, in his effort to win over the military, seems to have promised to rid it of ASU harassment, to sympathetically consider its anti-Soviet grievances, to put an end to social experimentation, to reinstate officers unfairly dismissed after 1967 and to refurbish the tarnished image of the army. As against this, General Fawzi's claim that Sadat was preparing to sell out to the Americans carried little weight, a sign of how impervious the army elite had become to radical ideological appeals; moreover, Fawzi's chances of carrying the army with him had been compromised by resentment of the strict discipline and overbearing manner of the Soviet advisory mission with which he was identified as the officer most responsible for the post-1967 reconstruction of the army. Instead, the bulk of the military preferred to follow Chief of Staff Sadiq, an officer known for his anti-Soviet views, and Sadiq was more than pleased to combine with Sadat to replace Fawzi as Minister of War. Once Sadat won, he did move to fulfill his promises to the military elite. But while their support was critical to Sadat's consolidation of power, the military needed him as much as he them, and he did not thereby become their creature (Haykel 1975: 122–38; Sadat Speeches 14 May 1971, 22 June 1971).

Sadat's military base remained, however, precarious in these years of stalemate along the Suez Canal and continuing Israeli occupation. On the one hand, Sadat had to contend with militant officers' dissatisfaction with Egypt's inaction in the face of the Israelis. While sometimes identified with the popular General Saad ad-Din Shazli, this trend was strongest in the middle and lower ranks of the officer corps; the Hussein mosque incident and the participation of young officers in the 1972 street demonstrations were signs of the danger. On the other hand, Sadat had to cope with a 'rightwing' tendency led by (the now) War Minister Sadiq, Air Force commander Baghdadi and several other senior officers. It was fueled by resentments at the Soviet failure to provide the offensive arms the army wanted and by the behavior of Soviet advisors. The Soviets did not hide their contempt of what they considered the incompetence of many Egyptian officers and a lack of seriousness in Egypt's war preparations. They tended to act as owners of the house in the military facilities they controlled; it was apparently the refusal of the Soviet commander to admit the Egyptian Chief of Staff to a Soviet base which triggered an overt anti-Soviet movement within the officer corps. Led by Sadiq, top officers asserted that the Soviets represented a greater threat to Egypt than the Israelis and lent their support to demands by political forces outside the army that Sadat remove the Soviet presence.

Sadat moved first to head off the most immediate threat, that from the right in the person of Sadiq and his followers. Sadiq's role in the defeat of Sabri and his Free Officer status had led him to consider himself as entitled to a real share of power rather than being content, as Sadat expected, with the role of obedient professional. Through anti-Sovietism and the control of rewards and promotions he was building a personal base in the officer corps. His anti-Soviet advocacy was seen by Sadat as an encroachment on the high policy Sadat considered a Presidential prerogative. Sadiq had links with Libya's Qaddafi which Sadat considered dangerous and incompatible with his own policies. Sadiq also objected to Sadat's strategy of trying to seize a strip of land across the Canal as a prelude to political negotiations; yet, believing Egypt unprepared for a more ambitious venture, he opposed any military action, and together with several other senior officers argued in a tense meeting with Sadat against initiation of a limited war; Sadat was afterwards to accuse him of insubordination in failing to carry out the military preparations he had ordered. Once Sadat expelled the Soviet advisors, he calculated that by removing the virulently anti-communist Sadiq he could both placate the Soviets whose arms Egypt still needed and rid himself of a troublesome threat.

Sadat's move against Sadiq was a classic example of his strategy of control over the military. He waited until he had first expelled the Soviet advisors, thus winning for himself the acclaim of anti-Soviet elements and taking the wind out of Sadiq's sails. He appraised the commanders of the field armies of Sadiq's 'dereliction of duty' in preparing for war. He secured the support of Chief of Staff Shazli who had quarreled with Sadiq over the division of authority in the high command and was impatient to break the military stalemate. Then in a sudden strike Sadat dismissed Sadiq and put General Ahmad Ismail Ali in his place. Ismail was a professional soldier who lacked political ambition, but got on badly with Sadiq. He had long time links to Sadat, being from the same military graduating class, and was beholden to him for reinstatement after twice having been fired by Nasir. Thus, he could be trusted to give loyal support. Even so, Sadat, with the help of Shazli and Mamduh Salim, had to foil a pro-Sadiq coup attempt. The replacement of the overtly political Sadiq with Ismail represented another step in the de-politicization of the top military elite (Haykel 1975: 48–51, 165–81; Sadat 1978: 234–37; Shazli 1980: 27–31, 144–57, 172–91; Shukri 1978: 161–2).

The threat to Sadat from those impatient for action against Israel was to a great extent effaced by the October 1973 war which conferred popular legitimacy on his rule, and, by allowing the army to regain its lost prestige, won him a large fund of support in officer ranks. Nevertheless, as Sadat embarked on his post-war strategy of negotiation with Israel under American auspices, he again faced opposition in the military elite. It was undoubtedly the political capital won in the war which allowed him to override such opposition and carry his course through. The first and most important such conflict was between Sadat and Chief of Staff Saad Shazli. They first quarreled over the conduct of the war, each holding the other responsible for the Israeli breakthrough. After the war, Sadat viewed Shazli as a leading opponent of the decision to rely on Kissinger at the cost of weakening the military option and Arab solidarity. As before, Sadat prepared the ground for dismissing his opponent by soliciting the support of other top officers, some of whom resented Shazli's rapid ascent in the hierarchy. In the showdown, not only did he have the support of General

Ismail, who could not stand Shazli, but also of Air Force commander Husni Mubarak and of General Abd al-Ghani Gamasi, the Chief of Operations who helped plan the limited war and who, delegated to be the first to negotiate face to face with the Israelis (at Kilometer 101), accepted Sadat's strategy of negotiation. Shazli was reputed to be very popular in the ranks of the officer corps, and the wave of transfers and dismissals which followed his demise, not sparing even corps and division commanders, suggests Sadat was anxious to break up this potential support base; but Shazli proved, given the alignment of the top brass against him, in no position to translate this support into a political resource. His dismissal marked the fall of the last top officer prepared to challenge the President. Along with the removal of many other like-minded officers, it decimated the potential leadership of any military resistance to Sadat's post-war policies; subsequently dissidents either forebore to express themselves openly or, when caught in doing so, were easily forced out of active service. Sadat duly consolidated the hold of loyalists at the top by promoting Mubarak to the position of Vice President, thereby bringing a major military leader into overt identification with the policies of the regime; General Gamasi took over Shazli's position, and on General Ismail's death, was promoted to Minister of Defense. Mubarak, whose Air Force had performed credibly in the war was an asset to Sadat in keeping the loyalty of the officer corps; Gamasi, the very model of the respected non-political professional prepared to defer to the authority of the President, became a key figure in further consolidating the principle of military non-intervention in political matters (Sadat 1978: 262–3; *al-Safir*, 22 Aug. 1973; Shazli 1980: 184–6).

The presence of loyalists committed to carrying the military establishment along whatever course Sadat set was undoubtedly crucial to Sadat's ability to maintain undisputed control over the military elite in the subsequent years. For the President's foreign policy forced radical changes in its traditional role and had a negative effect on its professional interests. The break in the supply of military equipment caused by the worsening of relations with the USSR, led to a very serious decline in the army's fighting capabilities; after Camp David, Sadat could promise his officers growing access to Western equipment, but this did not materialize on a significant scale till the eighties. As Egypt gradually withdrew from the conflict with Israel, the Egyptian army in effect relinquished its earlier claim to be the citadel of Arab military power. On the political level, the army was transformed from 'vanguard of the Arab revolution' into a conservative regional gendarmerie. Internally, it was called on to put down the popular disturbances of 1977; externally, it was engaged on the side of the right in Oman and Zaire, in action against radical Libya, and on polite terms with the historic enemy with whom it had fought four wars in 30 years. For the first time since the expulsion of the British, it was conducting joint maneuvers on Egyptian soil with a foreign army, the forces of the main backer of its historic enemy. There is no doubt that these changes generated unease inside the army. No army gladly accepts a deterioration of its fighting capability. For the many in the middle ranks of the officer corps recruited and socialized under Nasir's Arab nationalism, the jarring reversal of the army's role could not have been welcomed with enthusiasm. To some of the junior officers who risked their lives in the 'Crossing,' Sadat seemed to have sold out the gains won on the battlefield. Tracts distributed by a 'New Free Officers' Organization,' the penetration of the middle and lower ranks of the officer corps by Islamic fundamentalism, and arrests and dismissals well after 1974 were indicators of a significant measure of disaffection (*al-Mustaqbal*, 16 Dec. 1978).

In the wake of Camp David, there was another wave of turnover at the very top in which Defense Minister Gamasi and Chief of Staff Muhammed Ali Fahmi were replaced. Gamasi's fall resulted from his opposition to Camp David and growing personal rivalry with Vice President Mubarak; Fahmi was reportedly identified with those dissatisfied at the deterioration of the army's capabilities and elements displeased at being engaged against a fellow Arab army in the Libyan war. (Sadat may have had to scrap plans for a second action against Libya because of the opposition in the officers corps.) Gamasi and Fahmi did not overtly challenge the President and even after his dismissal Gamasi publicly reaffirmed the principle of military deference to Presidential authority. But Sadat wanted men untainted by doubts about his policies in the critical high command. As before, he found no difficulty in finding new men to replace those dismissed: the three defense ministers who served Sadat after Gamasi, Kamal Hassan Ali, Ahmad Badawi, and Abd al-Halim Abu Ghazala were all unquestioning loyalists willing to follow him without demur (*al-Ahram* 4 Oct. 1977, Rubinstein 1979: 36, Ya'ari 1980: 116).

For the bulk of the officer corps, whatever its reservations about his course, there must have seemed no viable alternative to Sadat. A change in leadership would have put in doubt the peaceful recovery of the Sinai and advanced the possibility of a war with an enemy it had no immediate prospect of defeating and which could wipe out the redemption won in 1973. Sadat was careful to promote the privileges of the officer corps as well as the interests of the favored social strata from which much of its top leadership was drawn; some officers went into business under *Infitah*, acquiring a stake in the new order (Shukri 1978: 450). The military could not have expected to do much better under another leader. And, even those who wanted rid of Sadat, could not have been unaware of the high risks and low prospects of opposition: no officer since 1970 had challenged Sadat and survived. By the end of the decade, the main concerns of the military elite seemed to be exclusively professional, namely, the re-equipping of the armed forces with sophisticated and expensive American arms needed to make it a credible fighting force again. The $1.5 billion military aid program scheduled by the Americans was no doubt designed to satisfy and preoccupy the military with its professional reconstruction.

Sadat thus presided over a thorough transformation in the role of the army in the political system. At the beginning of his rule, the military constituted a privileged ruling group dominating top elite posts. By the end, it had been reduced to a much smaller, weaker component of the elite. Its claims for a decisive role or veto even in its field of special responsibility had been repeatedly defeated. Indeed, every major foreign or defense policy decision under Sadat was a purely Presidential initiative, often taken without consultation or even against the wishes of top generals: this was true of the choice of limited war in 1973, the acceptance of the first and second disengagements and of the Camp David accord. The military still had some input, informally or through the consultations of the National Security Council, into defense policy, but its role had been reduced to that of simply giving professional advice. Top generals sat in the cabinet and the politburo of the ruling party, but were outnumbered by civilians. By the eighties, the military was merely one of a number of institutional interest groups and, if its claim on the budget, which slightly declined as a proportion of total spending and GNP, was any indicator, one carrying little privileged weight.

The de-politicization and conservatization of the military resulted partly from external pressures and the political struggle: the reversals suffered by the army under Nasir, the premium put on professional competence by the post-1967 conflict with Israel, Sadat's mastery of the politics of divide and rule, the lack of political solidarity in an increasingly large army. But reinforcing this was a gradual transformation in the authority system from the Nasir to Sadat eras, that is, the decline of revolutionary authority which sanctioned an active political role for the officers who made the revolution and its relatively complete routinization in legal–bureaucratic authority, above all in the Presidency. The institutionalization of the political system over the 30 years since 1952 had gradually narrowed the scope for overt military politics. But at a deeper level yet, the change in the orientation of the military was an expression of the widespread tendency observed by Huntington (1968) in the armies of new states. The military, acting in the earliest stages of modernization as vanguard of the rising middle class challenging a traditional agrarian elite, appears a radical force for change; but as the middle class is integrated into the political system, it becomes a conservative pillar of the status quo. By the end of the Sadat era this had unmistakably happened in Egypt (Huntington 1968: 221).

Technocratic–administrative elites and economic policy

Technocrats and the Sadat regime

Under Nasir, the technocratic–administrative elite constituted a privileged and favored group, largely recruited from the urban upper and upper middle class. Although there was a submerged current of liberalism in its ranks, its dominant attitude was elitist and etatist: technocrats viewed policy-making as properly the business of experts who, insulated from popular demands or the pressure of private interests, were best able to define the public interest. Pragmatic and adaptable, they became in the sixties, 'socialists by Presidential decree.' However, although prepared to serve in and favored by the Nasir regime, this elite was not happy with Nasirism as it evolved in the sixties and almost unanimously welcomed the victory of Sadat over the leftwing Free Officers. Although, unlike the military, the technocrats represented no direct threat to Sadat's position, he wanted their support and sought it through the pursuit of policies responsive to their interests and grievances. Ali Sabri's ASU had attacked their high salaries and privileges, accusing them of forming a 'new class' above the masses; Sadat freed them of ASU harassment. Western-trained and convinced that access to the most advanced technology was the key to development, few liked the dependency on the USSR symbolized by Sabri; Sadat won them access to the 'superior' Western technology they wanted. Nasir had not been illiberal with his technocrats; their salaries of £E2000–5000 per year, plus perks, separated them by an enormous gap from the incomes of workers and lowly white-collar employees. Yet, by the Western standards by which they measured themselves, and even by those of Egypt's private sector, their incomes were modest and most believed they deserved more. Sadat raised their salaries and lowered their taxes on the grounds that the state had to compete with high salaries available elsewhere. Nasir's nationalization measures and development program opened up many opportunities for career advancement for technocrats and administrators. But the private interests or opportunities of their families were also sometimes damaged or narrowed and by the late sixties the growth of new opportunities at the top had stagnated. Under *Infitah*, opportunities again began to widen. For those with political clout and connections the influx of foreign aid and business opened up opportunities, licit or illicit, for tax-free commissions and 'consulting work.' For those who had acquired business experience and connections in the public sector, there were now opportunities to join higher-paying private firms or go into business for themselves. Under Nasir, import controls greatly narrowed the elite's access to the Western consumer goods and life style they believed their due; under Sadat this access was restored. Under Nasir the military domination of power was resented by civilian elites; but as Sadat pushed the military out of top elite roles, opportunities for civilians to acquire power grew. For all these reasons, Egypt's technocrats and senior administrators generally supported Sadat (Ayubi 1980: 184, 370–90, 418–20, 447–81; Baker 1978: 110; Farid 1970: 16, 31, 40).

The politics of economic strategy

It does not follow from this support for Sadat that there was no intra-elite conflict over power and policy. While Sadat's authority to set the major lines of policy was accepted, technocrats did try to influence his decisions; and even once high policy was set, there remained considerable scope for conflict over its interpretation, the best way of implementing it and, when objectives conflicted, over priorities. And as high policy shifted over the decade, power flowed away from some elements in the elite and toward others.

In the early seventies, four divergent trends could be identified inside the technocratic elite. One, an etatist view best represented by Aziz Sidqi, stood for a continuation of the Nasirite strategy and wanted no more than a circumscribed, controlled role for foreign and private capital compatible with the dominance of the public sector. To the left of the etatists was a handful of Marxists like Ismail Sabri Abdullah and Fuad Mursi who favored a 'deepening' of the socialist experiment, and who served as Ministers of Planning and of Supply. A center–right tendency advocated the creation of new foreign and private capital sectors in competition with the public sector. The public sector would be confined to heavy industry, allowing light and medium industry to private investors. A small faction on the extreme right, in alliance with private sector interests, espoused full blown *laissez-faire* capitalism; Mustafa Kamil Murad who later appeared as leader of the rightist Ahrar Party, was an outspoken advocate of this position (Aziz 1972).

At the beginning of the Sadat era, the etatists still had the upper hand; the external conditions for *Infitah* hardly existed before the October War, and Sidqi, an ally of Sadat in the fight with Ali Sabri and the senior spokesman for the civilian technocracy, presided over economic policy. He was head of the Cabinet Economic Committee, Minister of Industry, and finally Prime Minister. But etatism was soon on the defensive. Sidqi's populist and etatist policies – from the progressive taxation of the private sector to the SUMED pipeline – encountered overt resistance from the private bourgoisie ensconced in parliament and the ASU. The President's distrust of Sidqi's political ambitions, and his desire to appease the bourgeoisie, led to Sidqi's removal in May 1973. The changed conditions following the October War further weakened the hand of etatists and increased the influence of those in the elite – not least the President's very close confidants Marei and Osman – arguing for a radical change; buttressed by his new political strength, the President was now prepared to innovate. The *Infitah* was declared, Law 43 issued giving incentives to investors, and Abd al-Aziz Higazi, a long time Treasury Minister and liberal economist with links to the Western financial community, brought in to preside over the new policy. In 1975 Ahmad Abu Ismail, a liberal economist from a wealthy bourgeois family who as head of parliament's budget committee had spearheaded attacks on the public sector's efficiency, was made Minister of Finance. Ismail Sabri Abdullah, who had argued that foreign investment should be submitted to the state development plan, was dismissed as Minister of State for Planning. Thus, once Sadat was convinced by objective constraints and opportunities and intra-elite arguments of the need for a change, he reconstructed an appropriate team to preside over it (Waterbury 1976c: 327).

While *Infitah* had by 1974 officially displaced Nasir's 'Arab Socialism', intra-elite conflict over economic policy did not cease. Below the top-elite level there was resistance to the concept of *Infitah*. A few in parliament had opposed the terms of the new investment law; Ahmad Taha, a Marxist, and Mahmud Qadi, an independent, argued for restrictions on the sectors open to foreign capital on the grounds that unrestricted investment would lead to foreign domination of the economy and the erosion of worker rights. However, Higazi's government successfully pushed the law through devoid of such restrictions. Important elements entrenched in the bureaucracy also resisted it and Sadat had to call on Mamduh Salim to root out those who, intent on hoarding their prerogatives or in the name of 'socialist slogans,' were obstructing liberalization of controls (Dessouki 1982b: 75–8; Rubinstein 1977: 37). But apart from this resistance to the concept of *Infitah*, there were also conflicts over its meaning. One view which accepted the Western argument that state intervention in the economy retarded growth and efficiency, expected that the norms of capitalism, introduced through the foreign capital sector should eventually spread to and engulf the whole economy. Then, for example, public sector firms would operate according to the norms of capitalist profitability and the state would cease to administer and subsidize prices. Another view saw *Infitah* as merely an opening to outside investment and freer trade necessitating no radical transformation of the internal economy; it had less faith in the unfettered operations of the market, believed in the continuing need for some state intervention, and saw a full liberalization as dangerous to state interests and social peace.

The first major conflict over the meaning and consequences of *Infitah* took place in 1976 over pressures from the IMF and foreign banks to cut subsidies and float (in effect, devalue) the pound as necessary and take logical steps in the liberalization of the economy; both Arab and Western money underlined their demands for these changes by holding up Egyptian requests for loans and aid at a time when the country faced a liquidity crisis. Sadat's key economic advisors, including the Ministers of Economy, Finance, Planning, and Industry opposed these demands chiefly because of the politically dangerous rise in the cost of living they would impose on the public. Economy Minister Zaki Shafa'i preferred to raise taxes than cut subsidies and defiantly declared that a wholly free market would be introduced 'when we deem it suitable; we will not submit to any pressure.' He seemed, in fact, to be having second thoughts about *Infitah*: the liberalization of imports, he complained, rather than filling supply shortages and raising customs revenue, was only fueling middle-class indulgence at a time when austerity was needed. Finance Minister Ahmad Abu Ismail, despite impeccable liberal credentials, wanted a more gradual paring of subsidies combined with price controls. Other economists, chief among them Abd

134

al-Munim Qaysuni, argued for a cut in subsidies. Qaysuni held that the subsidies did not really help the poor: those to the consumer durables industry favored the middle class and even subsidized popular consumption goods were so widely diverted to the benefit of black marketeers that they did not reach their lower-class targets. If Egypt wanted to revitalize her productive bases she could not afford such a massive welfare program. In the end, Sadat stepped in and opted to follow the IMF program. Egypt's budgetary distress had narrowed his options, but the logic of *Infitah* also demanded further liberalization: once a country opts to depend on foreign financing and investment it must take whatever measures are necessary to create a favorable investment climate and assure its creditors. The dependence of his foreign policy on Western goodwill also figured in Sadat's calculations. The personal access to Sadat enjoyed by top Western bankers and statesmen helped circumvent the opposition of his own ministers; persons such as David Rockefeller and William Simon visiting Egypt at this time were urging Sadat to go beyond half-measures if he wanted to make *Infitah* a success (Dessouki 1981; *The Middle East*, Nov. 1977).

Once Sadat opted for a deepening of liberalization, Shafa'i and Ahmad Abu Ismail were dismissed and a new team brought in from those elements who had argued for the IMF proposals. Qaysuni became Deputy Prime Minister for Economic and Financial Affairs, and his protégés, Salah Hamid and Hamid Sayyih, became Ministers of Finance and Economy. Qaysuni had served as Middle East director of the IMF and had strong connections with Western bankers while Hamid had worked for an Arab investment bank; thus, the new team was much more congenial to the capitalist market Egypt was coming to depend on (Dessouki 1981: 415). Qaysuni was as good as his word and promptly set out to cut subsidies. One minister privy to the decision-making process later revealed that the cabinet had to cut the budget and of the four basic items in it, defense, public sector investment, debt service and subsidies, cuts in the last seemed the most feasible; what he did not say is that this was so because while the first three had powerful international or elite constituencies, the last did not. 'The 'food riots' which followed however revealed that decision-makers had miscalculated their political environment. The speed with which the Prime Minister and the leaders of the ruling party disavowed the cuts and deserted Qaysuni, also showed how shallow was the support in elite circles for politically risky rationalization measures. Subsequently, the possibility of popular reaction was to be an important element in all economic decision-making. But so also would the contrary pressures of international bankers and investors and their local advocates (*al-Ahram* 3 Jan. 1977).

The 'food riots' put the break on liberalization, but they did not put an end to the covert tug-of-war between those who, backed by the international financial community, wanted – and frequently had a personal interest in – more liberalization and those who opposed it for fear of the political consequences or in defense of threatened local interests. External forces for liberalization were strengthened when Egypt's creditors and potential or actual investors came together in a united front, the so-called 'Consultative Group for Aid to Egypt'; they also acquired stronger semi-institutionalized access to the decision-making process as the practice took hold of making economic policy in 'workshops' between Western economic elites and Egyptian officials from the Ministry of Economy and private Egyptian investment lawyers and consultants. In 1977–8, Egypt signed several 'letters of intent' with international financial authorities promising to put the public sector on a 'sound commercial basis,' reduce the rate of growth of subsidies, devalue the pound and raise interest rates. The Consultative Group committed Egypt to further reduce public sector foreign trade monopolies and trade agreements with the Eastern bloc, reactivate the stock exchange and reduce government price controls. American aid agreements were also a lever of policy change: funds for a cement plant were made contingent on the sale of part of its stock to the private sector and reduction of subsidies on cement; a grant to the Ministry of Industry was tied to a reduction of subsidies on public sector products (Abd al-Khalek 1982: 445–50; Carr 1979: 47–8; Dessouki 1981: 413–14).

In 1977 a debate over proposals to amend the 1974 investment law, further increasing incentives to investors, showed the potency of these forces. Ahmad Shalkani, an Egyptian investment lawyer representing foreign investors, was brought into the ministerial consultations over the law. He argued that there must be no limits on the freedom of capital, no controls on profits or their repatriation, and generous tax exemptions and foreign exchange rates if Egypt wanted international capital, Arab petro-dollars, and even 'hidden local capital' to invest. American business groups held scores of 'seminars' with government officials, urging that an acceptable investment climate required a more liberal and guaranteed exchange rate, access by foreign firms to local foreign exchange reserved for the government sector, and an end to discrimination against firms producing for the local market rather than for export. In drafting a new law, the government conceded most of these demands. When the bill reached parliament, Mustafa Kamil Murad, head of the rightist Ahrar Party, told the deputies: 'The Paris Consultative Group is waiting for a positive answer from you.' A few demurred, arguing that more incentives would produce little additional investment and would discriminate against national industry. But the government, as usual, got its way. Indicative of the covert influences shaping decision-making was the fact that several persons strategically placed in it stood to benefit personally from the outcome: for example, Muhammed Ibrahim Dakruri, head of the parliamentary committee which championed these changes in the law, later became head of a bank operating under it. Thus foreign intervention in Egypt's decision-making process was facilitated by links to key local clients (Ajami 1982: 490–4).

The forces of liberalization were also aided by elements in the bureaucracy which appeared to join the fray for purely ideological reasons. For example, the Central Agency for Organization and Administration, whose role was to rationalize the bureaucracy, carried on an on-going guerilla war against overstaffing in government and the public sector and against the policy of guaranteed employment of graduates which produced it. In its periodic reports and news releases it charged that in Cairo alone there were 450,000 redundant employees, that only one-third of government employees worked while the rest looked on, and that 162,000 office boys employed to serve drinks and sandwiches and carry files, were a non-productive waste. Overemployment in the public sector raised the cost of production and resulted in budget deficits, thus fueling inflation. In 1979 an agency report openly recommended an end to guaranteed employment, causing an uproar among students who claimed its abolishment would lead to favoritism in recruitment (*al-Ahram*, 30 Mar. 1979; 11, 20 Sept. 1979).

The forces of liberalization were thus on the offensive from the middle seventies. But there nevertheless remained a gap between policy intentions and actual rationalization measures. Thus, the pound was floated, but debates over the pace and extent of subsidy cuts continued inside the elite. Qaysuni remained a strong advocate of fiscal austerity and a radical approach to subsidies. But the Minister of Supply, reporting on decisions inside the Economic Committee of the cabinet revealed that such views continued to meet resistance: 'It is easy to call for curbing consumption expenditure . . . but this is a problem the economic aspect of which is different from its political inside.' In 1978 the government again backed down, in the face of protests, from an attempt to cut subsidies and then went on to raise salaries; Qaysuni, his political position severely undermined, resigned. In early 1979, however, there were new price increases supposedly limited to luxury items, but which were taken as a signal for unofficial rises in many other commodities and services.

By the end of the decade, on the whole, the balance of forces seemed to be swinging against further rationalization. One sign of this was the rising tide of criticism from inside the establishment itself at the abuse of or poor implementation of *Infitah*. The Ministry of Industry began to criticize the effects of unrestricted imports on local public industry (*al-Ahram* 13 Sept. 1979) and new laws were proposed to raise duties on some imports. The role of foreign banks was called into question: Wagih Shindi (*al-Ahram* 14 Feb. 1980), chairman of the budget and planning committee of the NDP, declared that they had contributed little to investment and Central Bank officials, arguing that national banks could and did handle most transactions and that foreign banks were transferring local savings out of the country, called for a halt in the establishment of any new ones. The editor of *al-Ahram al-Iqtisadi*, the journal of economists, openly attacked the consumerism, inequalities and social strife

Infitah was generating (15 Feb. 1976). A rightwing journalist, Ibrahim al-Sada, declared in 1980 that Egypt had to 'clean up *Infitah*' since the special privileges and exceptions won by those with special connections gave the left the chance to tarnish the whole idea (*Akhbar al-Yom*, 14 June 1980). Sayyid Marei acknowledged that *Infitah* had to be modified to provide protection for local industry and prevent the exploitation of the state by private interests (*Egyptian Gazette* 15 June 1979). The Minister of the Economy had publicly to defend *Infitah*, asserting that it had proved its worth in projects, capital influx and employment, and that even if many of the investments had been in the consumer field, this still contributed to welfare. By 1980 even Sadat had joined the attack on the 'abuses' of *Infitah*: the private sector had to pay its fair share of taxes, middlemen who 'profited at the expense of the people's suffering' would be subject to a new price control offensive (*al-Ahram* 29 Feb. 1980; MENA, 3 June 1979). A string of 'populist' measures seemed to reverse the drive to rationalization: minimum wages were raised, taxes on the poor cut, prices on public sector commodities slashed, 'Sadat pensions' extended to craftsmen, small peasants and street vendors, and the budgetary cost of food subsidies allowed to climb to a staggering £E2 billion per year. Government commitment to appointment of graduates was reaffirmed and £E18 million set aside to employ 463,000 university and secondary school graduates out of school since 1977 (*al-Ahram*, 5 Jan. 1979, 23 Sept. 1979, 16 Jan. 1980, 2 Mar. 1980, 14, 15 May 1980; MENA 27, 30 Mar. 1980). This alteration in course may, in part, have been due to genuine distress in the elite at the negative side effects of public policy; but the primary impetus was the erosion in the regime's political base, and the need to deflect the growing influence of the opposition. The change was permitted by Egypt's new financial freedom resulting from the massive influx of American aid after the peace treaty; to avoid the high political costs of wholly dismantling populism Egypt apparently decided to ease the drive to rationalization and let the Americans pick up the tab. Sadat had not given up on *Infitah* and the recapitalization of Egypt; indeed he escalated the rhetoric of capitalism. But his economic policies remained caught between political expediency and the imperatives of rationalization.

Public sector managers and Infitah

Public sector managers remained an important social force under Sadat, but they seemed to take a back seat in the elite; they also seemed to be less enthusiastic proponents of his new order than other top officials. For many managers, the Nasir years were a time of expanding career opportunity when, as leaders of a public sector regarded as the cutting edge of development, they enjoyed great prestige. The etatist industrialization drive stagnated after 1967, but in 1973 one scholar found public sector managers more satisfied and committed than other public officials (Moore 1980: 189–204). Of course, managers had their grievances under the Nasirist order. Their authority was diluted by central control over decisions and resources, from the hiring and firing of workers, to product pricing and the disposal of the foreign exchange their firms earned. There were checks on them in the factory embodied in the ASU unit, the union, and the worker representatives on management boards. Some were recruited from families disfavored by the socialist measures and all resented leftist attacks on salary levels they considered inadequate. Few were sorry to see Ali Sabri and his allies deposed. Yet *Infitah* seemed to hold as many risks as opportunities for them, and they were more than a little ambivalent toward it (Baker 1978: 175–96; Farid 1970).

Most managers welcomed the strengthening of managerial authority which followed on the abolition of the frequently hostile ASU unit in the factory, and the marginally greater discretion permitted them over productivity incentives. Some welcomed the access to advanced technology and the chance to refurbish their often decrepit machinery which they anticipated would follow from joint ventures with foreign firms. Some were prepared to benefit from the commissions to be had from such firms and some were attracted by the prospects of much higher salaries by joining a foreign firm or entering a joint venture with it (*al-Ahram* 10 Feb. 1975, 23 Oct. 1978, 29 June 1979; Dessouki 1982: 79). Some saw new chances to utilize public connections and facilities to go into business on the side.[2]

However, as *Infitah* took form its threats and costs to managers became clear. The downgrading of the public sector from the main vehicle of development had negative implications for career prospects and prestige. In the years after 1974, the public sector suffered from a barrage of elite political hostility: from parliament issued attacks on its 'abysmal' productivity and calls to sell off the good as well as the badly run firms to private industry; from the Ministry of Finance came complaints at the subsidies received by some public firms; from the press, notably from the pens of the rightwing crusaders like Mustafa Amin, came a drumfire of attack: the managers wouldn't accept responsibility when their firms lost money, they falsified accounts or hid them from the public, they tried to cover up rather than correct the mistakes of their subordinates, the same firms which had made profits under private owners now lost money under public management (*al-Akhbar* 24 Jan. 1979, 5 Feb. 1979, 20 July 1979). So far did the campaign of denigration against the public sector go that Sadat (Speech 22 July 1977) himself had to warn against this 'dire campaign' and assure managers that the regime wanted to 'reform, not sabotage' the public sector. But in elite circles, the views of economists and of the Investment Authority in its advocacy of foreign investment seemed to carry all the weight, while the Ministry of Industry was ignored; it appears, for example, to have been excluded from the crucial joint workshops with the IMF and the 'Consultative

Group' (Ajami 1982: 490). Perhaps most important of all, however, were the changing economic conditions under which the public sector was having to operate. Some managers feared *Infitah* because of the greater risks of operation they potentially faced on a competitive market. Moreover, while most Egyptian industrial products probably could not compete with the influx of cheap foreign goods which accompanied *Infitah* under any conditions, the customs and tax laws which exempted new foreign and private firms, put the heavily taxed public sector at a big disadvantage (*al-Ahram* 19 Feb. 1979; Handoussa 1979: 102–3).

In the initial years of *Infitah* the managers seemed impotent or unconcerned to protect their threatened bases. Liable to removal without redress, lacking much cohesion due to career rivalries and their diverse sources of recruitment, and perhaps neutralized by the generally favorable impact of *Infitah* on the class most came from, they acquiesced in the new course. Ministers of Industry, their spokesmen, seemed ineffective and none was prominent in elite circles. Moreover, the Ministry and the managers were sometimes at odds: thus, in 1976 the Ministry carried out a wave of transfers and dismissals which, believed by managers to be done on the basis of politics and patronage rather than competence, left a feeling of bitterness and insecurity in managerial ranks (*al-Ahram* 31 May 1977).

It was not until the late seventies that the managers began to fight back. One thrust of their effort, that against unrestricted *Infitah* and for greater protection from foreign imports, was essentially defensive. In 1979 general assemblies of scores of public sector firms met under the chairmanship of the Minister of Industry, Ibrahim Atalla, to pass resolutions against imports, citing precipitous declines in sales due to foreign competition and warning of the threat to thousands of jobs from it. Insisting their products were up to international standards, they attributed their troubles to unfair tax and customs laws: for example, they held that the tariffs on intermediate products imported for local industry were so high that they alone raised the cost of the local product above that of lightly taxed finished imports. In a kind of on-going indirect debate, the Minister of State for Economic Cooperation, Gamal Nazir, countered that foreign competition was good for the public sector since it would force it to operate more efficiently and raise the quality of its products. The Minister of Supply defended imports as a way of filling shortages on the local market (*al-Ahram* 24 May 1979, 6 June 1979, 13 Sept. 1979, 22 Sept. 1979, 10 May 1980). Hassan Tawfiq, the head of the Central Agency for Organization and Administration joined the fray by declaring that the problems of the public sector were due to red tape and mismanagement (*al-Ahram*, 14, 30 May 1979). Wagih Shindi, at this time director of the Arab Investment Bank, accused public sector workers of having the highest absentee rate in the world (*al-Ahram* 31 Jan. 1978).

The case of the Amiriya project was a prime example of the growing intra-elite conflicts between the forces of *Infitah* and the public sector. This was a huge new textile joint venture sponsored by Bank Misr and supported by the Central Bank and the Investment Authority. The Ministry of Industry (joined by the labor unions) opposed the project on the grounds that current textile plants already could not sell their output and that the need of the new plant for an estimated 28,000 technicians would denude the public sector (already suffering from shortages) of its skilled manpower; also at stake was Egypt's tariff-free quota to the Common Market which the public sector feared the new project would encroach on. Amiriya, the Minister of Industry declared, would ruin the public textile industry. It later came out that the World Bank agreed with this assessment, that no serious feasibility study had been done, or the project even submitted to the industrial planning authorities, that the machinery for the project would be sold to Egypt at a high mark-up over normal price, and that, as parliament found, Bank Misr went beyond the bounds of the law in 'offering facilities' to the investors. The Bank's enthusiasm for the project seemed not unrelated to the fact that the officials who negotiated the project reaped extremely large commissions and that one was a relative of the local representative of the foreign firm involved. Yet the deal went through, though possibly on a reduced scale, a sign of the continued limited clout of statist interests as opposed to those promoting *Infitah*. Customs duties were raised on some imported goods, however, and at the end of the decade more draft laws to protect local industry were under consideration (*al-Ahram al-Iqtisadi*, 1 Nov. 1978, 15 Jan. 1979, 15 Feb. 1979; *al-Ahram*, 6, 16 Feb. 1979; Ajami 1982: 501–2).

Managers also began to fight more aggressively for the means to adapt themselves to the new order. Many managers wanted to operate according to the norms of economic rationality and to self-finance the development of their firms. The Ministry of Industry, speaking for them, demanded that managers be given the discretion to raise prices with costs, authority over personnel policy and the ability to 'link incentives to production.' The National Council on Production recommended a reduction in public sector taxes, the abolition of price controls on its products and the extension to it of the same privileges enjoyed by the private and foreign sectors. Given that the IMF and USAID were arguing along similar lines, the managers finally seemed to have a strong hand. Prime Minister Khalil publicly endorsed at least some of the proposals. If a major reform in the public sector was in the offing, it was set back by Sadat's sudden 'populist' intervention in economic policy, which cut prices of public sector commodities and recommitted the regime to hire unemployed graduates. Yet, in the last Sadat cabinet both the Ministers of Economy and Industry were proposing greater autonomy and rationalization of finances in the public sector (*al-Ahram* 23 Oct. 1978; 4 Dec. 1979; MENA, 27 Apr. 1979; *al-Ahram al-Iqtisadi* 6 Oct. 1980).

Thus, at the end of the Sadat era, the position of public sector managers remained as uncertain as at the beginning of *Infitah*. Their desire for lowered tax burdens clashed with the treasury's need for revenue. Their desire to raise prices with costs and dismiss excess labor frightened politicians fearful of popular reaction. Their calls for tariff protection and import restrictions had to battle the regime's desire to promote foreign investment, the stake of agents of foreign firms and merchants in free trade and the insatiable consumption demands of the bourgeoisie as a whole. Unable to win public sector reform or fight *Infitah*, many managers sought to join it. By linking parts of their firms in a joint venture with a foreign firm they could acquire the privileges of the foreign sector (e.g. greater freedom to hire and fire, set prices) (Handoussa 1979: 103). Although some managers continued to believe the government should finance the sector's investment, the view of Izz ad-Din Hilal (*Middle East Economic Digest* 28 Oct. 1978) a prominent technocrat–minister close to Sadat, suggests that many viewed joint ventures as the wave of the future and did so with increasing equanimity. In his view, there could be no objection to the unlimited expansion of the private and foreign sectors, but the public sector would remain the pillar of heavy industry and through joint ventures with foreign capital would find the key to its own continued growth.

Agrarian policy and intra-elite politics

Public policy on land tenure and agricultural investment also evolved under Sadat through the intra-elite political process. Under Nasir the basic policy conflict was over the proper tenure form for newly reclaimed lands. On one side were radical officers who, for reasons of ideology or empire-building, advocated state ownership; on the other, more conservative civilian technocrats led by Sayyid Marei wanted to distribute the land to peasant cooperatives and were skeptical of the efficiency of state management.

Under Sadat, the terms of the debate rapidly shifted to the right as *Infitah* unfolded. The radical officer group was gravely weakened by the fall of Ali Sabri, but some officer–technocrats who had made careers in state agriculture survived the 1971 purge. Arguing for economies of scale and seeking to protect their own 'empires,' they advocated that 'state companies' be developed to reclaim and run the new lands. Marei continued to advocate the cooperatives his career was associated with. But in the atmosphere of *Infitah* new groups with new options also emerged. The Agricultural Engineers' Syndicate pressed for the distribution of the lands to agronomy graduates on the grounds that they had the required skills, even though a similar experiment before 1952 had produced absentee ownership. Some technocrats advocated leasing the land to private agro-business, while private landowners in the People's Assembly wanted it sold on the open market to the highest bidder (Springborg 1979a: 52–65; *al-Talia*, No. 12, 1975).

Policy shifted slowly in line with the balance of power between these forces. Initially, the officer–technocrats had the upper hand. Some enjoyed good personal links to Sadat and Osman Badran who served on-and-off as Minister of Agriculture or of Land Reclamation in the early to mid-seventies. Their organizations also had a prior claim on a large segment of an agricultural budget formulated through a process of aggregation and incremental bargaining inside the bureaucracy, and neither private farmers nor cooperatized peasants had much voice or influence in this process. In October 1971 the officer–technocrats' model of state companies was announced as official policy. However, after 1974, as *Infitah* took root and Sadat increasingly reached for support in the private sector, they lost ground. By the end of the decade, only three public companies had been formed. Other tracts were distributed to peasants as Marei had advocated and 100,000 *feddans* were given to the Agronomists' Syndicate. And not only was some auctioned off to the highest bidder, but the land reform ownership limit of 50 *feddans* was declared not to apply to reclaimed land. This potentially cleared the way for a re-emergence of the large capitalist farms destroyed by the 1952 reform (Ikram 1980: 73–4; Springborg 1979a: 52–65). The influence of landed interests, expressed by prominent personalities close to Sadat – notably Marei and Muhammed Hamid Mahmud – had apparently begun to prevail. By the late seventies, the swing toward the private – and then foreign – sectors accelerated. Arguing that the public sector had failed to efficiently manage reclaimed lands and lacked the capital to undertake reclamation, agricultural authorities deprived it of its old priority. Land reclaimed by the government, and even existent public sector farms, began to be sold off in 5–25 *feddan* plots at the pre-reclamation cost, that is, at low subsidized prices. Then, in a breakthrough, a foreign firm, Coca-Cola, was leased a tract of farmland to run on agro-business lines; the ice broken, other such firms were given sole or joint venture leases (which, to get them to commit their capital, ran for 50 years) (Hafiz 1980; Speech, Tawfiq Karara, *al-Ahram* 31 Sept. 1979; MENA 23 Nov. 1979; Sadat Speeches 28 Sept., Oct. 1977). According to the opposition leader, Hilmi Murad, the government was deliberately neglecting the public sector in order to have an excuse to totally abolish it; if current policy was not reversed, he charged, Egypt's agriculture would before long be foreign dominated (*al-Sha'b* 22 Apr. 1980). Yet, even in the midst of the *Infitah*, bureaucratic interests retained enough clout to keep a foot in the agricultural sector. A large proportion of public investment in the sector was diverted into the creation of the General Organization for Poultry Production which began to undertake large-scale capital-intensive broiler production (Ikram 1980: 201). And Osman Ahmad Osman was given responsibility to set up a public 'Food Security Company.' Thus, Egypt's land tenure policy seemed to be rather overtly shaped to satisfy the shifting influence of the various interests in the regime constituency.

Whether this patchwork represented a rational response to Egypt's agricultural needs, was questionable.

Interest group elites

Interest group elites are defined here as those leaders who 'represent' in councils of government the powerful private and semi-private interests in Egyptian society. These interests were chiefly, though not exclusively, part of the regime's main constituency, the bourgeoisie. Under the Nasir regime, which was not dependent on these groups and which mistrusted the effect of pressure groups on public policy, they carried little weight in the political system and were largely powerless to deflect the mounting assaults on private interests in the sixties. Sadat, in contrast, assiduously sought the support of the private bourgeoisie and in doing so shaped public policy in many ways to meet its demands. The burning of the tapes and the return of sequestered property was a first signal that henceforth private interests would be respected; subsequent policies – above all *Infitah* – meant, for the private bourgeoisie, virtually a new lease on life. In this climate, the scope of private interest group activity significantly expanded. On the one hand, *Infitah* revitalized these interests and expanded the stakes of the interest group game; on the other, the relaxation of state control over private life, and of the President and top elite over certain domains of the policy process, permitted interest groups more autonomy and greater input into the policy process. Increasingly, access points to decision-makers virtually non-existent under Nasir, opened up. Professional syndicates and chambers of commerce, used under Nasir more for control than interest articulation, became more autonomous and effective in pressing demands. Parliamentary committees became staging platforms for the articulation of interests. The Combined National Councils developed into arenas for institutionalized consultation between decision-makers and societal interests. Perhaps most important, a constellation of powerful personalities with links to the private bourgeoisie dominated the President's inner circle. The demands of private interests did not always find easy sailing; entrenched statist interests and the need of the regime to pacify the mass public sometimes conflicted with them; but, judging by policy outputs, these access points were very effective and enormously more so than under Nasir.

The business bourgeoisie

The social power of the business bourgeoisie grew rapidly under *Infitah*. To be sure, Egypt has as yet few of the big business magnates who wield great influence in older capitalist states, but in a relatively short time, *Infitah* spawned a new crop of millionaires. This bourgeoisie found a more sympathetic hearing in elite circles than ever before and access points which allowed it to lobby with great effectiveness on issues of importance to it. In Osman Ahmad Osman and Mansur Hassan the business world enjoyed direct access to the President, a link critical for ensuring a continued favorable policy climate for it. It also enjoyed more institutionalized channels of interest articulation. The Chamber of Commerce and the Federation of Industries spoke with increasing authority in defense of private interests against both the state and labor; committees of parliament and the National Council on Production were forums in which entrepreneurs pushed for the encouragement of private enterprise, for example, tax incentives and the revitalization of the stock market. The government even encouraged the formation of new business associations to express the interests created by *Infitah*, for example, a joint venture investors' association and an exporters' union needed to fill the gap caused by the decline of trade agreements with the Eastern bloc. The Ahrar Party was a constant advocate in press and parliament for *laissez-faire* policies. Businessmen enjoyed increasing tolerance of the use of personal, business and marriage connections with state elites to search for individual privileges and exceptions, to insert themselves as middlemen between the state and foreign firms, to use personal connections to win franchises and consultancies, or to corner import licenses or monopolies on state contracts. But private business did not always get its way, nor was it always united; the methods, effectiveness and consequences of its interest articulation can be illustrated by a look at several areas of conflict where business demands clashed with opposing forces.

The private bourgeoisie persistently lobbied for tax reductions and exemptions. Its argument was that the mobilization of savings and investment depended on tax breaks. Big entrepreneurs were in the forefront of this campaign, but by the end of the decade it had spread downward, taking the form of a tax rebellion among small workshop owners against arbitrary tax assessments. The government was largely receptive to this lobbying and cuts and exemptions on taxes and customs proliferated, reducing the high rates in force under Nasir. But the government had to balance its desire to stimulate investment with its need for revenue. Thus, in 1978 a fight developed over an effort by the Ministry of Finance to 'take back' some of the privileges the regime had already granted and to give customs officials the right to check the records of Free Zone merchants for 'irregularities.' The Suez Chamber of Commerce vigorously opposed this effort and even enlisted the local governor on its side (*al-Ahram* 31 Oct. 1977). This struggle was a sign of persisting conflicts between the interests of the 'state' and 'private' bourgeoisie. The drive to escape taxes also ran up against the advocates of equity. Sadat had laid down that progressive taxation on high incomes and luxuries should be the main tool of social justice under his regime, but, as he himself declared, the rich were not paying their fair share; subsequent campaigns by the tax department against tax evaders could not have pleased the business community (*al-Ahram* 20 Feb., 14 Oct. 1979; NDP Statement, 6 Mar. 1979; Sadat speech 1 June 1978). The legal opposition Labor Party began to make tax evasion and equity a major public issue toward the end of the decade. At a tax conference at Alexandria University in 1980 a number of delegates, encouraged by Sadat's position, called for restrictions on the excessive proliferation of tax concessions (*al-Ahram* 24, 27 Feb. 1980). Instead, the Finance Ministry bowed to demands to grant tax exemptions on savings accounts (up to £E5000) and on dividends from shares purchased in public companies (*al-Ahram* 24 Feb. 1980, 11 Mar. 1980, 17 Apr. 1980); and the cabinet approved and sent to parliament a bill further reducing progressive rates levied by the income tax (Bentley 1981). The government was clearly caught in a contradiction: while it was committed to progressive taxation in the interest of social justice and political stability, its decision to rely on private investment for development made it extremely vulnerable to the demands of capital for investment incentives.

Another issue of concern to the merchant wing of the bourgeoisie was government price-fixing. As *Infitah* accelerated, and with it inflation, traditional government measures to stabilize prices became increasingly ineffectual, and popular discontent alarming. In an effort to find a middle position between merchants and the mass public, a 1977 Ministry of Supply decree fixed a 30% profit ceiling on hitherto unregulated imported commodities. The Chamber of Commerce lobbied against and defeated it. Before long, however, as its popularity eroded the government was forced to come out more strongly against 'profiteering.' Sadat attacked 'market sharks' who 'exploited the people's suffering,' and Fikri Makram Ubayd, appointed head of an NDP price enforcement committee, accused merchants of trying to absorb the cost of living bonuses given public employees as fast as the government scoured the hard-pressed treasury to pay them. Government price-control efforts began to take the form of arrests and confiscations and, in a throwback to the strategies of the sixties, Sadat proposed to set up a public company to distribute food in order to undermine middlemen (*al-Ahram*, 22 Dec. 1979; Sadat speech 2 Mar. 1980). These measures could only have unsettled the hitherto excellent relations between the state and the merchant community.

Labor issues, also of concern to the bourgeoisie, were a focus of political conflict. The Chamber of Commerce wanted market forces to set wages. This would probably, except for certain skilled categories, have been very low in a labor surplus economy. While sympathetic, in principle, to the market mechanism, the government could not easily ignore labor expectations that it set minimum wages; indeed traditionally, the Minister of Labor, picked from pro-government syndicalists, was not only an advocate of labor demands in the cabinet but presided over periodic negotiations between employers and labor associations. It was a measure of the strong bargaining position of employers, however, that even in the aftermath of the 1977 riots when the government was trying to sooth popular unrest and when 25–30% inflation was translating into big profits, that the Chamber of Commerce could only be brought to concede a 7% pay raise, and that on condition that the government never again make such a demand. In an atmosphere of high inflation and popular unrest, the government could not, however, be held to this promise and in 1978 and again in 1980 the Labor Minister extracted another 10% increase in wages (*al-Ahram* 4 Jan. 1980). Thus, even under *Infitah* there were elite spokesmen for the interests of the mass public which, strengthened by the regime's instinct for self-preservation, carried some weight against the claims of the bourgeoisie and the operations of the market. But the limits of their influence can be measured by the fact that, at the end of the decade the minimum wage was still a dismal £E15 per month.

The construction industry was perhaps the most powerful segment of the business bourgeoisie under Sadat. Informally headed by Osman Ahmad Osman, it had the best of connections inside the regime. Flourishing on the *Infitah* building boom and the reconstruction contracts to be had from government, it was, not surprisingly, mostly on the offensive under Sadat and for this very reason, seldom out of the center of controversy. One measure of its political clout was its ability to commit the government to the investment of scarce public funds in a network of flyovers and highways chiefly of benefit to well-off motorists at a time when public transport was deteriorating. It weathered all criticism of this and of its frequent cost-overruns (*al-Ahram*, 8 Feb. 1979). A not untypical controversy erupted over its plan for slum clearance in inner-city Cairo. Operating through the Housing Committee of the People's Assembly, construction and real estate interests pushed for the demolition of lower-income neighborhoods to make way for luxury hotels and housing, parking lots, and offices for *Infitah* firms. Local neighborhood groups fought back, charging that they were not being guaranteed better housing elsewhere and that the compensation being offered was trivial compared to the profits developers stood to gain. When their own parliamentary deputy and the Governor of Cairo proved indifferent to their case, neighborhood leaders took it to the press. Public exposure won them promises, at least, that they would be given better new housing (*al-Ahram*, 4 Nov., 27 Dec. 1979). Another curious controversy, illustrative of the appetite of contractors, was a proposal to level the Cairo zoo to make room for tourist development. A storm of protest erupted in the press where developers were told to build in the desert not on the green; the zoo grounds, declared the Minister of Agriculture were a 'lung' for 10 million Cairenes. For the time being, at least, the proposal was allowed to drop (*al-Ahram*, 11 Mar., 26 June 1979). A similar case, involving foreign as well as local developers, was the notorious Pyramid Plateau scandal; it, too, aroused too much public resistance to be sustained. An aroused public opinion could thus put some limits on even the most powerful lobbies. Another issue, however, demonstrated the growing 'softness' of the state in the face of such interests. Over the years, large tracts of public land had been taken over by builders, but when public officials attempted to expel squatters or collect rents, they found that the protection given the offenders in high places made it impossible to enforce the law. Builders openly challenged officials to prove that the land was public property, an attitude which in Nasir's day would have invited instant confiscation (*al-Ahram*, 27 Dec. 1979, 3 Apr. 1980).

Another issue, rent control, pitted construction and real estate interests against the wider public and put the government in the middle. Rent was traditionally controlled, but was evaded on new apartments by requiring new tenants to pay 'key' money. The housing committee of parliament began to push for the abolition of the law against key money since it couldn't be enforced. The Ministry of Housing, long virtually a colony of the construction industry, joined in, calling for an end to rent control as allegedly the cause of the housing shortage. It wanted the government to leave housing to the private sector and encourage it by tax and customs exemptions. These initiatives let loose a storm of protest in the opposition press, which predicted they would only increase the availability of housing for the rich while inflicting major hardship on modest income tenants. The proposals were consistent with the market logic of *Infitah*, but a government facing growing discontent was not prepared to antagonize the significant part of the public living in rent-controlled flats. Private capitalist interests still ran up against entrenched consumer 'rights' left behind by Nasirite populism (*al-Ahram* 23 Jan. 1980).

Finally, the case of private Egyptian industrialists suggests some of the divisions inside the bourgeoisie and the ambivalence which part of the private bourgeoisie felt toward *laissez-faire* policies promoted under *Infitah*. Local industrialists did seek to profit from the new climate favorable to free enterprise. They won tax exemptions on new investment comparable to that given foreign investors. Their confidence renewed, they launched a campaign in parliament to roll back the public sector monopolies from fields where they wished to invest and even secured a government investigation of such monopolies in the plastics field (*al-Ahram* 23 Jan. 1980). However, by the end of the decade, they were alarmed by the unrestrained influx of foreign commodities. Joining hands with the public sector, the Federation of Industries came out against tariff laws favoring finished commodities over intermediate products and spare parts. It attacked the 'import complex' which led Egyptians to buy foreign as a 'badge of sophistication,' and cited the threat to hundreds of small knitwear factories from cheap foreign goods. Devaluation had raised costs and stable East European export markets had been lost (*al-Ahram*, 20 Nov. 1979, 12 Mar. 1980). Indicative of the extent of business disaffection was the charge of the Chamber of Commerce that because the government had failed to define priorities for foreign investment, it had gone into quick-profit consumer ventures, which, it implied, should have been left to local industry (Dessouki 1982b: 78). However, by this time, foreign investors had their own pressure groups which, backed by their finance and technology, were perfectly capable of defending themselves; indeed, taking the offensive, they announced they would press for an extension of customs exemptions beyond the five years initially conceded (MENA, 3 June 1979). Thus, the classic cleavage between national and international capital had re-emerged in Egypt.

The agrarian bourgeoisie

The agrarian bourgeoisie seemed no less well equipped than its business cousins to advance its interests in Sadat's political system. In Sayyid Marei, one of their number, they had access to the very top. Though an architect of the land reform and the cooperative movement, Marei was, by the late seventies, arguing that the reform had limited production by rewarding poor peasants with a high propensity to consume, and that to get agricultural growth, the regime had to favor the investment-prone agrarian bourgeoisie. The Agronomists' Union and segments of the Ministry of Agriculture could also be enlisted in behalf of this social class. But it was in parliament, especially the Agricultural Affairs Committee, (which by the end of the decade was headed by Marei's son) where its real strength lay. This committee had a string of victories to its credit. In 1972, it deflected an attempt by the statist Sidqi government to tax fruit trees, the lucrative cash crops on which the agrarian bourgeoisie was enriching itself (Lachine 1978: 14). The committee also won land rent increases and a watering down of the agrarian relations law which reduced the security of tenants (Lachine 1978: 18). In an unprecedented 1979 *coup*, agrarian interests brought the Minister of Agriculture to announce compensation of up to £E500,000 for landowners expropriated under the 1969 land reform from a £E79 million fund to be financed through the selling and leasing of this land (MENA 24 Dec. 1979); this remarkable concession, at the expense of both the peasants and the state treasury, indicated the potency of the agrarian lobby. While it usually got its way against peasants, the agrarian bourgeoisie did not win every round against the state. The Agricultural Affairs Committee mounted attacks on the cooperatives and the system of compulsory state marketing of cotton and other vital crops. But although the cooperatives were enervated by the regime, and wheat was pried loose from the state marketing system, the bourgeoisie failed to abolish compulsory marketing of cotton; here it ran up against the vital interests of the treasury and the state bourgeoisie. It had to compromise, too, on its drive to remove some of the consequences of the land reform law. It won the right to bid for reclaimed state land unrestricted by reform ownership ceilings, but a proposal to allow peasant land-reform beneficiaries to sell their land was vetoed

– not because it would lead to the reconcentration of land – but because the government would lose revenue it still collected in payment for these lands (*al-Ahram*, 13 June 1979; MENA 29 Dec. 1979).

The free professions

The free professions carried power and influence in the Egyptian political system, and much more so under Sadat than before. Their access to ministerial posts, always liberal, expanded under Sadat. The professions each had syndicates to articulate their interests in elite councils. Under Nasir these syndicates had some clout in defense of professional interests (the Medical Syndicate defeated socialized medicine in 'socialist' Egypt), but in the sixties the regime made serious efforts to subordinate them to the ASU, and sometimes imposed leadership from above (Springborg 1978). Under Sadat their autonomy and effectiveness significantly increased. ASU controls were dismantled and intervention in their elections became less overt. In 1979 some syndicates took to supporting their own candidates for parliament. Some syndicates, closely tied to the regime, continued to seek prominent regime personalities as their heads, in the apparent belief that such personal access to the center counted for a lot. A few staked out positions independent of the regime and had to be warned by Sadat that their proper role was to defend their members' welfare, not to advocate political positions. Nevertheless, most professionals welcomed Sadat's political and economic liberalization and he, in turn, anxious for their support, usually trod warily in dealing with them.

The Engineers' Syndicate was closely tied to the regime and largely conservative. In the early seventies under the conservative Abd al-Khalek al-Shinnawi, it challenged the Sidqi government, insisting on the right of the association to review all Soviet-aided development projects; Shinnawi also signed the famous statement against the Soviet advisors (Springborg 1978: 284–5). Subsequently, the Syndicate was headed by regime stalwarts Mustafa Khalil and Osman Ahmad Osman. Engineers, chiefly recruited from the Westernized upper classes, saw in *Infitah* opportunities for their oversupplied profession and were among its staunchest advocates. So adept did they prove in taking advantage of the need of foreign firms for Egyptian middlemen and consultants, that Sadat chose a speech to the Engineers' Syndicate to warn against commission-taking (MENA 11 Oct. 1979). However, engineers soon became alarmed at competition from foreign experts who began to flood the Egyptian market. Osman, speaking for the professional interests of his constituency, demanded that the Syndicate be given a role in supervising and reviewing the work of foreign consultants and that foreign firms be required to employ a quota of Egyptian engineers (*al-Ahram* 19 Mar. 1979). On a different track was the separate Society of Engineers; more autonomous of the regime, it was in the vanguard of forces warning against the Pyramid Plateau project.

The Medical, Dental and Pharmacists Syndicates were pro-regime. The head of the Medical Syndicate, Hamdi Sayyid, was a leading member of the government party, and the chief of the Pharmacists' Syndicate had served as Governor of Fayyum. Their concerns centered on protecting the professional interests of their members, the main threat to which was the indiscriminate expansion of professional schools. Thus, the head of the Medical Syndicate in letters to the Minister of Health, predicted 40,000 surplus doctors in five years and, because the new schools lacked faculty and equipment, a precipitous decline in the quality of graduates (*al-Ahram* 16 Sept. 1979).

The Journalists' Syndicate, on the other hand, was generally on bad terms with the regime. Since Sadat's succession, it fought to expand journalistic freedoms against regime controls. Adding asperity to the conflict was the strong leftist ideological influence in the profession. In the mid-seventies, a Sadat confidant, Yusuf Sabai headed the union and tried to discipline it; but somewhat later a leftwing journalist, Kamal Zuhayri, was elected. This, press criticism of the government, and the opposition political activity of some journalists, led Sadat to attempt to abolish the Syndicate. It deflected this threat, but could not prevent creation of a watchdog 'Higher Council for the Press' to make sure journalists adhered to Sadat's political 'code of ethics' (*al-Ahram* 12 Nov. 1979; *al-Akhbar* 10 Mar. 1980; *Egyptian Gazette*, 23 Jan. 1980; Sadat speech 10 May 1980).

The Lawyers' Syndicate also became an independent force troublesome to the regime. To be sure, lawyers generally applauded Sadat's liberalization measures. They had disliked Nasir's disregard for legality, and the Judges' Club, a power in the profession, was a center of anti-regime hostility in the sixties. Sadat's restoration of the rule of law pleased them and put their depressed profession in demand again. *Infitah* opened up a wealth of new opportunities for them as legal advisors and consultants to foreign firms trying to negotiate webs of regulation. But Sadat's liberalization apparently did not go far enough for them, and their Syndicate turned into a troublesome pressure group disrespectful of government authority. In 1972 it supported the student and worker demonstrations. It published a book on the Pyramid Plateau scandal at a time when the government was trying to hush it up. It gave Wafdist leader Serag ad-Din a forum for his blistering attack on the revolution, helped him resurrect the Wafd as a political force, and denounced its 'unconstitutional' repression; in spite of the defeat of a Wafd candidate in subsequent Syndicate elections as a result of pressures on government-employed lawyers, the Syndicate became a center of anti-regime sentiment in the last years of the Sadat regime. It fiercely attached Sadat's Law of *Aib* and burned an Israeli flag at its headquarters to protest normalization of relations. So incensed was Sadat with the lawyers that he refused to attend a ceremony honoring the law faculty of Cairo University and finally purged the Syndicate leadership.

Academic elites occupy a special place in the Egyptian political system. They enjoy only limited autonomy and, like other state employees, can be arbitrarily removed. Yet, under both Nasir and Sadat, large numbers of them were recruited into the ministerial elite. Perhaps for these reasons, Egyptian academia was not the anti-government force it is in many Third World countries. To be sure, there is a sprinkling of Marxist professors. Some academics were active in opposition parties. But many prestigious professors were also prominent in the ruling party and the regime's chief ideologue, Sufi Abu Talib, was a chancellor of Cairo University. Some university administrators and professors zealously cooperated in government efforts to rid the campuses of leftist and Islamic influence. The dominant sentiment among academics was undoubtedly liberalism and as such most applauded Sadat's liberalizing reforms. Some were in the forefront of those urging a maximum of political liberalization during the debates over Egypt's political future. In his last years, however, Sadat's relations with academics deteriorated: many were antagonized by the retightening of controls over political freedoms and government efforts to push them into relations with Israeli counterparts.

Educators were also active in defense of their purely professional interests, which on occasion became issues of conflict. Controversy arose over the effort by administrators to restrict the leaves of absence taken by professors which threatened to denude Egypt's already understaffed universities at the expense of students. Academics insisted that these leaves of absense – often to Gulf countries – were part of their professional work or were needed to supplement their low salaries. The solution to the problem proposed by the Minister of Higher Education, evidently speaking for academics, was to raise salaries; the alternative, to restrict travel abroad, was rejected as incompatible with *Infitah* (*al-Ahram* 31 Oct. 1978). Another educational issue symptomatic of the *Infitah* era was the proposal to create a new private university. This project, pushed by the education committee of parliament and endorsed by the Minister of Education, would, its advocates claimed, produce a better quality education and relieve the state of some of its burden. 'We should apply the Open Door to Education,' they argued. Some critics of the plan did come forward from academia. They argued that it would destroy the principle of equal opportunity of access to education and deplete existing public faculties, that resources should go into technical and vocational education and that it was a scheme to serve the children of the rich since anyone who could pay was to be admitted, regardless of grades. Yet, many educators from the public university system, notably ones from regional campuses, testified in favor of the project: the chance for higher-paying jobs out of the boondocks must have seemed irresistible to them (*al-Ahram* 1, 2 Mar. 1979; *Egyptian Gazette*, 11 Jan. 1979; MENA 8 Feb. 1979). The debate over the issue deadlocked, but the demand to privatize education was wholly consistent with the trends encouraged by *Infitah* in every sphere of social life.

The religious elites

Egypt's religious elites have frequently played a political role. Appointed, dismissed and subsidized by the state, they have proven responsive to the demands of the authorities. Under Nasir they legitimized socialism as Islamic. Under Sadat they were also repeatedly mobilized to legitimize controversial policies. In 1975 the Shaikh al-Azhar entered the debate over economic inequality and *Infitah* on the side of capitalism; Islam, he declared, was for private property and demands for equalization were heresy. It was relevant that some of Azhar's top figures enjoyed considerable personal wealth and were not above investment in business (Ajami 1981: 186). The religious elite also legitimized Sadat's foreign policies. The trip to Jerusalem was endorsed on the grounds that it would lead to the recovery of the Holy City, and though in fact the peace treaty failed to return the city, the religious elites held that it did in principle! Equally credible was the comparison of the treaty with Muhammed's peace with a defeated enemy. Signaling its deference to secular authority the Shaikh al-Azhar declared that the leader alone was authorized to decide on matters of peace and war. Religious leaders also obliged Sadat by declaring that communism (not Israel) was the main enemy of the Islamic world (*al-Ahram* 11 May, 23 June 1979).

On matters of Islamic regulation of social life, the clergy was less passive and frequently attempted to influence legislation; but, in this effort it was not united. The main tendency at the top of the religious establishment was 'modernist.' The Shaikh al-Azhar – who in the late seventies actually held a doctorate from a British university – usually endorsed a liberal interpretation of Islam, including such things as support for freedom of individual conscience, women's rights, and the use of interest in the banking system; occasionally top religious authorities took on Islamic fundamentalists in defense of the regime. Other religious figures, including a contingent of clergy in parliament, were advocates of a greater Islamization and won the designation of Islam as the main source of legislation in the constitution (Humphreys 1979). But the practical legislation expected by less liberal clergy to flow from this – such as the prohibition of alcohol or the death penalty for apostasy – was either stalled in parliament or, if passed, never seemed to be enforced. Such measures were strenuously opposed by Copts. The prohibition of alcohol was opposed by influential elements – including the President's brother – with an interest in nightclubs. Moreover, such measures were hardly compatible with the open liberal atmosphere of *Infitah*.

One of the most bitterly fought contests involving the religious elite was over the law of personal status. In 1974, the Minister of Social Affairs, Aisha Ratib, an advocate of women's rights, proposed a new law of personal status which made modest reforms in favor of women, for example, providing that husbands could only divorce their wives or take another wife with the permission of a judge. Conservative religious forces mobilized against the proposal with street marches to parliament and threats of assassination. Her hand weakened, Ratib could not prevent the Ministry of Justice from assuming control over the issue. It proposed a diluted reform providing only that the husband must inform his wife of divorce and that she could sue for divorce if the husband took a second wife. The balance of power, however, shifted in favor of reform when Sadat himself, at the behest of his wife, intervened. Sadat warned against the 'misuse of religion as a mask behind which man hides his vindictive desire to maintain absolute supremacy over women.' He proposed a new law which made taking a second wife grounds for divorce, required men to register divorces in court and entitled divorced wives to generous alimony. Sadat was able to enlist the support of top figures in the religious elite, but opposition remained so strong in the middle ranks and in the religious affairs committee of parliament, that he had to promulgate the law by decree (*al-Ahram* 23 June, 3 July 1979; Nowaihi 1979).

The leadership of the Coptic Church proved less amenable than its Muslim counterparts to the wishes of political authority. Initially, it welcomed Sadat's more liberal Western-oriented policies, but in the later seventies relations between church and state dramatically deteriorated. Coptic leaders were displeased by the Islamization measures and official leniency toward, if not encouragement of, Islamic fundamentalist harassment of Copts. In 1978 Pope Shenouda canceled Easter celebrations in protest. Copts in the US publicly criticized the regime, to the embarrassment of Sadat for whom a favorable American image had become a major foreign policy asset. An anti-Zionist, Shenouda – in striking contrast to his Islamic counterparts – refused to support the peace treaty, meet Begin, or permit Coptic pilgrimages to occupied Jerusalem. This tarnished the image of pro-peace unanimity Sadat wished to project. He soon counter attacked. In an aggressive public speech, he declared that Egypt was an Islamic state and denounced the Coptic leadership for trying to create a 'state within a state.' Later he removed Shenouda as pope, a dramatic reminder that no social force in Egypt is ultimately autonomous of the Leviathan state (Sadat speech 14 May 1980). Despite a century of secularization, both religious leaderships remained in the anomalous positions they occupied in the traditional Islamic state: they were expected to refrain from overt political activity; yet they were also expected to legitimize government policies, indeed to act as a virtual propaganda wing of the state.

Elite politics and interest groups under Sadat

In Sadat's Egypt, as in Nasir's, the big decisions continued to issue from struggles in restricted elite arenas decided by Presidential authority and the informal influence of personalistic cliques and bureaucratic factions. This was especially so in the critical domains of foreign policy and military politics. The major direction of domestic high policy – *Infitah* – was a response to external pressures and the covert lobbying of bourgeois elites, but it also was decided in a small elite arena in which Sadat's close confidants seemed to carry formidable weight. In lesser questions of socio-economic policy where, as compared to foreign policy, the President was less personally identified with a specific course, less threatened by elite opposition and less interested in expending political capital, he permitted policy to be shaped by a more open process of intra-elite conflict, although, as in the case of the law of personal status, he reserved the right to impose his will even in such matters. Even these decisions, however, were usually settled in small elite arenas where individuals and groups sought to win over the President or key ministers. Sometimes debates between experts as to what was needed if the government was to reach its objectives may have decided the outcome. Sometimes, as in the Amiriya case, decisions were dominated by small self-interested groups with personal pull or the promises of a payoff. Normally, as in the land tenure case, both kinds of resources – pragmatic arguments as to what would work best and personal influence – probably contributed to the outcome.

The importance of small arena clique politics in Egypt may, in part, be a reflection of a personalistic semi-traditional culture or of the relative weakness of classes and functional groups which could form the basis of larger more impersonal political forces with the power to force open the political game. But policy conflicts, even when ostensibly fought by *shillas* over spoils, were seldom random or divorced from class ideology, interests and power. In the land tenure case it was chiefly the rise of the *Infitah* ideology and of the private bourgeoisie, as much as personal influence, which shifted agrarian policy from statist toward private solutions. Decision-makers' perception of the relative power of social forces also figured in the decision to cut the subsidies. But, as the subsidies case showed, what small arena politics did was to bias the game against social forces lacking strong representation in elite circles. The case also suggests that small arena politics may enhance the weight of foreign interests, when they get access to decision-makers, since countervailing mass domestic pressures are absent. Even when some elites are prepared to defend mass interests, as in the subsidy debate, the rules of the game prohibit them from trying to mobilize popular support which might match elite or foreign interests.

The fact is that small groups carried so much weight in the political process less for cultural or social reasons than because of the authoritarian state, that is, the controls over activism and the weakness of political infrastructure needed to aggregate mass opinion into the policy process. That this is so is indicated by the fact that the limited relaxation of control and opening of the political system in the late Sadat period resulted in a significant proliferation and activation of interest groups representing constituencies well beyond elite circles and trying to use a broader mobilization of opinion, not simply bureaucratic or personalistic resources, to affect decisions. The Industry Ministry mobilization of public sector firms indicated a new tolerance for efforts by interests disfavored by decisions to overtly lobby for their modification or reversal. The aggressive battles of business groups with the public sector and the customs authority signaled a growing ability of private interests to check state authorities. Sadat's relative patience with the lawyers' and journalists' syndicates indicated a greater tolerance even for mobilization around broader political issues. These were symptoms of a growing though still limited pluralization of the Egyptian polity.

The cases also suggest, however, that pluralization in an only semi-institutionalized state can have important negative side effects. One was an apparent growing 'colonization' of the state by private interests. Even under Nasir, conflicting vested interests sometimes paralyzed the making of coherent policies; but under Sadat the revitalization of private interests and the weakening of forces with a commitment to a definite vision of the public interest, seemed to produce an ever more 'soft' state. The Ministry of Housing seemed little more than a creature of the construction lobby; the police, feared under Nasir, proved powerless to defend the public land and treasury against protected interests. Even the Ministry of Finance which almost everywhere can be depended upon to defend the revenue base of the state, was sometimes actually in the forefront of campaigns to grant tax exemptions to privileged interests. Secondly, a limited pluralization which opens access points to those with resources but provides no effective means for the mobilization of the have-nots accentuates class bias in the policy process. The interest group game unmistakably favored the haves. At the very time the Minister of Housing was declaring that the government lacked resources to build low-cost public housing, well-connected interests brought it to sink millions in highways and flyovers, liberally hand out tax exemptions, pay compensation to expropriated landlords and recommend increases in professors' salaries and the building of a private university. This outcome was of course partly the consequence of a development strategy relying on foreign and private capital which to provide the needed incentives cannot avoid favoring privileged groups. But the combination of limited pluralization and an *Infitah* strategy seemed to result in an especially soft and biased policy process. This is not to say that the state had been reduced to nothing more than an 'executive committee of the bourgeoisie.' Its persistent autonomy could be seen in the continuing instinct for survival which it frequently put before the special interests of segments of the bourgeoisie: its efforts to control rents and prices and to raise wages reflected a determination to protect its popular base. Nor did it always fail to defend its revenue base: some of the claims of the agrarian bourgeoisie, for example, were turned back. Moreover, other forces than the bourgeoisie could sometimes bring some competing input into government circles. A disinterested public opinion, mobilized and channeled through the press, checked some of the more audacious 'smash and grab' efforts of pressure groups at the expense of the public or the poor in the Pyramid Plateau, Cairo zoo, and perhaps the slum clearance cases. Within elite circles, the Ministers of Labor and of Social Affairs seemed to speak for have-nots. Moreover, in time, a biased policy tended to provoke a reaction which could sometimes partly redress it; thus, the food riots showed that when its interests were damaged the mass public could mobilize, and if in-system channels were closed it could make its point outside them, in the streets. But in the long-run this could not substitute for institutionalized mass participation. For the masses, partial pluralization for the haves was probably worse than no pluralization at all.

Chapter 6

The political infrastructure

This section examines the changing role of Egypt's political infrastructure, namely, the established political party system, parliament and parliamentary elections, the press and the legal and judicial systems insofar as they helped shape political activity. Under Nasir, the political and legal infrastructures were overshadowed by the Presidency and its bureaucratic appendages. Under Sadat, they remained 'subordinate' systems unable to compete effectively with the executive as a source of public policy or to hold it accountable. But the limited pluralization of the system allowed them a somewhat greater measure of autonomy from the executive and, hence, enhanced their effectiveness as channels for the articulation of interests.

A changing party system

Egypt's party system under Sadat evolved gradually from the all-embracing official party, the ASU, under Nasir. The first step was a change in top leadership, the 1971 displacement of leftist officers who had tried to make the ASU an instrument of mobilization and control by, conservative Sadat loyalists; also, rural notables pushed aside in the sixties recovered their positions in local branches. Many of these elements, as well as centrist and leftwing intellectuals, wanted a widening of political freedoms inside the party and in 1972 Sadat appointed Sayyid Marei as party chief, charged with trying to accommodate these demands. Marei presided over debates on the role of the party in which critics charged that, dominated by the government at the top and paralyzed by mass indifference below, it had failed to function as an effective elite–mass link. Marei was in sympathy with these views and subsequently tried to open the ASU up, encouraging educated middle-class elements in it to criticize the government. This, however, brought him into conflict with Premier Sidqi who viewed the party as an instrument for explaining the government's policy to the people rather than a mechanism for holding it accountable; Sadat decided to end the experiment (Marei 1978a: 664–79). Once he consolidated his legitimacy in the October War, however, Sadat evidently decided that a liberalization of the party system would serve to differentiate his regime from Nasir's, satisfy participatory pressures, win support from liberal elements of the bourgeoisie, please the Americans on whom his diplomatic initiative depended and encourage the economic liberalization he was launching. In the *October Paper*, Sadat raised the possibility of permitting a greater diversity of viewpoints inside the ASU and, at the urging of liberal confidants, notably Mahmud Abu Wafia and Marei, allowed the debate over a proper party system for Egypt to be reopened. In 1974, Abu Wafia presided over parliamentary hearings on the subject and thereafter a Committee on the Future of Political Life chaired by Marei carried the discussion further. The debates revealed several distinct tendencies in elite opinion. The liberal wing of the bourgeoisie, composed chiefly of businessmen and professionals, argued for the replacement of the ASU by a multi-party system; this would permit them greater political freedom and a distinct political identity, separate from the leftwingers and the workers and peasants with whom they were thrown together in the ASU. Leftist intellectuals wanted a 'National Front' in which the left would be permitted an autonomous existence. Some argued for the maintenance of the ASU as it then existed, notably 'Nasirites,' several peasant and trade union delegates wary of any change in a system which, in principle, guaranteed them 50% representation, and some ASU officials led by the then Secretary General, Rifa'at Mahgub. High officialdom opposed a multi-party system, fearing the challenge to authority and the fragmentation of the regime's base which might ensue from it, but they were prepared to support greater diversity of views within the ASU. Some army officers in alliance with Mahgub viewed the formation of parties as a project to foster civilian political forces at the expense of military influence in the regime, and had to be warned by Sadat that the military no longer had a role in politics. Sadat himself initially rejected a multi-party system as harmful to national unity and reaffirmed the need for the 'alliance of popular working forces' in which all groups were bound by a common ideological and organizational framework. Eventually, however, he was brought to support a compromise in which separate tendencies or 'platforms' (*manāber*) would be allowed to crystallize within the framework of the ASU. As many as 40 different platforms were proposed, but, unwilling to accept such fragmentation, the regime approved only three *manāber*: a liberal 'right' one, a center one – in effect the pro-government faction – and a 'left' one. These three platforms were then permitted to compete in the 1976 parliamentary elections, the results of which were an overwhelming victory for the government center faction: the center won 280 seats, the right 12, the left 4 and independents 48. The success of the government platform evidently convinced Sadat that the experiment could be safely carried further, and the *manāber* transformed into full-fledged independent parties (Dessouki 1978: 14–17, Marei 1978b: 38–41; Sa'id 1977). Under this arrangement the parties of the right and left would act as safety valves satisfying the participatory demands of elements on these two fringes of the regime constituency and might even coopt those who could not have been satisfied by a single centrist party into the system. Their relegation to separate parties might make it easier for the government to share power with its own supporters in the center party. The party experiment was, however, to be carefully controlled. The constitutional prerogatives of the President would not be affected; the President, representing the whole people and above the parties, would continue to set the broad lines of policy, within which the parties would offer 'constructive alternatives.' Finally, Sadat was persuaded to approve in principle the right of new parties to form under carefully controlled conditions: they had to secure the support of 20 deputies in parliament, a provision meant to limit if not exclude their actual emergence; they could not be formed on a class, religious or regional basis disruptive of national unity; they could not deviate from the basic principles of the regime or 'threaten social peace' and they had to be approved by the government (*al-Ahram* 21 June 1977). In practice, the regime denied requests from Nasirites and Islamic fundamentalists to form their own parties, evidently fearful that they might mobilize wide support, but in 1978 it did permit a fourth party, the New Wafd, to form. As it turned out, however, neither the New Wafd nor the leftwing party, the NPUP, were willing to play the game as Sadat envisioned it, and in May of 1978 the Wafd was forced to disband and the NPUP banned from open political activity. In place of the NPUP Sadat encouraged the formation of a new left of center party, the Socialist Labor Party. In order to give it greater authority, he took over personal leadership of the government party, now named the National Democratic Party. At the end of the Sadat era, therefore, three parties made up the established party system, the government party and two 'loyal opposition' parties of the right and left.

The government party

The pro-government party was born from the efforts of Mahmud Abu Wafia to put together a liberal but pro-Sadat political coalition in parliament. Because the 1976 parliamentary elections held at the time this was happening were relatively free, this coalition tended to incorporate notables enjoying local bases of support. Simultaneously, however, the ASU was being disbanded and, with the exception of the slivers which split off to form the left and right parties, its remnants merged with Abu Wafia's deputies to form the center *manbar* soon named the Arab Socialist Party of Egypt (or Misr Party); in the process several top government leaders were imposed from above on the party, including Prime Minister Mamduh Salim, who was named its president. Then in 1978 when Sadat decided to head the government party himself, the Arab Socialist Party of Egypt (ASPE) was transformed into the National Democratic Party. Sadat brought in new leaders to help him run the 'new' party, notably Fikri Makram

Ubayd and Mansur Hassan. In 1980 Vice President Mubarak took over the running of the party.

In social composition, the party leadership, though a descendant of the ASU, was significantly altered. In place of the military-politicians and leftist intellectuals who had dominated it in the sixties, the leadership was now made up roughly equally of technocrats, professionals and military or police elements. Some had made their careers chiefly in government, some were chiefly private sector notables and some combined public careers with private sector assets. The party sub-elite, as with the ASU, was largely drawn from three overlapping groups: officialdom, professionals and the rural notability. The typical government party stalwart came from a middle-sized landowning family, was educated as a professional, made a career partly in the bureaucracy or in farming and was elected to parliament. The party leadership thus incorporated wide segments of the bourgeoisie which made up the regime's support base.

The successor parties of the ASU were less ideologically disparate than the parent organization, having rid themselves of the leftwing elements which had been forced to coexist with the center and right in a single organization during the sixties. The ideological center of gravity had moved, by the end of the Sadat period, firmly to the center–right. Nevertheless, the official program was still vague enough to accommodate a fairly heterogeneous spectrum of political attitudes and too vague to determine government policy except in the most general way. Perhaps for this reason the program of the party often appeared divorced from the policy of the government it supported and the actual attitudes of its membership.

In the field of foreign policy, the government party officially stood for priority for the Arab cause, Palestinian rights and non-alignment. Yet the party supported a government, which, in practice, subordinated the Arab and Palestinian causes to Egypt's immediate particular interests and swung her squarely into a Western anti-Soviet alliance. Party members justified this gap between declared intent and actual policy by the plea of necessity. Egypt could neither afford nor hope to escape disaster in another war and had no choice but to rely on the American alliance to extract itself from the Israeli grip. Some party members were uneasy over Egypt's growing isolation from the Arab world. But most were 'Egypt-firsters'.

In the socio-economic field the official program stood for the preservation of the public sector and the 'socialist achievements' of the Nasir regime. Yet it also stood for *Infitah* and a widened role for the private sector. In fact there was considerable disparity of views in the party over economic policy and not a little dissatisfaction with the way government had translated the program into policy. There was considerable criticism of the way *Infitah* was implemented, for example, complaints that it had stimulated consumption and speculation, and allowed well-placed groups, including high officials, to enrich themselves at the expense of the state and the majority. There was discontent over the threat to national industry. But there were also those who wanted more *Infitah* free of government red tape or restrictions. Some elements wanted to reverse Nasir's populist measures while others wanted to keep them. Differences sometimes took factional form. Mahmud Abu Wafia was identified for a time with a 'progressive' trend which fought landlord efforts to raise rent for tenants, while the party's Fayyum branch was on a *laissez-faire* tack challenging government control over cotton marketing. Significantly, Abu Wafia later joined the left–center Labor Party while the Fayyum deputies defected to the right–liberal Wafd Party.

Attitudes toward Nasir, perhaps the best indicator of real ideological attitudes, varied dramatically. Many governmental partisans were openly hostile to Nasir, supporting the regime precisely to the extent it undid his work. They saw Nasir's rule as an ideological dictatorship, blamed him for putting persons in power on the basis of connections rather than competence and criticized him for ruining private business and closing Egypt to the West. But others were far more generous toward him, arguing that he had taken the first big steps in the modernization of Egypt.

The attitudinal heterogeneity in the party reflected the many potential conflicts of interest which divided it: 'Egypt-firsters' vs those with a stake in the Arab world, those who made their careers under Nasir vs those who suffered under his rule, those with a stake in the public sector vs those in private business who wanted it dismantled, those concerned with national industry vs those with a stake in free trade and foreign investment. Many of these elements did share the perception of a threat from the left. But they were brought together less by ideology than by personal connections, pragmatic concerns for patronage and career, and a willingness to follow President Sadat. Just as many of them were prepared to follow Nasir left in the sixties, so in the seventies they followed Sadat right; in a country where power and opportunity is so concentrated in the hands of the ruler and state, such adaptability is perhaps not surprising.[1]

The structure and functioning of the government party continued in the seventies to manifest its descent from the ASU, but several important alterations in both were apparent. The party organization, forged, as before, from the top down, was headed by a politburo presided over by a chairman or president, one or more secretary generals and their various deputies; there was also a party parliamentary caucus, an addition from the Nasir days made necessary by the appearance of opposition parties in parliament. From the capital, the organization reached downward to provincial and district level committees headed by secretaries, but, in contrast to the ASU, the party appeared to lack formal presence at the village level (Egyptian Arab Socialist Organization 1977; *al-Ahram*, 24 Sept. 1978). Under Nasir, the ASU functioned chiefly as an 'auxiliary' of the government, as one Egyptian leader put it, as a kind of Ministry of Political Propaganda. Under Sadat, the ruling party continued to play a far less central role than in other political systems. But it did perform some indispensable functions for the regime and these were somewhat different from those under Nasir.

Under Nasir, the party never functioned as a leadership recruitment channel, and this remained largely so under Sadat. Presidential cooptation from the civil and military bureaucracies and academia remained the dominant recruitment channels. Moreover, movement upward inside the party itself depended more on cooptation from above than cultivation of constituencies below. In principle, party leaders were elected, but elections were infrequent; there was a round in 1971 and again in 1980. Moreover, nominations, appointments and purges from above played a greater role in establishing party leadership. The President was free to remove party leaders at will and often did so; top party leaders were invariably nominated or at least approved by him, and not infrequently coopted from outside the party structure (as in the appointment of Fikri Makram Ubayd as NDP Secretary General) or appointed on the basis of high government office. However, when parliamentary elections were left free (as in 1976) the party sub-elite in parliament did at least partly emerge from local support bases. Moreover, recruitment data (see chapter 4, table 5) suggest that party service had become more important in cooptation to ministerial roles from government and academia, a critical access channel into the elite for those in the private sector, and as an apprenticeship for recruitment to the Prime Ministership. These were signs that the party might have been developing into a recruitment mechanism at the end of the Sadat era.

The party was also intended to function as an elite–mass linkage for the mobilization and control of a support base. Formally, the party did link a wide array of social forces to the regime, but, in practice, this linkage was relatively brittle and of limited effectiveness. The party embraced large numbers of government employees but many were purely nominal members who paid their dues to protect their jobs. The NDP set up a youth organization and a religious branch meant to recruit religious-minded youth, but the NDP youth had difficulty, even with the help of university administrations, in holding its own against Islamic youth groups. The party successfully ran pro-government candidates in several professional syndicate elections, thus helping to keep large segments of the professional middle class in the government fold, but it failed to keep the journalists and lawyers in line and generally its control was far looser and less effective than in the sixties. Nor was the party very successful in protecting the government's bourgeois constituency from the New Wafd Party. The party coopted the top leaders of the trade union movement – such as Abd al-Latif Bultiya who was a member of the NDP politburo in the late seventies – and was able to prevent the victory of anti-regime candidates in elections at the top of the union hierarchy, but opposition candidates sometimes won at lower levels. The party was able on occasion to mobilize segments of the working class on Sadat's side but generally could not neutralize the special appeal of leftist ideology to workers. In the countryside, the local notability – landlords, *umad* and rich peasants – often belonged to the government party and, to the extent they represented the natural leadership of the village, helped link the peasant masses to the regime. In contrast to Nasir's ASU, however, Sadat's party lacked village committees and leadership units, evidently content to rely on the personal ties of the notability to the peasants; this was seemingly a contraction in the political penetration of the countryside from the sixties. As its own leaders admitted, the party was, in its support-mobilization efforts, severely handicapped by its lack of ideological solidarity, by the very little headway it made in developing a corps of voluntary activists and by a ramshackle organizational structure impotent to overcome the gap between center and base typical of the ASU. Even by comparison to the limited mobilizational efforts of Nasir's ASU, the government party under Sadat manifested a disinterest in mass mobilization if not an actual preference for de-mobilization. If the party was meant to fill the ideological vacuum resulting from the decline of Nasirism, it failed. But as an organizational bond between the top regime elite and the sub-elites which represented its core support and its informal linkage to wider social forces, the party served an important purpose.

The elimination of the military dominance characteristic of Nasir's ASU and the relegation of leftwing dissidents to a separate party should, in principle, have made it easier to develop the government party under Sadat into a mechanism of interest aggregation for the regime's constituency. This, however, did not happen to any significant degree. The party program did apparently emerge from intra-party consultations, but it had little direct role in shaping government policy. Many of the most crucial decisions – from the trip to Jerusalem to the decision to cut the subsidies – were taken without any intra-party consultation, and the party did not seem to play a significant role as an arena for the debate of lesser issues or policies. The only known instance of an overt challenge by the party to the government, the clash between the Sidqi government and the ASU under Marei in 1972, was a result of Sadat's appointment of a powerful close confidant to the head of the party, rather than a symptom of an emerging party role in holding the government accountable. In the late seventies, the government, responding to complaints from party members that they were ignored, promised that government legislation would henceforth scrupulously be discussed in the party parliamentary caucus. Moreover, Sadat did subsequently seem to take pains to turn the NDP politburo into a consultative body which overlapped with – and perhaps competed with – the cabinet. But even if these tendencies were developed and institutionalized, there still appeared to be no mechanisms for including the bases of the party in the aggregative process. On the other hand, as mechanisms of individual interest articulation, party channels were probably of some utility to those with access to them. In particular, local notables seemed to find party membership worthwhile in enhancing their access to local officials and in enforcing their prestige and authority in the community.[2]

In conclusion, the government party helped in a rather desultory fashion to hold the regime's coalition together. It may have been developing into an arena for ambitious personalities to accumulate the political credentials needed to move up in the regime. It may have functioned in a limited sense as a patronage machine for the regime's constituency. But it seemed no less subordinate to the government or ineffectual in channeling broad political participation than Nasir's ASU and it was palpably more feeble as a mechanism of control and mobilization. Egypt was not a no-party state, but its ruling party remained a very weak one.

Hizb al-Ahrar: the right–liberal loyal opposition

The Ahrar (Liberal) Party emerged from a rightwing sliver of the old ASU. The regime's expectation was that it would function as a loyal opposition capable of coopting into the system both the secular liberal right (e.g. ex-Wafdists and other *ancien régime* forces) and the religious right (the Ikhwan and its off-shoots). Sadat asked several of his close supporters to join it as a way of ensuring its loyalty and giving it the official stamp of approval.

In spite of its mission to appeal to elements to the right of the government establishment, there was in its social composition little to distinguish the Ahrar from the government party. Its president, Mustafa Kamil Murad was a former army officer and chairman of a public sector company. Its Secretary General, Abd al-Fattah Shurbagi, was a classic survivor of the Nasir era. A landowner and originally a Wafdist, he adapted to the Nasir regime, joining both the National Union and the ASU because, as he put it himself, 'everyone rode the wave.' In the sixties, Ali Sabri's faction pushed him out of the party, but after Sadat's 'Corrective Revolution' he returned. A number of other representatives of the landowning, professional or merchant classes who had been pushed out of politics in the fifties also appeared in the party leadership, but these were also common enough in the government party.

In keeping with its mission to appeal to the whole rightwing of the political spectrum regardless of the secular–religious divide, the party presented itself as both the party of capital and the party of God; its slogan was 'God, Freedom, Country'. It was a vigorous advocate of economic *laissez-faire* and a dominant role for private capital as the motor of development. It denounced Nasir's socialism as a socialism of poverty and sequestration. Except for public utilities and a few strategic industries, the party wanted the public sector to be sold to private capital or transformed into joint ventures. The party was also a strong supporter of *Infitah* and of international investment. 'Capital is international,' asserted Mustafa Kamil Murad, 'there is no longer room for small business; we need the multi-nationals and thus we must have low taxation and high profits.' The party called for an end to subsidies and to cooperative marketing of crops. In the political field it also stood for liberalization: it advocated competitive election of the President and of governors, a stronger legislature, judicial independence, an end to Presidential appointment of newspaper editors, and – except for communists and other advocates of class strife – full freedom of political activity. In contrast to the government party, it argued that political democracy could not take root until the government divested itself of its control over the economy. In its effort to appeal to the religious right, the party advocated the serious implementation of the religious law (*sharia'*), including the prohibition of alcohol and of usury; but evidently mindful of the secular caste of much of the bourgeoisie, it distinguished its position from the 'rigidity' of the Ikhwan. Finally, the Ahrar was an even more vigorous supporter of Sadat's pro-Western foreign policy and of his peace initiatives than the government party itself; indicative of this was the fact that Murad accompanied Sadat on his trip to Jerusalem while his own foreign minister declined. (Hizb al-Ahrar 1977).

While the Ahrar started out with promise, winning 12 parliamentary seats in 1976 and later picking up nine more adherents, it conspicuously failed to become a major party of the right. As a party headed by an army officer loyal above all to Sadat, it had little appeal to the old liberal bourgeoisie, and only in the absence of an independent liberal party were some prepared to work through it; in 1978, however, when the New Wafd Party was formed, 12 Ahrar deputies and many more partisans defected to it. The Ahrar was even less successful in attracting the religious right which was unimpressed by its leadership, its essential liberalism and, after 1977, its embrace of the Israeli connection. The ideological combination of religiosity and property is a familiar stamp of conservatism elsewhere, but in Egypt, where the bourgeoisie is traditionally liberal and the religious right illiberal, the attempt to combine them was not, apparently, viable. The Ahrar's potential to speak for the right was also undercut by Sadat's own continuous movement to the right, a development which made the government party an ever more promising vehicle of rightwing interests; thus when Sadat formed the NDP all but two Ahrar deputies bolted to join his party. It is clear that many of the party's own leaders accorded it little loyalty.

For a small group of its leaders, however, the Ahrar apparently had some *raison d'être*. In the 1979 elections, the party elected only three deputies and its leader was defeated (*al-Ahrar* 1 July 1979); yet the rump of the party declined Sadat's suggestion that they join the NDP. Less contaminated by the statist interests and the need to keep a mass constituency which diluted the economic liberalism of the government party, the Ahrar could be a vigorous advocate of *laissez-faire*; yet, its unquestionable loyalty to the President allowed it to operate without fear of the repression that the Wafd's confrontation policies had brought down on itself. Thus, the Ahrar could think of itself as the 'vanguard of liberalism' in Egypt; and could plausibly argue that, in spite of its small size, its views enjoyed a much wider response among the public and inside the government itself. In fact, the Ahrar was able to play a modest role as a liberal advocate. Among the small victories for property it claims to have had a hand in was the defeat of a government proposal to limit the number of flats an owner could sell (and thus avoid rent control), the extension of the tax exemptions granted foreign capital to Egyptian private capital and the broadening of incentives to foreign investors in 1977. Generally, the Ahrar was careful not to stray from the role of loyal opposition, but occasionally it took liberal political stands independent of the government; thus, it opposed the dismissal of Shaikh Ashur Nasr from parliament for his criticism of Sadat, and backed Nemat Fouad's exposure of the Pyramid Plateau project. Always careful to avoid criticizing the President himself, it occasionally attacked the government's alleged unwillingness to tolerate a constructive opposition. The chief function of the Ahrar in the political system seemed to be that of a pressure group for political liberalization and economic interests especially opposed to statism and with links to international capital.[3]

The Socialist Labor Party: the center–left loyal opposition

Following his 1978 crackdown on the Progressives, Sadat made another attempt to create a constructive opposition to the left of the government party. To head it, he called on Ibrahim Shukri, an ex-leader of the old nationalist party, Misr al-Fatat, and an early advocate of land reform, who Sadat respected and trusted and who had served the regime as Land Reclamation Minister. In addition to Shukri and his old Misr al-Fatat colleagues, Sadat's brother-in-law, Mahmud Abu Wafia, joined the party along with a contingent of followers from his Misr Party days and was made the number-two man in the party. Sadat clearly hoped that the new party would both draw off the constituency of the NPUP and coopt liberal and social democratic elements unattracted to an increasingly rightist government party, and that his personal ties to its top leaders and the presence of a faction in it from the old government party would keep it loyal to the regime (*al-Ahram* 24 Nov. 1978).

In social composition there was little to distinguish the SLP from the ruling party. Its two leaders were both scions of big landed families. It was, of course, devoid of the many top government leaders prominent in the NDP. But its largely middle- and upper-middle-class membership, made up of professionals, state employees, and even a contingent of rural notables, was little different from the NDP's. Politically, its leadership was, especially at the outset, quite as heterogeneous as the government party. Its Misr al-Fatat core had a long tradition of radical populist nationalism, not at all dissimilar to Nasirism, although these sentiments had undoubtedly mellowed over the years. Until he left the party, Mahmud Abu Wafia headed a group of '100 *feddan* landowners' who, though perhaps centrist by ruling party standards, represented in the SLP a kind of conservative social anchor. On the other hand, as Sadat moved right, many of his disenchanted former centrist supporters, though unprepared to join the radical opposition, seemed to find in the Labor Party an ideological home; Layla Takla, for example, had been a prominent member of the Misr Party's foreign affairs committee in parliament, but finally broke with Sadat over the separate peace with Israel. Yet another familiar face of a totally different political coloration which surfaced in the SLP was Sayyid Gallal, a wealthy merchant and Islamic street boss from Cairo's *baladi* quarters, in disgrace under Nasir for his opposition to women's liberation, but rehabilitated under Sadat. In a relatively short time, thus, the party, increasingly a magnet for centrist and establishment elements disenchanted with various government policies, built itself a numerically respectable support base. In the 1979 elections it won 29 seats in parliament, by 1980 claimed 180,000 members, and through the sale of 60,000 copies of its weekly organ *al-Sha'b*, reached a significant segment of the 'attentive public.'

Ideologically, there were, in principle, no major differences between the NDP and the SLP. Both claimed to be centrist parties rejecting both the Marxist left and the extreme right, that is, unrestrained capitalism or Islamic fanaticism. Both accepted the legitimacy of the socio-political order, *Infitah*, and a 'just' peace with Israel. Their differences, according to Abu Wafia, were mainly over methods of implementation. In practice, however, the two parties were further apart: Sadat's actual policies were to the right of his party's official line, while despite a smokescreen of official conformity, the beliefs of many SLP leaders were to the left of their official program. In the foreign policy field, the party officially accepted the Camp David inspired peace treaty and even criticized the Arabs for attacking it without offering a viable alternative. But the party insisted that Egypt must ensure that Israel withdraw from all occupied territories and not allow the treaty to turn into a separate peace at the expense of Egypt's Arab links and identity. After a period of waffling it came out against the government's moves toward the normalization of relations with Israel in the absence of an overall settlement. As a symbol of protest it printed full page Palestinian flags in its newspaper and urged its readers to display them. It warned against Israeli attempts to penetrate Egypt culturally and economically, urged Sadat to suspend relations when the autonomy talks broke down, called for a boycott of Israeli visitors and products, and launched a campaign against Sadat's idea of channeling Nile water to the Negav. The SLP also criticized

Sadat's very close American alignment and his increasing identification of Egypt with the Middle East's most rightwing regimes; it called Egypt's refuge to the Shah a provocation to the Iranian people and complained about his delivery of arms to Morocco. The party officially supported *Infitah* and the mixed economy emerging from it, but was critical of its implementation. For a while the party's actual views were confused by the stands of Abu Wafia who often appeared 'more royalist than the King,' for example, when several NDP deputies criticized a government proposal to give certain foreign investors a 50-year tax exemption as excessive, he defended the proposal, declaring 'if we're not serious about *Infitah*, let's cancel it.' But, especially after Abu Wafia resigned, the SLP began to differentiate its stands from government policy. It complained that the government's failure to properly plan *Infitah* had made it an instrument of foreign penetration threatening local industry. It called for restrictions on consumer imports, less dependence on foreign capital and more stress on the role of the public sector. It also advocated a more populist policy package, including tighter price controls, the maintenance of subsidies, more welfare spending and more progressive taxation. In parliament, Shukri waged a campaign against the regime's housing policies, attacking the suggestion to eliminate rent controls and demanding that subsidized building materials be limited to use in low-cost housing. Finally, the party urged a further liberalization of the political system, for example, freer formation of parties, the end to government controls over the press, and a limited-term Presidency filled by competitive elections. It urged Sadat to withdraw from leadership of the government party and to stand above politics, allowing a government to be formed from a parliamentary majority and, in actual practice, be responsible to it (*al-Ahram* 10 Sept. 1978; *al-Gumhuriyya*, 22 Jan. 1979; MENA, 30 Jan., 2 Apr. 1979; *al-Sha'b*, 4 Dec. 1979; 8, 15 Jan., 5 Feb., 18 Mar. 1980).

In principle, the Labor Party leadership accepted its role as a loyal 'constructive opposition;' in Layla Takla's words, the Laborites wanted to 'correct the regime, not tear it down.' In practice, its differences with the government steadily widened and it was soon treading close to the arbitrary and constantly shifting line demarcating constructive from destructive criticism. Before long, party leader Shukri was admitting that he and the President had had a 'completely different image' of how the SLP experiment would develop (*New York Times* 12 Mar. 1980). The SLP had expected that its views would be taken into account in decision-making. When this failed to happen, it increasingly tried to mobilize public opinion on its side and against the policies it objected to. The party tried to distinguish between opposition to government policy and to the President, but because the President was the actual author of many of these policies and head of the government party, it was increasingly difficult to spare him. Before long, the party began to 'expose' various instances of corruption and abuse of power in the very highest places: it subtly linked Sayyid Marei to a scheme by foreign adventurers to exploit the public sector and accused Prime Minister Khalil of accepting commissions on a massive telecommunications contract (*al-Sha'b* 6 Nov. 1979). Mahmud Abu Wafia resigned from the party over this issue, charging the Misr al-Fatat faction with adopting a 'destructive' attitude toward the regime, trying to turn the party into a front for 'alien' ideas, and isolating him from party councils. Shukri accepted his resignation, imply-ing that he put his family link to the President above party loyalty (*al-Ahram*, 21 Dec. 1979). After a rebuke from Sadat, the party dropped the commission issue and accepted a government statement denying any wrongdoing. But, in its opposition to relations with Israel, it encroached on the foreign policy domain Sadat considered a Presidential prerogative, and in its opposition to the Law of *Aib*, it challenged a personal Presidential initiative. Evidently disillusioned by the party's growing antagonism, Sadat did not spare the SLP in his 1981 crackdown, arresting some of its members and closing its organ *al-Sha'b*. In short, the SLP seemed rapidly to develop into a pressure group just to the left of the government party expressing the growing disenchantment of centrist and even mainstream establishment elements with many of Sadat's policies. Unlike the NPUP it could not easily be dismissed as a fringe group.

The role of the loyal opposition parties

The effort to create a loyal opposition in Egypt ran up against certain apparently durable obstacles. To the extent the parties remained more loyal than an opposition, they could mobilize no significant constituency, since those satisfied with the regime had a natural home in the government party, especially as long as the opposition had no realistic chance of gaining power. To the extent the parties sought to mobilize a constituency among the disaffected, they had to stress their opposition to the regime and thereby risk the wrath of an elite whose tolerance for this was very limited; moreover mobilization of an opposition constituency was discouraged by the widespread belief that no opposition party would ever be allowed to translate popular support into power. Thus, opposition parties seemed relegated to the status of small 'parties of pressure' trying to sway but never able to displace the ruling 'dominant' party. In this 'dominant party system' both opposition parties played a role in helping to define the terms of political debate and in raising the big issues of public policy. But influencing this policy was something else. In this effort, they could rely on good connections with the government or on the mobilization of public support. The Ahrar Party chose the first course and appeared to win some liberal concessions from the regime, although this was only because the government was already, in principle, committed to liberalization. The SLP chose the second course. It may have played some role in checking the government's rightwing drive and in inducing its populist backpeddling at the turn of the decade; but as Sadat's 1981 crackdown showed, the government could always opt for repression instead of concession.

Parliamentary elections

Under Sadat, the electoral system underwent, at least by comparison to the sixties, a limited liberalization. This alteration, however, never authentically transformed the system, and electoral outcomes continued to be determined by the same two basic, sometimes countervailing factors operative under Nasir, namely, government intervention and personal resources of candidates. Government intervention could take the form of the overt screening of candidates often practiced under Nasir, but under Sadat it usually took more subtle forms such as the government monopolization of the media, intimidation of opposition candidates, the mobilization of local *umad* on the government's side, and the stuffing of ballot boxes. Most subtle of all was the government's reliance on the tendency of many voters, out of hope for advantage or deference to authority, to support candidates known to have government approval and avoid those in disfavor. To the extent that government intervention was minimized, outcomes were shaped according to the resources of candidates. The chief such resource was the ability to dispense economic rewards and punishments. This could take the form of personal wealth needed by a candidate to distribute favors, such as chickens, at election time, or to do something for his constituency such as renovate the local mosque; while by law candidates could spend no more than £E50 on their campaigns, in fact, an expenditure of £E10,000 was needed in many districts to win election. It could also take the form of the government connections needed to bring sanitary water, roads or electricity to the district, get public jobs for clients or intervene on behalf of constituents seeking services or redress from the bureaucracy. While land reform and urbanization had sharply cut into the ability of landlords to deliver the votes of hundreds of peasant dependents typical of the *ancien régime*, both landlords and employers could still often count on the votes of economic dependents. Another basic personal resource was family and local connections. Electioneering usually meant forging intricate patterns of family alliance, and some elections were chiefly battles between rival clans. Alliances with *umad* or their urban equivalents remained important for, although the hold of *umad* over peasants was greatly reduced under Nasir, sufficient numbers of people continued to respect or want to stay on the right side of such notables to allow them to act as vote-brokers. Personal prestige was also important: to be a professional, to come from a family with a good name, or to enjoy national level stature all helped candidates win acceptance as a local 'favorite son.' In some places, especially in upper Egypt, the use of armed gangs of 'toughs' to impress or intimidate voters remained a factor. What counted least, if at all, in elections were issues and ideology; this was because, except for the 1976 election, candidates were not permitted to run on an overtly programmatic basis and because, even to the limited extent that they were, most voters either lacked the political consciousness to respond or were unconvinced of the efficacy of issue voting in an authoritarian regime. Middle- and working-class voters when given the chance sometimes voted on an issue basis; but the great urban and rural masses rarely did. In sum, the electoral process in Egypt was essentially run on a controlled patron–client basis; the mass of voters lacking political or economic resources elected 'notables' who, because they possessed resources and government connections could promise to protect them or do them favors. In the rural areas the notable was normally a professional living in Cairo but with land and family connections in the village; in the city he might be a prominent professional or government official, or, notably in the '*baladi* quarters,' a wealthy merchant speaking the language of conservative Islam.

There were, however, some significant variations in the electoral process governed largely by the extent and form of government intervention which the evolution of the regime's political strategy dictated. In the 1969 elections which produced the first parliament inherited by Sadat, government controls were relatively strong. But there was some competition: two candidates were officially endorsed in each contest and independents were permitted to run, although only 7% of victorious candidates were independents. Sadat may have played a major role in screening official candidates, with the result that in the succession struggle his leftist rivals could not count on the support in parliament they enjoyed in the ASU (Binder 1978: 368).

The 1972 elections were, in contrast, left relatively open: no official candidates were endorsed and hundreds of conservatives deprived of their political rights under Nasir were permitted to compete. The election seems to have faithfully reflected the local social structure, producing the conservative parliament which clashed with the Sidqi government and urged Sadat along the road of de-Nasirization, *Infitah*, and the break with the USSR.

The 1976 elections represented a further step along the road to a more competitive and open electoral process. Not only were they relatively free of government intervention but three proto-parties and a score of independents were permitted to contest them on an issue basis and the regime largely refrained from taking sides between multiple candidates running on the pro-government label. To be sure, regime favoritism toward the government party was operative: it kept a near monopoly of the mass media, and sporadic police intervention and the mobilization of *umad* on the government side took place. Moreover, while the government party simply inherited the ASU's local network, the opposition parties, just formed, had little chance to organize or proselytize voters. Most voters were therefore little conscious of being offered alternative programs and the habitual politics of patronage and deference to the government-endorsed candidates biased the contest in favor of the government party. It won an overwhelming majority of 280 out of 350 seats. Nevertheless, in some urban working class districts leftwing candidates were able to turn the election into an issue contest in which class consciousness played a decisive role. The four NPUP deputies and many of the 48 independents elected made the 1976 parliament the most independent and issue-minded since 1952.

The 1979 elections, governed by Sadat's determination to remove 'those who exploited democracy' from their seats, represented a retreat from the liberalization of the electoral process. In a move widely seen as a purge intended to produce a more disciplined ruling party caucus, the NDP leadership carefully screened its candidates, discarding many of the deputies who had won on the government's ticket in 1976 in favor of a flock of some 200 newcomers. Opposition party candidates and anti-government independents ran up against a campaign of government containment and harassment. They were denied the right to hold public rallies or raise the basic issues, notably the peace treaty. A new opposition party, the SLP, was licensed in time for the elections but it had yet to really differentiate its program from the NDP. The Minister of the Interior, a ranking ruling party member who presided over the elections, made sure his subordinates – from governors to *umad* – understood that the government did not wish to see those who violated social peace or corrupted political life returned. Thus, for example, in Mehalla al-Kubra, a factory district, the streets were flooded with police and workers threatened with dismissal if they voted left. In Shubra the popular Marxist deputy, Ahmad Taha, was arrested before the election as a Soviet spy. In many districts NDP toughs and police prevented all but NDP supporters from going to the polls. Kemal ad-Din Hussein, for example, withdrew his poll-watchers in protest against the climate of intimidation they encountered. In some areas, ballot boxes were stuffed (*al-Ahram* 10, 11, 13, 18 June 1979). Even the loyal opposition complained of widespread irregularities. The turnout in the election was low, evidently indicative of these government pressures and voter recognition that it was not intended to be competitive. Finally, in a classic bit of patronage politics, Sadat announced a ten-day bonus for government employees and pensioners on the eve of the election. The result was that almost every prominent critic, including many believed to have strong support in their constituencies, lost their seats.[4] The lone major opposition candidate who survived, Mumtaz Nasser, apparently did so because he possessed a private army able to counter government forces. Compared to that of 1976, the 1979 parliament proved much less troublesome to the regime.

Thus, in spite of limited liberalization, the electoral process had not developed into a mechanism either of elite accountability or for the registration of policy preferences by citizens. When government intervened, as it would not refrain from doing if it faced a serious challenge, this possibility was completely defeated. When government intervention was restrained and the election relatively competitive, elections may have given client–constituents some leverage over patron–candidates. But even to the extent this mechanism was operative, it had high costs and limited benefits. Given the scarcity of resources needed to compete in elections, it tended to produce an unrepresentative parliament dominated by the upper classes.[5] Secondly, such an electoral process encouraged a politics of particularism while discouraging consciousness of issues and their consequences for broad social forces. Rashad Rushdi writing in *al-Ahram*, observed that the practice of candidates running on the basis of promised services to their local constituencies reduced the importance of party programs and noted that these services often turned out to be favoritism for a privileged few. Ahmad Bahgat wrote that voting for the candidate with the best contacts in high places merely produced deputies preoccupied with rendering petty services for favorites and serving personal ends, rather than concerning themselves with the public interest (*al-Ahram*, 6, 23 May 1979). The result was likely to be a compliant parliament engrossed in patronage concerns rather than issue politics. The imperfect extent to which such elections were reliable barometers of public sentiment was suggested by the fact that scarcely had the government won the elections of 1976, when major public disturbances broke out against it.

Parliament, government and society

Parliament was formally intended to function as a representative link between government and society. In fact, the election of deputies was the outcome of an encounter of sorts between societal forces and government efforts to manipulate them. Under Sadat, parliament did become more effective as a channel of access to government. But in practice it represented only a part of society, chiefly the bourgeois social base of the regime; and it remained subordinate to the government and lacked the power to hold it accountable.

Constitutional practice put parliament at a great disadvantage in relation to the executive. The President was above parliamentary authority. The cabinet was, in principle, responsible to and removable by a majority in parliament; but, in practice, governments were appointed by the President, without any concern for whether ministers enjoyed parliamentary support and they were changed exclusively at his will and never following a vote of no-confidence. The executive could also legislate independent of parliament by decree when it was not in session or through plebiscites which invariably were given overwhelming public approval. Sadat in fact so bypassed parliament on several occasions when he anticipated resistance to measures he wanted swiftly enacted. The Law of Personal Status, long stalled in parliament, was issued by Republican Decree; the 1978 repression of the opposition and the Law of *Aib* were first submitted to plebiscites. The cabinet and even individual ministers enjoyed, on the authority of very generally worded laws, what in effect amounted to decree power; the 1976 cut in subsidies and Law 600 of 1979 on the payment of customs fees in dollars, both very controversial measures, were unilateral decrees of the Minister of Economy taken without parliamentary consultation. The budget had to be accepted or rejected *in toto* by parliament unless the government consented to amendments. Defense and foreign policy matters were considered the 'reserved spheres' of the executive. The 1973 war was launched on purely Presidential authority and the defense budget was never debated in parliament. Parliament, in particular the foreign affairs committee, was allowed to discuss and even to pass resolutions on foreign policy, but as the government's dismissal of repeated parliamentary initiatives during the peace negotiations with Israel demonstrated, the executive branch felt free to ignore even a near parliamentary consensus;[6] when the peace treaty was eventually submitted to parliament it was a *fait accompli* which parliament could not reject without rejecting the President himself. Finally, the President possessed the ultimate weapon with which to dispose of a parliamentary challenge: the power of dissolution and, in practice if not theory, the ability to ensure troublemakers were not re-elected.

Under these conditions parliament could not develop a tradition of independence or collective solidarity *vis-á-vis* the executive. The great majority of deputies never viewed challenges to the executive in the name of alternative conceptions of public policy as part of their role. Rarely did the assembly rebel against government infringements on theoretically parliamentary prerogatives. Before 1976, parliament, lacking opposition parties, was not, of course, even organized to check the government; but even thereafter the government party possessed a large deferent majority. This majority could and was prepared to oust parliamentary peers who antagonized the government, and in four cases, those of Kemal ad-Din Hussein, Shaikh Ashur Nasr, the Nasirite Kamal Ahmad and the leftist Abd al-Aziz Hariri, it did so. Unsatisfied even with this, Sadat had parliament form an 'ethics committee' for disciplining deputies who transgressed on his code of political ethics (*al-Ahram* 21 Sept. 1979; MENA 15 Oct. 1979; 29 Apr. 1980). Finally, the government took care to ensure the appointment of trusted men to the speakership and chairmanship of committees where much actual legislative work took place. The combination of a constitutionally dominant executive and habitually deferent deputies translated into a subordinate legislative branch with a very modest capacity to check or hold government accountable.

Parliament nevertheless played an important and growing role in the political system. Even under Nasir, it was not purely a rubber stamp and on occasion became an arena for the clash of elite interests and ideologies. But because Nasir was an activist president, prepared to encroach, in the interests of the revolution or *raison d'etat*, on the societal interests represented in parliament, and little dependent on them for his power, parliament was in a very weak position. Sadat, in contrast, unconcerned to reshape society from above, and much more dependent on the bourgeoisie for support, was prepared to allow parliament to become a more effective vehicle of the interests of his constituency. At least two important changes in the position and operations of parliament took place under Sadat which revitalized it: government controls over it were significantly relaxed, permitting the deputies considerably more freedom of expression, and opposition parties were permitted to crystallize within it. The resulting expansion in the power of parliament was manifested in its increased exercise of at least four distinguishable roles in the political system.

Perhaps the most important function of parliament under Sadat was to serve as a channel through which the interests of the regime's bourgeois constituency could be articulated and conflicts between its various segments, particularly its state and private wings could, to an extent, be reconciled. The committees of parliament became breeding grounds of an endless stream of initiatives or responses to the government meant to advance or protect particular interests. From the education committee sprang the proposal for a private university. From the planning and budget committee came demands that the private sector get a fair share of foreign exchange and banking credit, proposals to sell shares of public sector companies to private investors, opposition to periodic increases in worker salaries on the grounds that they raised consumption and inflation, and calls to restrict the public sector to fields the private sector could not undertake. From the agricultural committee came proposals to change the land tenure law, opposition to taxes on fruit trees and proposals to allow landowners to buy government reclaimed land. From Port Said deputies issued a proposal to exclude foreigners and reserve to local merchants the right to import through the city. From the housing committee came pressure on the antiquities department to divest itself of lands coveted by developers. From the religious affairs committee issued a spate of proposals to advance Islamic orthodoxy: demands to ban the writings of Ibn Arabi, alcohol, anti-Islamic foreign films and belly dancing (*al-Ahram* 27 Feb. 1979, 1 Mar. 1979; Lachine 1978: 14–18).

Not all of these initiatives succeeded, of course, but many did, and two cases on which there is a record of parliamentary proceedings show how far the bourgeoisie succeeded in turning parliament into a vehicle of its interests. One case was that of the proposal introduced by the Sidqi government to tax fruit trees, the lucrative cash crop on which the agrarian bourgeoisie was enriching itself. In direct defiance of the government, an enlarged sitting of the agricultural committee defeated the bill by a vote of 90 to 2. The great majority of the deputies, perceiving the government as statist, socialist and urban-oriented, opposed the bill in principle as an attack on the rural private sector. Many had a personal stake in orchards or spoke for constituents who did. The lone two votes for the bill were cast by a small peasant and an ASU *apparatchek*. After this victory, landowners were able to keep any new tax measure off the agenda till the 1977 food riots, which, spurring the government to attempt a more equitable distribution of the tax burden, caused one to be proposed again. A broad agrarian coalition cutting across party lines emerged in opposition. It was led by NDP deputies from Qalyubiyya, Minufiyya and Sharkiyya where 80% of the fruit gardens were located, and joined by Wafdists and Ahrar deputies; for once, the leftist NPUP voted with the government. Although the rates proposed were lower than those in 1972, the bill could be passed only after direct Presidential intervention and in much diluted form; while the 1972 bill would have raised £E7 million in revenue the one approved raised only half a million (Nizar 1979).

The second case was that of the 1975 session which changed the agrarian relations law raising the rent burden on peasant tenants and reducing their security of tenure. Despite its importance, the bill was pushed through in a mere six hours. But the session was especially significant as an indicator of the climate of opinion prevailing in parliament. Speaker after speaker detailed landlord grievances against peasants: they were rebellious and needed no government protection; they lived in luxury while the landowners went hungry; the peasant who was once oppressed had become the oppressor. One speaker declared that the slogan of the Land Reform, 'The land to he who works it' was communist in inspiration. Without suffering contradiction, the landlords claimed that the peasants profited £E100 per *feddan* per year while the owner received only £E20 in rent, neglecting to mention that the peasant paid out much of his 'profit' in expenses. Only three deputies – all intellectuals – spoke against the bill; if there were any peasants in the assembly which by law had to be 50% peasant and worker in composition, none dared raise their voice in defence of their class. The measure was also passed without a legal quorum. The government did not oppose this measure even though, by raising costs for peasants, it would make it more difficult to get them to cultivate the 'strategic crops' needed by the state without giving them higher prices (*Ruz al-Yusuf* 24 June 1975, 3–7).

A second function performed by parliament under Sadat, if only in a modest way, was governmental oversight. In this capacity it often spoke for a wider constituency than the bourgeoisie. Oversight took the form of criticisms from the floor, interpolation of ministers, and committee investigations and reports. While it is true that, as deputies complained, ministers sometimes failed to appear as scheduled before parliament, the government was far more on the defensive before parliament under Sadat than it ever was under Nasir. And the emergence of opposition parties added a whole new dimension to parliamentary oversight; indicative of this was Prime Minister Mamduh Salim's complaint that the opposition was paralyzing the government with 'hundreds of inter-polations.'

One common form of oversight was parliamentary queries calling attention to shortcomings in the performance of the government bureaucracy or speaking for constituents with problems or grievances. Complaints in parliament over shortages in the supply of certain commodities were frequent occurrences. Deputies attacked the Minister of Housing over cement shortages, the Minister of Industry over the inability of the public sector to meet the demand for refrigerators, the village bank authority over shortfalls in the delivery of fertilizers. The Committee on Public Works accused the Cairo Water Board of violating water standards and called its chairman and the Governor of Cairo to appear before it; though contriving to blame the problem on a lack of funds and improper performance by a private contractor, they promised to improve the situation. Local deputies voiced the objections of Alexandria to the siting of a nuclear power plant in the vicinity of the city though they were rebuffed by the Minister of Power who claimed that 'experts' had agreed on the site. A deputy from Kom Ombo complained to the Minister of Industry of the environmental dangers in discharges from a sugar factory. A group of deputies, speaking on behalf of disadvantaged public sector workers, urged the government to eliminate the large discrepancies in raises and promotions between different categories of employees, and was promised remedial action. The agrarian affairs committee occasionally spoke for the less well-situated in the village as when it recommended small peasants who could not pay their debts to village banks be given easier terms. A deputy speaking for squatters, challenged the right of the Ministry of Awqaf to evict them from land under its management (*al-Ahram*, 13 Dec. 1977, 28 Nov. 1979, 8, 31 Jan. 1980; MENA 29 Dec. 1979, 12 Mar. 1980). All deputies did not, of course, conscientiously represent their constituents; the deputy for Bulak accused by his constituents of ignoring their interests, was content to reply that they were 'always grumbling' (*al-Ahram* 1 Apr. 1980). Nor did the government necessarily respond favorably to such interventions. But such activity seemed to make up a great deal of the activity of those deputies who took their role seriously, and appeared to have some impact on government.

Parliament sometimes went even further and attacked the probity of actions by government. The Sidqi government suffered from a campaign of attacks against irregularities in the arrangements of the SUMED pipeline project. Inquiries into irregularities in public sector companies were periodic occurrences. Parliament held hearings on charges of improprieties by the Khalil government in the award of a massive telecommunications contract. The Amiriya case was investigated in parliament and aired in heated debates in which opposing party leaders Ibrahim Shukri and Mustafa Kamil Murad exchanged insults and charges which 'astonished' the assembly (*al-Ahram* 16 Feb. 1979). The Pyramid Plateau case was perhaps the most significant example of the liberties parliament had begun to take by the late seventies. This project had received the personal approval of the President and had been arranged by his close associate and Minister of Reconstruction, Osman, whose company received the contract; the government was clearly anxious to silence critics of the project. Nevertheless, parliament played a major role in exposing and then forcing the government to back down on it. Independent Mumtaz Nasser first raised the issue. It was proposed to refer the matter to the tourism committee but since a number of those on the committee were themselves implicated, parliament voted to set up a special investigatory committee. In its sessions, deputies took issue with the cavalier way the government had issued decrees approving the project without consulting parliament on the grounds that it was a technical matter within ministerial discretion and despite the fact that the decrees actually violated existing laws; parliament's reaction represented a minor but rare rebellion against executive encroachment on its already constricted prerogatives. But the substantive case against the project – the conflicts of interest, violation of law, and sacrifice of the public interest – were also so damaging that opposition and government deputies joined hands against it; the deputy speaker of parliament, Gamal al-Utaifi, representing the parliamentary consensus, played a major role in bringing the President to cancel the project (*al-Ahram*, 29 Mar. 1978; Fouad 1979; Gami' 1979). If kept within bounds, oversight activity was by no means without utility for the President: it represented an instrument for controlling his bureaucracy and a safety valve for the venting and perhaps redress of grievances which might needlessly arouse public discontent. But, it is clear that Sadat was increasingly irritated by what he considered to be the ever more corrosive character parliamentary activity assumed; the dissolution of the 1976 parliament was his response (Sadat speeches, 10, 14, 18 May 1979).

Periodically, parliament assumed yet another function, that of an arena for the debate of major policy issues. To be sure, parliament has no record of having decided those issues. But on occasions when government was considering a change of policy or when the top elite was divided on a course, parliament was sometimes encouraged to debate alternative courses or to discredit past policies. More rarely, pressures welled up from parliament for alterations in the government's course. At least three separate cases can be identified when parliament became involved in debate of the regime's high policy. In 1972–3 parliament became a base, tolerated if not encouraged by Sadat, for attacks by the conservative private bourgeoisie on the statist Sidqi government. This came as close to an authentic executive–legislative cleavage as the Egyptian political system can admit. The period seemed to be a prelude to Sadat's decision to veer right and, indeed, parliamentary criticism did give Sadat an excuse to dismiss the Sidqi government. After the October War, from 1974 to 1976, again encouraged by Sadat, parliament played a major role in discrediting the record of Nasirism and delineating the lines of regime liberalization. On the one hand, everything from the public sector to the conduct of the 1967 war to the High

Dam was suddenly vulnerable to criticism; on the other, parliamentary pressures helped push the regime along the road of economic liberalization and played a role in defining the shape of the emerging party system. Then after 1976, once opposition parties appeared in parliament, government high policy, from *Infitah* to the treaty with Israel, was increasingly subjected to challenge in the name of alternative courses. This campaign was initially led by the NPUP and the New Wafd; after they were purged the SLP took over their role. Its effectiveness was, of course, strictly limited by the government's overwhelming majority, the frequent press blackouts on coverage of parliamentary proceedings through which the regime attempted to isolate the parliament from the wider arena of public opinion, and the regime's ultimate ability to purge its critics. But the opposition did succeed in seriously embarrassing the government and, by 'throwing doubt on everything,' as Sadat put it, to undermine confidence in the regime's course.

Finally, parliament began to develop into an elite recruitment and preparation pool. This tendency remained limited, but by comparison to the Nasir period when over 18 years only three ministers were picked from parliamentary careers, under Sadat parliament became more of an apprenticeship for cooptation into government and in a few cases – like Mansur Hassan and Fikri Makram Ubayd – a springboard for rapid ascent to the very inner elite core. On the other hand, parliament increasingly also served as a repository for high officials out of office who wished to remain politically active, a symptom of the growing influence associated with a parliamentary seat.

Despite the subordination of the legislature to the executive, parliamentary seats, judging from the number of candidates who sought them, remained desirable. For most who sought them they were seen as a base from which to cultivate strategic connections in the power elite and to build or consolidate roles as brokers and patrons in their constituencies; for a few they were platforms for the articulation of ideological differences with the regime. Sadat was, within limits, content to allow parliament to develop into a vehicle to so satisfy his constituency and placate his opponents.

The political role of the press

There was no major transformation in the political role of the press from the Nasir to Sadat periods. No less than Nasir, Sadat regarded the press as chiefly an instrument for shaping public opinion in the government's interest. The mechanisms of government control over the press changed little. The President continued to appoint trusted editors who were expected to self-censor their product and when they did not, were removed. The Ministry of Information, a press watchdog, was abolished in 1977, supposedly heralding a new era of press freedom, but by 1980 a 'Higher Press Council' charged with enforcing a 'code of ethics' on journalists, had taken its place. Sadat repeatedly rejected suggestions that the government divest itself of control over the press in favor of private ownership on grounds that this would allow special interests to dominate public opinion. The press seemed to be no more effective under Sadat as an instrument for the debate and shaping of public policy. Under Nasir, when identifiable papers of the right, center and left were published, there was probably as much variety of opinion on basic issues. Moreover, there is evidence that Nasir, a voracious reader, was affected by what he read; not only did the editorial page of Haykel's *al-Ahram* seem to carry significant weight with the President, but criticisms in the leftwing press appeared to play a role in his leftward drift. Under Sadat, who did not read much, there is no evidence that the press carried similar influence at the top. Nevertheless, the changing orientation of the regime under Sadat was reflected in two clear alterations in the operations and character of the press.

First, in his effort to foster a press which was compatible with limited liberalization of the political system, Sadat experimented with strategies which departed from the practice under Nasir. The scope of permissible criticism of the government was widened. The penalties for transgression of these limits were also lightened; whereas under Nasir offending journalists were sometimes jailed, under Sadat they simply lost their jobs. As the risks of challenging the limits of journalistic freedom decreased, the willingness of writers to do so increased. Sadat also experimented with an opposition party press. Secondly, however, greater liberalization was accompanied by an attempt to reorient the press toward the political right. Under Nasir, the left had carved out a significant place for itself, notably in *al-Talia'* and *Ruz al-Yusuf* and leftist journalists often wrote in the mainstream press as well. Under Sadat, the scope of opportunity for leftwing journalists was steadily narrowed. Both of these developments, however, unfolded in a zig-zag process symptomatic of the President's effort to create a press that was both 'free' and 'responsible.' Buffeted between the desire to please liberal opinion and the determination to keep press opposition within bounds, Sadat periodically alternated between liberalization and retightening of controls over the press; and in periods of liberalization, leftwing opinion often found ways of making itself heard.

Following his victory over Ali Sabri, Sadat encouraged journalists to expect greater press freedom. But after a period of openness led to rising criticism from the left, he launched a major purge of leftwing journalists. By 1973, most had been pushed out of the mainstream press. After the 1973 war, the government again announced a new era of press freedom and conservative journalists proscribed under Nasir began to reappear. But the fall of the centrist Muhammed Hassanein Haykel at *al-Ahram* for allegedly trying to turn the paper into a 'center of power' showed the regime was unprepared to tolerate a major journalistic voice at variance with its basic policy. The installation of the

Amin brothers, anti-etatist leftovers from the *ancien régime* charged with CIA connections in the sixties, at *al-Ahram* and *al-Akhbar* signaled the new ideological direction the regime wished to give the press. They and other conservative journalists were responsible for the de-Nasirization campaign of the mid-seventies. When the widened latitude for the right led to attacks on the government itself, the Amin brothers, who had a chip on the shoulder toward the whole 1952 revolution, were removed from their editorships. Yet the press continued to take increased latitude in investigative reporting and was responsible for breaking the 'Boeing Scandal' implicating influential ex-Ministers. The 1977 riots touched off a government purge of the last remaining bastions of the left, *al-Talia'* and *Ruz al-Yusuf*. But shortly thereafter, the new left and right opposition parties were allowed to publish independent organs, *al-Ahali* and *al-Ahrar*, respectively. *Al-Ahali*, which, recognizing no limits, exposed scandals in the President's entourage and waged a relentless campaign against *Infitah* and the regime's foreign policy, was soon closed down. *Al-Ahrar*, by contrast, published a series of articles exposing the Pyramid Plateau scandal, but was tolerated. Another lurch to the right accompanied the deterioration of Egypt's relations with the USSR and the Arabs in the second half of the decade. Typical of this period was the appointment of Ibrahim al-Sada, a man who made his career as an anti-Soviet and anti-socialist publicist, to the editorship of *al-Akhbar* (*al-Ahram*, 11 Dec. 1979). Under the direction of Sada and likeminded colleagues, the mainstream press launched waves of anti-Soviet propaganda while filling their pages with the most uncritical pro-Americanism. After the trip to Jerusalem, the Arabs also increasingly became objects of press attack: the rejectionists were mere Soviet agents and the oil Arabs ungrateful and uncivilized; but Begin was a man who 'worked for the good of his country.' By this time, *al-Sha'b*, organ of the SLP had taken the place of *al-Ahali* with left-of-center readers. It took issue with the regime's anti-Arab policy, exposed the flaws of *Infitah* and even accused the incumbent Prime Minister of taking commissions. After the peace treaty, it was joined in its criticism of the regime by the organ of the Ikhwan, *al-Dawa* which rejected the treaty and the growing Western penetration of Egypt. Finally in 1981, both *al-Sha'b* and *al-Dawa* were closed.

Thus Sadat failed to develop a press which was both 'free' and 'responsible.' In the process of trying he did permit the press, if only sporadically, a greater autonomy than it had enjoyed under Nasir. But, essentially, it continued to take its cues from the regime: as Sadat's policies drifted right so did the terms of discourse in the press, from a contest between 'radical' left and 'moderate' views to one between the center and right. And it was this discourse which to a great extent framed the policy alternatives considered by the 'attentive public.' The biggest change in the press under Sadat was not so much in the degree of freedom to write as in *who* enjoyed this freedom.

The judiciary, civil rights and the rule of law

According to Sadat, Egypt passed after the May 'Corrective Revolution' from revolutionary to constitutional legitimacy, from the rule of men to the rule of law. That the courts and the rule of law protected the rights of Egyptians more effectively than under Nasir was one of the indisputable major achievements of Sadat's reign. But if a constitutional state is meant to denote one in which the political elite is effectively bound by the law and every citizen enjoys basic political rights, Egypt's constitutional evolution has just begun.

The judiciary under Sadat achieved a very substantial measure of autonomy from the executive. Judges became a vigorous force defending and expanding the legal rights of citizens against the government. Although he was often annoyed by their rulings in political cases, Sadat, in contrast to Nasir, steered shy of any major purge of independent-minded judges. Toward the end of the decade he did propose to create exceptional courts for political offenses, staffed by political appointees; but it was a measure of the vigor and influence of the judiciary that it forced the regime to concede to trained judges a majority of appointments to these courts (*al-Akhbar*, 20 Mar. 1980).

Non-political personal and property rights, much restricted under Nasir, were effectively restored under Sadat. Restrictions on the right to travel were abolished. Private property rights were again considered invioiable. Indeed, judges leaned over backwards to favor private rights, often at the expense of the state. Striking a blow for the sanctity of private property which could cost the treasury a pretty penny, judges ruled some of the nationalizations of the sixties unconstitutional and their victims entitled to compensation. A 1975 decision dismissed charges against 50 persons for violating foreign exchange laws on the grounds that the illegal operations had subsequently been made legal. And the courts were palpably anxious to protect the legal rights of persons charged with abuse of public property (Waterbury 1976a).

Political rights were far less secure under Sadat but by comparison to the Nasir era they were significantly broadened. Under Nasir, the political police became a feared 'state within a state' practicing torture and running detention camps; any criticism might – often rightly – be taken as counter-revolutionary. Sadat put an end to this, and the best indicator of his achievement was the much reduced fear of the police in his Egypt, even among opposition elements. Private criticism of the regime was no longer guarded and often quite openly expressed. Rights of public assembly and expression were however less observed. Draconian laws against even peaceful protests such as demonstrations, strikes and sit-ins were passed after the 1977 riots. Even the possession, much less the distribution, of 'subversive' political tracts sometimes made persons liable to arrest. The 'Socialist Prosecutor General,' a political watchdog, was one of the few parts of Nasir's political apparatus retained by

Sadat. The courts frequently dismissed charges against political offenders but for precisely this reason Sadat took to referring political cases to military or exceptional courts. Finally, it must be observed that the ability to exercise political rights varied widely according to a person's political and social status.

The extent and limits of political rights under Sadat can be illustrated by a brief look at several recent cases. The first, that of Nemat Fouad, the writer who almost single-handedly defeated the Pyramid Plateau project, illustrates the expanded scope of political rights enjoyed by some Egyptians. Despite the fact that this project had patrons in the highest places, she was able to wage an extensive public campaign against it. She published six newspaper articles and a book, toured the country delivering 28 lectures before faculty, professional organizations (including the Engineers' and Lawyers' Syndicates), the Higher Council for Arts and Science, the Rotary, and the Cairo Women's Club. To minimize the chance of being charged with political agitation, she avoided speaking to student groups, political parties, or the public at large. Finally, she appeared before the People's Assembly. The foreign company involved in the project sued her three times for libel and each time judges dismissed the case, one declaring that every citizen must have the right to defend the public interest. She then sued the government itself for having illegally disposed of public property. This remarkable campaign is virtually unimaginable under Nasir. Yet Nemat Fouad was no ordinary person: from a good family, on the conservative side of the political spectrum, the author of 21 books, and General Director of the Higher Council for the Promotion of the Fine Arts, she was almost a part of the establishment itself. Carefully confining her activity to elite circles, and with an impeccable case which aroused wide sectors of the bourgeoisie, she could not readily be silenced without provoking resentment in the regime's own constituency (Fouad 1979: 137–57).

The other cases illustrate the unequal treatment meted out to less well-placed persons. One case was that of Iglal Ihsan who was jailed for allegedly smuggling subversive literature into the country. Because the charge could not be substantiated, she was ordered to be released by a court; nevertheless, she spent two more weeks in prison before Sadat confirmed the court order. A second case concerns five students and workers charged with plotting to overthrow the government because of their possession of Marxist literature; again a court dismissed the cases, noting that possession of literature openly distributed from eastern bloc culture centers hardly demonstrated an intention to overthrow the government; but the case took seven years to decide, part of which the accused spent in prison (*al-Ahram*, 19 Dec. 1979). A third case was that of 156 students charged with provoking the 1977 riots. All but 20 were acquitted; yet those found guilty were sentenced to 1–3 years in prison for nothing more than the distribution of 'provocative' leaflets or displaying a poster on campus (*al-Ahram*, 20 Apr. 1980). Another case was that of 200 leftist candidates competing in the 1979 trade union elections. On the basis of the 1978 plebiscite which banned atheists from any kind of political office, the Socialist Prosecutor-General banned them from competing; the courts, however, overturned the ban. These cases suggest that ordinary persons on the left wing of the political spectrum could expect far less tolerance of their political activity by the government than a Nemat Fouad. The courts tried to maintain basic standards of justice, but many of these persons were still made to pay a high price for the exercise of their political rights, something that was likely to be a strong deterrent to others like them. Finally Sadat's sweeping 1981 crackdown on dissidents in which at least 1500 persons were arrested, academics and journalists fired, newspapers banned, religious societies dissolved and the Pope of the Coptic church removed showed that if the regime wanted badly enough to put an end to dissidence, the courts were no effective barrier to it; ten years after the 'Corrective Revolution,' the rule of law remained a fragile growth.

Another dimension of the rule of law is the extent to which officials must make their decisions within the law. The Pyramid Plateau case again gives a revealing glimpse of the extent to which this was so. Relying on their wide official discretion and the protection of personal connections, elites ignored and manipulated the law. Government decrees authorizing the project violated no less than five statutes: Law 250 of 1951 protecting public property containing antiquities, Law 61 of 1958 governing concessions of public land, Law 129 of 1947 limiting the period of concessions, Law 43 of 1974 regulating investment, and Law 89 of 1976 on ownership of land by non-Egyptians (Gami' 1979). Elites had become accustomed, in their use of decree power, to ignoring or overriding the tangled and uncodified accumulation of legal enactments. But it is also remarkable that counterforces, especially lawyers, strengthened by the respect for legality which exists in public opinion and in the establishment itself, were able to use legal arguments to make an unanswerable case against the project. Equally significant, it was an arm of the state itself, the Central Auditing Agency, which first blew the whistle on the malefactors. Lawyers, intellectuals, and even public officials were learning to use the law to check arbitrary power. In the West, the rule of law was not born overnight, but from just such a struggle and it can probably only triumph in Egypt in a similar way. This struggle was, itself, only possible because the regime was committed to steering Egypt into an era of 'constitutional legitimacy.'

Chapter 7

Counter-elites and the pluralization of the political arena

Perhaps the most striking transformation in Egyptian politics under Sadat was the growing pluralization of the political arena as a result of expanding anti-regime opposition. This contrasted with but had its seeds in the Nasir period. Before 1952, the political arena though small was already quite pluralized. But Nasir, through a combination of charismatic legitimacy and coercion, imposed a nationalist–populist consensus on it, bringing nearly all social forces into a grand coalition organized by the single official party, and balanced and reconciled by the leader. By the late Nasir period, however, divisions were developing in this coalition between a new bourgeoisie seeking to advance and protect its interests and those speaking for a mass public increasingly conscious of its own rights. The post-1967 stagnation made these conflicting interests increasingly difficult to reconcile and when Nasir died the main force holding the coalition together was removed. Sadat, neither wishing to continue Nasir's nationalist–populist course nor able to balance the disparate forces in the regime coalition as he had done, sought to build a strong base in one strategic part of this coalition, the bourgeoisie, and ultimately permitted the 'alliance,' incorporated in the ASU, to disband. His own support was absorbed into a succession of new government parties. At the same time, his pursuit, in the absence of overwhelming legitimacy, of controversial rightwing policies which reversed much of Nasir's work, provoked growing opposition from the nationalist-left wing of the Nasirite coalition. The party experiment gave this force a chance to organize in a separate party, the NPUP. To balance the left, Sadat permitted forces on the right, first the Ikhwan, then the liberal Wafd, to partially re-emerge. Sadat hoped the greater freedom granted these political forces would allow him to play them off against each other, perhaps even coopt them into the established system. But ideological conflicts increasingly separated them from the regime and they used the opportunity to mobilize constituencies of their own and to challenge his policies. Thus was set in train a growing repluralization of the political arena. This section will examine the three main opposition forces, the NPUP, the Islamic movement, and the New Wafd, and analyze the consequences of their emergence for the political system.

The National Progressive Unionist Party: nationalist–left opposition

Leadership

The Progressive Party can legitimately be considered the heir of the left wing of the nationalist movement in Egypt. It emerged from the left wing of the Nasirite alliance; it has brought together a coalition (*tagammu'*) of veteran leftists and nationalists with newer elements formed under Nasir and still loyal to his course. The socio-political composition of its leadership embodied in its top organs, the secretariat and its more powerful inner 'executive committee', clearly reflects this (see tables 1 and 2). Politically, Nasirites dominate and the sprinkling of Arab Nationalists and Misr al-Fatat elements strengthens the nationalist coloration of the party elite. Marxists are also well represented at the top, however, and, after them, social-democratic or liberal independents. In occupational and class composition, the party leadership was made up of two distinct social forces: middle-class intellectuals or professionals and workers or trade union cadres of modest class origin. Information available on the middle and lower levels of the party leadership suggests a similar social composition except that the worker contingent is larger, representing about half of the total and the middle-class group commensurately smaller (Hinnebusch 1981: 334–5). Generally, the proportion of peasants, workers and trade unionists decreases toward the top of the organization pyramid while that of those in non-manual occupations increases. While the two groups were nearly equally represented at the local and provincial level, professionals made up 70% of the general secretariat and 88.3% of its 'inner executive committee.' In sum, the NPUP leadership does seem to represent a continuance of the middle-lower-class coalition forged under Nasir; in this respect and in the significant role played by activists of working-class background, it differed substantially from the ruling elite.

To a great extent the party leadership is indeed a product of political developments in the Nasir era. Though small in number, ex-Free Officers play a critical role in the top leadership. Party leader Khalid Muhi ad-Din is a Free Officer known for his Marxist sympathies. Socially, he comes from a politically prominent family of that rural middle stratum which constituted much of the social base of the Nasir regime. Although on the peripheries of the Nasirite establishment after his stand with the left in 1954, he served in the sixties in the leftwing media and the ASU. He enjoys the prestige of one of the leaders of the revolution as well as a popular image as a kind of 'tribune of the people.' Until his death, Kemal ad-Din Rifa'at, another prominent political officer, was number-two man in the party and leader of its more mainstream Nasirite current. Under Nasir, he was close to the center of power and, as a long-time Labor Minister, ideologue of Arab Socialism and ASU chief of political

Table 1. *NPUP general secretariat by occupation and political trend**

Member	Nasirite	Independent or social democrat	Marxist	Arab** nationalist	Misr Al-Fatat	Enlightened religious	Occupation Totals
Ex-Free Officer	2		1				3
Bureaucrat	1			1			2
Journalist	6	1	3		1		11
Trade Union leader or worker	4	5	5		1		15
Religious Shaikh	1					1	2
Ex-ASU or Socialist Youth Cadre	3						3
Peasant	2						2
Other professional	6	4	6	1			17
Contractor	1						1
Student	1						1
Political Totals	27	10	15	2	2	1	57

* No data available for three members

** Denotes former Ba'thists or members of the Arab Nationalist Movement

Table 2. *NPUP 'Inner' Ex-com. by occupation and political trend*

Member	Nasirite	Independent	Marxist	Arab Nationalist*	Occupation Totals
Officer	I		I		2
Bureaucrat				I	I
Journalist	2		2		4
Trade unionist or worker		I	I		2
Youth leader	I				I
Religious Shaikh	I				I
Other professionals	2	I	2	I	6
Political Totals	7	2	6	2	I7

* Denotes former Ba'thists or members of the Arab Nationalist Movement.

indoctrination, identified with the Nasirist left; he brought many of his followers in the ASU and labor movement into the party. Lutfi Wakid, a second-rank Free Officer who served on Nasir's presidential staff, emerged as the leader of more centrist Nasirite elements in the party after Rifa'at's death. These officers are the last remnant of the original radical current in the officer corps which produced the revolution. The great majority of the officer corps, either supportive of Sadat or politically inactive, was conspicuously absent from this party of Nasirism.

The largest social element in the leadership were 'professionals' many of whom came from 'good families.' Journalists represented the largest professional contingent, indicative of the radical tradition in Egyptian journalism, including that fostered under Nasir in journals such as *al-Talia'*, *Ruz al-Yusuf* and *Gumhuriyya* during the sixties when large numbers of Marxists joined the media establishment. Rifat Sa'id, the party's first Secretary General and its main organizer, is a Marxist journalist. The second largest element, the trade unionists, indicates the extent to which the trade union movement fostered under Nasir did produce a cadre of political militants. Only a few representatives of the civil and party (ASU) bureaucracy forged under Nasir surfaced in the NPUP leadership, indicative of the incorporation of much of the bureaucratic elite into Sadat's base and of the extent to which the ASU elite was made up of careerists and 'bureaucrats on loan,' rather than ideological militants. However, in some provinces, the 'roots' of the Socialist Vanguard

Organization formed by Ali Sabri joined the NPUP and many veterans of the ASU Youth auxiliary and the Socialist Institute man its middle- and lower-level organs; these militants, chiefly of worker, peasant or petty bourgeois origin, are the durable evidence that Nasir's mid-sixties political radicalization was not wholly without consequence. Not surprisingly, businessmen and landowners are almost absent in the leadership although many of the latter were prominent in the ASU. But the presence of one contractor suggests that some elements of the national-capitalist class may still favor a Nasirite course over the current open economy. Also conspicuously under-represented are the peasants, evidently indicative of the small extent to which their support for Nasirism was translated into durable activism.

Ideology[1]

The NPUP saw its mission as the 'completion of the national-democratic revolution' by which it meant national liberation from world imperialism, modernization and socio-political democratization. According to the NPUP program, Egypt took major strides along this road under Nasir but, partly because Nasir did not sufficiently mobilize the masses to defend these accomplishments, in the aftermath of the 1967 war, Egypt's progress was checked. Subsequently under Sadat a 'parasitic bourgeoisie' was able to take power and compromise with imperialism, thereby threatening all Egypt's previous strides toward the national-democratic revolution. As such, the NPUP's immediate task was to mobilize and organize a counter-coalition to defend the Egyptian revolution against the course followed by the Sadat regime.

On the foreign policy level, the party's program follows from two basic propositions. The first is that Egypt's main enemies are world imperialism, led by the United States which seeks to control the Middle East in its own interests, and Israel, which in addition to pursuing its own racist brand of 'little imperialism,' is a bridgehead of world imperialism, aiming to play the role of agent for capitalism in the Arab world. The second is that Egypt is an inseparable part of the Arab world: only through pan-Arab solidarity can Egypt and the other Arabs hope to defend themselves from imperialism and Zionism and only as part of a complementary Pan-Arab economy can Egypt hope to gain access to the markets and resources to build a national economy free of imperialist dependency. It follows that Egypt's natural role is to lead the anti-imperialist forces in the Arab world as it did under Nasir. The party conceded that in the current stage, at least, Egypt had to seek a settlement of the Arab–Israeli conflict, but only on condition of complete Israeli withdrawal from the occupied lands and creation of a Palestinian state. Such a 'settlement' would not, however, lead to relations with Israel for this would allow her to act as agent for international capitalism in the area; nor would it mean the end of the struggle with Zionism, for it would change neither Israel's racist nature nor her role as imperialist bridgehead. Moreover, such a settlement could hardly be reached by reliance on American diplomacy, but only through negotiation from strength based on Arab solidarity, the oil weapon and the preservation of the war option. By relying on American diplomacy and by breaking with the USSR and thereby forfeiting the war option, Sadat, as the NPUP saw it, bargained from a position of weakness. Thus, he squandered away the bargaining strength the Arabs had acquired as an outcome of the October War and obtained only a separate peace which ignored Palestinian rights, broke Arab solidarity and thereby fatally weakened the Arab world's resistance to imperialism and Zionism.

On the economic level, the NPUP charged that Egypt was suffering from a severe crisis of development for which *Infitah* was in great part responsible. *Infitah* meant the abandonment of the effort to plan and a surrender to uncontrolled market forces and foreign penetration. Far from stimulating investment in productive enterprise, it merely fueled the growth of speculative non-productive ventures and middleman operations and opened Egypt to an invasion of foreign consumer goods which hurt national production, and foreign banks which siphoned off her savings. The result was growing foreign debt and dependency; rampant inflation, eroding the living standards of the vast majority on limited income; the enrichment of a tiny parasitic bourgeoisie; and the corruption of public life. The only solution to the crisis, the Progressives held, was a return to Nasir's strategy of planned industrialization through the public sector. Much of the resources for this effort could be mobilized domestically through rigorous planning, a more efficient public sector, high taxes on the wealthy and an end to non-essential consumption; although a role for national capitalism would be preserved, a sound strategy required the renationalization of banks and foreign trade. Development had also to be accompanied by social justice, that is, a return to the populist policies devised under Nasir to increase the share of labor in the national income at the expense of property. Price controls, higher wages for workers and another land reform to wipe out the exploitation of peasants by landowners were all needed.

On the political level, the Progressives argued that Nasir had, through the redistribution of social resources and the recruitment of peasants and workers into the assemblies of state, made an important contribution to democratization. But he did not fully solve the problem of democracy and, thus, full democratization was a basic goal for which the Progressives had to fight against those who wanted to impose a rightwing dictatorship on Egypt. The Progressives' model of democracy was Western-style political liberalism, including full freedom of political activity, competitive elections for all offices including the Presidency, and strong legislative and judicial powers to check the executive. The NPUP pledged that it would pursue its goals within the legal–constitutional structure, that is, by trying to mobilize a popular and parliamentary majority. In its advocacy of a liberal regime, the NPUP departed from the Nasirite model. A constitutional regime admitted far greater opportunities to pursue its goals than the authoritarian alternatives plausible at the time.

Organization

Organizationally, the NPUP was born as the 'left' *manbar* within the ASU. Khalid Muhi ad-Din brought his following of Marxist intellectuals and Kemal ad-Din Rifa'at his 'Nasirite' supporters. They were joined by a heterogeneous collection of groups – local factions of the moribund ASU, trade union leaders and independent intellectuals – in a 'founding congress' held in 1976. This congress elected a provisional leadership which appointed provincial leaderships to organize local branches. Within three months the *manbar* had enrolled more than 150,000 members and was allowed to become a fully independent party.

The organizational development of the party nevertheless encountered many obstacles. Some resulted from its birth as a sliver of the official state party: initially many leftist militants, not seeing it as an authentic opposition party, remained aloof from it. Others, however, joined only because they believed they were expected to join one of the three *manāber* or to acquire office, and a few were planted by the government as a means of control; their commitment to the party ideology was, at best, luke-warm. The party's break with the regime over the 1977 'food riots' and a subsequent campaign of harassment and arrests against it, led to a serious organizational contraction. Those who had joined out of convenience quit, anxious to put a distance between themselves and a party out of favor with the government; many others, sympathetic to the party, but unprepared to pay the costs of opposition, allowed their memberships to become inactive. But the conflict with the regime marked the party's development from an 'official opposition' into an authentic one; it was subsequently able to attract many new, more-committed members.

Other organizational problems resulted from the party's origin as a collection of previously existing separate groups. Ideological cleavages between Nasirites and Marxists, some of whom wanted to maintain separate organizational and ideological identities, was a threat to party integration. In fact, some Marxist and Nasirite elements remained apart from the party, frustrating its efforts to unify the whole nationalist left. There were conflicts between former ASU elements who stuck together in order to dominate local branches, and excluded 'outgroups.' Other problems stemmed from inexperience, a lack of resources, government harassment and, perhaps, cultural traits. The tendency of many members to be active in spurts, leaving the burden of most work on a few individuals, scarcity of full-time cadres, and negligence and poor discipline made it difficult to maintain sustained collective party work. Communications gaps between the top leadership and the base sometimes resulted in decision-making isolated from the problems facing lower-level cadres.

In spite of these problems, however, the NPUP developed an impressive organization. Although its strength remained quite uneven across the country, it was able to create hundreds of basic units in villages, neighborhoods and factories manned by a very respectable corps of basic-level cadres; except for the Ikhwan no other political force in Egypt was organized on a comparable grass-roots scale. These local units combined in district sections (*qism*) and provincial level branches; in 1978, the party was able to hold provincial branch conferences of 35 to 150 delegates elected from these bases which in turn elected provincial leadership committees and secretaries. In March 1980 the organizational structure was completed when the party held its first national congress of 401 elected delegates. The congress elected a 235-man central committee which in turn elected a 44-man general secretariat, the top decision-making body, and from this a 17-man executive committee to administer the party on a day-to-day basis. Khalid Muhi ad-Din, elected leader without opposition, was assisted by Lutfi Wakid, as secretary of the central committee, two assistant secretaries for organization (Dr Rifat Sa'id) and inspection (Abd al-Azim Maghrabi), and various staff offices, for example, political affairs, Arab affairs, finance, the press, education, mass work.[2]

Social base and mobilizational performance

The NPUP considered its potential support base to lie in the middle-lower-class coalition of forces which had supported Nasir. In addition to nationalist–left intellectuals, the party specifically targeted middle- and lower-class elements which benefited under Nasir and were hence thought to have a stake in defending his revolution. These included public sector workers, peasant beneficiaries of land distribution and tenancy laws, and the sons of workers and peasants who got access to education and public jobs under Nasir. In its effort to mobilize this support base the party enjoyed some definite assets, but it also labored under certain liabilities and faced formidable obstacles.

The party's image and its stand on major issues were both an asset and a liability. Its commitment to the Arab and Palestine cause at least initially actually seemed to be a liability in spite of a generation of Nasirism: many middle- and lower-class Egyptians, sensitive to the high costs of the prolonged war with Israel, were receptive to the government's effort to portray Pan-Arabism as a matter of asking Egyptians to fight for the rich and 'ungrateful' Arabs. Indicative of this was the popular isolation and even rebellion in the party bases encountered by the leadership when it opposed the trip to Jerusalem. However by the end of the Sadat era, as peace brought isolation from the Arab-Islamic world rather than the promised prosperity, the power of a Pan-Arab appeal seemed to revive. If the zeal with which the government tried to portray the party as Marxist, hence anti-religious and anti-national, and the care the party took to refute these negative connotations are any indication, the party's Marxist image was probably a liability (Shukri 1978: 247). Identification with Nasir's 'socialism,' which among the lower classes was associated chiefly with populist benefits, equalization and fixed prices, was probably an asset. Moreover, the party's critique of the government's socio-economic policies and of foreign penetration of Egypt enabled it to express the grievances of the many who were paying the heaviest costs of *Infitah* while a minority visibly enriched and culturally differentiated itself from the masses. Its attempts to identify itself with Nasirism, which enjoyed a large, if latent popular appeal, was also an asset. The potential threat to the regime should socio-economic discontent merge with Nasirite nostalgia and reaction against foreign cultural penetration was amply demonstrated by the chants of the crowds for Nasir during the 1977 disturbances.

Translating the potential appeal of its program into support, however, depended on access to the masses and here the party faced formidable barriers. Competing political forces stood in its way. Through the personal legitimacy of the ruler, corporatist structures controlling the union movement, and patron–client networks reaching down to the village, as well as the traditional deference to authority and economic dependency of the masses, the regime was able to maintain a mass constituency in the face of the opposition. Other opposition forces also helped contain the party, particularly the Islamic fundamentalist movement; in its absence the campuses would have been a fertile field for the nationalist–left, and in the villages and *baladi* quarters of the city it was the main opposition alternative to the Progressives. The party was also handicapped by the lack of an efficient machine experienced in mass political work. It did make a start at mass proselytization, holding public meetings exposing government corruption and raising issues of concern to the masses such as supply shortages or government-proposed changes in the labor law. But for a long time, it was chiefly engrossed in organization-building and internal politics 'far from the daily problems of the masses,' as one self-criticism put it. Even these modest efforts encountered growing government containment and repression. Constant governmental harassment of its members – ranging from arrest to dismissal, transfer or demotion at work – discouraged proselytization. For a brief period, the party published its own paper, *al-Ahali*, which quickly attained a circulation of 100,000, reaching a respectable portion of the 'attentive public,' but this very success soon invited the paper's repression. A new order of magnitude was added to government containment efforts in 1978 when the party was virtually banned from public political work. It had subsequently to develop a private network of hand-to-hand distribution of political tracts which, only with great effort, can hope to substitute for open political work. The party was given to understand, in fact, that it would be tolerated only as long as it did not become a threat, and that success in mobilizing public support, only invited full-scale repression; in this way the regime hoped to make the party leadership timid, discourage the membership and render the party impotent as a political force.

In spite of all obstacles, the NPUP nevertheless did manage to carve out a modest place for itself in the political arena. The party claimed a membership of 150,000, but this figure includes many who were only sporadically or nominally associated with it; evidence suggests that its active or hard-core membership was of the order of about 20,000 (Hinnebusch 1981: 339). Its membership was strongest in urban and more modernized areas where there were above average concentrations of workers, intellectuals and public employees. Thus the party had about 3000 members in Cairo and 1100 in Alexandria. In provinces such as Qalubiyya (about 4000), Gharbiyya (2000) and Buheira (878) which were close to urban centers and/or with their own smaller industrial centers, it also had a respectable presence. The party was weaker in more agrarian provinces especially in upper Egypt, but, significantly, the rural areas were not wholly immune to its penetration; for example, in Minya it had about 600 members and even in tiny Wadi Jedid, about 400. Much of the variation in party support can be explained by the greater receptivity of socially mobilized areas to modern ideological appeals. But certain political factors also affected recruitment. The party was strong in Dakhaliyya owing to a history of radical activism and the relatively strong impact of agrarian reform there; in Minya its weakness was partly due to a Muslim–Christian conflict there, which polarized the population between Islamic fundamentalists and the Coptic Church, squeezing out the secular parties. In Qalubiyya, the home province of Khalid Muhi ad-Din, the party benefited from his personal stature.

The party entered several electoral contests, the outcomes of which are an indicator of its mobilizational capacity. The most important such contest was the 1976 parliamentary election. The NPUP's electoral performance was very modest; it nominated 61 candidates, only four of whom were elected (out of 350 seats), and obtained no more than 8% of the popular vote.[3] The party nominated candidates in constituencies where either a party leader enjoyed good family connections or personal standing or where there was a tradition of radical sentiment and/or a concentration of workers; thus, it tried to mix 'modern' and 'traditional' electoral strategies and both were indeed reflected in the electoral victories it scored. In Fayyum, a peasant candidate won largely owing to the support of local party leader Lutfi Sulaiman, a prominent physician and former ASU boss, who enjoyed wide local prestige. A second victory was scored by a trade union activist in a working-class district of Alexandria, and a third by a worker in the central Cairo constituency of Kasr al-Nil which embraces contiguous lower-class areas and the wealthy downtown business district. The fourth case, the easy victory of party leader Khalid Muhi ad-Din in his rural Qalubiyya constituency, was more complicated. His opponent, the incumbent government candidate, enjoyed the prestige and patronage connections which come with this role. But Khalid, notwithstanding his leftist background, was also perceived by some to have the connections and sympathizers in government to help out clients. Khalid's opponent was his cousin Safwat, so the great prestige of the Muhi ad-Din family in this area was presumably neutralized as an electoral factor. The decisive factors in Khalid's victory appear to have been some barely separable combination of personal stature and issue politics. As one of the original Free Officers, Khalid enjoyed a national stature far overshadowing his cousin, as well as a reputation as a kind of 'tribune of the people.' While many of his supporters showed no sophisticated understanding of the NPUP program, they could understand his attribution of socio-economic problems like inflation and inequality to regime policy, and were responsive to his populistic campaign style. His major handicap was the regime's monopoly of the media which it used to attack his party as atheistic and communist. In this district the party was able to counter the media campaign through the use of public meetings to which Khalid, as a major public figure, drew large crowds. But the government campaign did hurt him among those most concerned with religion; in the one part of the constituency where he lost heavily, local preachers had attacked him in the mosques and the religious students of a local al-Azhar school had generated a strong hostile current of Islamic fundamentalism.

As long as elections turn largely on a combination of government interference, mass deference to authority, and local patronage resources, a party such as the NPUP can never make more than a modest showing. The 1976 elections were by no means free of government interference against the NPUP but by comparison to most such contests, it was local patron–clientage which largely shaped the outcome to the party's disadvantage: the NPUP lacked access to government patronage and although the local prestige of its candidates was important in two of its victories, the great bulk of the local notability stood with the regime. To be sure, the party's success in two working-class districts where it turned the election from competition between rival clans into issue contests, suggests that as the masses are more socially mobilized traditional politics is giving way to a class politics more favorable to the NPUP. But, in any election for the foreseeable future, the government will probably be able to swamp, with a mass of peasant votes, the more limited though more politically conscious vote which the party might be able to mobilize among workers, intellectuals and employees.

The party's electoral performance in smaller political arenas was similarly modest. Even in trade union elections, government controls and the dominance of pro-regime syndicalists over the central union structure, confined Progressive victories to the lower levels, such as management boards in several factories, or to particular unions such as the trade workers and textile unions. Except in the journalists' union, it did poorly in professional syndicate elections. It was surprisingly weak on the main student campuses dominated by Islamic fundamentalists and government supporters, although on some regional campuses, for example Mansura and Zagazig, and in the higher technical institutes, it fared better. Finally, it had little success in local council elections due in part to government interference.

In summation, the social base of NPUP was concentrated among the ranks of industrial workers, intellectuals and small government employees. The NPUP successfully rooted itself in the middle- and lower-class social forces which make up the base of progressive parties, and within the limited arena composed of the politically active or attentive public, it represented a significant political force. But in the far wider arena, made up of the whole population, its weight was very limited. Its main weakness was its modest ability to mobilize peasants; even when it penetrated the rural areas, the local school teachers or agronomists were likely to make up a disproportionate part of its support, and where it did have a sizable peasant following this was more the result of party support among prominent village families than an intensive politicization of the peasantry. While the party could, no doubt, expand its base considerably under more open, competitive conditions, such liberalization is unlikely.

The NPUP and the regime

When Sadat launched his party experiment, it seemed possible to NPUP leaders that the new parties would be allowed to freely offer alternatives within a broad minimum consensus (an Arab–Israeli peace but with provision for Palestinian rights, an *Infitah*, but with a leading role for planning and the public sector, global non-alignment). The President, they hoped, would withdraw a little above politics or at least steer a centrist course within the minimum consensus. Sadat, however, wanted a 'constructive' opposition that would not challenge his right to set basic policy. Moreover, he quickly set Egypt on a course to the right in total disregard for the positions of the NPUP, presiding over a separate peace, unrestricted opening to foreign capital and a close American alignment. The NPUP, unable to accept this course, and anxious to establish a credible claim to leadership of the nationalist left, came into growing confrontation with the regime.

The first clash resulted from the party's involvement in the demonstrations which were part of the 1977 food riots, the first major popular reaction against *Infitah*. The party insisted that its protests had been peaceful, but the government accused it of having engineered the disturbances and the violent turn they took. Some government leaders wanted to repress the party, but Sadat, reluctant to put such an early end to his party experiment, contented himself with the expulsion of the party's Alexandria deputy from parliament and a campaign of increased police pressures against it. There were also conflicts with the regime in parliament. There the party, with its small representation, could initially be little more than a gadfly. However, after the formation of the New Wafd, the two opposition parties increasingly joined hands in attacks on regime policy, submitting the government's legislative program to sustained criticism and a systematic campaign of interpolations. Inside and outside parliament, they played a role in mobilizing middle-class opinion against the Pyramid Plateau project, attacked activities of the President's close personal associates and, in their criticism of the trip to Jerusalem, encroached on the foreign policy domain Sadat considered his personal prerogative. Sadat was increasingly angered by the NPUP's open opposition to his basic policies; lumping together Nasirites and communists as 'haters,' and attacking Nasir's heritage ever more openly, he increasingly abandoned any effort to appease the left wing of the political spectrum. Alarmed at the party's potential to mobilize mass discontent if allowed to operate unchecked,[4] Sadat finally cracked down in May 1978. Denouncing the Progressives as unbelievers and disloyal agents of the USSR who were stirring up class warfare, he staged a plebiscite which banned from open political activity and public employment all 'communists' and 'unbelievers.' 'You have no place among us,' Sadat told the Progressives, a clear invitation to disband (Speech 14 May 1978). The NPUP refused to dissolve itself voluntarily and Sadat stopped short of wholly repressing it, but its paper was banned, its holding of open public meetings forbidden and the pressures on its members increased. Sadat encouraged the formation of a new left-of-center party, the SLP, to replace the NPUP and staged new parliamentary elections in which the handful of NPUP deputies lost their seats. The NPUP did survive as a going organization but the government blockade around its access to the public greatly tightened, making it harder than ever for it to develop into a major political force. By the end of the Sadat era, the NPUP had been confined to the status of a counter-elite 'party of pressure' on the peripheries of the political arena. Possessed of a viable cadre organization and still able to speak for an articulate segment of the attentive public, it could not be wholly ignored by the regime; but only in concert with other opposition forces, could it seriously challenge it.

The Islamic fundamentalist opposition

The emergence of an Islamic movement in Egypt increasingly at odds with the regime was perhaps the most important ingredient in the pluralization of the political arena: it added a depth to the opposition of which neither the left nor liberal right was capable. Its emergence was partly rooted in an accumulation of rapid, unbalanced, social change. Massive urbanization was uprooting a growing number of persons from the land and village community who could not be absorbed by the modern urban sector of the economy. Set adrift from the security of family and village, searching for a wider identity and solidarity, yet barely removed from traditional life and values, their heightened aspirations frustrated in a system dominated by a Westernized bourgeoisie, urban migrants were especially susceptible to recruitment by a nativist social protest movement. The unbalanced development of education, producing graduates far in excess of the absorptive capacity of the economy, reached crisis proportions in the seventies, making the campuses a special breeding ground for oppositional movements. The Islamic movement on campus was also fed by another kind of social dislocation: the massive movement of women out of the protected home environment into higher education and public spaces, helped produce the movement toward Islamic dress and deportment partly as protection against male molestation (al-Guindi 1981: 479–81). But, that the main opposition movement should have taken an Islamic, rather than a secular nationalist or leftwing form, and that it emerged when it did, cannot be explained without reference to political factors. The Ikhwan, powerful before 1952 had, after all, been contained under Nasir through a combination of efficient repression and the popular legitimacy of the leader. It is clear that the decisive political event which revived the fortunes of the Islamic movement, was the 1967 defeat; as Guindi put it, the peoples' faith in Nasir as a symbol of Arab dignity and strength and in the secular nationalist and socialist mix which made up his ideology, was shattered, leaving a leadership and ideological vacuum. It was not unnatural that Egyptians, suffering from a loss of self-esteem and security, and apparently failed by imported secular ideologies, should turn back to the indigenous and familiar: religion provided a comprehensible world-view which satisfied people's need for inner security in the face of uncontrollable disaster. The disaster could be made bearable by resignation if it was seen as God's will; religion offered hope too, for if Egyptians returned to the Islamic path, God would favor them and give them the moral strength to redress the defeat. The 1973 'Ramadan war,' seen as an Islamic victory, and the sudden rise in the wealth and prestige of apparently 'Islamic' regimes like Saudi Arabia and Libya reinforced this view. The growing contact of Egyptians with these more conservative societies as well as the funds made available by them to religious groups in Egypt helped stimulate religious revival (Dekmejian 1980; Dessouki 1982a: 22–3; al-Guindi 1981: 469, 481). Finally, Sadat's policies played a decisive role in the broadening of an Islamic opposition. His relaxation of police controls and the encouragement he initially gave to Islamic revival as a way of winning mass legitimacy and defeating the threat from the left, gave Islamic groups the opportunity to proselytize and organize without government molestation. But it was Sadat's economic and foreign policies which mobilized the movement against the regime. The Westernization and inequality spurred by *Infitah* were perceived as a threat to Islamic values and Islamic social justice, the alliance with the United States and peace with Israel as capitulation to infidel powers. Thus, the very factors which accounted for Nasir's ability to contain Islamic opposition – efficient repression and nativist–populist legitimacy – were decisively weakened under a less repressive, more cosmopolitan regime.

Leadership, ideology, strategy

It is appropriate to speak of an Islamic movement in Egypt which shares a common orientation. All Egypt's Islamic groups seek the creation of an Islamic state headed by a pious Muslim and enforcing Islamic law and social justice. All believe that in the true implementation of the social blueprint supposedly contained in the Koran and *sharia'* lies the solution to Egypt's problems. They share a rejection of foreign ideologies – whether liberal capitalism or Marxism – and attribute Egypt's disasters to attempts to imitate these foreign models. In varying degrees they all combine puritanism in matters of personal morals with public activism in search of a truly Islamic social order. The movement, however, possesses no united leadership, overarching organization or common program, and is, indeed, divided into a multitude of autonomous groups. These groups can usefully be classified along a spectrum ranging from those more conservative and tolerant of the status quo to the more radical activist groups which reject the established order and seek its violent revolutionary transformation (Dessouki 1982a: 12).

On the conservative side of the spectrum were traditional but politically active *ulema* and neighborhood leaders who spoke the language of Islam and projected an image of Islamic piety. Their main concern was the enforcement of the *sharia'* in matters of personal morality. Although they sometimes used populist rhetoric, most were little concerned with the social equality which agitated other Islamic militants; indeed many profited from *Infitah*, and were not only violently anti-Nasirite and anti-Marxist but were alarmed at radical Islam as well (some denounced Khomeini's regime as a communist front). A good example of this type of figure was Sayyid Gallal, a wealthy merchant and pious *Hajj* powerful in Cairo's *baladi* quarters. This group was generally satisfied to work through the regime (e.g. through parliament) and was, in fact, long allied with Sadat. In time, however, as Sadat's commitment to Islamization failed to take concrete forms, particularly when he threw his weight behind a liberalized law of personal status, many of this group were disillusioned with him; nor did his separate peace with Israel go down well with them (*al-Ahram* 10 Aug. 1977; *al-Akhbar* 16 Feb. 1978; *al-Gumhuriyya* 10 Feb. 1978).

Toward the center of the spectrum were the various factionalized remnants of the once powerful Muslim Brotherhood. Imprisoned, broken, or exiled under Nasir, and amnestied under Sadat, most of the former brethren avoided open confrontation with the regime in favor of the peaceful evocation of Islamic goals and the rebuilding of their movement. Least activist was the 'Murshid Jadid' faction led by Rahman al-Misiri, which argued that the Ikhwan was in a 'period of weakness' during which God did not demand *jehad*; eschewing, thus, any confrontation with the state, it concentrated on building a new generation of preachers. A second faction led by Zeinab al-Ghazali, was chiefly distinguished by its opposition to this 'passive' policy. The dominant remnant of the Ikhwan, clustered around the paper *al-Dawa* and its editor Omar Tilmisani, initially cooperated with the regime. Some of its members sat in parliament where they advocated Islamic legislation. It opposed the anti-regime violence of the radical wing of the movement (and was accused by these radicals of informing to the police) and long avoided any overt criticism of the regime. After the peace treaty, however, its relations with Sadat deteriorated and in 1981 Tilmisani was among those arrested for opposition (Altman 1979; *al-Dawa*, July 1979).

The ideas advocated in *al-Dawa* give a representative view of the program of the mainstream Islamic movement. The Ikhwan was much concerned with personal Islamic morality, advocating a value system which was, by Western standards, conservative, if not reactionary. It opposed birth control, arguing that God was capable of providing food for all Egyptians. Holding to an authoritarian–patriarchal view of the family, it opposed liberalization of marriage and divorce laws, defended polygamy and the unrestricted right of husbands to divorce their wives, and held that the place of women was in the home, not with men in offices. It called for the replacement of Western law codes by Islamic law, and wanted the state to enforce the daily acts of Islamic worship and the observance of Ramadan. It called for banning of the indecent books, films, nightclubs and alcohol consumption which it took as symptoms of imported Western immorality (*al-Dawa* Jan. 1978, Jan. 1979; Dessouki 1982a: 20).

The *Dawa* group did not accept the principle of separation of religion and politics preached by Sadat. It advocated, albeit cautiously, its own conception of an Islamic state in which the ruler would enforce and be bound by the *sharia'* and rule through a single 'Islamic' party. Although it denounced Nasir's socialism as repressive and a failure, it advocated a welfare state capable of closing existing class gaps without resorting to class struggle; the prohibition of usury, enforcement of *zakat* (charitable contributions) and a full-employment policy were the primary envisioned instruments of equalization and social justice, but neither land reform nor nationalizations were ruled out in principle. *Dawa* also deplored the corruption of the state which it attributed to Western influence. *Infitah*, at least as it was being implemented under Sadat, did not meet with its approval. In social policy the *Dawa* group was thus vaguely populist (Altman 1979: 93–4; *al-Dawa*, Jan. 1978, Nov. 1979). In the field of foreign policy the group, supported by and sympathetic to Saudi Arabia, applauded Sadat's alliance with the conservative Arab states and the break with the USSR. But, it rejected the separate peace with Israel. A peace treaty with a state which still usurped the land of Muslims, including sacred Jerusalem, was, it declared, unacceptable. Sadat's treaty had returned but one-tenth of the usurped land and Israel showed, in its attacks on Lebanon and its West Bank settlement policy, that far from wanting peace, it was still intent on expansion; thus, Sadat's argument that the peace was justified by Muhammed's injunction to make peace with those who wanted it, was invalid. Nor could the Jews, loyal only to their own kind, be trusted to keep a treaty. The Arab–Israeli conflict was inherently irreconcilable. It had its origins as far back as Muhammed's conflict with the Jews; today, Israel was an instrument of both the capitalist West (which provided it with weapons and funds) and the Soviet Union (which provided it with migrants) to dominate the Arab–Islamic world. The treaty, opening the door to Jewish cultural and economic penetration, and destroying the Arab front against Israel, put the Arab world in danger of being swallowed up. As against Westernized groups which advocated Egypt's withdrawal from Arab affairs, *al-Dawa* vigorously reaffirmed her Arab–Islamic character. Finally, although *al-Dawa* denied the appropriateness of a Khomeini type revolution for Egypt, it supported Khomeini and criticized the refuge given by Sadat to the Shah (Altman 1979: 95; *al-Dawa*, Jan., July 1979).

A second grouping in the center of the spectrum were the individual Islamic preachers whose sermons in mosques or circulated by cassette tape, attracted wide popular following in the traditional urban quarters. These preachers, combining a charismatic appeal with a populist message, denounced official corruption, immorality and the growing gap between rich and poor. Among them may be counted the blind Shaikh Iman, Shaikh Abd al-Hamid Kishk, Shaikh Salah Abu Ismail and Shaikh Ashur Nasr. All had run-ins with the regime which feared their agitation (Dessouki 1982a: 12).

Also in the center, but larger and more activist than the aging Ikhwan leaders, were the youth groups which sprang up in the mid-seventies under the label of *Gama'at al-Islamiyya*. Espousing an alternative Islam disdainful of the religious establishment, they concentrated on creating an Islamic order on campus. This meant adopting Islamic dress, and sometimes the veiling and segregation of women, a goal pursued in conflict with secular-minded university authorities. In upper Egypt, campus Islamic groups were involved in clashes with Copts. Gradually, however, the *Gama'at* began to mobilize the campus against Sadat's policies. They attacked the corruption and inequality supposedly caused by the *Infitah*; a famous leaflet, distributed by the group, decried the lack of public buses and food for the poor while others feasted on champagne and drove limousines. They also adamantly opposed the peace treaty and hailed Khomeini's revolution. Insofar as the *Gama'at* had a socio-political program, it did not seem to differ much from that of the mainstream Ikhwan, but they were less circumspect in their dissent from the status quo (Altman 1979: 96–7).

Finally, at the radical end of the spectrum were the smaller activist factions which believed the regime totally illegitimate and were prepared to challenge it openly and with force. Messianic and paramilitary, they deplored the mainstream Ikhwan as weak, opportunistic and burnt out. There were at least a half dozen such groups but significant evidence is available on only two of them.

The first such group to appear was the Shabab Muhammed, an offshoot of the Islamic Liberation Party, a group which traditionally deplored the Ikhwan's compromise with authority. Led by a Palestinian, Dr Salih Siriya, and supported by Libya, this group was spurred into opposition to the regime by Sadat's move toward accommodation with Israel and the West which it considered to be ungodly treason. The group attacked the Military Technical Academy in 1974 as a prelude to a *coup d'etat* against the political leadership assembled at ASU headquarters. But it failed and its leaders were executed or imprisoned (Ibrahim 1982a: 118–25).

More radical and messianic was the *al-Takfir wa'l-Hijra* group led by the charismatic self-styled *Mahdi*, Shukri Mustafa. Believing the totality of Egyptian society to be infidel, it denied any legitimacy not only to the regime, but to the whole social order, including the religious establishment and even the *fiqh*, the corpus of religious jurisprudence. So alienated was this group that it attempted to totally withdraw from society and create new communities in the desert in which all modern innovations were rejected in favor of a return to natural simplicity. The group did not intend, however, to remain an isolated sect and prepared itself for a conquering 'return' for which it engaged in paramilitary training and the collection of arms. The regime, however, uncovered and arrested many of its members, forcing its hand before it was fully prepared; when, to secure the release of its comrades it kidnapped and (when its demands were ignored) killed the Minister of Awqaf, Muhammed al-Dhahabi, the government smashed the group. Of the 465 members who stood trial, five, including its leader, were executed in 1978. Two years later, however, remnants of the sect surfaced again, involved in attacks on police stations (Altman 1979: 110; Ibrahim 1982a; Shukri 1978: 317–22).

Although radical in their activism and rejection of the established order, the socio-political views of these two groups differed little from the mainstream Ikhwan. They adhered to the standard positions on the status and segregation of women; accepted the traditional view of the ideal political system as a pious ruler implementing the *sharia'*, and wanted a non-aligned self-sufficient Egypt. They denounced usury, extravagance, excessive wealth and poverty, called for state collection of the *zakat* and regulation of the economy in the interest of justice and welfare. But no less than established Islam, they accepted private property, inheritance, profit and social distinctions, provided they resulted solely from the expenditure of labor (Ibrahim 1982a: 119–25).

Thus, in spite of its opposition to Sadat's socio-economic policies, and the radicalism of at least parts of the Islamic movement, almost the whole spectrum of political Islam combined an acceptance of the principles of a capitalist economic system with a moral code which denounced its inegalitarian and materialistic consequences. Only on the very fringes of the Egyptian Islamic movement was there any sign of an evolution beyond this traditional stance. A small off-shoot of the Ikhwan, the *Muslim al-Muasir* group, developed a doctrine combining Islamic and Marxist ideas, arguing that without socialism an Islamic social order could not be realized. It was attempting the synthesis which inspired the radical guerilla movements in Iran. It was, however, only a tiny fragment of the Islamic movement and had yet to enter the stage of political activism; this was a good indicator of the considerably lesser extent of radicalization of the Egyptian Islamic movement as compared to that in Iran.

Social base and mobilizational performance

Traditionally, the Ikhwan was recruited from modest social strata, notably the urban lower middle classes which, socially mobilized enough to be conscious of religio-political issues, but too far down in the social system to be securely integrated into established institutions, were most vulnerable to political mobilization. The successor groups of the Ikhwan seemed to recruit from a similar social base; but there are also signs that the appeal of political Islam was beginning to embrace groups both further up and down in the social system.

There is scattered evidence on the social composition of the Ikhwan mainstream. Letters to the editor columns of *al-Dawa*, one rough indicator of activism, were dominated by lower civil servants, provincial teachers and university students. Recent urban arrivals from the village seemed, according to casual observers, to be well-represented in the movement, and the provincial university campuses, its most secure strongholds, were dominated by new rural arrivals; this suggests significant recruitment from elements on the verge of moving up from the lower to the lower middle class (Dessouki 1982: 23). The movement penetrated the small towns and even the villages. The mosques of the *baladi* quarters of the big cities were also Islamic breeding grounds; not only did the populist preachers find their most receptive audiences in the poor backwaters of Cairo and Alexandria, but two of them – Abu Ismail and Ashur Nasr – were elected to parliament from such areas. This suggests that the influence of the movement was seeping down to the lower classes.

More precise evidence is available on the small radical factions. Shukri Mustafa was an agronomist and his closest colleagues included an ex-police major, a small bureaucrat and a bricklayer. Of a sample of radical sects studied by Ibrahim, two-thirds were recent arrivals in the city for university education. Two-thirds had fathers in the middle and lower grades of the civil service, while only a handful were from high-status professional families or working-class families. Though cut off from their families and uprooted from their accustomed milieu, they were nevertheless mostly high achievers, potentially upwardly mobile through education, yet, given the approximately 30,000 unemployed graduates on the market, many must have regarded their future prospects with frustration (Ibrahim 1982a: 125–33; MENA 9 Nov. 1977, 19 Mar. 1978).

The campus-based *Gama'at* appeared to be of higher social status than the Ikhwan or the radical sects, for their recruitment seemed to reach children of the upper and upper middle classes as well as the middle class. Indicative of this was their power in the engineering and medical faculties (al-Guindi 1981: 480) traditionally recruited from higher social strata, and the not uncommon complaints of sophisticated Westernized mothers against the veiling of their daughters. It seems thus that the 'ruling class' itself was not immune to the appeal of radical Islam.

The mobilizational capacity of the Islamic movement, while perhaps still falling short of its peak in the thirties, had, by the late seventies, produced one of the most formidable political forces in Egypt. A radical group such as *Takfir* was estimated to have had 3000–5000 members with cells in upper Egyptian villages, urban mosques, campuses and the desert (Merriam 1982: 6; Shukri 1978: 222–3). Circulation of the Ikhwan paper, *al-Dawa*, (though evidently restricted by the regime) reached between 80,000 and 150,000. The *Gama'at* commanded around 100,000 members and the allegiance of one-fifth to one-third of the student body, allowing them to dominate the student unions (Buttner 1979: 66). Although the organized strength of the Islamic movement was centered on the campuses, its appeal spilled over into the *baladi* quarters of the city, the rural towns and even the villages, where it organized around mosques and religious schools and in some places developed its own clinics, cooperatives, and small industries. It seemed to have a growing cross-class appeal. Given the religiosity of the Egyptian masses, its potential for broad political mobilization seemed better than that of any other political force in Egypt. Equally significant were signs that it had even penetrated the armed forces; though mostly confined to the lower ranks it is known that even a few field-grade officers were recruited. Finally, not only was the movement numerically strong, but the activism and ideological motivations of its following were exceptionally high. Their distinctive dress and forms of address were, to some extent, the outward signs of a total rejection by recruits of the values of established society, the adoption of an alternative value system and incorporation into a new community for which some were actually prepared to sacrifice themselves (al-Guindi 1981: 473–5). While few Islamic groups took this as far as the *Takfir*, many were made up of true believers in the cause.

The Islamic movement, the regime and the political arena

Sadat enjoyed good relations with much of the Islamic movement for at least the first half decade of his rule. His more traditional outlook as compared to Nasir, his portrayal of himself as the 'believing President,' his expulsion of the Soviet advisors, his alignment with the more Islamic Arab states and his support for the Islamization of legislation pleased Islamic leaders. Sadat released many Ikhwan leaders from prison, and allowed them to preach and organize so long as they eschewed opposition politics, violence and secret cells. In 1976 *al-Dawa* was allowed to start publishing and in 1977 the regime abstained from obstructing the movement's capture of the student unions. For a while, there were even pro-Sadat factions in the movement. For Sadat, the political benefits from this policy were substantial. It enhanced his legitimacy as an Islamic ruler. The spread of political Islam weakened the nationalist–left in which, until the end of the seventies, he saw his main opposition. The movement swept the campuses where otherwise dissidence would have probably taken a leftwing form while the mass religious revival it encouraged undercut the threat of a mass reaction to de-Nasirization.

The first signs of divergence between the regime and political Islam were the 1974 attack on the military academy, the attacks of fundamentalists on nightclubs during the 1977 riots and the *Takfir wa'l-Hijra* incidents. Thus aroused to the oppositional potential in an independent Islamic force, the regime rejected Ikhwan requests to form an Islamic political party, and insisted on the separation of politics and religion. As Western penetration, the American alliance and Sadat's accommodation with Israel became more overt, regime relations with the movement soured; the peace treaty and the break with Saudi Arabia, patron of the center–right of the movement, marked a watershed in this development (Altman 1979: 88, 93).[5] Sadat at first tried to contain rising Islamic opposition through overt Islamic symbolism and the sponsorship of Islamic legislation. But, encouraged by the Iranian revolution, it spread and intensified: criticism in *al-Dawa* invited its frequent confiscation; demonstrations against the treaty, and the asylum offered the Shah, spread. Minya and Assuit were turned into centers of nearly constant anti-government and anti-Copt agitation. Sadat finally began to reimpose coercive controls on Islamic political activity: the leadership of the Islamic-led student unions was purged, and a Supreme Islamic Council proposed which would bring all Islamic associations under establishment tutelage (*al-Ahram*, 9 Nov. 1981; Sadat speeches, 14, 15 Apr. 1979; 19 May 1980). But the scale of disturbances and violence escalated. In 1981, sectarian rioting spread to Cairo. In the summer of 1981, Sadat cracked down, arresting large numbers of Islamic leaders, including the moderate Tilmisani, and ordering the takeover of mosques controlled by fundamentalist preachers. The Islamic movement, he declared, had become a state within a state and would no longer be tolerated; the break between Sadat and his former allies seemed complete. It required only the assassination of the President by Islamic dissidents in the army and massive Islamic attacks on police stations in upper Egypt in which more than 100 policemen were killed or injured, to complete the story (Merriam 1982).

The development of relations between regime and political Islam exposed something of the changing role of religion in Egyptian politics. Under Nasir, the political system seemed to tame and subordinate religion to its own purposes. The smashing of the Ikhwan, the confiscations of extensive Waqf lands, and the secularization of the schools and courts radically curbed the political influence of religion; the takeover of al-Azhar, and the supervision, subsidization and appointment of the personnel of the main mosques narrowed the autonomy of Islamic institutional life (Berger 1970). Although religious elites were brought to lend public approval to regime policies, its legitimacy rested mainly on nationalist grounds. Under Sadat there was a re-Islamization of politics. Unwittingly, he contributed to it by relaxing state control over mosques and religious societies. He insisted that they eschew political activity and that religion and politics remain separate. But he himself constantly tried to use religious legitimacy and Islamic forces, established or not, against his opponents. As Sadat's policies went beyond what they could accept from an Islamic ruler, Islamic activists rejected the separation of politics and religion, and sought to recreate the city of God on earth. The very dearth of legitimate means of political expression at odds with official policy turned many to the mosque and Islamic associations as outlets for their dissidence. This re-Islamization threatened to shift the balance of power in Egypt. Because Islam was the idiom most comprehensible to the masses, the movement had powerful potential to mobilize mass opposition and to do so on an intensely moral–ideological basis. In short, it promised to broaden the scope and deepen the intensity of conflict between a Westernized elite and a nativist mass. Its diffuseness and natural mass roots made it very hard to decisively repress. The effect of this seemed to be to put vague but real limits on what the elite believed it could safely do, a lesson reinforced by the assassination of Sadat. By the eighties, there were signs that this was beginning to check, even upset, the game of interest group politics which throughout the Sadat era had been played chiefly at the expense of the have-nots. It may also have begun to destroy mass tolerance for the normalization of relations with Israel and the Americanization of Egypt and thus to put in place domestic constraints on foreign policy-making which seemed largely absent for much of the Sadat era. But the potential of the Islamic movement seemed largely limited to such negative power. Barring regime acceptance of an Islamic party, it had no legitimate means to translate support into the shaping of policy. It lacked the organization and unified leadership to make a forcible bid for power on its own; the limited appeal of its program to the secular educated and to Copts, exacerbated by its own sectarian agitation, was an obstacle to formation of the broad opposition front needed to really threaten the regime and, indeed, allowed the regime to play the politics of divide and rule.

The New Wafd: the liberal opposition

In February, 1978, a group of Egyptian elder-statesmen joined together to resurrect Egypt's liberal–nationalist independence movement, the Wafd. Prior to the 1952 revolution, the Wafd was Egypt's most durable and electorally successful party. Led by the bourgeoisie, it mobilized a broad cross-class coalition around a program of national independence and political and economic liberalism. By the 1952 revolution, however, it had exhausted much of its political capital and, along with other political forces, could not forestall the banning of parties and establishment of an authoritarian regime. Nasir achieved many of the things Egyptians wanted but which the Wafd could or would not do – from the expulsion of the British to land reform. Through a combination of repression and legitimacy, he relegated the leaders of Egypt's greatest political party to political obscurity (Cantori 1975; Deeb 1979). The de-Nasirization and liberalization of the Egyptian political system under Sadat, however, set the stage for the re-emergence of the old Wafdists. The leading force behind the resurrection of the Wafd was its former Secretary General, Fuad Serag ad-Din. An ex-minister, big landlord and representative of the conservative wing of the party before 1952, he was an archetypical figure of the old *Bashawāt* (Pashas) proscribed under Nasir. His reappearance, with mansion and a modest estate intact, and new business interests afoot, was a symbol of the survival and revival of this social force under Sadat. In a famous 1977 speech to the Lawyers' Syndicate, Serag ad-Din defended the record of the Wafd, attacked Nasirism and called for the formation of a fully independent liberal party (Serag ad-Din 1977). Taking advantage of the new party law, he and his colleagues worked to assemble the required 20 deputies in parliament, to establish a founding committee of nearly 1200 persons, and to prepare a party program. When, in spite of government pressures, the 20 deputies were assembled and the program altered to give lip-service to the 1952 revolution and Sadat's corrective movement, the party, the New Wafd, was officially approved. The Wafdists set out to challenge the Sadat regime for the loyalties of Egypt's upper and middle classes and in consequence were repressed within four months; yet that short experience permitted a valuable glimpse of Egypt's liberal opposition.

Table 3. *Occupations of New Wafd leadership*

	N	%		N	%
Lawyer	6	18.2	Engineer	1	3.0
Minister,			Farmer,		
politician	5	15.2	landlord	5	15.2
Academic	6	18.2	Merchant	1	3.0
Doctor,			Military	2	6.0
pharmacist	2	6.0	Religious		
Bureaucrat	4	12.1	Shaikh	1	3.0
			No Data	2	
		Total: 35			99.9%

Leadership

Data on the background of the New Wafd leadership and a sample of party activists (presented later) provides a socio-political portrait of the New Wafd-ists. The New Wafd leadership was by occupation chiefly a coalition of 'free professionals' and landowners (table 3). Out of 35 members, 22 were trained in law (table 4), and three-quarters reported a professional skill or practice (table 5). More than half reported owning land, and as 70.6% reported provincial births, it is likely many more came from land-owning families. The Wafd leaders were clearly men of substance and property. They were also highly educated: 13 out of 35 had Ph.Ds and only three lacked any higher education. The Wafdists seemed to represent successful stories in social adaptation and mobility: while almost three-quarters were born in the provinces, all now live in Cairo and Alexandria, evidently having used family land ownership as a ticket to the higher education needed to move up in a post-traditional Egypt. However, if the small number reporting business interests (14.6%) (table 5), is accurate, they did not appear to constitute an entrepreneurial bourgeoisie. Finally, 88.3% were Muslims and 11.7% Copts.

This social profile is very similar to that of the Wafd leadership of 1919–26. In that group, 57% had professional skills, 78.6% reported owning land (30.9% were pure landlords) and only 11.9% had commercial or industrial interests (Cantori 1975). As might be expected after half a century of modernization and land reform, the current Wafd leadership reports more education and professional skills and numbers fewer landlords than the older one. But, in view of the great changes in Egypt during the last 50 years, the social characteristics

Table 4. *Education of New Wafd and Sadat leaderships*

	Wafd Leadership		Sadat Ministers	
	N	%	N	%
Military or military-technocrat	2	5.7	43	24.7
Engineer or agronomist	2	5.7	46	26.5
Medicine or pharmacy	2	5.7	9	5.2
Law	22	62.8	35	20.1
Economics or commerce	1	2.9	23	13.2
Humanities or social science	2	5.7	7	4.0
Natural science	0	0.0	5	2.9
Religion	1	2.9	5	2.9
No university education	3	8.6	1	0.6
	35	100.0	174	100.1

Table 5. *Economic interests of the New Wafd leaders*

	N	%
Land only	7	20.6
Professional practice only	13	38.2
Commercial or industrial only	1	2.9
Land and professional	9	26.5
Land and commercial or indus.	1	2.9
Commercial/industrial and professional	2	5.9
Land, commercial/industrial and professional	1	2.9
No data	1	
Total	35	99.9

of the New Wafdists seem remarkably little different from their predecessors. Many of the 'new Wafdists' were, of course, also old Wafdists.

Several basic contrasts between the Wafd and Sadat leaderships give a glimpse of the social cleavages which underlay their political differences. First, at least a decade separates them by age; the typical Wafdist was in his sixties, while Sadat's men were in their fifties. By education they were different; in contrast to the lawyers dominant in the Wafd a majority of Sadat's men were officers and technocrats (table 4). While the Wafdists were concentrated in the private sector, Sadat's men made their careers through the state. The Wafdists thus seem to represent the first generation of Egyptian modernizers: liberal, humanistic and legalistic in education, rooted in the private professions and land ownership, they bridged the traditional agrarian milieu and the Westernizing city. Sadat's men represented a later generation, more distant from the land and traditional professions, based on the great central institutions of state, and more technocratic, military and statist in orientation.[6]

In political background, most of the New Wafd leaders had roots in the Old Wafd: a quarter were leaders in the old Wafd, another third members, and almost two-thirds came from pro-Wafd families. While only 20% were politically inactive before 1952, 79.4% were so under Nasir and 29.4% report imprisonment, arrest or deprivation of political rights during that time. Thus, the New Wafd leadership was dominated by the old pre-revolutionary generation which, unwilling or unable to adapt to the Nasirite order, suffered at its hands. A minority, however, had a different political background and 20.6% did hold public office under Nasir. Among these were many elements who for one reason or another subsequently fell out with Nasir or Sadat. Hilmi Murad, the number-two man in the party, for example, was a former partisan of the radical nationalist Misr al-Fatat movement, served as a minister under Nasir, but resigned in protest against a purge of the judiciary; thus he combined 'progressive' nationalist and liberal credentials and was reportedly recruited by Serag ad-Din to broaden the appeal of the party to younger non-Wafd elements. Mahmud Yunis was head of the agricultural cooperatives until purged in the early Sadat years, allegedly for corruption. Several landowning deputies from the government party defected to the Wafd over quarrels with the local governor and the regime's failure to liberalize agricultural marketing. A few ex-officers, blamed for the 1967 defeat, found in the Wafd a channel for their grievances. Ahmad Taha, a Marxist independent, joined the party chiefly as a vehicle of opposition to the regime. The one thing that held the old and new elements of the Wafd leadership together was opposition to the regime forged under Nasir and inherited by Sadat.

Ideology[7]

The leaders of the New Wafd saw their party as a force seeking the dismantling of the regime created by Nasir and the creation of a liberal–democratic capitalist system in Egypt. In his famous speech, Serag ad-Din expressed the dominant Wafd attitude toward Nasir. Nasir's seizure of power was, in contrast to the Wafd-led 1919 revolution, a mere *coup*, not a popular movement. While the

Wafd had forced the British out of Egypt, he declared, Nasir had brought on the Israeli occupation of Egyptian land. Nasir's repression of political and economic liberties was, in fact, responsible for virtually all Egypt's economic and foreign policy reverses. Of all the Wafd leaders, only Hilmi Murad was prepared to give Nasir any credit: for failed good intentions. Most of the Wafd's rank and file activists agreed with their leaders; asked whether they believed Nasir was a great leader who had put Egypt on the road to modernity and national pride, or had ruined Egypt, destroying her economy and political liberties and losing the war with Israel, three-quarters picked the latter opinion, 7.5% the former and 17.5% had mixed feelings. Toward the Sadat regime, on the other hand, the Wafdists were ambivalent. They praised Sadat's de-Nasirization and liberalization measures, but in claiming that Egypt suffered from a political vacuum, and that the pro-regime parties lacked popular roots, they did not spare him. Their calls for trial and purge from office of those guilty of corruption and repression under Nasir was a threat to the large part of the Sadat elite which had held office under Nasir. The Wafdists could not, it seems, put their animosity to the 1952 revolution behind them. For want of a practical alternative, they did pledge themselves to the established order and the constitution in force; but within this order they saw their role as the genuine opposition to whom it fell to hold the government accountable and ultimately to transform it.

'Democracy' was the central plank in the Wafd's program. Specifically, the Wafd wanted the removal of all restrictions on political parties, full freedom of expression for citizens, an end to government control over the press, absolute sovereignty of law, and free elections. The Wafd favored a parliamentary–cabinet system, but if a Presidential system were maintained, it wanted competitive Presidential elections. Whichever system was chosen, the Wafdists insisted on a strong legislature able to check or hold government responsible; by contrast, they described the Sadat regime as one wherein the President ruled but was not responsible while the cabinet was responsible but did not rule, and parliament carried little independent weight. Expressive of the Wafd's secular–liberal orientation, was its call for the modernization of the (Islamic) law of personal status and the separation of the religious establishment from government control.

In the socio-economic field, the Wafdists pressed for an even more thorough liberalization and opening of the economy than that sponsored by Sadat. They considered the state-dominated economy forged under Nasir to be inefficient, corrupt, an obstacle to authentic national capitalist development and of benefit only to a parasitic officialdom. The public sector, they argued, should be confined only to the largest projects. The medium and small industry over which the government still retained certain monopolies under Sadat, should be reserved for private capital and even public utilities should be opened to private investment. State industries which could not be run at a profit without subsidies should be de-nationalized. In agriculture, while the party insisted it would not reverse the land reform, it did advocate the abolition of the state agency supervizing land reform cooperatives and of the state-run cooperative marketing system. In place of Nasir's effort to make Egypt the heavy industrial center of the Arab world, a course which they considered economically inefficient and to have resulted in state domination of the economy, the Wafdists advocated that Egypt concentrate its efforts in medium and light industry, agriculture, and tourism where it had a comparative advantage. They also wanted administrative intervention in the economy, such as price controls and popular consumption subsidies, reduced or abolished, thereby liberating market forces. The bloated state bureaucracy needed to be reduced, shedding, in particular, high-ranking and high-paid officials; the top-heavy expansion of education restricted by a halt to open admissions and the opening of new campuses; and the guaranteed employment of graduates ended. These measures, the Wafd argued, would make possible a balanced budget and reduce inflation while a free market would raise wages. The Wafd called for progressive taxation to contain the growth of class gaps, but also argued for tax incentives for private investment. It supported the rights of workers, but in a critique of the poor labor discipline encouraged by Nasir's populism, demanded that they meet their duties as well. Finally, the Wafdists were strong supporters of *Infitah*. Their program urged that the economy be further opened to the world capitalist market, through the reduction of tariffs and customs on the grounds that foreign competition was needed to improve local enterprise and prevent (chiefly state) monopolies. When asked whether they believed *Infitah* necessary to bring in capital and technology or viewed it as likely to lead to Egypt's colonization by foreign capital and enrichment of the wealthy at the expense of the poor, 69.4% of a sample of activists deemed it necessary. Only 8.3% cited negative results such as inequality, excessive importation of luxury consumer goods, inflation and dangers to social peace or national industry. And while 22.2% had mixed feelings, their reservations had chiefly to do with the regime's implementation rather than the principle of *Infitah*, that is, its distortion by excessive red tape, or its manipulation by officials who took bribes to favor one company or interest over another.

In its foreign policy stance, the Wafd was more ambivalent and less united than on its domestic program. Officially, the party called for global non-alignment, and even declared Sadat's antagonism of the USSR dangerous; in fact Wafdists felt a strong affinity with democratic capitalist America, saw no dangers to Egypt from Western 'imperialism,' and feared the Soviet Union. Most Wafdists were Egypt-firsters without interest in Pan-Arabism, but all wanted strong economic links with the Arab world. Wafdists favored a peace with Israel which would result in a solution to the Palestine problem, but were divided or ambivalent on how to reach such a settlement. Serag ad-Din backed Sadat's trip to Jerusalem, but Hilmi Murad argued that his course, breaking Arab solidarity, was unlikely to result in a just or permanent peace. A half of a sample of activists queried considered the trip to Jerusalem a victory, but a quarter asserted it had destroyed the Arab bargaining position and another quarter had mixed feelings. A half considered peace more important than Palestinian rights, while another third put these rights first. But as Sadat moved toward a separate peace with Israel and broke with the Arabs, the Wafd, arguing that Egypt could not do without Arab economic resources, decisively parted company with him.

This ideology appears to have been an authentic expression of the interests and outlook of the liberal more private-based cosmopolitan wing of the bourgeoisie which the Wafd apparently represented. Political liberalization could only enhance its political influence, chiefly at the expense of the state establishment. Its socio-economic program was a classic liberal prescription for private capitalist revival which would presumably create new opportunities and a more favorable business climate for private investors, at the expense, at least in the short-run, of other social forces. Its call for balanced budgets, for cuts in the bureaucracy and public sector, and for dismantling of most state controls over the economy, threatened both the state bourgeoisie and the bureaucratic middle class. The elimination of state agricultural marketing would deprive the state of the ability to extract a surplus from agriculture and shift this opportunity to private farmers and merchants. An end to food subsidies, public employment and open higher education would threaten the living standards and opportunities of workers, peasants and the petty bourgeoisie. The Wafd saw itself as representing a resurgence of entrepreneurial national capitalism in opposition to a parasitic bureaucratic state, but its unreserved advocacy of an open economy, including the reduction of tariffs, suggests that the interests of traders, agents for foreign firms, joint venture partners and rich consumers overshadowed that of local industrialists in its ranks. Finally, the Wafd's ambivalence toward Sadat's Arab policy seemed to reflect the understanding of the private bourgeoisie that without a Middle East peace, business prosperity and political liberalization were in jeopardy, but that a separate peace could cut it off from the tremendous opportunities and resources of an oil-rich Arab world.

Organization, social base and mobilizational performance

The organizational core of the New Wafd was made up of a General Assembly of about 1200 'founding members,' a high board elected from this, and a parliamentary caucus. The high board was headed by a president, Fuad Serag ad-Din, three Vice Presidents, Hilmi Murad (also head of the caucus), Abd al-Fattah Hassan and Waheed Rifaat and, a Secretary General, Ibrahim Farag. Provincial and local committees reaching downward from the central core were barely formed when the party was repressed (Hizb al-Wafd al-Jadid 1977). The 1200 members included in the party general assembly probably reflected its active membership in 1978; it also claimed, plausibly, to have attracted up to 10,000 supporters in a short four months.

Although the Wafd experiment was prematurely cut short, there is evidence as to the likely social base and mobilizational capacity of the party had it been permitted to continue. The Wafd clearly drew most of its support from the liberal upper and middle classes, and there is evidence it had the potential to mobilize a significant segment of these classes to its side. The party's mobilizational strategy certainly focused on these strata. Its program and its militant stance toward the 1952 revolution, were clearly designed to appeal to them. Its call for democracy, in particular, had a powerful appeal to educated Egyptians from these classes. Its attack on the Ahrar Party as an artificial creation headed by an army officer and undeserving of liberal support was an effort to detach elements of the liberal bourgeoisie coopted by the regime and indeed many Ahrar leaders and members did defect to the Wafd. The regime itself clearly perceived the Wafd as a dangerous rival for the loyalties of the upper and middle classes it was itself courting. It feared the Wafd would attract not only committed liberals, but, capitalizing on the poor organization of the ruling party, mobilize all disaffected elements among the educated classes; such a split in the bourgeoisie between the regime and the Wafd, would, it feared, open the way to the left and the religious right.[8]

Data on a small sample of the party's activist membership reinforces evidence that its social base was rooted in the bourgeoisie.[9] A great majority of the sample came from professional (32.2%), bureaucratic (22.6%) or private business (32.2%) families. Most had higher education in liberal arts (20.9%), law (30.2%) or commerce/economics (16.3%) (table 6); and by occupation, were either private professionals (16.2%), government employed professionals (16.2%), bureaucrats (32.4%) or businessmen (16.2%) (table 7). They also reported sufficient professional, business and landed interests (table 8) to rank them in the upper or upper middle class.[10] By comparison to the top leaders, activists reported somewhat less control of land and lower education. Moreover, evidently reflective of the growth of the government sector and the depression of the professions and business under Nasir, half of the activists were actually employed in government; this was an indicator of the extent to which the Wafd's appeal had actually penetrated the government establishment itself. But there is little doubt that, like their leaders, most Wafd activists were drawn from the property-owning bourgoisie; indeed only 15.9% could be considered as far down as the lower middle class and none lower in social status.

Table 6. *New Wafd activists by education*

	N	%
Liberal Arts	9	20.9
Law	13	30.2
Commerce/economics	7	16.3
Medicine	3	7.0
Military/police	1	2.3
Agronomy	1	2.3
Engineering	2	4.6
Education	1	2.3
No higher education	6	13.9
Totals	43	99.8
No data	1	

Table 7. *New Wafd activists by occupation*

	N	%
Professional (private)*	6	16.2
Professional (gov't)*	6	16.2
Bureaucrat	12	32.4
Merchant	2	5.4
Contractor	3	8.1
Foreign company agent	1	2.7
Teacher	1	2.7
Student	1	2.7
Housewife	1	2.7
Retired	4	10.8
Totals	37	99.9
No data	7	

* Professional refers to lawyers, doctors, engineers, economists, etc. They are differentiated according to their employment in the private or government sectors.

On the other hand, there is evidence that not all elements of even the liberal wing of the bourgeoisie were prepared to throw in their lot with the Wafd. Some stood with the regime. Some stayed with the small rightwing Ahrar Party, believing the Wafd's hard line toward the regime was bound to be suicidal. Even

Table 8. *New Wafd activists by estimated class*[10]

1.	Upper (Large professionals plus economic interests or high position)	36.4%
2.	Upper Middle (Large professionals only or economic interests only)	47.7%
3.	Lower Middle (Small professionals or employees without interests or top positions)	15.9%
		100.0%
N = 44		

some liberals critical of the regime found the Wafd no more attractive; thus Mahmud Qadi, a leading liberal independent, objected to the domination of the new party by pre-1952 politicians, to its attack on Nasirist populism and the public sector and to *laizzez-faire* policies he considered inappropriate to Egypt's stage of development (*al-Ahram* 5 Apr. 1978).

Beyond the liberal bourgeoisie, the Wafd did have some, but, it appears, a far less potent appeal. Many Christians were attracted to this secular refuge in a time of rising Islamic militancy (Shukri 1978: 324). The inclusion of leftwing and Islamic elements in the Wafd leadership was an effort to build bridges to these segments of opinion. Muhammed Anis, a Marxist academic, saw his mission as the reconstruction of the old Wafd's campus left wing; but in this effort, he would have faced formidable competition from Islamic fundamentalists and the left itself. A leader like Shaikh Ashur Nasr gave the Wafd a foothold in Islamic circles, but the Wafd's secular program and a history of animosity between it and the Ikhwan limited its appeal to Islamic fundamentalists. Among the mass public discontent with the government, and the Wafd's identification with the illustrious leaders of Egypt's independence movement could probably have been turned to its advantage. But its anti-populist program and its image as a 'party of pashas' were liabilities. Certainly the government made much of the Wafd's supposed opposition to land reform, popular education and 'the gains won for workers and peasants by the 1952 revolution.' It played up the vulnerabilities in the Wafd's nationalist record such as the 1936 Anglo-Egyptian treaty and the 1942 collaboration with the British (*Jaridat Misr*, 7, 14 Feb., 4 Apr. 1978). The roots of many Wafd leaders in the village gave them the means to recruit peasant clients and, in fact, the Wafd presented the regime with a list of some thousand such followers in its effort to gain approval; but pro-government notables, with their access to the levers of government patronage and pressure could play this game as well or better. Given the chance, the Wafd could have mobilized a significant base. Its liberal-democratic stance could, in the short-run, have rallied wide sectors of the upper and middle classes discontented with authoritarian rule. But, in this effort, it would have faced stiff competition from the left, the regime and political Islam, all of which had their own support bases. Given its anti-populist and very lukewarm nationalist stance, it would, in the long-run, probably have ended up as chiefly the party of the liberal wing of the bourgeoisie.

The New Wafd and the regime

After Serag ad-Din's overt attack on the 1952 revolution, Sadat must have had his qualms about letting the Wafd reorganize; government leaders certainly warned him of the risks. But he probably wanted to please liberal opinion and silence critics who questioned the authenticity of his liberalization experiment. He may have thought the new party would serve as a safety valve for the pent up political frustrations of the old liberals, help reconcile them to the regime and balance the power of the left. He may even have thought to strengthen his personal position by stimulating rivalry between the Wafd and the state party for his favor. But, in fact, from its inception, Sadat and the New Wafd clashed repeatedly.

Although with its mere 22 deputies, the Wafd lacked the strength to directly influence legislation, it was able to make its presence in parliament a serious irritant to the government, subjecting its program to a barrage of criticism. Some of its initiatives expressed the ideological stance typical of an anti-statist party of the private bourgeoisie; it helped stall government proposals to tax the fruit gardens of the agrarian bourgeoisie and, though blocked by the Irrigation Minister, tried to force an investigation of the High Dam's negative side effects. But it often appeared intent on simply embarrassing the government. Its lone Islamic populist deputy, Shaikh Ashur Nasr, was a constant thorn in the side of the government, criticizing it on treatment of the poor in state hospitals, abuse of public funds, the public transportation crisis and other matters more of interest to the mass public than the Wafd's bourgeois constituency. In March 1978, when denied the right to speak in a debate over the quality of bread, Shaikh Ashur Nasr called the assembly a 'puppet theater' and when expelled from the session for having insulted it, he denounced Sadat. The regime chose to consider this a grave breach of conduct making him liable to loss of his seat. The Wafd argued that to punish a deputy for an expression of opinion would render parliament impotent, but the government party used its big majority to expel him. Sadat seems to have been personally affronted, considering it a 'shameful' violation of traditional Egyptian values to insult the 'head of the national family.' The denunciation of the President was a bad precedent which the regime felt, if left unpunished, could only encourage others. It was, no doubt, happy to rid itself of this gadfly, but other Wafdists remained vocal. The

Pyramid Plateau project was not, in principle, incompatible with the Wafd's support of *Infitah*, but, perhaps sensing the regime's vulnerability in the matter, the Wafdists played a major role in mobilizing public and parliamentary opinion against it; in this attack on his close associates, Sadat must have seen a personal animosity toward him on the part of the Wafd. Wafdist leaders also charged that Sadat's concessions in the peace negotiations with Israel were isolating Egypt from the Arab world. In parliament, they joined hands with the NPUP against the regime. In a by-election to fill Shaikh Ashur Nasr's vacant seat in parliament, Serag ad-Din's attack on the regime evoked an enthusiastic response among the Shaikh's Islamic constituents. In the Wafd-influenced Lawyers' Syndicate open anti-regime discourse was escalating. To the regime, this was all taken as evidence that the Wafd would not be self-disciplined in its criticism of the regime, and that disparate opposition forces, instead of fighting each other, were linking up and mobilizing a sizable anti-regime coalition on their side.

In May 1978 Sadat cracked down, banning from political activity 'those who corrupted political life before 1952,' that is, Serag ad-Din and several other Wafd elders. The Wafd charged that this was a violation of the spirit of the constitution and of the regime's promise not to again resort to deprivation of political rights and that it was a sign the regime failed to understand opposition as a normal part of democratic life (Bayan Hizb al-Wafd al-Jadid, 12 June 1978). Rather than submit to a purge of its top leaders, the party voted to disband. Sadat, in defending the repressive measures, stressed three themes. He attacked the corrosive 'unconstructive, dishonest' nature of the Wafd's opposition; by 'casting doubt on everything,' exploiting the people's suffering, they sought to make the people lose faith in the regime. He defended the 1952 revolution and depicted the Wafd's attacks on it as an effort to turn back the political clock and distort the historical record: 'They claimed there was no feudalism in Egypt, which shocked me.' The revolution had not been a mere *coup* by power-hungry soldiers, but a response to the people's despair at the failure of the *ancien régime* to solve their problems. In spite of his own criticisms of Nasir, Sadat was not prepared to dissociate himself from the 1952 revolution and regarded attacks on it as attacks on himself: 'I have declared . . . my responsibility for every decision that was taken and any . . . short coming . . . of the revolution. The May 15 (1971) revolution was not a counter-revolution but a correction of the mother revolution of July 23.' Finally, Sadat declared, 'I will not resort to bargaining.' He would not be swayed by opposition pressures in exercising his Presidential prerogative to decide for Egypt (Speeches, 2, 15, 23 May 1978).

Even after its disbandment, a rump of Wafdist deputies remained in parliament, still critical of the government, but in the 1979 elections they all lost their seats. In one last contest with the regime, a Wafdist ran against the government candidate in elections to the Lawyers' Syndicate. But in spite of pro-Wafd sentiment among lawyers, divisions among the opposition and pressures on government employed lawyers were enough to defeat him. Even after this, however, elements of the Wafd remained covertly active, hoping for another chance to resume public political activity.

The New Wafd was the representative of a very specific social force, namely, the most liberal, Westernized, outward-orientated and 'private,' that is, landowning, professional and commercial-based wing of the bourgeoisie. This was suggested by the composition of its leadership and social base, as well as its program which, jettisoning the vague populism and nationalism of the old Wafd, expressed the most uncompromising advocacy of political liberalism, economic *laissez-faire* and global cosmopolitanism of any force in the Egyptian political arena. This not only differentiated it from the more populist–nationalist orientations of the left and Islamic oppositions, but from other elements of the bourgeoisie as well. It did not seem to speak for local small-scale 'national capital': few of its leaders or activists seemed to have such interests, and its opposition to protectionism suggested little concern with developing an autonomous local capitalism. The Wafdists spoke for that wing of the bourgeoisie chiefly outside of or constrained by the state establishment in opposition to those who made their careers in it. The Wafd's attack on the 1952 revolution and Sadat's defense of it, the threat in its program to statist interests, the continuing gap between the Wafd's unmitigated liberalism and the more authoritarian–statist leanings of the ruling elite reflected a lingering cleavage between the 'old bourgeoisie' and the 'new state bourgeoisie' in Sadat's Egypt.

The Wafd's ambitions, however, went beyond being a mere 'party of pressure' on behalf of the liberal bourgeoisie. It attempted to present itself as an alternative to the regime for the loyalties of Egypt's upper and middle classes. When the Wafd's militancy showed it was intent on pushing liberalization to its conclusion at the expense of the regime, and that it could indeed deprive the regime of a significant portion of its bourgeois constituency, Sadat foreclosed on this alternative. The ostensible ease with which the Wafd was pushed back into political obscurity suggested that much of the bourgeoisie was prepared to accept limited authoritarianism as the price of social peace and a capitalist course. But, for some elements of the bourgeoisie, the honeymoon with Sadat had ended. The persistence of powerful, if latent, liberalism in the bourgeoisie weakened the regime's support among its primary constituency.

The pluralization of the political arena

Sadat's policies resulted in a remarkable pluralization of the political arena, the consequences of which he found very difficult to control. The erosion of the Nasirite coalition as leftist and centrist elements went into opposition, the relaxation of political controls permitting the re-emergence of the hitherto suppressed liberal right, and the growth of autonomous religious associations, set off the process of pluralization. Sadat attempted to adapt the authoritarian state to this pluralization of its political environment; the party experiment, the greater freedom for political expression and the tolerance of growing Islamic proselytization, were meant to provide safety valves which might control participatory pressures in a non-violent, semi-institutionalized form. This attempt resulted in the emergence for the first time since 1954 of overt independent and organized opposition forces with ideologies and constituencies distinctive from the regime. However, the incorporation of these forces into the system proved less than successful. Sadat's unabated pursuit of controversial policies, which ignored the interests and views of the opposition, and persisting historical animosities, combined to polarize relations between regime and opposition. When some opposition forces attempted to mobilize public support in a challenge to his policies, and others resorted to anti-regime violence, Sadat responded with varying levels of repression; the former had their political activity curbed or ended, the latter suffered imprisonment and even execution. The intolerance for challenges to its authority of an elite raised in an authoritarian tradition; the fondness of the President for power; his unwillingness to compromise his mission for Egypt which to him took precedence over all other petty concerns; the breadth of the ideological cleavages between regime and opposition; the fear of the elite and its constituency that if allowed to operate unchecked the opposition would reduce the country to political strife and jeopardize the course which so favored them – all these factors combined to put the brakes on political liberalization.

Yet the regime did not wholly reverse the political relaxation or fully repress most opposition elements which, in fact, persisted in varying degrees of organization and activity. Their place in the political system remained fluid and uninstitutionalized. Some, such as the NPUP and parts of the Islamic movement seemed to assume, to some degree, an informal status as 'parties of pressure' (alongside the Ahrar and SLP) articulating ideals and interests unrepresented in the dominant party and able, to the degree these views threatened to capture wider support, to force the elite to at least partially accommodate them; Sadat's various reversals of course on economic rationalization, at least, seem to have been attempts to pre-empt the further spread of opposition sentiment among the masses. But this tendency remained rudimentary; on many basic issues, Sadat would not even permit the expression of opposition demands, much less accommodate them. Thus to a great extent, the opposition forces seemed increasingly to turn into counter-elites, trying covertly to build popular support at the expense of the regime, and, occasionally resorting to 'anomic' interest articulation – protests, demonstrations and, more rarely but especially on the part of Islamic groups, violence. Their ability to so threaten the regime was sharply constrained by its repressive capabilities and their limited access to the masses. Only together did they seem to have the potential to put the regime in serious trouble, but their historical rivalries and incompatible objectives long enabled it to play them against each other. Toward the end of Sadat's regime, there were increasing signs that they were coalescing in an anti-regime front, and it is partly for this reason that in 1981 Sadat cracked down harder than ever before. This however, was only a short-run solution; and so Sadat left to his successor the unsolved problem of a remarkably resilient and dissatisfied spectrum of counter-elites, who for the most part, were quite unabsorbed into legitimate channels of political participation.

Chapter 8

The regime and the mass public

Egypt under Sadat remained an authoritarian–bureaucratic state devoid of effective institutions for mobilizing mass political participation. A large proportion of Egyptians, lacking political resources or the cultural habits of a participant public, simply remained outside the political arena. Nevertheless, the steadily widening politicization of the mass public since the nineteenth century generated growing pressures for participation and heightened mass vulnerability to the appeals of counter-elites. This politicization made some form of elite–mass linkage through which the regime could generate legitimacy, control opposition, and satisfy at least some of the demands of some of the public an indispensable requirement of political stability. This chapter will explore how the regime tried to absorb and control the participatory propensities of the mass public and how and to what extent the public was able to influence the decisions of political elites.

The changing social bases of mass political participation

Egypt's historical experience shaped a political culture traditionally hostile to mass political participation. The dependence on the state of a hydraulic society, and the ease of government control over the country's narrow, densely settled riverine communities generated a strong tradition of passivity and deference to the state. A history of rule by foreign conquerers accustomed Egyptians to expect harsh government as almost a natural phenomenon about which little could be done except to adapt to or evade its exactions; 'the government – it doesn't matter, God is above it,' expressed the dominant fatalism regarding things political. The strand in Islam ascendant since the Middle Ages mirrored and reinforced acceptance of authoritarian rule; religious teaching permitted the ruler the widest discretion and regarded rebellion as a greater evil than tyranny. The authoritarian patriarchal family reproduced attitudes of dominance and submission generation after generation. Autonomous social bodies capable of checking the ruler or acting as vehicles of participation comparable to the Free Cities or estates in the West remained rudimentary. Encapsulated in their segmentalized little communities, lacking the basic means of understanding or communicating with the wider world, notably literacy, the mass of the people lived apart from the state and each other. The big social cleavages which might have formed the basis of large-scale political association were underdeveloped: familism and localism retarded class consciousness and solidarity, while in this rather ethnically and culturally homogeneous society, vertical cleavages provided few vehicles of political organization or action. For all these reasons, development of a civic culture, a sense of public obligation and concern for public issues was retarded and Egyptians had little opportunity to develop habits of 'secondary' association. Hence, when they were released from their little communities into the wider political arena dominated by a Leviathan state intolerant of organized activism, they tended to operate as individuals, in small personalistic groups (*shillas*), kin groups, or patron–client networks. Pragmatic and oriented toward short-run particularistic benefits, they showed no great taste for ideological conflict or attraction to the idea of systemic change through political action (Ayubi 1980: 77–136; Fawzi 1969; Fouad 1978; Moore 1974: 216; Springborg 1975; Yassin 1978). Much of this traditional political culture persists today, retarding political consciousness and participation, in part because some of the objective factors which shaped it continue to reinforce it. Government not only continues to show the most limited tolerance of autonomous political activity, but today enjoys much enhanced technological capacity to control it. The massive role of the modern Egyptian state in the economy continues the tradition of dependency of the hydraulic society on government and sharply limits the social pluralism which elsewhere provides the social base of autonomous politics. Per capita income, a key indicator of the availability of the resources needed for participation, remains very low and few Egyptians enjoy freedom from pressing preoccupation with economic survival. Only 40% of those over ten years old possess literacy without which a critical political consciousness and efficacious activism are impossible. The opportunity cost of political participation for Egyptians is thus very high. Only a transformation in these conditions can bring a transformation in their participatory propensities.

Nevertheless, objective conditions have altered, diluting the anti-participatory propensities of the inherited culture and making Egyptians more susceptible to political mobilization. As Egypt turns from a segmented agrarian society into a large-scale class society, an educated bourgeoisie, a large, salaried middle class and an industrial working class, have emerged, possessed of a significant measure of political self-consciousness. Access to education and literacy and mass communications have steadily expanded, widening the social base of political participation. That this 'social mobilization' is undermining traditional culture is evidenced by the greater political activism of those milieux – the campus, factory and urban street – most exposed to it. The state, though still authoritarian, has changed too: now indigenously recruited, its legitimacy based on popular sovereignty, it has tolerated and even advanced mass politicization. The pre-1952 regime gave some scope for autonomous activism and electoral participation for the new educated classes. The Nasir regime made the first serious effort to identify the mass public with the state and spread popular understanding of the principle of citizenship rights at the expense of traditional deference to the ruling class. The effect of these experiences could be seen in the rapid spread, once government controls over the political arena were relaxed under Sadat, of autonomous political activism, and in the growing readiness of the masses to resist perceived encroachments on their acquired 'rights', for example, in the 1977 'food riots;' cultural hostility to participation seemed rapidly to dissipate in the absence of continuous coercive reinforcement. Politicization has pushed latent strands in the Islamic tradition which legitimize political activism to the fore: increasingly, Muslims are prepared to oppose the ruler if he is perceived to depart from the obligations incumbent on a legitimate ruler, namely, the protection of the community and the ensuring of social justice and Islamic law. The periodic participatory crises which, with increasing frequency, have punctuated Egypt's recent history whenever the legitimacy or control of the ruler slackens – the Urabi revolt, the 1919 revolution, the anti-regime activism from the thirties to 1952, the crisis of 1967–73, the 1977 riots and the rise of opposition in the late seventies – all indicate Egyptians are ever-less immune to political activism. The increasingly assiduous efforts of elites to generate legitimacy and to forge more sophisticated instruments of control show how little confidence they place in mass passivity and deference.

The political arena has thus been expanding; yet even by the seventies it remained limited and highly stratified. Political activists, that is, the combined active membership of the government and opposition political forces could not have much exceeded 200,000 or around 1% of the over-15 population (as compared to 5–10% in developed countries). The politically attentive public, if measured by the proportion of college or higher institute graduates, might have amounted to 5% of the population over-12 (compared to 15–20% in developed countries). The politically relevant population, defined as those who though not normally active or attentive, are susceptible to periodic mobilization, might, if measured by the more readily mobilizable occupations (students, industrial workers and government white-collar workers) make up 15% of the over-10 population, if measured by literacy or by urban residence, then about 45%. All of these categories have steadily widened over the last half-century and will continue to grow; but most of Egypt's masses still remain outside the 'participant' public.

Elite–mass linkage

The main aim of elite–mass linkage under Sadat as under Nasir, was to contain public demands and control opposition in order to allow the regime to pursue the policies it thought best and only secondarily to provide channels to keep it in touch with public opinion. The basic difference between the two was that Nasir feared and sought to control the political activity of the educated classes, the bourgeoisie and the intellectuals, while viewing the masses with more ambivalence and occasionally trying to mobilize them against his upper-status opponents. Sadat tended to view the bourgeoisie as a friendly force and attempted to accommodate its participatory demands, but feared the demands and vulnerability of the masses to counter-elite appeals, and sought to de-politicize them. Sadat continued to make use of many of the mechanisms of control developed under Nasir, but the differences in his political assets and objectives dictated alternative strategies of control.

Given the weakness of political institutions in Egypt, the personal legitimacy of the ruler has always been the decisive link between governors and governed. The distinctive characteristic of Nasir's regime was the tremendous personal legitimacy enjoyed by the ruler which enabled him to minimize other mechanisms of control. Because it fell to Sadat to temper the national and egalitarian enthusiasms which made Nasir a popular hero, he could not, even had his personality been suited, become a charismatic leader in Nasir's mold. He could and did develop personal legitimacy of a different kind. But it fluctuated greatly over his reign and he could never take it for granted. Sadat began with a fund of inherited legitimacy in assuming the mantle of Nasir and was careful to keep it until he had developed his own. The October War was the basic well-spring of his own legitimacy and initially the apparent successes of his drive for peace and the recovery of Egyptian lands enhanced it; a massive cult of personality, far more overt than under Nasir, was created around these achievements. Sadat shrewdly tried to tailor his image to different targets; thus, to the Westernized bourgeoisie, he portrayed himself as an advocate of freedom, secularism and modernity and allowed his wife Jihan to project the image of an educated Westernized woman. To the masses, he portrayed himself as a patriarchal leader and a pious Islamic ruler frequently observed in public prayer. Sometimes though, the signals got crossed: the modernized bourgeoisie disdained the patriarchal Sadat while the Islamic masses disliked his Westernized wife. To all, however, Sadat promised great things, unprecedented economic prosperity once Egypt was through the 'bottleneck' into the land of peace and capitalism, and the great hopes he aroused certainly buoyed his stature. By the end of his reign, however, he had expended much of his political capital. As hopes for prosperity turned sour for many, they held Sadat responsible for their frustrations.[1] The corruption and inequality fostered by the regime undermined his support. The peace with Israel and the break with the Arabs eroded it further. For a while, Sadat traded on Egyptian resentment of the 'rich' Arabs and fostered Egyptian separatist feeling, but as peace translated into isolation from the Arab–Islamic world rather than prosperity and its separate character became manifest, Sadat became vulnerable to charges that he had betrayed the national honor and the trust of an Islamic ruler (Fahmi 1983: 291–2). The contrast between his funeral and Nasir's symbolized public disillusionment with their fallen President.

The regime was also linked to society by an array of structural mechanisms. The ruling party, parliament, syndical structures and local government councils were, as channels for absorbing participatory demands and mobilizing support, at best efficacious only for the regime's educated propertied constituency and hardly at all for the mass public. But they did link the top elite to local sub-elites who to varying degrees, had personal, social or patronage connections to the mass public. The bureaucracy was an important link: it embraced thousands of employees, its structures were relatively dense and penetrative and the people were more dependent on it than in less government-dominated societies. Overlapping these structures a clientage network extended downward. Sadat himself frequently played the role of chief patron, directly dispensing favors to his people; whether it was reclaimed lands given to peasants, new housing to slum dwellers, or a bonus to government employees on religious holidays, Sadat took care to be seen as personal benefactor of the common man. The President received personal petitions in periodic tours of the country and on occasion dispatched his ministers to hear the grievances of their particular constituencies. At the base, local notables coopted into the ruling party or parliament, were also, to a modest extent, able to dispense patronage, and local officials were in a position to grant favors or divert public goods into private hands. This 'network' hardly constituted a continuous or systematic chain between apex and base, but it was a tissue of shared interest and personal connections which linked the top elite to local power structures. The Sadat regime also made growing use of the orthodox religious establishment as a link to the lower classes, particularly in the cities. Top religious leaders legitimized government policies, denounced the opposition, and were expected to mobilize local preachers on the side of the government and to control religious dissidence. Sadat declared that the role of religion was to 'restore spiritual peace within man and social peace within the homeland,' and told the Minister of Waqfs and the Shaikh al-Azhar to prepare plans to confront 'invading intellectual currents.' The orthodox establishment did seem to constitute an effective elite–mass link, although once it became too closely identified with the legitimation of religiously controversial policies, it began to lose control over its own base to dissenters. The controlled mass media was another potent instrument of linkage, bringing a pro-government and frequently biased or even false message into remote villages; a half-literate public often exposed to no alternative views was very susceptible to such media manipulation. If all else failed, the ultimate instrument of control was the repressive apparatus. As compared to the Nasir regime, police control over the political arena was relaxed under Sadat and opposition no longer invited instant repression. Yet the opposition faced police harassment and a concerted effort to contain its access to the masses. Those who tried forcefully to challenge the regime were swiftly repressed. And, as Sadat's legitimacy declined in the late seventies, he greatly expanded the security forces, relying on their massive presence in the cities as a deterrent to active opposition (*al-Akhbar* 27 Aug. 1979). Repression was a weapon held in reserve which, as the 1981 crackdown showed, could be reintroduced at need into the political equation. Finally, the regime actively fostered divisions in the public as part of a strategy of 'divide and rule'. It fostered, even financed and armed the Islamic right in the early seventies against the left (Shukri 1978: 75–6); it allowed the rebirth of the Wafd for the same reason. Until the late seventies, this policy proved very effective.

The political arena

The political arena can be roughly defined by locating social groups in it along two dimensions. First, they can be differentiated according to their power, that is, located in a political stratification system made up of three rough strata: at the top was the regime's favored constituency, the bourgeoisie; in the middle, three relatively active social forces, students, government employees and organized workers; and at the bottom, the most numerous but least powerful groups, the urban and rural masses. Secondly, groups can be located according to their political alignment, namely as liberal–right, Islamic fundamentalist, pro-Sadat, center–left and nationalist–left.

The bourgeoisie: a favored constituency

Before 1952 the 'old' semi-feudal bourgeoisie was the dominant socio-political force in Egypt, ruling through its control of the land, commercial wealth and education, an ideology combining Egyptian nationalism and liberalism, and its monopoly of local leadership, parliament and cabinet. Under Nasir, it was subordinated to a salaried middle-class political elite, which excluded it from the apex of power, rejected much of its ideological world-view and curbed its control over wealth-producing assets. But Nasir also fostered a new state establishment which was either recruited from the bourgeoisie or used its power to get rich. Moreover, the middle bourgeoisie of medium landowners and merchants largely escaped unscathed or benefited from the Nasir era and was, in good part, incorporated into the regime's base. Under Nasir there were sharp divisions between the 'old' private-based big bourgeoisie and the 'new' state bourgeoisie; these social differences were reinforced by ethnic and cultural differences since elements of Turkish, Levantine or European ancestry were concentrated in the old bourgeoisie and the new bourgeoisie was dominated by Egyptians, and because, though both groups were partially Westernized, the most Westernized elements were part of the old bourgeoisie. However, by the Sadat era, the marriage, political and business ties between the various wings of the bourgeoisie far overshadowed their differences and much of the bourgeoisie was establishing a foot in both the private and state sectors. Thus these factions gradually merged under Sadat into an increasingly cohesive social force conscious of itself as a class distinct from others.

It had not yet, of course, become a political monolith. The New Wafd episode revealed that elements of the old bourgeoisie remained on a liberal–right tangent apart from the regime. The rapid evolution of the Socialist Labor Party into an opposition force reflected the center–left orientation of other elements, notably those who made their careers under Nasir. Parts of the middle bourgeoisie – merchants, workshop owners, middle landowners – were susceptible to Islamic fundamentalism. Interest group politics exposed the multitude of distinct particular interests which divided the bourgeoisie, for example, the conflict between the agrarian and state bourgeoisies, and between protectionist-minded local manufacturers and groups with a stake in *Infitah*. Nevertheless, the bulk of the bourgeoisie appeared to be united behind Sadat and his course. The vast majority of the bureaucratic elite, and of the rural notability incorporated into parliament or the ruling party, were with him. His cooptation of elements of the urban private bourgeoisie into the political elite was a symptom of his success in winning over significant segments of this hitherto hostile force. The great majority of the bourgeoisie favored the main lines of Sadat's policies – *Infitah*, peace with Israel, the Westward tilt – whatever reservations they had about particular forms of implementation. And of course, the main alternatives to Sadat's course – a return to Nasirism, a turn left or toward the Islamic right – could only be to their great disadvantage.

Under Sadat, the reconstructed bourgeoisie clearly re-emerged as Egypt's dominant socio-political force. Needing its support, Sadat tailored his policies in good part to its wishes. The political elite was drawn from its ranks. By virtue of personal connections to and social affinity with the elite, and because the most effective political channels – parliament, the professional syndicates, the ruling party – were dominated by it, the bourgeoisie enjoyed highly privileged access to the center of power. Its greatly disproportionate command of social resources such as higher education and wealth decreased the opportunity costs and increased the effectiveness of its political activity. Its wealth and prestige, which under Nasir carried little weight in the decision-making process, once again translated into political influence.

An attitude survey of the Westernized bourgeoisie

Empirical data is available on the attitudes of a sample of students drawn from the more Westernized, higher strata of the bourgeoisie on which Sadat relied for some of his strongest support.[2] As the most strategically situated social force in Sadat's Egypt, even its attitudinal nuances and ambivalences are of major consequence for the course of Egyptian politics, and are thus worth examination.

Social background By class, the sample is clearly of the highest social status: 22% of respondents claimed to be from upper class or 'aristocratic' families, 70% from the upper middle class, 8% from the middle class and none from the lower classes. Of total families, 38.6% were employed in the public sector, 42.1% in the private sector, and 19.3% bridged both sectors. The sample included a wide variety of professions and occupations: the fathers of 22% were 'free' professionals; 23.1% private businessmen; 9.9% academics; 7.5% diplomats; 10.4% engineers or agronomists; 9% bureaucrats; 5.3% public sector managers or officials; 8.3% army officers; 3% solely landowners and 1.6% politicians or ministers. Roughly half reported stable social fortunes, roughly a quarter downward mobility and another quarter upward mobility. As for religion, 80.7% were Muslim and 19.3%, Christian. Although they had been raised in Egypt, ethnically their background was mixed: 47.2% reported purely Egyptian backgrounds; 8.4% Turkish; 7.6% Arab (Levantine); 2.1% European or Armenian; 17.4% mixed Egyptian and Turkish or Arab ancestry and 17.4% mixed Middle Eastern and European ancestry. Thus, in background, the sample appears to represent most of the major components of the bourgeoisie. Some groups are, however, probably overrepresented, notably Christians, those with non-Egyptian ancestry, and perhaps, those in the private sector, while others, such as Muslims, pure Egyptians and those in the state sector, especially the 'new bourgeoisie' which moved up in the social system under Nasir, are probably underrepresented. The attitude analysis will try to take account of and control for this bias.[3]

Political identity Respondents were asked several questions designed to elicit their personal political identity and their views of Egypt's identity (table 1). Respondents' orientation toward the Arabic–Islamic world was relatively weak. It is true that 71.1% believed Egypt a part of the Arab world, but only 42.2% thought of her in chiefly Arab–Islamic terms, while a majority subordinated her Arab identity to a distinctive Egyptian 'Pharaonic' or even 'Mediterranean' identity. A great majority saw themselves as 'Egyptian' and only 11% as Arabs. Ethnic distinctions accounted for some variations in this overall pattern (table 2).[4] Pure Egyptians and 'Arabs' were more oriented toward the Arab world. Those with European ancestry strongly preferred a 'Pharaonic' identity for Egypt and 43% of them did not even see themselves as Egyptian. Those with Turkish ancestry mostly (89.3%) saw themselves as Egyptians. They also preferred either a Pharaonic or Islamic identity for Egypt (table 2). Several

Table 1. *Political identity*

1. Which of the following best describes your political identity, that is, 'Who am I?' 'To what community do I belong?'
   a. Egyptian   71.3% N–97
   b. Arab   11.0% N–15
   c. Muslim (or Christian)   9.6% N–13
   d. Other (Turkish, Armenian, etc.)   8.0% N–11
   e. NA   N– 9

2. Which of the following *best* describes your view of Egypt's political identity?
   a. Egypt, part of the Arab nation   34.4% N–44
   b. Egypt, part of the Mediterranean world, outpost of Western
      civilization   3.9% N– 5
   c. Egypt, Islamic heartland   7.8% N–10
   d. Egypt, land of the Pharaohs, oldest nation in the world   53.9% N–69
   e. NA   N–17

3. Does Egypt belong to the Arab nation?
                          Yes: 71.1% N–91   No: 28.9% N–37   NA N–17

Table 2 *Ethnic background and perceptions of Egypt's political identity*

Ethnic background	Arab world	Egypt's identity (in percent) Mediterranean	Islamic	Pharaonic	N
Egyptian only	37.1	4.85	4.85	53.2	100% 62
European blood	28.6	7.1	0.0	64.3	100% 14
Arab blood	44.4	0.0	5.6	50.0	100% 18
Turkish blood	17.4	4.3	26.1	52.2	100% 23
N	39	5	10	63	

questions suggested that Westernization had left a powerful impact on the political loyalties and identities of the sample. As many as 15.2% reported wishing they had been born in a Western country; 66.7% preferred employment in a Western to an Egyptian establishment and 74.2% preferred Western to Egyptian films; these responses suggest a considerable level of cultural alienation. All this adds up to much ambivalence in political identity for many respondents. Many seemed pulled to the West by personal tastes, ties, and ambitions. There was no strong identification with the Arab–Islamic world, but

Table 3 *Foreign policy attitudes*

===

1. Which best describes your view of Egypt's proper strategy toward Israel?
   a. Egypt should join the rejectionists and continue to struggle against Israel because she is an illegitimate intrusion by foreigners into the Arab world.　　7.9% N–11
   b. Egypt should make peace with Israel only on condition that she returns *all* the occupied Arab territories, including the Golan Heights of Syria and permits creation of an independent Palestinian state on the West Bank of the Jordan.

      60% N–84
   c. Egypt should make peace with Israel if Israel returns *all* Egyptian territory, but it doesn't matter about Syrian or Palestinian lands　　29.3% N–41
   d. Egypt should make peace with Israel even if Israel won't return all Egyptian lands　　2.9% N– 4
   e. NA　　N– 5

2. Which of the following statements best describes your view of the proper policy for Egypt to follow toward the Palestinians?
   a. Let the Palestinians help themselves; Egypt has sacrificed enough for them already and should not feel obligated to them.　　26.4% N–37
   b. Egypt should support the Palestinians diplomatically, but not support them to the extent of risking war with Israel.　　55.0% N–77
   c. Egypt should refuse any peace settlement that does not give the Palestinians an independent state on the West Bank, even if it means another war with Israel.

      12.9% N–18
   d. Egypt should support the Palestinians actively in liberating their homeland, because Israel has usurped their national rights to their land. Egypt should never make peace with Israel.　　5.7% N– 8
   e. NA　　N–5

3. President Sadat's visit to Israel was a good thing.
   a. Agree: 64.3% N–92　　Disagree: 10.5% N–15　　Mixed Feelings: 21% N–30
      No Opinion: 4.2% N–6　　NA: N–2

4. Egyptians and Israelis can live together in peace if only they overcome the psychological barriers between them, since there are no irreconcilable conflicts of interest or principle between them.
   a. Agree: 27.5% N–39　　Disagree: 38.7% N–55　　Mixed Feelings: 25.4% N–36
      No Opinion: 8.5% N–12　　NA: N–3

5. President Sadat should coordinate his negotiations strategy more with the other Arab states.
   a. Agree: 44.7% N–63　　Disagree: 24.8% N–35　　Mixed Feelings: 22% N–31
      No Opinion: 8.5% N–12　　NA: N–4

6. Egypt can do without the Arabs who have only caused trouble for her.
   a. Agree: 23.9% N–34　　Disagree: 38.7% N–55　　Mixed Feelings: 33.1% N–47
      No Opinion: 4.2% N–6　　NA: N–3

Table 3 *cont.*

7. It was a mistake for President Sadat to fight with the Russians.
   a. Agree: 22% N–31   Disagree: 51.1% N–72   Mixed Feelings: 16.3% N–23
      No Opinion: 10.6% N–15   NA: N–4

8. It is silly for Egypt to rely on the Americans, friends of Israel.
   a. Agree: 16.3% N–22   Disagree: 50.4% N–68   Mixed Feelings: 27.4% N–37
      No Opinion: 5.9% N–8   NA: N–10

9. What position do you think Sadat should take toward the great powers?
   a. Strongly pro-USSR   0.7% N– 1
   b. Non-aligned but leaning toward the USSR   2.9% N– 4
   c. Absolute non-alignment and neutrality   42.1% N–59
   d. Non-aligned but leaning toward the USA   50.7% N–71
   e. Strongly pro-USA   3.6% N– 5
   f. NA   N– 5

Table 4 *Ethnic background and foreign policy attitudes**

Ethnic background	Trip to Jerusalem good (in percent)			Silly to rely on US (in percent)		
	Agree	Disagree	N	Agree	Disagree	N
Egyptian only	69.7	6.1	66	15.6	45.3	64
European blood	60.0	6.7	15	7.1	50.0	14
Arab blood	38.1	33.3	21	36.8	36.8	19
Turkish blood	78.6	00.0	28	4.0	68.8	25
N	85	12		19	60	

*The percentages of those claiming 'mixed feelings' or 'no opinion' are omitted

respondents' cultural heritage seemed reflected in the belief of almost three-quarters that Egypt does have an Arab role. A majority seemed to seek a center of gravity in an Egyptianness distinct from but blending elements of both the Arab–Islamic and Western worlds. The lukewarm Arabism of the group seems quite compatible with the disengagement from Pan-Arabism and inter-Arab entanglements pursued by Sadat. Its Western orientation fits well into his opening of Egypt to the West.

Foreign policy attitudes Respondents indicated substantial but qualified support for Sadat's foreign policy (see table 3). Few wanted to continue the

Table 5 *Political alignments, leadership and political system preferences*

---

1. Try to 'place' yourself in the following political spectrum.[5]
   Left   Communist   1.8% N–2   Center or NDP   29.7% N–33
          Socialist   5.4% N–6   Right Liberal
          Nasirite   2.7% N–3   or New Wafd   56.7% N–63
          Labor   0.9% N–1   Muslim Brothers 2.7% N–3   Right
          NA 34

2. What, in your view, is the appropriate political system for Egypt?
   a. A strong presidency and single party system as under Nasir   5.3% N–7
   b. A strong presidency and multi-party system as under Sadat   36.8% N–49
   c. A fully liberal multi-party system with competition in the
      election of the President, as in France or the USA   48.9% N–65
   d. A powerful revolutionary single party, as in China   9.0% N–12
   e. NA   N–12

3. Regarding the late President Nasir, which of the following best describes your view
   of him:
   a. Nasir was a great leader who restored Egypt's national dignity
      and set her on the road to modernization   8.2% N–11
   b. Nasir achieved some important advances for Egypt, but his
      excessive ambitions exceeded capabilities   54.5% N–73
   c. Nasir ruined Egypt   37.3% N–50
   d. NA   N–11

4. How well, in general do you think President Sadat is doing his job?
   a. Very well   21.3% N–30   d. Not very well   7.8% N–11
   b. Well   38.3% N–54   e. Very badly   5.0% N–7
   c. Fair   27.7% N–39   f. NA   N–4

5. Due to their heritage of authoritarian rule, Egyptians are not properly prepared to
   make liberal democracy work.
   Agree: 43.7% N–62   Disagree: 22.5% N–32   Mixed Feelings: 29.6% N–42
   No Opinion: 4.2% N–6   NA: N–3

6. The communists are the cause of most of Egypt's internal political troubles.
   Agree: 34.5% N–49   Disagree: 38.7% N–55   Mixed Feelings: 14.8% N–21
   No Opinion: 12% N–17   NA: N–3

7. If Islam were really implemented, many of Egypt's problems could be solved.
   Agree: 34.8% N–49   Disagree: 31.9% N–45   Mixed Feelings: 25.5% N–36
   No Opinion: 7.8% N–11   NA: N–4

8. The political party experiment is setting Egypt on the road to democracy.
   Agree: 27.9% N–39   Disagree: 25.7% N–36   Mixed Feelings: 32.9% N–46
   No Opinion: 13.6% N–19   NA: N–5

Table 5 *cont.*

===

9. Getting enough food for people is more important than experiments with political parties.
   Agree: 58.7% N–84   Disagree: 11.9% N–17   Mixed Feelings: 23.1% N–33
   No Opinion: 6.3% N–9   NA: N–2

10. Egyptians should take Col. Qaddafi's ideas more seriously.
    Agree: 4.9% N–7   Disagree: 77.5% N–110   Mixed Feelings: 6.3% N–9
    No Opinion: 11.3% N–16   NA: N–3

===

Arab–Israel conflict. Only 7.9% rejected the principle of peace with Israel (Q1); only about one in five were prepared to take risks for the Palestinian cause (Q2); only one in ten opposed the trip to Jerusalem (Q3); and few thought it was foolish to rely on the Americans in the search for peace (Q8). On the other hand, responses suggested considerable unease over the particular strategy pursued by Sadat to reach a peace settlement; a significant minority (31.5) had at least misgivings over the trip to Jerusalem (Q3); less than a third favored a separate peace (for which Sadat ultimately opted) (Q1); only 27.5% accepted the claim that only psychological barriers separated Egyptians and Israelis (Q4); only 23.9% believed Egypt could do without the Arabs (Q6); and only a quarter rejected the suggestion that Sadat should coordinate his negotiations strategy more with the other Arab states (Q5). On the global level, there was significant support for Sadat's reorientation of Egypt's alignments. Less than a quarter blamed Sadat for the break with the Russians (Q7); less than 4% favored a pro-Soviet alignment, and a majority favored non-alignment but leaning toward the US (Q9). On the other hand, however, 95.7% favored some brand of non-alignment and only 3.6% the strongly pro-US policy Sadat in practice pursued (Q9).

Social differences acounted for some small but consistent variations in foreign policy attitudes. As table 4 suggests, those of Arab ancestry were generally more opposed to Sadat's strategy, the Americans and Israel, while the Turko-Egyptian 'aristocracy' stood out for exactly the opposite views. The policy preferences of Christians were more pro-Western and less pro-Arab than Muslims; thus, for example, about 40% of Christians thought Egypt could do without the Arabs, but only 20% of the Muslims did, and while no Christian thought it silly for Egypt to rely on the US, one in five of the Muslims did. Finally, those employed in the government sector were less enthusiastic about Sadat's policies than those in the private sector; thus while almost 50% of the former rejected the idea that only psychological barriers divided Egyptians and Israelis, only 27.1% of the latter did.

Political alignments The questions detailed in table 5 were designed to explore political alignments. It is clear a vast majority of respondents (Q1) were clustered on the center–right end of the political spectrum. There was, on the one hand, strong support for political views to the liberal–right of the Sadat regime: a majority actually identified with such political forces, and 48.9% preferred a fully liberal political system compared to 36.8% favoring the Sadat model of limited liberalization (Q2). Yet respondents were also clearly ambivalent toward liberalism: a strong plurality believed Egyptians weren't prepared to make it work (Q5), and few considered the political party experiment of high priority or likely to succeed (Q8,9). Most seemed to prefer a liberal regime in principle yet feared that in practice the masses would abuse it and the ruler was unprepared to permit it. In any case, it is clear that most respondents did not allow their liberal views to prejudice them against the Sadat regime. A respectable 29.7% were actually partisans of the ruling party (Q1). More important, a majority (59.6%) gave Sadat very good or good marks as President, and only 12.8% poor marks (Q4). When asked to rank ten Egyptian leaders in order of their esteem for them, respondents ranked Sadat third, behind only Egypt's greatest national heroes, Sa'ad Zaghlul and Mustafa Kamil (table 6). Finally, only small minorities supported radical Islamic, leftist or Nasirite alternatives to Sadat's regime. The low support for the left can be seen in the political alignments (7.2%), and the substantial minority which accepted the implausible government assertion that the communists were the cause of most of Egypt's troubles (Q6). The low support for political Islam can be seen in the tiny number (2.7%) identifying with the Muslim Brotherhood (Q1), the low ranking of the Ikhwan leader, al-Banna (table 6), and the light regard in which Colonel Qaddafi was held (Q10). That Nasirism also fared poorly is evident from the few who considered themselves Nasirites (2.7%) (Q1) and the modest regard for Nasir among respondents (table 5, Q3; table 6); they ranked him eighth of ten leaders in esteem, only 8.2% thought he was a great leader and 37.3% believed he ruined Egypt. A majority (54.5%) conceded that he had achieved some important advances for Egypt but agreed his excessive ambitions had exceeded her capabilities.

Social distinctions within the sample were associated with few major attitudinal variations. One of the most striking findings, indeed, was the absence of any variation among social groups in preferences for a political model (Q2); if the attitudes of their children are any indicator, neither pure Egyptians, army officers nor public employees are less receptive toward liberalism than the minorities, civilians and private sector families. This suggests that even inside the state establishment support for authoritarianism has been significantly diluted. The minor variations in attitudes which could be identified were much as might be expected. Thus, pure Egyptian Muslims employed in the public sector were a bit more likely to be partisans of the

Table 6 *Ranking of Egyptian leaders by esteem*[6]

1. Sa'ad Zaghlul	326	6. Mustafa Nahas	44
2. Mustafa Kamil	277	7. Hassan al-Banna	−98
3. Anwar Sadat	259	8. Gamal Abdul Nasir	−103
4. Muhammed Ali	133	9. Ismail Sidqi	−112
5. Ahmad Lutfi as-Sayid	72	10. Khedive Ismail	−218

Table 7 *Attitudes toward Nasir by social differentiation*

	Sectors*			Class			
	Public	Private	N	Upper	Upper Middle	Middle	N
Great leader	13.5%	3.6%	9	10.0%	7.7%	11.1%	11
Some achievements	61.5	49.1	59	33.3	60.4	66.7	71
Ruined Egypt	25.0	47.3	39	56.7	31.9	22.2	48
	100.0%	100.0%		100.0%	100.0%	100.0%	
N	52	55		30	91	9	

*Those reporting careers spanning the public and private sectors are excluded.

government party, while those privately employed or of Christian background, or with Turkish, Levantine or European ancestry were more likely to be more to the liberal right. The small leftist and Nasirite components of the sample were exclusively Muslim and two-thirds of Colonel Qaddafi's few sympathizers, of Arab ancestry. Variations among respondents were greatest in their assessment of Nasir, a symbol associated with strong emotions and concrete policies which benefited or hurt many people. As table 7 shows, there is a definite association between more favorable attitudes in the public and less in the private sector, more favorable attitudes among the middle and less among the upper classes; these relations of course, correspond to the tendency of Nasir's policies to favor or disfavor the particular sub-group. As table 8 suggests, ethnic ancestry made some difference too: the less favorable attitudes taken by Europeans and Turks and the more favorable attitude by Egyptians cannot be unrelated to the differential effects of 'Egyptianization' policies; but the more favorable view taken of Nasir by the Arabs suggests that his reintegration of Egypt into the Arab world was for some enough to outweigh the harm done to this minority by 'Egyptianization.'

Table 8 *Attitudes toward Nasir by ethnic differentiation*

	Arab	Egyptian	European	Turkish	N
Great leader	15.8%	11.3%	00.0%	3.9%	11
Some achievements	63.1	59.7	42.9	34.6	64
Ruined Egypt	21.1	29.0	57.1	61.5	46
	100.0%	100.0%	100.0%	100.0%	
N	19	62	14	26	

Table 9 *Socio-economic attitudes*

1. What, in your view, should Egypt's economic policy be?
   a. Increase the size of the public sector, reverse the open door policy and build socialism   13.4% N–18
   b. Keep the present balance between the public and private sectors and keep the current open door policy   37.3% N–50
   c. Decrease the public sector, expand the private sector, and broaden the open door policy   49.3% N–66
   d. NA   N–11

2. There is too much inequality in the distribution of wealth in Egypt.
   Agree: 77.6% N–111   Disagree: 7% N–10   Mixed Feelings: 12.6% N–18
   No Opinion: 2.8% N–4   NA: N–2

3. The Open Door has caused the rich to get richer and the poor poorer.
   Agree: 50.0% N–71   Disagree: 16.9% N–24   Mixed Feelings: 25.3% N–36
   No Opinion: 7.7% N–11   NA: N–3

4. Egypt never really gave socialism a chance to work.
   Agree: 26.5% N–36   Disagree: 27.2% N–37   Mixed Feelings: 21.3% N–29
   No Opinion: 25% N–34   NA: N–9

Socio-economic policy preferences Questions on socio-economic preferences suggested that respondents overwhelmingly either supported Sadat's economic liberalization or wanted more of it (table 9, Q1). This was so almost regardless of social category. There was little variation in attitude by ethnic ancestry, in spite of the greater concentration of minorities in the private sector; indeed, those in the public sector were hardly less favorable than those in the private sector. In order to distinguish between the attitudes of those who benefited and suffered under Nasir's etatist policies, respondents were broken down into six categories

Table 10 *Economic policy preference by employment sector* and social mobility*

		Policy preference			
	Socialism	Current Infitah	More Capitalism		N
Public sector + upward mobility	30.0	20.0	50.0	100%	10
Private sector + upward mobility	8.3	50.0	41.7	100%	12
Public sector + stable status	15.4	30.8	53.8	100%	26
Private sector + stable status	18.5	25.9	55.6	100%	27
Public sector + downward mobility	8.3	41.7	50.0	100%	12
Private sector + downward mobility	8.3	41.7	50.0	100%	12
N	15	33	51		

*Those reporting careers spanning the public and private sectors are excluded.

by father's employment in the public or private sector, and social mobility, as indicated in table 10. All groups supported liberalization, even those who experienced upward mobility through the public sector under Nasir. As might be expected, those who did well under etatism were the most likely to favor a return to 'socialism' while those who experienced downward mobility, regardless of employment sector, were least favorable to it. But the little support for socialism among public sector respondents certainly supports the view that Nasir tried to 'build socialism without socialists'; their support for liberalization suggests that, far from seeing it as a threat to their positions, they viewed it as an opportunity, for example, for commissions, better jobs, joint ventures, etc. A survey of the attitudes of 30 prominent Egyptian businessmen done by Mokhtar is largely consistent with these findings (Mokhtar 1980). Of her respondents, 57% favored a totally free economy, 43% a mixed economy; 33% believed in some role for state planning of the economy and most were tolerant of a state role in heavy industry. Almost all welcomed foreign capital. However, the 16.5% who formerly were public sector officials were more likely to oppose a total dissolution of the public sector, while private businessmen hurt by the nationalizations were more likely to favor its sale to the private sector. These results suggest a strong bourgeois consensus behind liberalization, regardless of sectoral distinctions, but some disagreement over the lengths to which it should be carried, and with a small minority remaining favorable to etatism. Responses to questions 2–3 (table 9) also suggest some ambivalence concerning the consequences of liberalization: a vast majority believed there was too much inequality in Egypt and most feared that *Infitah* was increasing it. A majority of Mokhtar's businessmen also believed that the current distribution of wealth was unjust. That only 20% of them favored redistributive taxation and a big majority of both samples nevertheless wanted liberalization, suggests that either they put their private fortunes first or believed all Egyptians would ultimately benefit from liberalization; thus, for example, Mokhtar's businessmen held that increases in employment from new business would improve the lot of the masses. But it is suggestive of the weakness of the bourgeoisie's ideological commitment to a capitalist model that only a minority of the student sample was convinced that socialism in Egypt had been given its fair chance and had failed (table 9, Q4).

Finally, it is possible to explore what differences there may be between this sample which overrepresents the more Westernized, the more educated, the minorities and private sector families, and the bourgeoisie as a *whole* in which one could expect pure Egyptian Muslims employed in the public sector on the one hand, and less-well-educated landowners, traditional merchants and workshop owners of the middle bourgeoisie on the other, to be more heavily represented. An effort was made to obtain a glimpse of the attitudes of the public-employed pure Egyptian Muslims by comparing the attitudes of such elements represented in the sample with the sample as a whole. The analysis found no great differences between the whole sample and this 'Egyptian' sub-group. There were few differences in attitudes toward either political or economic liberalization or in the high levels of support for Sadat. But, there was one major and several minor but consistent differences regarding political identity and foreign policy preferences (table 11). In contrast to the whole sample, the Egyptian sub-group was more likely to see Egypt as primarily Arab in character (Q1, 2). It is slightly but consistently more anti-Israeli, and pro-Arab, e.g. less willing to make a separate peace with Israel, less willing to do without the Arabs, and less willing to accept that Egyptians and Israelis can live together (Q3, 4, 5). The sub-group is less pro-American and more pro-Nasir than the whole sample (Q6, 7). As for the non-Westernized middle bourgeoisie, since it is virtually unrepresented in the sample, little can be said with confidence about its attitudes. But its political identity and foreign policy preferences probably resemble those of the Egyptian sub-group. It is likely to be less politically liberal than the highly educated elements which dominate the sample, but to be favorable to economic liberalization. In conclusion, the attitudes of the bourgeoisie as a whole seem shifted in a more pro-Arab, anti-Israeli, less pro-Western, and less liberal direction than those of this sample.

These findings suggest some conclusions regarding the role of the bourgeoisie

Table 11 *Attitude differences between whole sample and 'Egyptian' sub-group*

Question	Whole sample	Subgroup
1. Egypt's political identity:		
Arab	34.4%	48.6%
Mediterranean	3.9%	8.1%
Islamic	7.8%	8.1%
Pharaonic	53.9%	35.1%
	100.0%	99.9% N–37
2. Egypt belongs to the Arab nation:		
Yes	71.1%	79.5%
No	28.9	20.5
	100.0%	100.0% N–39
3. Strategy toward Israel:*		
Peace only if *all* Arab lands returned	60.0%	70.0%
Peace if only Egyptian lands are returned	29.3	20.0% N–40
4. Egyptians and Israelis can live together:**		
Agree	41.5%	34.5%
Disagree	58.5%	65.5%
	100.0%	100.0% N–29
5. Egypt can do without the Arabs:**		
Agree	38.2%	35.0%
Disagree	61.8%	65.0%
	100.0%	100.0% N–20
6. Silly to rely on US:**		
Agree	24.4%	29.6%
Disagree	75.6	70.4%
	100.0%	100.0% N–27
7. Attitudes toward Nasir:		
Great leader	8.2%	13.2%
Some achievements	54.5	65.8
Ruined Egypt	37.3	21.0
	100.0%	100.0% N–38

*Percentages of the other two choices given in this question are excluded.
**Mixed Feelings and No Opinion responses are excluded from the calculation of percentages.

in the political arena. Sadat's effort to forge the bourgeoisie, particularly its Westernized wing, into a base of support was, it seems, largely successful. It was personally supportive of his leadership and repulsed by the alternatives to him. It largely supported his reintegration of Egypt into the Western capitalist market and state system, and his lower profile in the Arab world; its moderate nationalism, strongly diluted by Westernization and largely an inward looking 'little Egyptian' variety divorced from the Pan-Arab messianism which disrupted Nasir's relations with the West, was certainly no obstacle to these policies. The modest extent of variation in this supportive orientation associated with distinctions in ethnic or religious background, public and private sector, suggests that the divisions between these groups under Nasir had been, by Sadat's time, significantly bridged and that a new conservative consensus based on common upper-class interests was emerging.

The findings do, however, suggest some soft spots in the support of the bourgeoisie for Sadatism. The bourgeoisie had considerable misgivings about Sadat's go-it-alone policies toward Israel and his isolation of Egypt from the Arab world; after all, part of the rationale for *Infitah* was to gain Egyptian access to Arab investments and markets all of which were jeopardized by Sadat's policies. Sadat clearly went much further in accommodating Israel at the expense of Egypt's Arab ties than even his strongest supporters would have done. Large segments of the bourgeoisie preferred a more liberal political system and a greater share of political power than Sadat was willing to permit. That a majority of respondents placed themselves to the liberal right of Sadat's government party was a measure of the threat to his support represented by the liberal New Wafd. However, their strong support for Sadat personally, and their ambivalence regarding the feasibility of a fully liberal model suggests why most accepted his repression of the Wafd in the name of social peace. Finally, there seemed to be some unease, even among those most benefiting from it, at the growth of inequality under *Infitah*; given the strong stake of the bourgeoisie in liberalization this is unlikely to translate into much opposition to the regime but it could result in a moral 'failure of nerve' in some future class conflict. On the whole, these soft spots did not seem to seriously threaten Sadat's command of the loyalty of the bourgeoisie; but they were enough to explain the ability of the New Wafd on the right and the SLP on the left to carve out support among smaller segments of this class.

Finally, because these 'cracks' in the support of Sadat's main constituency were undoubtedly magnified in the strata below the bourgeoisie, the survey findings give some suggestive glimpses of the wider political arena. The lack of enthusiasm among this most Westernized group for a separate peace with Israel and for a strongly pro-American policy suggests how shallow support for these policies must be in the wider Egyptian public. That significant support was expressed among this most Westernized group for an Arab–Islamic identity for

Egypt, and even more so among pure Egyptians, suggests the strength of such an appeal among the less Westernized masses. The greater Arab orientation and lesser appeal of Sadat's foreign policy among the pure Egyptian Muslim government-employed sub-group suggests that in these issue areas Sadat was out of step with the bureaucratic bases of his own regime.

The middle strata: the breeding grounds of activism

The middle layer of the political pyramid was made up of elements which lacked the formidable political resources and the privileged access to decision-makers enjoyed by the bourgeoisie, but which were much more politically attentive and susceptible to political mobilization than the bulk of the mass public. Students, organized (largely public sector) industrial workers, and public sector white-collar employees were the main constituents of this stratum. These groups all had more education than the rest of the mass public; concentrated in urban areas, for example, the campus or factory, they were more organized and mobilizable. Endowed under the Nasir regime with certain rights threatened by liberalization, and with higher expectations susceptible to disappointment, they were more conscious of grievances than the rest of the mass public. Thus they were the typical pool from which opposition movements drew their activists. As such, the regime had to take care either to control or respond to their demands.

Students The students were a vanguard of political activism. Student opinion carried special weight because, as a broadly recruited group, students expressed the views of a wide public. While some students, such as those from bourgeois families concentrated at the American University, were pro-government and many others were politically apathetic, there was considerable student activism under Sadat and it usually took an anti-government form. Students were susceptible to dissidence because of their greater politicization and their high expectations at a time when career outlooks for many surplus graduates were bleak. As if to make trouble for himself, Sadat continued the expansion of higher education, opening many regional campuses which spread student dissidence from the big cities to rural towns like Assiut and Minya.

Student activism seemed inversely related to the legitimacy level of the regime. The student movement of 1972–3 which reached unprecedented levels, was a product of the post-1967 disillusionment and Sadat's apparent inability to face the Israelis. Nationally humiliated and faced with interminable military service, students wanted serious preparation for war. The left, swelled by the recruitment of students from lower-class families and American support for Israel, dominated the movement, but there was also an anti-Soviet student right wing. Having lost confidence in the regime, students of all persuasions demanded democracy. Their weapons were posters, leaflets, sit-ins, petitions and, when these failed, massive demonstrations. Even officially sponsored student union leaders were carried away by the demands of their constituency. Sadat jailed student leaders and sent the police onto the campus, but then, in a gesture of appeasement, released the leaders and deputized ASU boss Sayyid Marei to devote his full time to assuaging student discontent (Marei 1978a: 662–8; Shukri 1978: 110–29). After 1973, however, as the legitimacy of the regime soared and student preoccupation with conscription and American imperialism faded, the wind went out of the sails of the movement. De-Nasirization inspired only sporadic, tame student protests. Leftist student leaders were loath to challenge the newly legitimized regime (Shukri 1978: 253–6); their influence on campus shrank. Sadat, encouraged, removed police from campus and relaxed controls over the student unions. Before long, Islamic power began to fill the vacuum. In 1977, Islamic students swept student union elections in most faculties at the expense of both pro-government and leftist candidates (*al-Ahram* 27 Dec. 1977). Then, as the regime's legitimacy was eroded in the late seventies, student dissidence reignited, this time in an Islamic form. Students trying to impose an Islamic order on campus clashed with administrators. At Cairo University posters openly critical of Sadat, his wife and advisors went up. The head of the student union openly accused Sadat of lying to the people about the terms of the peace treaty. In Assiut and Minya student demonstrations took a violent turn. Most opposition was ideological but official calls for an end to public employment of graduates inflamed students' personal grievances. Finally, the regime cracked down. Police were returned to campus, student unions purged and 'advisors' appointed to screen nominees for new elections. Sadat ruled campuses off limits to political activity and told politically active students to join the established political parties. The Ministry of Youth, defunct since the 1973 war, was reactivated and set about organizing sports to divert students from religion and politics. Student power was weakened by the reimposition of controls and by conflicts between Islamic militants and Coptic or secular students antagonized by the moral puritanism the latter were trying to impose. But unless the regime could restore its credibility with students, they were in a unique position, drawn from every social force, from top elite to rural town, to further undermine its remaining legitimacy (*al-Ahrar* 10 Sept. 1979; *al-Gumhuriyya*, 25 Feb. 1979; *al-Sharq al-Awsat*, 28 Mar. 1979).

Industrial workers Because of their relatively high levels of political consciousness, strategic concentration and history of activism, 1.2 million workers carry some political weight in Egypt. Although many workers can afford to do little more than concentrate on earning a living, their class consciousness is more developed than that of most other social forces. A feeling of bitterness toward the rich and educated encouraged and legitimized by Nasir in the sixties has left a permanent imprint on them. The identification of the government with state managers who many workers regard as a virtual class enemy, resentment at the absence of a right to strike, and the failure of wages to keep up with inflation have kept alive and turned worker class-consciousness in an anti-regime direction (Sayed 1978: 45–65). Instances of worker activism hostile to the regime dot the seventies. Worker activists were largely ranged on the side of Ali Sabri in the 1971 conflict with Sadat and were thereafter punished by the regime (Marei 1978a: 650–1). A workers' movement paralleled that of the students in the pre-1973 years. Workers protested the effects of economic liberalization in sporadic strikes and marches on parliament in the mid-seventies. In 1975, police repression transformed a protest over frozen wages and personnel matters into a major uprising in Mehalla al-Kubra. Workers set up a 'commune', seized the factories and the managers and were only put down after 50 died and 2000 were arrested. In 1976, there was a major disturbance in Kafr al-Dawar (Shukri 1978: 256–60). Working-class districts stood out in electing leftwing NPUP candidates to parliament in 1976. Workers provided many of the cadres of the NPUP, and in general showed a greater receptivity to the left than any other social force. Workers were involved in the 1977 'food' protests.

The regime tried to control and absorb the demands of labor through the established corporatist–syndicalist structure. Government intervention in union elections and its power to purge syndical leaders ensured pro-government syndicalists dominated the top of the union structure and they, in turn were coopted into the ruling party and into the government as Ministers of Labor. In the public firms, labor 'representatives' served on management boards. This arrangement permitted the labor movement to act, within narrow limits, as a kind of interest group in the system. The Minister of Labor's role in the wage-setting process gave workers a voice in this critical matter. Syndicate conferences in the seventies became arenas for articulating the special interests of workers and even for expressing their views on wider issues such as equality, defense of the 'gains' of the Nasir era and of the public sector. The 1976 National Congress of the General Federation of Labor demanded the public sector be protected, urged that only projects which local capital and technology could not undertake be admitted under *Infitah*, called for labor-intensive investments, asserted that inflation fighting measures should not be aimed at wage-earners only and that high and 'parasitic' incomes should pay their fair share, called for wage increases commensurate with inflation, the maintenance of price subsidies and price controls, and the extension of the rights enjoyed by the public sector workers to those in the private sector. Unions opposed the removal of parts of the public sector from the provisions of the labor law through establishment of joint ventures, they stood against the Amiriya project as a threat to public sector jobs, and opposed, through their positions on company boards, the hiving off of the best parts of public firms in foreign joint ventures.

Syndicalists expressed concern over proposals to amend the Labor Law giving management the right to fire workers receiving a grade of inefficient two years in a row and to unilaterally decide the hours of work; in general, they feared the drive of managers for greater power and autonomy (*al-Talia* Feb. 1977). To be sure, as the syndicates themselves complained, their demands often appeared to have little effect on decision-making (*al-Ahali*, 15 Feb., 3 May 1978); food subsidies were cut right after the 1976 conference called for their maintenance, Amiriya was approved, and *Infitah* administered without discrimination. But the regime did concede periodic wage increases against the arguments of economists and the private bourgeoisie that they were inflationary.

The regime had some success in containing the labor movement. As long as workers made their demands through the controlled unions, they were diverted from overt anti-system activity. Pro-regime syndicalists had a modicum of credibility with some workers. They helped contain worker participation in the 1977 riots (*The Middle East* Nov. 1977, p. 106) and were always able to mobilize contingents of workers for pro-regime demonstrations. Yet the head of the Labor Federation was once held prisoner by angry workers who accused him of being a tool of the regime (Shukri 1978: 60) and many workers viewed their representatives on management boards as collaborators (Sayyid 1978: 43). At lower levels of the union structure where government intervention was less effective, leftwing candidates won some elections and in 1979 an alarmed government tried to prevent leftists from standing (*Guardian* 22 Oct. 1979). Ultimately, it was the stick and the carrot which really kept workers in line: public sector workers knew that their wages were several times those of private sector workers and that a huge reserve army of unemployed coveted their jobs.

White collar employees   Middle- and lower-rank public employees were a third group which enjoyed greater political assets than the broader masses. They were better educated, concentrated and socially mobilized. Sheer numbers (about 2 million) lent them weight. Some of them, at least, had access to patrons higher up in the bureaucracy which most citizens lacked. In many ways the regime's policies, if not its survival, depended on their compliance.

However, at least by comparison to workers and students, public employees were less politically active and less involved in overt opposition. They made up, it is true, significant segments of all the opposition parties; but many others were members of the government party. Some were incorporated into trade unions which made up part of the Labor Federation, but Egypt's white-collar unions were not the vanguard of militancy they are in many Third World countries. If the government's complaints can be believed, many public employees put up covert resistance to Sadat's liberalization policies, and many may have disliked his foreign policy as well (see p. 243); but they were not in the forefront of challenges to the regime on issue grounds. Rather they were more likely to act in defense of their particular interests. Much of their political influence was expended in individual efforts for upward mobility. They used both parliament and the government party to seek increased salaries and redress of career grievances. Their negative power as a group seemed sufficient to deter the government from long-overdue reforms of the bureaucracy.

The regime had several levers of control over them which, no doubt, muted their political activism. It could depend on the heritage of bureaucratic submission to authority as well as the threat of dismissal. Some civil servants, at least, were a 'bought' clientele: in return for loyalty, the regime tolerated their petty corruption and the indiscipline and poor job performance for which the bureaucracy had become famous (Waterbury 1976a: 435). Thus, as parasites on the public and the state treasury, they had a stake in the regime. Yet, if little was demanded of the bureaucrat, little was also given to him. Not only were lower- and even middle-level civil servants badly paid, but the gap between them and the top bureaucratic elite was enormous. Moreover, no social force suffered more from the rapid inflation unleashed by *Infitah*. As their relatively fixed salaries fell behind inflation, many saw the amenities they believed themselves entitled to – notably housing – slip out of reach. Because their frustrations were undoubtedly more acute than those of the poor who never had a hope of rising out of poverty, they were much more susceptible to political discontent. But there was little sign that their discontent had been channeled into a united anti-regime direction.

The lower strata

The urban masses Egypt's urban mass public is not, of course, an undifferentiated monolith. It is stratified internally. At the top are middle and small merchants, artisans, petty contractors, small workshops owners and other small-scale 'entrepreneurs' who shade imperceptibly into the middle bourgeoisie. At the bottom are legions of underemployed beggars, peddlers and laborers who eke out a bare existence. This public is also segregated according to somewhat self-contained *baladi* neighborhoods composed of a multitude of small family-owned establishments knit together through kinship and inter-marriage, common religion and place of rural origins, traditional life style and social controls. To be sure, the isolation of these communities is breaking down, for roughly half of urban workers must now seek employment outside their quarter. But the solidarity of neighborhoods remains strong and the stratification which divides them is bridged by ties of clientage and kinship. Internal segmentation and differentiation and the vertical ties which link the masses to the bourgeoisie retard class consciousness in the *baladi* quarter. A tradition of individual entrepreneurship reinforced by the prospect of self-betterment

247

through work in the Arabian Gulf also works against it. Yet as the urban masses are increasingly exposed to and made dependent on wider society, and as, under *Infitah*, their perceptions of societal inequality are sharpened, class consciousness is no doubt developing. The distinctions between *baladi* people and the Westernized upper and middle classes along lines of dress, life style, values and self-perception could provide the basis for a politically operative division between the urban mass and those above them (Rugh 1979: 34–53).

The urban quarters are only tenuously linked to the larger political system. The penetration of governmental bureaucracy is weak. Government provides few municipal services; on the contrary, it makes an onerous demand on the local community, military conscription, which today as in the past is feared and evaded because of its threat to the economic viability of the family. The government party lacks formal presence in the local neighborhoods and is content to coopt local notables to committees situated at Cairo's seven very large urban districts, each of which encompasses hundreds of thousands of people (Cantori and Benedict 1979; Rugh 1979: 72–4) The urban public is also only tenuously linked to the regime through its parliamentary deputies. Many deputies were prestigious Westernized professionals nominated by the government and dutifully elected by the urban masses, but hardly representative of their district. Others were traditional notables. Typical of the latter was Sayyid Gallal, a rich merchant from the al-Azhar area who stood at the head of a clientage network reaching into every back alley of his quarter. As a pious builder of mosques and a provider of petty welfare services, he had won the trust of his constituents, but he certainly did little to bring them into the world of modern issue politics (Springborg 1975: 89–90). Only a handful of deputies, such as the working-class activists elected on the NPUP ticket, or the likes of Ahmad Taha, an educated professional and Marxist who enjoyed wide support in Shubra, were outside these traditional molds. They may have symbolized the beginnings of class politics in Egypt's cities, but the bulk of the urban masses continued to be linked to the political establishment through the patron–'gatekeeper' typical of the historical Middle Eastern city. Most of these notables profited from and thus supported government policy; they therefore played a major role in the political control of the urban mass.

The urban masses were among the most powerless social forces in the political system. Their modest social resources, their low political consciousness, segmentalism, and propensity to clientalism, retarded organized political activism among them. The patron–client network which linked them to the top was by its nature asymmetrical, affording those at the bottom little leverage over those who represented them in the system (see, e.g. the attitude of the deputy from Bulak, Chapter 6). Yet, the urban mass could be said to enjoy, at least since the 1977 riots, a kind of negative power. In this uprising, elements of the urban poor demonstrated a readiness to resort to violent action and a hatred of the rich and powerful alarming to the regime. Equally alarming was the growing receptivity of the *baladi* people to the appeal of Islamic fundamentalists. Hence, the regime's care in tampering with subsidies on popular consumption commodities, Sadat's greater effort to deport himself as a pious Muslim, his periodic distribution of largesse on Muslim holidays, and the growing presence of security forces on Cairo's main streets.

The peasantry   The peasantry is not a uniform or solidary social force. It is segmented by family and village, and internally stratified into 'rich' and 'poor', while lines of kinship and clientage cut across economic differences linking peasants to the rural bourgeoisie. Dispersed in hundreds of self-contained villages and lacking political organization, or much class consciousness, peasants hardly functioned as a unified political force. The peasants possessed the fewest politically usable resources; their average income was the lowest of all social groups and they had the least command of literacy: in the seventies, 70% of the rural population remained illiterate and 97% of the poor peasantry had not even completed primary school (Radwan 1981: 122). Peasants were the most politically crippled by the traditional political culture of passivity, deference and particularism. Possessing the least capacity to influence or to threaten the powers-that-be, peasants were the easiest ignored of the forces competing in the political arena. As the ties which once linked the power elite to the village withered away, it was less inclined as well as little constrained, to consider peasants' interests in its decisions.

This does not mean that the countryside remained politically unchanged since 1952, for the Nasir regime's effort to bring the village into the national political system did leave a durable impact. Land reform broke the overwhelming dominance of the landlord over the peasant, and the penetration of the government apparatus, checking the sway of traditional notables, produced a more pluralized local power structure. The peasant was, in principle, welcomed into political life as a citizen with rights, and sporadic limited efforts made to mobilize peasant political activism. These changes left some imprint on peasant political consciousness. Observers have noted a dilution of the old culture of servility to landlord or official and some have reported an assertiveness on the part of peasants in some places (Harik 1984: 60). In a few places the change has been dramatic: in some of the same areas of upper Egypt where before 1952 landlords could expect peasants to kiss their hands, in the seventies fear of peasant violence kept them from their estates. One 1979 study of an Egyptian village discovered a substantial difference between the attitudes of generations. The older generation felt powerless, fatalistically attributed the outcome of elections to the will of God, dutifully voted for a candidate from a notable family because he was the most outstanding 'son of the village,' believed the government could or would do nothing for peasants, preferred to settle problems and disputes privately, and being illiterate, neither followed nor discussed political issues. In contrast, members of the younger generation expressed a greater sense of efficacy, asserted that they would take grievances to the authorities, were much more likely, being literate, to follow and discuss political issues and explained their support for electoral candidates in terms of specific services promised the village (Hamid 1980).

The central government reform drive in the village was not, however, sustained under Sadat. As a result of the rural penetration drives of the Nasir regime, government presence in the countryside was still formidable. But the mobilizational and service dimensions of that activity disappeared, leaving only the control dimension and a growing tolerance for the restoration of old or the emergence of new power structures and social inequalities. A huge apparatus of agricultural officials remained in place, which, though sometimes both corrupt and incompetent, had the right to tell the peasant when and what to plant and harvest, and to secure or obstruct his access to credit, seed, water and fertilizer; for the peasant, the hydraulic society was, in some respects, more a reality in the late twentieth century than ever before. A line of coercive control ran downward from the Ministry of Interior to the district police station and the local *umdeh*. The persistence of traditional fear of and deference to authority is hardly surprising (Critchfield 1978). To be sure, a series of service ministries like health and education also maintained local offices in the countryside, but this, as opposed to the control dimension of government activity, contracted in the seventies: there was a perceptible decline in the provision of services by local officials, whether those running the combined health and social service unit or teachers staffing village schools, and a corresponding increase in 'private' provision of these same services for a fee; this neglect and privatization of public services resulted in part from financial constraints and a decline in control, but also from a decline of interest at the center in servicing the village (Rashid 1980). There was a similar atrophy of the socio-political institutions created under Nasir in part to represent and stimulate local peasant activism. The ASU had so acted to a modest degree, but it was allowed to decline in the village. In 1972 the peasant affairs committee of the organization reported that links between the party center and the village had disappeared leaving a political vacuum in the countryside; the government parties which replaced the ASU neither penetrated as far down nor made comparable efforts to recruit mainstream peasants, being content to coopt local landlords, *umad* and rich peasants. The cooperatives, which in the sixties had sometimes served as political bases for middle peasants, also declined. After 1968 they were increasingly neglected by the regime, in good part, owing to the hostility of landlords and some local officials, and the lagging support of the peasants themselves who resented their use increasingly to extract a surplus from them. The regime's failure to hold periodic elections to cooperative boards, to raise the meager salaries paid officials appointed to cooperatives, or seriously to prosecute abuses led to widespread corruption in the system; the regime then used the results of its neglect to justify the further enervation of the cooperatives (*al-Ahrar* 11 Feb. 1980; Harik 1984: 49–53; *al-Talia*, May 1976, pp. 87–92). The cooperative superstructure, the one linkage to the national level speaking solely for a peasant constituency, was abolished. Then the cooperatives' responsibilities for marketing and the provision of credit and supplies were entrusted to 'Village Banks' which had no peasant representation and were expected to run on a purely 'commercial' basis. Practically all that remained of the coop was the agronomist charged with control of the crop rotation system. Not surprisingly, cooperative membership steadily declined from 3.2 to 2.5 million between 1972 and 1977. Similarly, the agrarian arbitration system, since the fifties in the hands of village committees on which peasants were represented, was abolished and its functions assigned to the local judiciary; few peasants could hire the legal aid needed to make this institution work for them (*al-Ahram* 20 May 1980; NPUP 1978; Osman 1980).

The one institution linking village and center which persisted and was even revitalized under Sadat was local government. As part of a strategy of de-centralization, local mayors were given authority over all 'line' ministries operating in their locales, presumably at the expense of the central government. Local governments were also given widened powers to raise and keep local tax revenues. Elected local councils were, at least formally, given a share of power *vis-à-vis* the appointed executive, for example, the right to disapprove the mayor's budget (*al-Ahram* 20 May 1980; Harik 1984: 54–62). In a major departure, local public bodies were encouraged to invest in local economic enterprises alone or in partnership with private investors. These changes were designed to encourage local political participation. But they also aimed to contain local demands on the central treasury by encouraging communities to raise the revenues to finance their own services; to some extent this happened but the soaring deficits of local government budgets (Bonander reports they went up 110% from 1978 to 1979) suggest that elected local councils often became platforms for making local demands on the government (Bonander 1980; Rashid 1980; Springer 1980). A third purpose of the local government experiment – supported vigorously by USAID – was to stimulate local capitalist enterprise, complementing economic liberalization on the national level. By all accounts, it did, in fact, encourage a new alliance between government employees and local investors which paralleled that on the national level. Since the mainstream of the peasantry had few resources to invest, the benefits of these enterprises tended to go disproportionately to the 'haves', increasing inequality at the local level as at the national level (Bonander 1980, Harik 1984:63; Springer 1980). Power on the local councils also seemed to be in the hands of local officials and well-off peasants. The end result of the experiment seemed likely to be increased prosperity for some and, as on the national level, a refusion of power and wealth which were, to some extent, separated under Nasir.

Parallel to the decline of local institutions in which the mainstream peasantry was represented, there was a perceptible revitalization of the traditional power structures curbed under Nasir in the sixties. The village *umdeh* recovered some of his old power. To be sure, he remained checked by the officers of the district police station appointed from outside the area. But the *umdeh* was chiefly responsible for security in the village, and for mediating relations between it and the police. The old dominance of the landlords was not restored – and could not be without a restoration of the great estates and a retreat of the government presence from the countryside. But, while diluted, peasant economic dependency on landlords had far from disappeared; 200–300 *feddan* estates on which peasant laborers live at the sufferance of their employer can still be found in Egypt. Moreover, the government had ceased to challenge, and had become an ally of landlord power; in this changed political climate they acted with much greater confidence than under Nasir.

Parliamentary elections, the basic political institution through which the political preferences of the rural population is registered at the political center, clearly reflect this resurgence of traditional power and the persistence of the old politics. Families and clientage networks were the basic units of political action in these contests. *Umad* in some places could still deliver the votes of practically whole villages. Conversely, issues were of little importance, and the opposition parties which tried to fight them on such grounds found limited receptivity; indeed, typical of the little extent to which peasants understood or welcomed issue politics was the opposition of some to party competition on grounds it was likely to take the form of rivalries between families which would split the village. Elections run on a clientalist basis inevitably reproduced the local power structure in parliament; thus, in the seventies the countryside was almost exclusively represented by notables, the contingent of mainstream peasants coopted under Nasir largely disappearing. This shift in representation appeared to have a significant impact on political outcomes, that is, in the bias in agrarian legislation which favored the interests of the rural bourgeoisie at the expense of the mainstream peasantry.

Many peasants had good reason to be discontented. Increases in rent, restoration of land to landlords, the gutting of the cooperatives, the reduction in subsidies for agricultural inputs, low state prices for compulsory crop deliveries and the rapid rate of inflation, higher in rural than urban areas, hurt peasants and were readily attributable to government policy. Poverty, inequality and landlessness in the countryside all grew during the seventies. Passive resistance to the regime did seem to be on the rise; in 1976 there were, according to one source, 302,000 cases of violation of the crop rotation plan and 118,000 of failures to make compulsory crop deliveries (*al-Ahram* 14, 17 Jan. 1980; *al-Ahram* 17 Dec. 1979; NPUP 1978: 20–3, 34–5). There are a few incidents of overt rebellion on record, such as anti-landlord riots in Biyala against attempts to recover land forcibly from tenants. There are reports of destruction of machinery by peasants facing displacement by mechanization (*al–Ahali* 5 Mar. 1978). But such incidents were localized and sporadic. More significant was the fact that the regime was consistently able to fall back on the weight of peasant votes and soldiers to contain the largely urban opposition. The reasons are clear. Peasant culture, poverty, and ignorance kept most non-participant and quiescent. Bureaucratic controls were pervasive. The rich peasantry and notables who benefited from regime policies supported the regime; to the considerable extent they represented the natural leadership of the village, they linked much of the peasantry to it. With the exception of Islamic fundamentalism which did begin to spill over into the village, this network was quite resistant to opposition forces. Sadat probably enjoyed some personal legitimacy as a son of the village who made good but continued to identify himself as a peasant and to articulate traditional village values. Even some poor and middle peasants advanced themselves under his new order: those living in labor-scarce areas got higher wages, a few received redistributed reclaimed land, and those who got the chance to work in oil rich countries returned with savings and consumer goods hitherto inaccessible to the rural masses. The only danger to the regime seemed to lie in the potentially explosive combination of growing rural inequality and spreading rural access to education which was bound, over time, to raise rural politicization and expectations.

Political alignments under Sadat

While no precise depiction of the political arena in Egypt is possible in the absence of survey data, there is enough evidence to attempt a rough depiction of it around 1976–8, a time when the legitimacy of the regime was neither at its highest nor lowest points, and when, political freedom being at its maximum, a reasonable assessment could be made.

The Sadat regime itself was the only political force which enjoyed a base cutting across all political strata and social classes. It enjoyed its most solid support among the bourgeoisie which dominated the political infrastructure; but the bureaucracy and labor syndicates linked a big segment of public employees and industrial workers to it and a combination of clientage and deference to legitimate authority translated into substantial mass acquiescence in the established order. The regime thus had strong support from the strongest social force, the bourgeoisie, and softer but wider support in the mass public. The bases of the opposition were all smaller, but, recruited on an issue basis from the most active political strata, they were also more mobilized and committed. The New Wafd mobilized a following of committed liberals from the bourgeoisie and was a major threat to the regime's base among its strongest supporters. The center–left, incorporated in the SLP, rallied elements of the bourgeoisie and the educated middle class; loyal to the regime, it was not a direct threat but its significant latent appeal inside the establishment itself made it a potential rival of incumbent elites. The nationalist–left (mainly the NPUP), though small, cut across two strategic social forces, the educated middle class and industrial workers and was well-organized and motivated. The Islamic opposition was the largest and perhaps the most intensely committed of the opposition forces; rooted in the active middle strata, it also had a potentially wide mass appeal. Under conditions of free competition all these opposition forces would have had good chances to expand their bases, probably at the expense of the regime, but it was precisely for this reason that Sadat eschewed full-scale liberalization. Without it, they threatened the regime only to the extent they acted in concert; however, divided by deep historical animosities, they long permitted Sadat to divide – and hence – rule them. Only at the beginning of the eighties were there serious signs of a coalescence of an all-opposition front which could pose a significant threat to the regime, and it proved fleeting.

The mass public in the Egyptian political system

The role of the public in the political system was shaped in part by the participatory resources and propensities of the public itself. Traditional habits of deference, segmentalism and the scarcity of the resources of participation limited the size of the politically active, attentive, and relevant publics to a minority of the population. The unequal distribution of resources translated into unequal propensities and capabilities to participate. But the political arena was not unchanging. On the one hand, the expectations of the educated classes, especially the bourgeoisie, for a share of power steadily mounted. On the other hand, the slow diffusion of participatory resources downward widened the social base of political participation. Thus, participatory pressures from below on the regime did grow, albeit slowly.

The strategies and capabilities of the regime for coping with its changing political arena also shaped the role of the public in the system. In essence, while under Nasir the regime minimized the ability of the haves to translate their greater resources into power, under Sadat it attempted to accommodate their demands, and thus, reinforced the inequality in the distribution of power resources between social groups. In an authoritarian regime, the responsiveness of the elite to political groups is a decisive factor in determining the distribution of power. Nasir, a populist who sought to build mass support in the face of opposition from the haves, frequently chose to put the expectations of his mass constituency above the interests of the bourgeoisie. Sadat, in contrast, rested his rule and his policies on the support of the bourgeoisie and the Western powers; the need to accommodate their demands introduced powerful influences potentially, although not always, in contradiction with the expectations of the have-nots. The embourgeoisement of the elite, in part an outcome of deliberate recruitment policies, also shifted the balance of sympathy in elite circles in favor of the haves. The structures of elite–mass linkage also biased the distribution of political influence. Employed under Nasir more to control than channel demands into the decision-making process, they gave little effective influence to any social group. Under Sadat, they were opened up for the bourgeoisie, but remained largely closed to those below; while this alteration did widen the scope of participation, because it did so unequally, it actually reinforced political inequality. Thus parliament and the professional syndicates, though still subordinate to the executive, became much more effective mechanisms of interest articulation for the bourgeoisie than heretofore, while efforts to use the student unions, mosques, or trade unions as comparable channels for other interests or values enjoyed little tolerance. The webs of clientalism which interlocked with formal institutions similarly favored the haves over the have-nots; thus, while bourgeois families, through intermarriage and personal connections to the Presidency, literally captured the apex of these networks, those at the bottom of the long chains of patrons and clients stretching downward, lacked the leverage to extract more than petty benefits. Even to the extent the masses were incorporated into the clientage system, they were thereby deterred from the activism and horizontal solidarity which alone might have made up for their individual lack of resources. Finally, the multi-party system, which, in principle, might have become a mechanism of mass influence and elite accountability, was not permitted to evolve in a competitive direction for precisely this reason. The regime's structural alterations were an effective adaptation to the growing bargaining power of the bourgeoisie, but not to the diffusion of political consciousness to those below this politically privileged stratum.

The experience of Egypt indicates that, so long as the legitimacy of the ruler is high, participatory pressures in an authoritarian regime are readily contained. However, to the extent it declines, opposition activism increases; if legitimate channels for such activity are lacking or clogged, groups deprived of access may nevertheless affect government decisions through the threat or actual resort to 'anomic' political activity outside of and against the regime. Up to 1973 Sadat had to cope with such pressures; the legitimacy won in the war gave him a free hand to pursue his policies, relatively unconstrained by them for several years. By the end of the seventies, however, discontent with policy consequences had begun to spark a reaction below. The regime responded to these pressures with a mixture of repression and concession. The concessions were a symptom of a measure of 'negative' power to constrain government decisions possessed by those outside the regime's privileged constituency. But even such negative power was unequally distributed: students, workers, public employees and the urban masses had some, peasants apparently very little. Moreover, it is clear that while mass reaction was able to slow down the implementation of regime policies, it was insufficient to force a major redirection. The consequent persistence of anti-system forces unabsorbed by the regime was evidently perceived by 1980 as a sufficient threat by Sadat to significantly heighten the level of repression. But repression was no permanent solution; by the end of the Sadat era, the regime seemed to face a mini-crisis of participation which was threatening to take 'praetorian' forms.

Chapter 9

Public policy and the political economy of development

The public policy orientation of the Sadat regime

If under Nasir the 'socialist transformation' of Egypt lagged well behind the formal adoption of 'Arab Socialist' ideology, so under Sadat change in public policy lagged behind the 'de-socialization' of elite ideology. In fact, so far did the actual development of new policies and practices lag behind intentions that a coherent new economic order which could effectively substitute for etatism had not yet crystallized by the end of the Sadat era. This was, in part, because, aside from agreement on the desirability of a more mixed and open economy, the elite possessed no coherent shared conception of the goals or means of reform. Neither was there a unified and committed leadership team needed to see it through. Moreover, decision-makers, hemmed in by constraints, faced no easy choices. The regime could, in principle, have charted an austere egalitarian road to reform, equally and strictly disciplining the appetites of all social forces and carefully tailoring *Infitah* to serve planned development objectives. But such a course was, in practice, impossible for it. It would have required a large scope of authoritarian government control and would have antagonized the very forces *Infitah* depended on: foreign investors who wanted less government and a wholly open Egypt, a local bourgeoisie seeking redress from the egalitarian privations imposed under Nasir. On the other hand, the regime could have insisted on a thorough return to the market, an end to statist and populist intervention, and a radical reform of the bureaucracy which would have put the burden of change squarely on the public sector and the poor. The regime did move in this direction, but faced with vested interests or popular anger proved wanting in commitment or ruthlessness. Buffeted by conflicting pressures, the regime increasingly took a third 'easy' way out: it declined vigorously to impose the burden of change on any social force and fell into reliance on foreign aid as the main vehicle of the economic takeoff needed to satisfy its bourgeois constituency and contain popular discontent. Apparently painless, this course led to rising debt and dependency.

As a result, policy was a patchwork compromise between the old etatist order and the favored new capitalist direction. Under Nasir, the public sector was

257

considered the motor of development. Under Sadat, the foreign sector, alone or in partnership with local firms, was to assume this role. The private sector was revitalized and much public investment diverted to services in support of private capital. Generous tax and tariff incentives put foreign capital at an advantage, and virtually no field, including strategic sectors such as heavy industry and banking, was immune from penetration. Yet, a huge unrationalized public sector persisted and continued to absorb a large proportion of all investment. Under Nasir, government operated on the assumption that public policy could ensure both growth and equity, and pervasive intervention in the economy sought to allocate resources for state-set investment priorities and to redistribute them through direct expropriation, progressive taxation, subsidies and the extension of welfare services. Under Sadat, it was accepted that the private entrepreneurship needed for economic recovery would have to be disproportionately rewarded in order that all might ultimately benefit from growth, and that the market could more efficiently allocate and distribute resources. Administrative intervention was indeed cut back (e.g. price controls, ceilings on income), taxation was reduced, welfare services neglected and property redistribution eschewed. Yet much administrative intervention persisted, and despite all 'reform' efforts, the total volume of subsidies continued to grow. Under Nasir, the state took over most of Egypt's foreign economic links with the aim of curbing the extroversion of the economy and pursuing a strategy of import substitution industrialization and agricultural intensification. Under Sadat, the economy was reintegrated into the world capitalist market, and development strategy began to stress Egypt's role as a middleman between the West and the Arab world and as an exporter of services and labor. Thus, state controls over foreign economic relations were sharply cut back: most foreign trade was returned to private hands which, under greatly liberalized conditions, permitted a massive influx of foreign imports; the allocation of scarce foreign exchange according to public priorities virtually ceased; the pound was 'floated'; and bi-lateral state economic agreements with the Eastern bloc phased out. This was perhaps the most thorough change from the Nasir era. Yet, the two regimes shared a heavy reliance on foreign loans and aid as a substitute for the extraction of a large internal surplus. In summary, both regimes sought a third or middle road to development which they hoped would relieve them of the high costs of pure capitalism or communism; they differed in that while Nasir sought to minimize the inegalitarianism and extroversion of the market economy, Sadat accepted these, insofar as it was politically feasible, as the costs of greater efficiency and foreign assistance.

Leadership, bureaucratic capabilities and policy implementation

The success of Sadat's new socio-economic order depended in great part on the capability of the administrative leadership and structures which were expected to design and carry it out. Sadat did not inherit an efficient apparatus of policy implementation from Nasir. The bureaucratic elite was infected with patrimonialism. The bureaucratic machine was bloated, overburdened, corrupted and lacking in effective planning and control mechanisms. Enveloping society in regulations, and drawing off resources for its upkeep, it threatened to be an obstacle rather than an aid to the new course. Because so much of the economy was state controlled, economic reform depended on bureaucratic reform; if the advantages of *Infitah* were to be maximized and its costs contained, and private initiative neither stifled nor diverted from productive channels, the bureaucracy had to be made more efficient, less burdensome and more deft in managing society. If the burdens of change were to be equitably distributed, public support for the new order maintained and a climate favorable to initiative and responsibility created, it had to be made more efficient and honest. But, reforming the accumulated bureaucratic pathologies of decades was a mammoth task. In practice, the Sadat regime not only failed to reform the state apparatus, but allowed it to deteriorate further. There were some reductions in the functions of the bureaucracy, but from 1971 to 1980 it grew 75% in size. By the mid-seventies, it was probably more fragmented, sluggish, and undisciplined than in the fifties and sixties. It was certainly more colonized by a mushrooming array of private interests, and, according to one prominent student of Egyptian public administration, corruption had become the rule rather than the exception (Ayubi 1979). The deepening of these pathologies was, ironically, partly a consequence of *Infitah* itself. In short, both economic reform and social equity became, to a great extent, victims of a persistent gap between policy goals and the administrative capabilities of the state.

A key factor in the failure of reform was the weakness of political and administrative leadership. The lack of strong unified direction from the top was one dimension of this weakness. Once Nasir's hard-driving presence was removed, a cohesive, motivated leadership team was needed to fill the vacuum. The purge of the 'centers of power' presented the opportunity to construct such a team, but it appears to have been missed. Sadat himself did not provide firm leadership for internal economic reform; he was too preoccupied with foreign policy, too unwilling to expend the scarce political capital needed to see through his foreign policy on economic reform, and perhaps too naively optimistic that a mere return to the market, more foreign resources and technology, or peace, would almost automatically bring prosperity.[1] Prime Ministers lacked the authority to provide the needed drive and cohesion. The heterogeneity and rapid turnover in the elite undermined the unity and continuity of leadership. There was little palpable effort to develop a more effective planning mechanism or better fiscal and monetary instruments needed to give coherence to economic management. As a result, decision-making was often fragmented among scores of agencies and committees, policies determined by bureaucratic rivalry and empire-building, and implementation retarded by a lack of coordination. These inefficiencies often had direct economic costs. Approval of projects of foreign investors was inordinately lengthy and bogged down in conflicts between various agencies. Resources were often poorly allocated, or linkage between projects sponsored by different agencies lacking. Limited resources were often spread too thinly among conflicting bureaucratic claimants, seriously lengthening project completion. *Infitah* seemed, in fact, to fuel bureaucratic empire-building; public agencies got in the habit of seeking partial funding from external sources for a project, then putting pressure on the treasury to match it (Ikram 1980: 63–4; Kanovsky 1981: 362).

Perhaps even more enervating was the growing corruption and 'colonization' of the administrative elite by special interests. There were, of course, many individuals of integrity in high official posts, but the names of those engaged in corrupt practices reads all too much like a roll-call of the top elite. The taking of commissions on state contracts with foreign firms and outright embezzlement were the chief and most overt forms of corruption. This corruption had major costs. Commission-taking not only raised the costs of contracts at the expense of the treasury, but often smoothed the way for deals inappropriate to Egypt's needs. The bribery of officials allegedly led to the purchase of the wrong kind of aircraft at excessive prices by the Aviation Ministry, to the purchase of trams for Alexandria at very high costs and without provision for the supply of spare parts and to the purchase of defective buses for Cairo. Commissions to officials helped conclude the Amiriya deal without serious study of its effect on local industry and fees to the Minister of Tourism paved the way for the Pyramid Plateau project. According to Waterbury, the cost of rebuilding the Canal cities may have been raised 30–40% after officials took their cuts. Outright embezzlement became more frequent and involved larger sums. The chairman of the Bank of Alexandria was charged with misappropriating a quarter of a million pounds and the head of the Cairo Water board with more than a million pounds. Officials are known to have exploited the public sector in less direct ways. Some officials used public facilities to set up their own businesses or stole public commodities for sale on the black market. They accepted kickbacks on contracts with the private sector in which poor goods or services were purchased at inflated prices, or set up their own firms to do business with the public sector on similar terms. Merchants using personal connections or bribery were granted concessions, monopolistic import licenses, exemptions from taxes or customs, or from the law, all at the expense of the treasury or consumers (Ayubi 1982; *al-Ahram* 16 Feb. 1979, 13 July 1979, 21 Nov. 1979; *al-Gumhuriyya* 18 Feb. 1979; *Ruz al-Yusuf* 19 Jan. 1976; Waterbury 1976a: 440). These crimes were rarely punished. The practice of keeping top officials on the public payroll long after they had left public service was a blatant example of the abuse of power for private interest. According to *Ruz al-Yusuf* (Ali 1977), of 1285 persons in ministerial, vice ministerial, or general director rank in the mid-seventies, only 94 were active; their salaries and fringe benefits amounted to £E13 million, twice the cost to the treasury of raising the minimum wage for 300,000 low-ranking employees from £E9 to £E15.

Less overt, but equally costly to reform, was the willingness of the elite to tolerate the growing colonization of public policy by vested interests at the expense of a coherent design. The previous discussion of the economic policy process showed how far they allowed policy to be shaped by pressure groups and how, under *Infitah*, they repeatedly tailored the law to meet the demands of foreign investors and donors. As Salacuse (1981) has argued, this legitimized the notion that the law could be bent for the sake of special interests and, as such, increased the vulnerability of the state to private colonization. In short, the state center was too fragmented, corrupted, and colonized – in a word, too 'soft' – to provide strong leadership in bureaucratic and economic reform.

The spread of corruption and colonization at the top resulted in part from the demoralization and privatization of the elite after 1967, in part from the unleashing of long pent-up appetites after 1973. It was also stimulated by the combination of a bureaucratic state and an open economy produced by *Infitah*. On the one hand, the influx of foreign aid and investment greatly expanded the rewards and temptations of corrupt practices; on the other hand, because the state remained a major customer, supplier and regulator of the economy, officials were in a strong position to 'sell' economic decisions on the revitalized market. The mechanisms of elite accountability proved far too feeble to contain these forces. The President tolerated (if he did not positively encourage) corruption as a mechanism of elite control, since those implicated developed a major stake in the preservation of the regime. Bureaucratic control mechanisms were weakened when honest auditors or inspectors who blew the whistle on malefactors were transferred or harassed. Criticism in the opposition press was too often repressed and public opinion too inattentive to be an effective deterrent. Parliament occasionally exposed corrupt practices but lacked the power to do much else and too often parliamentary elites were collaborators in these practices. Even the court system, zealous in the defense of individual private rights, proved lenient and sluggish in dealing with abuses of the public interest (Ayubi 1979; Hanafy 1976; *Ruz al-Yusuf*, 11 July 1978; Waterbury 1976a: 427, 435).

In this environment, it is scarcely surprising that the middle and lower ranks of the state machine were also plagued by costly pathologies. Corruption, if on a pettier scale, was no less pervasive at the expense of bureaucratic effectiveness, the treasury and the public dependent on the state for welfare services or legal protection. When officials of state stores diverted subsidized goods to the black market, the public was forced to subsidize the fortunes of black marketeers and fewer goods were available for the needy poor. When building inspectors took bribes to neglect the building code and buildings collapsed, the public was deprived of a basic security; when they took them to declare a sound building unsafe so the owner could sell the property on the booming real estate market, they deprived ordinary people of a place to live. When teachers insisted their students pay for private lessons, the poor were deprived of equal educational opportunity. When tax assessors took bribes to underestimate professional or business income or property values, the cost was born by the treasury and the wage earners whose taxes were deducted from their pay. The exaction of a bribe for every petty service from acquisition of a ration card to a passport, discriminated against the poor (*Ruz al-Yusuf* 12 Dec. 1978; Waterbury 1976b: 429–30, 442).

Added to the problem of corruption was the inertia, inefficiency, indiscipline and lack of initiative of much of the bureaucracy. To be sure, there were conscientious and innovative public officials. The agronomist of the state-owned Beheira Company who introduced a new line of small mechanized instruments suitable to Egyptian agriculture, represented the Egyptian official at his best (*Egyptian Gazette*, 13 Sept. 1979). But the spirit of *ihmal* (negligence) was rife in the state machine. The officials who came to work at ten o'clock and left at one, and spent their time reading newspapers, the busdrivers who passed up bus stops or stopped their buses for sandwiches while their passengers waited, the air traffic controllers who turned off their transmitters and refused calls from aircraft, were all too typical. Although the government employed thousands of surplus employees, the deterioration of public streets and buildings was pervasive, heaps of garbage cluttered the streets, broken sewage lines went unrepaired and manholes left uncovered. Citizens had to wait in long lines to buy in the cooperatives, pay public utility bills, deposit savings in banks, or conduct business in public offices (*al-Ahram* 24, 25 Oct. 1978; Nov. 1978; 14 June 1979; *al-Akhbar* 12, 15 Dec. 1978; 28 Feb. 1980). Laws went unenforced.

These pathologies had their roots in the Nasir era, but they seemed to take on a new order of magnitude under *Infitah*. The failure of leadership was undoubtedly decisive: a corrupt elite could hardly care to provide administrative leadership or fail to demoralize many honest officials at lower levels. But there were institutional and environmental problems, too. Even top officials who cared lacked instruments to energize and control those below them. The bureaucracy suffered from a scarcity of information – systematic files, data banks – with which to monitor policy performance. The personnel system had become largely *pro-forma*, incapable of rewarding the efficient or penalizing underperformers. The Central Agency for Organization and Administration (CAOA) claimed that 90% of public officials were regularly rated 'excellent' and a mere handful 'poor' by superiors who wanted no trouble from their subordinates; employees themselves attributed corruption to this poor personnel rating system (*al-Ahram*, 19 Oct. 1979). The Labor Law, making the dismissal of employees extremely difficult, greatly weakened discipline. For example, education inspectors were prevented by it from taking measures against teachers found forcing private lessons on their pupils (*al-Ahram* 10 June 1979). Public employees themselves attributed corruption to weak supervision, 'loose' regulations, organizational laxness and the lack of punishment (Abul Ghar 1979). The twin ills of overstaffing and underpay also contributed to bureaucratic pathology. In offices with numerous excess employees charged with the same job, nobody cared to take responsibility and supervisors could not differentiate between the efficient and inefficient. Low fixed salaries in the climate of inflation and conspicuous consumption produced by *Infitah* eroded employee motivation, forced them to hold two jobs, and made them ever more vulnerable to corruption (Abul Ghar 1979; *al-Ahram* 19 Oct. 1979). If, as the CAOA charged, most officials cared for little but promotions and allowances, this climate must have been partly responsible. Finally, much of the inertia and lack of responsibility of public officials was due to the over-centralization of decision-making and the excessive webs of regulations which constrained them; but in an era of growing official abuse of power, a significant relaxation of control or greater discretion for lower officials was risky. Sadat did try to shift powers downward to governors and public sector managers. But at the end of the decade, central authorities, believing lower levels infected with local particularism, and incompetent or dishonest, continued to hoard their powers over the smallest details, while lower-level officials were still passing responsibility upward (*al-Ahram* 11 Sept. 1979, 18 June 1980; *al-Akhbar* 10 Nov. 1978).

Effective policy implementation depends, ultimately, on habits of public compliance. But even as the ability of the bureaucracy to enforce public policy was enervated, indiscipline and *incivisme* grew among the public. The indifference and passivity toward public affairs bred by an overly bureaucratized state, no doubt, nurtured these tendencies. The shattering of regime legitimacy and the demoralization of the public in 1967 was a big step along this road. The relaxation and enervation of state controls in the atmosphere of privatism unleashed by *Infitah* was another. *Incivisme* took many forms. It was partly a lack of concern for public affairs, an unwillingness to accept the responsibilities of a citizen. As journalists frequently complained, Egyptians either took the view that everybody's business was nobody's business or that it was the government's business, that is, birth control was the problem of the Health Ministry, and law and order that of the Interior Ministry (*al-Gumhuriyya* 28 Apr. 1980). It was also expressed in a growing disregard for the law: traffic rules were ignored, books never returned to public libraries, taxes evaded. The neglect of obligations, however, was not paralleled by any lessened preoccupation with rights and privileges. Under Nasir, 'rights' to free education, public employment and subsidized food had been extended to the mass public and it was not prepared to give them back; under Sadat, the bourgeoisie sensed the time was right to press for the concessions and privileges they believed themselves deprived of under Nasir (e.g. unlimited consumption, lowered taxes) or for 'freedom' from public duties imposed on them (e.g. the year medical graduates were supposed to devote to rural service). These public attitudes constituted major constraints on government. It could expect little active support for policies; it could not even take compliance for granted or pursue strong consistent policies without resort to coercion and this it was largely unable or unwilling to do.

The combination of bureaucratic pathology and public *incivisme* often seemed to leave the government virtually paralyzed. Efforts to enforce policy seemed to come in frenetic campaigns which, once the push from the top ceased, rapidly subsided. In 1977 Mamduh Salim launched an 'administrative revolution' designed to reduce the bureaucratic red-tape and obstructionism which threatened to strangle the *Infitah*. But when it ended there was no evidence that much had changed and by 1980 organizational incapacity had replaced capital scarcity as the biggest constraint on Egypt's development (MENA 28 Sept. 1977; *Events* 4 Nov. 1977). In 1979 Prime Minister Mustafa Khalil launched a 'law and order' campaign to re-establish some public discipline: in one day of 'crackdown' 107 unlicensed street vendors, 112 litterbugs, 184 jay walkers, 15 pickpockets, 20 beggars and 40 'lechers bothering women' were arrested and 139 illegally parked cars towed. But only a month later, as one newspaper put it, 'chaos reigns supreme' (*Egyptian Gazette* 4 Jan., 14 Feb. 1979). Similar crackdowns on tax evaders and price gougers came and went, leaving little durable change behind them. The chaos on Egypt's roads was only the most visible example of the results of a return to 'market freedom' in a climate of official laxity and public indiscipline. On the one hand, a *laissez-faire* import policy flooded Egypt with more cars than its streets could accommodate. On the other, the public lacked habits of disciplined driving, and the police the capacity to enforce traffic regulations, often because well-off motorists could count on evading penalties. Cars were parked haphazardly, blocking streets and sidewalks, forcing pedestrians into the streets where they slowed traffic, traffic signals were ignored, and reckless driving was often the norm. The result was a very inefficient traffic flow and very dangerous streets; according to the Ministry of Transport, in 1977 Egypt had the highest death rate per automobile in the world (*Egyptian Gazette* 30 Apr. 1979; *Egyptian Mail*, 7 Apr. 1979). Unfortunately analogous situations prevailed in many other spheres of socio-economic life. Egypt's governmental incapacity had high costs for both equity and development.

The deterioration and apparent immunity to reform of the state's administrative capabilities was no accident. It was, rather, a natural product of the character of the regime and its relation to its environment in Egypt's particular circumstances. First, the enormous expansion and penetration of the state into a society where rational legal norms of achievement and loyalty to a 'public interest' were strongly diluted by particularistic attitudes was bound to make it vulnerable to infection by these cultural propensities. Secondly, delayed dependent development created a strong propensity to colonize the bureaucracy for the sake of private interests: because social mobilization and education outran economic development, pressures to turn it into an employment agency for the middle class were irresistible (and indeed are common to countries in Egypt's situation); because of the limited possibilities of indigenous capitalist development, the bourgeoisie was led to seek wealth through political influence. Thirdly, the structural dominance of the political system by the bureaucracy, and the lack of effective countervailing party organization, parliament or judiciary, deprived the system of institutional means to check official abuses of power or the capture of policy by vested interests, and of the instruments to mobilize the public support needed to pursue a strong policy in the face of such interests; in the absence of strong political channels capable of aggregating conflicting demands, the political process was bound to be channeled into a search for administrative exceptions and privileges through 'pull.' For a while, charismatic leadership and the ideological-nationalist impulse at the top could contain these tendencies, but once they were exhausted the system was bound to slip back into some form of 'neo-patrimonialism.' Last, but not least, *Infitah* inevitably exacerbated all these problems.[2] It stimulated appetites and eroded the rudiments of civic culture fostered by the revolution. It created or unleashed a multitude of private pressure groups and opened Egypt to powerful external pressures which further eroded the regime's capacity to enforce a coherent policy.

Public policy in practice

This section will attempt to assess, by focusing on several strategic policy areas, the performance of the political system in carrying out its policies. It will analyze the impact of policy on development in both its growth and distributive dimensions.

Public finance

Public finance – expenditures and taxation – is a strategic key to the assessment of system performance because it is a sector under relatively immediate government control. It is an indicator of the priorities, distributive intent and extractive capabilities of the regime.

Let us look first at the distributive impact of public finance, that is, the question of who bore the burden of government and development in Egypt. Taxation under Sadat was regarded not just as a revenue mechanism but as the sole legitimate means of containing income inequality (Dessouki 1982b: 79).

But did it in fact perform this function effectively? The evidence is strong that taxation lost under Sadat any progressiveness it had hitherto. Income taxes under Nasir reached a rate of 95% on incomes over £E10,000. In 1978 the tax rate on £E10,000–15,000 incomes was reduced to 35%, rising to only 80% on incomes over £E100,000; in 1980, the cabinet proposed legislation to further reduce the rate to a maximum of 50% on incomes over £E75,000 (Bentley 1981: 21–2). Ineffective tax collection in the private sector which shifted the burden to wage earners may have actually made the income tax regressive. High-income professionals and businessmen frequently evaded paying taxes. There was no effective capital gains tax to capture part of the spectacular windfall gains in fields such as real estate and construction typical of the *Infitah* period. In addition, the growing tax and customs exemptions granted investors, and incomes from shares and interest, narrowed the tax base at the expense of wage earners (Bentley 1981: 21; Ikram 1980: 49, 320; *Ruz al-Yusuf* 1 Mar. 1976; 25 Apr. 1977). The incidence of taxes on foreign trade and on consumer durables may have fallen more heavily on the rich, adding a progressive element to the system, but many indirect taxes also fell on popular consumption commodities. Implicit taxes, which were clearly regressive, must also be considered. Implicit taxes on compulsory crop deliveries which fell disproportionately on poor peasants, reached very high rates in the mid-seventies: 80% on income from cotton, almost 40% on rice; on the other hand, lucrative profits on the fruits and vegetables sold on the free market by well-off farmers went untaxed. Also, taxes and surpluses from the public industrial sector which in the mid-seventies reached a quarter of the value of the typical firm's output, could be considered a tax on public sector workers and perhaps the lower-income consumers of 'national' products. The evidence, therefore, appears strong that the tax system was regressive and became increasingly so. The concessions to capital meant to stimulate investment, and the administrative incapacity of the regime to enforce a progressive tax on private incomes and its consequent reliance on more easily collected or disguised 'implicit' taxes, explain this outcome.

Public spending tells a somewhat different, more ambiguous, story. Two major categories of expenditure, namely defense and development investment, presumably benefited the common good. The apparent decline in defense spending (from 15% to 10% of the GNP) in the seventies, and big increases in investment, can be taken as a welfare gain and an impetus to future growth; both can be considered positive aspects of regime policy. The other two major budget items were public salaries and consumer subsidies. Much of this was channeled to the middle and lower classes. A study by al-Edel argues that if subsidies, which grew rapidly in the seventies, are considered negative taxes, the overall effect of the tax system under Sadat was slightly progressive; but this study did not consider implicit taxes. Also, high-income groups received a higher per capita share of both public salaries and subsidies. And, the unofficial leakage of public funds through commissions and embezzlement disproportionately benefited higher income groups (al-Edel 1982: 132–73; Kanovsky 1981: 370).

As for the extractive capability of the state, it rose steadily. Government revenues as a proportion of GDP rose from 33% in 1962–3 to around 40% in 1976 and perhaps 50% in 1980–1, reflective of the strategic position of the state in the economy and growing oil revenues. Tax revenue also increased from around 15% of GDP under Nasir to between 20% and 25% in the mid-seventies, although it may later have declined as the government reduced taxes for the wealthy (Mabro 1974: 167, 226–7; Mead 1979). Despite this high extractive performance, revenue lagged well behind expenditures and Egypt was plagued with budget deficits in the seventies. The deficit, which Nasir had reduced from £E200–250 million (10%–15% of GNP) in the early sixties to £E5 million by 1970, reached 17% of GNP in 1977, 25% in 1978 (Kanovsky 1981: 372, Mead 1979), and exceeded £E3 billion by 1981–2. Part of the deficit was caused by inflated international prices, especially for imported food, and the willingness of the regime to bear these costs (if only for reasons of political survival) can be seen as an indicator of responsiveness to the mass public. Some of it was due to the regime's ambitious investment program. But it was also partly due to the inability of the tax system to capture a bigger share of the most rapidly rising incomes. The deficits were 'covered' by foreign aid and 'borrowing' from the central bank. The consequent inflationary effect fell heaviest on the lower-middle and lower groups, diluting if not wiping out, any progressive impact of public spending (Ikram 1980: 324).

On the whole, public finance under Sadat did not seem to have the progressive impact which might have diluted the inegalitarian effects of the newly unleashed market forces. Moreover, the declining ability of the regime to manage deficits, which compared unfavorably with the Nasir period, indicated a growing inability to face squarely the issues of who pays and who gets what.

Manpower and education policy

Another field of public policy under relatively direct government control was education and manpower. The Sadat regime inherited a system of expanded and open public education which was not particularly well-suited to Egypt's manpower needs and which, in its system of financing and access, resulted in a subsidization of education for the middle class by both the upper and lower classes (Abd al-Fadil 1982). It also inherited a policy of guaranteed public employment of graduates which put a big unproductive burden on the state. The positive impacts of the system were a reduction in illiteracy from 77.2% in 1947 to 56.5% in 1976, and increased social mobility for a portion of the middle and lower classes (Mead 1979). The Sadat regime, far from reforming the system, accentuated its defects and allowed its benefits to be eroded. The top-heavy development of secondary and higher education accelerated, while primary education was increasingly neglected. From 1969–70 to 1976–7, university students and graduates grew 16% per year, almost doubling in numbers from 1974 to 1977. Regional campuses sprang up all over Egypt, and by the end of the decade, there were 500,000 students in 13 universities (Kanovsky 1981: 374). This expansion was at the expense of quality, for not only were faculty and facilities stretched thin among all the new campuses, but *Infitah* permitted a wholesale drain of professors from Egypt. The result was a student–faculty ratio of 1 per 700 over Egypt and on one campus, Assiut, 1 per 1500 (*Ruz al-Yusuf* 4 Dec. 1978). The 100,000 graduates produced yearly were not, of course, readily absorbed into productive occupations and many had to wait more than two years for their appointment to redundant positions in the bureaucracy (*al-Ahram* 10 Dec. 1978, 8 Oct. 1979; *Akhbar al-Yom* 21 Sept. 1979). In the same period, primary education grew at less than 2% per year (compared to 6.3% from 1952 to 1965), well below the rate needed to absorb the school age population; only 78% of those eligible were initially enrolling in the mid-seventies and only 60% in rural areas, while only half of enrolled students reached the sixth year needed to achieve literacy (Ikram 1980: 117, 125–7; Kanovsky 1981: 374). Thus, while from 1947 to 1967 literates grew faster than population (289% compared to 98%), in the seventies the growth of literacy flagged and the absolute number of illiterates increased (from 18.3 million in 1960 to 20.7 million in 1976 (Ibrahim, 1982b: 405; Mead 1979). The quality of primary education also declined as most schools resorted to double shifts with 3–4-hour school days. As the quality of public education declined, the need for costly private lessons grew and state subsidized private schools serving the upper and middle classes expanded (*al-Ahram* 10, 12, 16, Dec. 1978, 27 Dec. 1979; *al-Akhbar* 22 Jan. 1979).

This educational policy was economically irrational since the cost of university education was 15 times that of primary education, and since the economic rate of return on primary education was much higher (Mead 1979; *al-Talia* 9 Sept. 1973). Moreover, a good portion of university graduates became a social burden rather than a productive asset; for although the regime did allow the real income of new entrants into bureaucratic jobs to decline, in spite of its ostensible commitment to rationalization, it made no determined attack on the policy of guaranteed employment. The policy was also inegalitarian since the neglect of public primary education at a time when the haves were acquiring greater relative access to education, increased the gap between them and the illiterate masses. In short, the regime exhibited no impressive capacity for reform in the field of education and manpower; indeed, responsive to the needs of more powerful social forces to the neglect of the poor and the weak, it permitted the evolution of education from a force for equality to one enhancing inequality.

Managing the public industrial sector

The performance of the regime in managing the huge public industrial sector had enormous and obvious consequences for Egypt's economic health. Since its inception, the record of the public sector has been mixed. The defects in the industrial decision-making system were a major liability. Because the big decisions on investment levels, prices and employment were centralized in government hands and public firms were required to channel the great bulk of their earnings to the treasury in the form of taxes or dividends, managers could not pursue policies rational or innovative from the micro point of view of the firm. Because the government lacked a sophisticated planning mechanism and often allowed socio-political considerations (keeping prices low or employment high) to influence its policies, economic rationality at the macro level was also weak. Overstaffing, a permissive labor law, foreign exchange scarcities, poor supply planning, and investments in projects in which Egypt lacked a comparative advantage, kept productivity low. On the other hand, the public sector did deliver a growing surplus to the public treasury; for every one Egyptian pound of production in the sector in 1977, the state extracted 0.25, compared to 0.15 devoted to salaries. In the seventies, at least, most companies, except for a few losers like the Iron and Steel Company, were making a profit (at an average rate of 9% in 1976–7) and quite a few were reasonably efficient (Handoussa 1979: 102–3). But, because the public sector could not retain its surplus, it lost not only the capability to finance expansion, but also to refurbish its depreciating equipment and in many cases, even to operate at full capacity. The financial crunch in the public sector was a main motive behind *Infitah*.

Yet, for the public sector, *Infitah* was, at best, a mixed blessing. The more ready availability of foreign exchange in the late *Infitah* years eased the problem of idle capacity and opened the door to some new expansion. But, unwilling to divest itself of control over industrial revenues and decisions, the Sadat regime made no real reforms in the defective system of economic decision-making. Managers were given somewhat more discretion over incentive payments in their firms and were relieved of the supervision of the holding companies which used to stand between them and the government. But the government continued to make the big decisions, and to extract the surplus for its own uses, and even less than under Nasir was this linked to a coherent economic plan. On political grounds, it continued to keep prices low, failed to improve labor discipline and still expected managers to maximize employment. Burdened with high taxes, tariffs, and manpower costs, increases in costs of imports due to devaluation, and constrained by set prices, many firms still labored under revenue constraints. Moreover an unreformed public sector was put at increasing risk in the climate of *Infitah*. Skilled managers were lured away by higher-paying foreign or private firms. Many firms could not compete with foreign competition: tariff rates on materials they processed were frequently higher than on manufactured foreign imports competing with them, and new foreign investment in Egypt enjoyed lower costs made possible by tariff and tax breaks, and exemption from employment policies (Handoussa 1979: 102–3; MENA 27 Apr. 1979). To escape political controls and capital constraints, many public firms sought to enter joint ventures with foreign companies. This may boost production and efficiency, but it also has high costs and risks. Frequently the most profitable parts of the public enterprise were separated from the parent firm to form such ventures, and because the public sector was often a minority participant in the new joint venture, foreign interests were literally acquiring control over some of the choicest morsels of the public sector (*Ruz al-Yusuf* 5 May 1980). Ultimately this could result in an outflow of profits, narrowing the locally produced economic surplus and exacerbating foreign dependency. Thus, rather than reforming its national public industry, the regime seemed prepared to let foreigners do the job, but at the possible price of its national character.

Housing and public services under Infitah

Government in Egypt, either as provider or regulator, has a direct impact on the availability and distribution of housing and public services such as medical care and transport. Generally, under Nasir, government intervention in these fields, in the form of measures such as rent control and modest efforts in public housing and medical care, favored lower-income groups, although it was sometimes inconsistent, diverting scarce resources to the benefit of upper- and middle-income groups as well. Under Sadat, the tendency was to pare back government regulation of the market and the commitment of resources to public services targeting the poor.

Housing offers an illustrative example of the effect (or ineffectiveness) of these differing approaches. Under Nasir, rent control reduced rents to the advantage of tenants. This discouraged private investment in housing which, however, basically targeted the 'haves' anyway. The state made a modest effort to fill the gap; it built some low-cost popular housing, but also diverted resources to middle- and upper-income projects (Mabro 1974: 162). Its effort peaked in 1963. Rapid urbanization in the absence of either a strong public or private construction effort, resulted in a housing scarcity which by the seventies had become a crisis. From 1960 to 1975, new households formed at a rate of 90,000 each year, but new housing units at a rate of only 28,000. The proportion of the population without proper housing grew from 21.7% in 1970 to 31.9% in

1977 and the shortage may have reached 1.5 million units by 1979. *Infitah* only worsened matters. The influx of foreigners and workers returning from abroad with money, raised demand. It set off a luxury building boom driving up the costs of real estate and materials. All this sparked a surge in the rents and prices of all housing which made fortunes for a few and put housing beyond the reach of many. Evasion of rent control became the norm: landlords charged large fees for the right to rent (key money), kept flats off the market waiting for rich Arabs or foreigners or took to selling them at exorbitant prices, and conspired to oust tenants from rent controlled buildings so they could sell the land at big profits. In spite of rent control, the rent of a four-room apartment increased six times between 1960 and 1979 (*Egyptian Gazette*, 24 Mar. 1979, 1 Feb. 1980; *al-Sha'b*, 18 Sept. 1979, 2, 9 Oct. 1979; Waterbury 1976b: 177–94). With the exception of a formidable project to reconstruct the Canal cities which may relieve some pressure on the main cities, the Sadat regime lacked the will or resources to cope with this crisis. It was unprepared to launch a major popular housing drive; indeed its modest public-housing program did not even target the poor, for, after 1973, 60% of new units were reserved for the army, public employees and persons returning from abroad, regardless of income (Ikram 1980: 149–50). By the end of the decade, the Minister of Housing was proposing, in the name of *laissez-faire*, that rent controls be abolished to stimulate new private investment and that the housing problem be left to the private sector (*al-Ahram*, 10 Jan. 1979). But the private sector was unprepared to construct low-cost popular housing. For the poor, for whom the housing crisis translated into life in mushrooming shanty-towns, and for the middle class for whom it meant postponed marriages and endless frustration, this policy offered no likely relief.

The effects and biases of regime policies could also be seen in the field of transportation. In the sixties, Egypt limited the import of personal automobiles and invested in a bus industry which produced 1500 units for public transport in 1965–6. In the seventies, by contrast, public transport was neglected in favor of private cars. The bus industry was allowed to deteriorate for lack of foreign exchange. While the number of passengers increased by 15% yearly, the growth of the bus fleet peaked at 1800 units and, by the end of the seventies, 25% of it was out of service. As skilled labor departed for higher-paying jobs abroad or in the private sector, maintenance could no longer be kept up. The overworked, overcrammed and undermaintained bus service limped along, occasionally getting an injection of new American buses. Meanwhile, large quantities of foreign exchange was made available for a massive import of private cars and millions of pounds were funneled into construction of new highways, bridges and overpasses to accommodate them; plans were soon afoot to uproot *baladi* neighborhoods in Bulak to make room for parking garages. As the streets of Cairo were progressively paralyzed by the excess of private cars, the ensnared public buses also ground to a halt. Thus, to service the desires of the 5% of the population that could afford a private car, public policy sacrificed the welfare of the vast majority dependent on public services (*al-Ahram*, 22 Mar., 23 May, 4 Oct., 21 Dec. 1979, 31 Jan. 1980; Waterbury 1976b: 145–75).

A similar story was apparent in the field of medical care. The Nasir regime made a major effort to extend health services to the poor, including those in rural areas. By the seventies, these services were contracting. Public hospitals fell into abysmal squalor; standards of sanitation were appalling, quality nursing almost absent, and equipment old and deteriorating. In the insane asylum of Abbassiyya, a handful of doctors and nurses were responsible for 5000 patients, violence went uncurbed, and lavatories were left out of order. Egypt did not, by Third World standards, lack trained medical personnel, but their level of performance and motivation was very low (*Egyptian Gazette* 23 May 1978; *al-Gumhuriyya* 6, 7 Mar. 1980). Unable to reform or upgrade the public medical service, the strategy of the Sadat regime was to neglect it and encourage the development of a quality private sector. Thus new private clinics opened with expensive imported equipment and a new project was put forward to build a major private hospital (*Egyptian Gazette* 23 May 1979).

In conclusion, it appears that the strategy of the Sadat regime in the field of housing and services was to neglect the public services and regulation on which the poor depended, while permitting the private sector to develop quality facilities for those who could pay (Waterbury 1976a: 162–4). If, as seemed likely, this return to the market translated into quality health care, private cars and private schools for the wealthy, and less and less public services for the have-nots, the result was likely to be an increasingly dualistic society.

Macro-economic policy: the Infitah

The economic Open Door Policy was the center-piece of the Sadat regime's development strategy and its success or failure is the ultimate test of the regime's whole redirection of Egypt. As the name suggests, the essence of *Infitah* was a cutback in etatist controls permitting an opening of Egypt's economy to trade and investment relations with the international capitalist market. First, it sought to stimulate investment. Law 43 of 1974, amended by Law 32 of 1977 opened Egypt to foreign investment in virtually any field, provided guarantees against nationalization, exempted new investment from taxes and tariffs for at least five years (and in the free zones indefinitely), and allowed the repatriation of profits and capital after five years (and without restriction in the free zones). Egyptian private investors were also guaranteed against expropriation and soon given the same tax and customs exemptions. Secondly, foreign trade was liberalized. Law 118 of 1975 dismantled public control of foreign trade except for certain basic commodities. The private sector was allowed to freely import most goods, Egyptians were allowed (under Law

93 of 1974) to act as agents for or hold franchises of foreign firms selling in Egypt, and traveling individuals (tourists or those working abroad) were permitted, under the 'own import' regulations, to bring commodities back into the country. Law 97 of 1976 permitted a free market in foreign exchange, and dismantled controls over access to and use of it; in 1977, even foreign firms were allowed to buy foreign exchange with Egyptian pounds. Thus, the government relinquished its earlier effort to control the amount and type of imports, and to set priorities for the use of scarce foreign exchange. Gradually also the pound was 'floated,' that is, official attempts to set the exchange rate for foreign currency were abandoned to the market; in consequence the value of the pound rapidly declined. Bi-lateral trade agreements which had previously been used to promote exports, mostly to the Eastern bloc, were phased out as Egypt's trade shifted Westward (Abd al-Khalek 1978, 1979, 1982; Carr 1979; Kanovsky 1981: 354, 372). At the same time, Egypt developed into a major exporter of labor to the Arab world. Finally, *Infitah* implied that, as the internal economy was exposed to the international market, the administered economy would gradually give way to market forces, and, indeed, public policy tried, with mixed success, gradually to pare back such interventions as subsidies, price controls and income ceilings. It was the expectation of policy makers that these measures, in the aggregate, would induce a sufficient mobilization of resources – foreign aid, investment, and technology and local investment – to spark an economic takeoff. In most immediate terms, therefore, *Infitah* can be assessed in regard to its effectiveness in so mobilizing resources at acceptable cost.

By the end of the seventies, *Infitah* had produced only a modest influx of the foreign investment it aimed to make the motor of development. Official sources claimed £E2.2 billion worth of projects had been approved by September 1979 under the investment laws and that at least three-quarters of approved projects had begun. However, it is clear that actual investment expenditures ran well behind approved investments; in 1975–8 they amounted to much less, a mere £E400 million over four years, (compared to public sector investment of £E900 million in one year) and, by 1981, Law 43 projects underway were capitalized at only £E900 million. Moreover, 60% of this total was Egyptian contributions, much of it from the public sector, to joint ventures. In fact, only about one-tenth of new investment in the late seventies could be directly attributed to *Infitah* (*al-Ahram al-Iqtisadi* 16 Mar. 1981; Dessouki 1982b: 79–80; Ministry of Economy 1979; Montasser 1979).[3] Even much of this was not in the 'productive sectors' (industry and agriculture) likely to lay the basis for sound economic recovery: in the seventies only one-half was in manufacturing, the rest in banking, housing, and – a large 25% of it – in tourism. Much of the investment in manufacturing was in light consumer industries which merely competed with existing Egyptian industry (Dessouki 1982b: 78–81; Ministry of Economy 1979); thus, foreign investors set up plants producing matches, soft drinks and tires which, rather than exporting as the government anticipated, merely encroached on the market share of national industry. Other investors actually insisted on market monopolies as a condition of investment. Some *Infitah* projects did bring, as the government hoped, new technology and equipment into Egypt; but even this had its negative side. Much of it was so costly and so capital intensive that it was of doubtful rationality in a labor surplus economy, and by 1980 *Infitah* projects had produced only 20,000 new jobs (Carr 1979: 87; Dessouki 1982b: 79–80). Finally, the foreign banks which were supposed to channel investment into Egypt and make Cairo an international banking center, showed little sign of playing such a positive role. They did finance some local development projects, but these remained modest and mostly in the trade and service fields. Worse, banks seemed to be siphoning local capital abroad; for example, in 1977 20 foreign banks brought in only £E26 million in foreign capital, but transferred 160 million abroad. 'Off-shore' banks, offering higher interest rates than local ones, seemed specifically designed to draw off Egyptian savings. The only real contributions the banks could be said to have made was the confidence their presence gave investors and the fact that without them part of the remittances of Egyptians working abroad would probably not have returned to the country (Carr 1979; 58; Dessouki 1982b: 81; MEED, 18 Aug. 1975; Ministry of Economy 1979).

There were many reasons for the disappointing response of investors. In spite of the many concessions granted to them, many did not like the investment climate. A decrepit infrastructure posed big obstacles to doing business. Protective labor laws (on minimum wages and dismissals) and generous social insurance provisions, though relaxed, deterred some investors. Local 'partners' did not always operate according to Western business practices; for example, the Chase Manhattan Bank explained its failure to finance local ventures on the grounds that Egyptian companies, to avoid taxes, failed to keep the public accounts which would make possible the identification of profitable projects. Many Western firms preferred to sell equipment and expertise rather than risk capital locally (Bentley 1981: 33–4; Carr 1979: 93; Waterbury 1976b: 229). Before the peace with Israel, many investors feared the renewal of war would sour the investment climate; after it, they were put off by Egypt's isolation from the lucrative Arab market many had hoped to exploit from Egyptian bases. The rise of domestic opposition to *Infitah* could not have assured investors, either. Not least, bureaucratic red-tape remained a formidable, seemingly intractable obstacle to business. According to Carr (1979: 93–100), incorporation of a new enterprise took 180 separate official steps. Multiple approvals were needed for most undertakings and because criteria were often vague, and official agencies each on their own tangent, inter-agency conflicts could paralyze business. The customs authority, controlling the vital links to the outside market, remained a formidable, often unresponsive hurdle to foreign firms, operating, at times, like a state within a state (MENA, 20 Feb. 1979). Thus the state itself, apparently incapable of self reform, was one of the biggest obstacles to its own policy.

Infitah was also supposed to spur local Egyptian investment, since local enterprise shared in the legal concessions to foreign business, could now operate more freely and would gain confidence from the foreign presence. The private sector did revive. Its share of total investment increased from about 10% before *Infitah* to about 15% in the late seventies. Private output went up 15% from 1974 to 1976, and the sector's share of the GDP went up 7% from 1974 to 1978. But the role of the private sector as an engine of development remained, to the end of the seventies, modest. Of gross investment in 1975–8, 82% was still by the public sector (Ikram 1980: 58–60; Kanovsky 1981: 363; Mead 1979). Private savings remained low; an important segment of it appears to have been channeled abroad and another big part squandered on a consumer buying spree. Much private investment continued to go into the traditional sectors it had long exploited such as fruit and vegetable cultivation, luxury housing and building materials, and, as such, would probably have been forthcoming regardless of *Infitah*; only one-third of private investment was actually under Law 43 (Ministry of Economy 1979). The private sector's share of industrial investment increased only slightly. The modest response of local investors to the new policy could be attributed to insufficient liberalization of the market: interest on savings was still too low (below inflation), and taxes too high, price and profit controls were still not wholly removed, the stock market had yet to be revived, and the government controlled share of domestic credit sufficiently reduced (Ikram 1980: 58–63). To the extent this is so, it suggests that a halfway liberalization, stopping short of a thoroughly capitalist course, may not be compatible with a major expansion of private enterprise. The high levels of official corruption probably discouraged productive investment, too; when big returns are to be had from corrupt practices and black marketeering, while legitimate investors must make payoffs to do business, incentives for invest-ment are weakened; in these respects, too, the state was an obstacle to its own policies. But, one may also question the utility of the *Infitah* model itself, at least as implemented in Egypt, in promoting private investment in productive sectors. When large profits are to be made in real-estate speculation, housing and importing, and secure returns are available in overseas banks, while local industry faces unrestrained foreign competition, major long-term investments in productive fields are unlikely to seem attractive. *Infitah* may have actually steered local investment away from industry and into tertiary activities. The NPUP claimed more than 1000 medium and small industries and 1500 crafts-men closed down (Shukri 1978: 423–4), and of the businessmen studied by Mokhtar (1980), those who started under Nasir were twice as likely to go into industry as those who began under *Infitah*.

The second major dimension of *Infitah*, the liberalization and expansion of

Egypt's economic relations with the capitalist (Western and Arab) market, also had, at best, mixed results. It did relieve the economy of some of the bottlenecks and scarcities caused by inefficient state foreign-trade bodies. But the liberalization of foreign trade and foreign exchange, by replacing state-set priorities with the profit motive and consumer demand as the determinant of imports, set off an explosion in the importation of consumer goods, frequently luxury items, which ate up big chunks of Egypt's potential savings (Abd al-Khalek 1978: 380; Ikram 1980: 47–50; Ministry of Economy 1979: Rifat 1978). The shift away from trade with the East cost Egypt export markets where she had received favorable prices, and forced her into Western markets where it was more difficult to compete; partly in consequence, Egypt's export performance was very poor (Kanovsky 1981: 366; Ministry of Economy 1979). Egypt did become a major exporter of labor to the Arab world, of course, and the remittances of some million Egyptians working abroad were a major source of foreign exchange and savings. Thus Egypt was successfully trading a factor of production of which she apparently had a surplus, labor, for one which was scarce, capital. But even this turned out to be a mixed blessing. The export of school teachers may have earned sufficient benefits to overshadow the cost in the deterioration of mass education (Messiha 1980). But, because many of the migrants were in skilled, labor-scarce categories, emigration drained Egypt of many of her most productive elements and introduced major bottlenecks into her own development. And, a good part of earnings came back in the form of luxury goods contributing little to development (Birks and Sinclair 1979).

In spite of the disappointments of *Infitah per se*, however, the regime's policies did produce a dramatic influx of financial resources in another form, foreign assistance. Arab grants, in part a reward for Sadat's move away from the USSR and his economic liberalization, soared to $1.2 billion in 1974 alone. Loans included, Egypt received about $7 billion in aid from Arab states in the 1974–7 period (Weinbaum 1983: 637–8). As Egypt withdrew from the Arab–Israeli conflict, it dropped off, but this withdrawal made Egypt eligible for massive aid from Western sources, especially the US, which more than made up for the loss (Kanovsky 1981: 364). By 1982, Egypt had received $4.1 billion in loans and $2.5 billion in grants from the US and several billion more in loans from Western Europe, Japan and international banks. In addition, Sadat's economic and foreign policy allowed Egypt to recover or develop several other major domestic sources of revenue, namely, the Suez Canal, petroleum (partly from recovered Sinai oil fields), and tourism. Together with workers' cash remittances, returns from these sources pushed foreign exchange earnings from $385 million in 1970 to more than $5 billion in 1980–1 (Kanovsky 1981: 364; Merriam 1982). Thus, although it did not come in the precise form anticipated, there is little doubt that Sadat indeed engineered a massive influx of capital which relieved Egypt of her financial crisis and, if properly used, could serve to spark economic take off.

The influx of these enormous amounts of new resources gave a double-barreled stimulus to the Egyptian economy and enabled Egypt simultaneously to pursue a massive expansion in both investment and consumption. This expansion had positive consequences for both growth and welfare, as will be seen. But it was not without costs. The expansion was of such a magnitude that, even given the big influx of revenues, it could not be financed without costly imbalances. Egypt's deficit in its balance of payments (for goods and services) grew from $250–300 million per year in 1964–69 (Kanovsky 1981: 363) to around $1.7 billion in 1978. A deficit of around 4–5% of GDP had turned into one of the order of 15–20%. The savings–investment gap ballooned: while about 70–80% of investment in the sixties was financed by domestic savings, this was true of only about 14% by 1979 (Ikram 1980: 44–54, 340–51; Mead 1979, Radwan 1974: 209). Only part of the deficit was covered by grants, the rest by loans which had to be repaid. As a result, Egypt's foreign debt grew from $1.6 billion in 1970 to $12.5 billion at the end of the decade, about three-quarters the size of the total GNP then (Merriam 1982). Debt service reached $1 billion a year by 1980 and a substantial 'hump' in repayments loomed in the mid-eighties (Ikram 1980: 53–4, 352–54; Merriam 1982: 7–9). Although his creditors were unlikely to foreclose on Sadat as they did on Khedive Ismail, such massive dependence made the country extremely vulnerable to outside pressures. To some it appeared that Sadat had mortgaged Egypt's policy and its future. The combination of high rates of consumption and investment was also responsible for the inflationary spiral which reached 25% or 30% a year with deleterious and unequal welfare consequences (Kanovsky 1981: 361).

These costs might have been avoided had the regime lived within its means; in practice, they were probably the inevitable consequences of its strategy. High investment levels were needed if *Infitah* was to be justified and the promised economic take off produced. High consumption resulted from the open economy desired by local traders and foreign sellers, and the need to satisfy the expectations of the bourgeoisie and appease the masses. In short, Egypt's leadership lacked the power and perhaps the option to choose between consumption and investment; the massive provision of foreign grants and loans relieved it, at least in the short run, of the need to do so.

The developmental consequences of Infitah

What were the concrete consequences of *Infitah* for development? The new resources mobilized by the regime's policies permitted a formidable expansion of investment from the mid-seventies on. In 1975–7, an extraordinary 26% of GNP was invested (compared to the previous high of 16 to 18% in the 1960–7 period) and similar rates continued thereafter (*Egyptian Gazette*, 12 Feb. 1980;

Kanovsky 1981: 361–2). This investment translated into a significant growth in capital stock (at a rate of about 5% per year between 1973–5, and higher thereafter), endowing Egypt with an expanded productive base. New investment sparked a new expansionary phase in the economy, enabling the country to break out of the stagnation of the 1967–73 period. Real growth in 1973–8 was 5–6% and in 1979–80 8–9%; this was a higher rate of growth for a longer period than the etatist expansionary period under Nasir which averaged 6% between 1960 and 1965 (Kanovsky 1981: 361; Montasser, 1979). This new expansion translated into a growth in per capita income of from 3% to 6% a year. Given that growth was its major objective, *Infitah* seemed, ostensibly at least, to be a major success.

A closer look at average yearly sectoral growth rates gives a more concrete picture of the direction and forces behind the *Infitah* advance. Much of the growth was in the tertiary sector. In the 1973–7 period, transportation and communication, a leading growth sector, grew at a rate of 19%; much of this was merely a result of the reopening of the Suez Canal. The stress on this sector, however, continued and at the end of the decade Egypt was investing massive resources in the renovation of her infrastructure. Trade and finance grew at a rate of 8%, a symptom of economic liberalization. Altogether, the tertiary sector grew by more than a third in the seventies. Industry grew at a good rate, perhaps 12% yearly. More than a third of this advance was attributable to the rapid growth in petroleum revenues, the basis for which had been laid in the sixties. In manufacturing, growth from 1973 to 1978 was around 6.5% to 8%, partly a result of new investment, partly from a growth in capacity utilization as supply bottlenecks were overcome. Agriculture, however, remained sunk in stagnation. After respectable rates of growth from the middle fifties to the early sixties, growth in agriculture had declined to 1.5% from 1967 to 1973, and in the seventies it declined further to less than 1%. This decline was due to the neglect of the sector. Failure to complement irrigation with investments in drainage led to salinity and a rising water table; urban encroachment on arable land, accelerated by the *Infitah* building boom, exceeded the very slow pace of land reclamation; low prices paid for crops marketed with the state discouraged the production of key crops; and investment in the sector plummeted precipitously from 24% of the total in 1963–4 to 7–8% in the seventies (Ikram 1980: 240; Kanovsky 1981: 355–57; Montasser 1979). The result was a growing and dangerous food deficit: of 7 million tons of wheat consumed in 1978, 5 million were imported, at great cost to the treasury. As population and demand rocketed ahead of production, Egypt's food dependence and her vulnerability to scarcities on the world market, mounted (Kanovsky 1981: 366; Waterbury 1976b: 112–24). In summation, the expansion of the seventies laid much less stress on the commodity producing sectors than had that of the sixties. And, little change in these priorities appeared projected for the early eighties. In the

1980–4 plan, the anticipated leading sectors were petroleum (12.8% growth), Suez Canal (16.7%), housing and utilities (12.5%), transportation and communication (11.7%), trade and finance (11%); 45% of all public investment was to be channeled into infrastructure. Industry, on the other hand, was anticipated to grow at only 10.8% and agriculture at 3.2% (MENA, 12 Jan. 1979). This sectoral pattern of development suggests that, though larger than the expansion of the sixties, that of the seventies may be less solidly based. To be sure, infrastructural expansion was endowing the country with tangible assets which could only increase the efficiency of the economy. But the fact that part of the expansion was based on a revitalization of previously developed productive assets and the relative neglect of the commodity production sectors in the seventies must qualify assessments of the *Infitah* developmental achievement.

The changed sectoral performances from the Nasir to Sadat eras were not wholly fortuitous. Part of it did result from accidents such as the reopening of the Canal and the urgent need to refurbish infrastructure neglected in the sixties. But a good part of it was due to changes in development strategy. Under Nasir, the regime tried to exploit Egypt's advantage in skilled but cheap labor to make her the industrial center of the Middle East and to crown her traditionally very productive, if slim, hydraulic agrarian base. Under Sadat, the regime began to envision Egypt as a kind of service *entrepot* between the West and the oil-rich Arab world. Labor was exported to the Arab world rather than employed in industrial development at home. The oil pipe-line and the widening of the Suez Canal, both priority projects, made Egypt a key transit point in the area. The new stress on tourism targeted both Westerners and rich Arabs. The massive allocations to infrastructure were needed to make Egypt a center of finance and a base for Western firms operating in the Arab World. Luxury housing, office construction, roadways for private cars, and a glittering life of consumption in the capital were all needed if Cairo was to become the new Beirut. But whether a strategy suitable for a small mountainous country with an entrepreneurial-minded population was appropriate for a large state with a massive depressed population, highly developed agricultural and industrial bases, and entrenched bureaucratic traditions was, to say the least, debatable.

The welfare and distributive consequences of Infitah

Not aggregate growth alone, but the uses to which it is put is rightly regarded as the test of development, that is, the extent to which economic modernization is accompanied by an equitable distribution of its burdens and benefits, and translates into increased welfare for an increased number of people. It is clear that the philosophy behind *Infitah* put a lower priority on distribution as compared to the Nasir era. It assumed that redistribution under Nasir had gone far enough or perhaps too far, and that in the new phase greater rewards needed to be given to those with skills and capital who, it was assumed, were capable of spurring growth; as the economy grew, the benefits of growth would 'trickle down' to the rest of society. In practice, the distribution of income and welfare was determined by an interaction between the forces of the market and public intervention in it. Given the unequal distribution of resources in Egypt, it is reasonable to expect, especially in view of Egypt's past experience, that a return to the market would allow the minority commanding such resources to increase their share of wealth at the expense of others; and given the change in public economic philosophy, one might expect government intervention to reinforce this market bias. While the evidence suggests that this was indeed the general tendency, it also suggests that there were countervailing forces – in fact, a certain 'trickle down effect,' and persisting populism in public policy – which checked and contained it.

There is plenty of evidence that the reactivation of the market rapidly resulted in new accumulations of wealth; that the haves were best situated to exploit the market, and that this was often at the expense of the have-nots. The bourgeoisie retained control of substantial wealth-producing assets even after Nasir's reforms and, once the economy was liberalized, it was able to put them to work again. Thus, for example, studies by Ajami (1982: 495–6) and Mokhtar (1980) of investors under *Infitah* indicate that most were either from the pre-1952 upper classes or those who made fortunes in the Arabian Gulf in the fifties and sixties. Under *Infitah* accumulated capital again began to reproduce itself. It is apparent, too, that it was the Westernized, more-educated upper strata which were best prepared to take advantage of opportunities under *Infitah* to enrich themselves as agents of foreign firms, middlemen or importers. Big money could again be made in foreign trade where merchants considered 30% markups too low and which, in fact often exceeded 100%. The liberalization of foreign trade also encouraged certain profitable abuses at the expense of the public; for example, publicly subsidized goods were smuggled abroad for hard currency to import luxury goods sold at big profits to the well off. Fortunes were also made in the relatively monopolistic internal wholesale trade: 20 large merchants controlled the meat trade, three the seed trade, nine the market in paper, 11 in pipes, 10 in soft drinks and four in automobile parts; in consequence of such monopolies, the price paid by the consumer for locally made goods was typically more than twice that paid by merchants to the producer (Issawy, 1982; Sahib 1976). Those with a corner on scarce housing or real estate enriched themselves. Building contractors flourished on the *Infitah* boom in construction, which typically diverted publicly subsidized building materials into luxury housing for the rich and foreigners. The liberalization of the foreign exchange market produced a dozen or so 'foreign exchange kings' making fabulous fortunes (*Egyptian Gazette* 23 Sept. 1979). The government had to raise the salaries of experienced top administrators and managers to prevent their moving to the higher-paying private or foreign sectors. The operation of the market did not exclusively favor the upper classes, however. Taxi drivers and tourist guides prospered from the influx of foreigners. Certain skilled workers, in increasing demand in an era of economic boom and migration, enjoyed rising wage rates. To a lesser extent, some low-income groups such as agricultural workers, also benefited from the growth in demand spurred by *Infitah* (Mead 1979). Those who got the chance to work abroad found new ways to raise themselves up. But the large majority of the lower-middle and lower classes indisputably suffered a decline in their living standards under pressure of the rapid inflation unleashed by *Infitah*.[4]

As regards public policy intervention under Sadat, there is plenty of evidence to support Sa'ad Ibrahim's 1982 claim that it shifted from favoring the have-nots to favoring the haves. The return of sequestered property to the rich increased inequality in control of assets; the conflicts between peasants and owners trying to reassert control over 53,000 *feddans* of formerly sequestered property indicates that this policy was sometimes at the direct expense of the have-nots. Legislated increases of 20-25% in rent on land and reductions in the security of tenancy favored landowners at the expense of tenants (NPUP 1978: 18–25). Tax incentives to capital benefited the wealthy at the expense of poor peasants and salaried middle groups which bore the burden of taxation. The neglect or de-nationalization of the public sector threatened to curtail its role as a source of superior benefits and income to those available to workers on the private labor market. Even as the regime raised salaries for top bureaucrats, it depressed those for new graduates in an effort to discourage them from flocking to government employment (Ikram 1980: 49; Radwan 1981: 133). The reduction and lax enforcement of price controls in an era of inflation hurt lower-income groups: for example, the tolerance of illegal key money for housing and of the black market in rent of agricultural land (£E72 per *feddan* compared to the legal rent of £E30 per *feddan* (NPUP 1978: 10–13). The neglect of public services aimed at benefiting the poor and the shift of investment into those chiefly benefiting the haves, such as roads and telecommunications, was an inegalitarian policy bias. There is some controversy over the extent to which state policy extracted a surplus from rural areas to the benefit of the urban center, but government bias against rural areas probably increased under Sadat; implicit taxation of the peasant through compulsory marketing (less subsidies on inputs), modest before 1967, was very heavy until 1978, while at the same time the proportion of state investment in agriculture plummeted (Ikram 1980: 175; Kanovsky 1981: 355–6; Korayem 1981: 426; Waterbury 1982: 307–25). Inside the rural sector itself, state regulations and operations increasingly favored the rural rich over the poor. The sale of reclaimed land at auction effectively excluded landless peasants from access to it. The crop rotation system put the heaviest burden of producing the low-priced compulsorily delivered crops on the poor peasants, while leaving bigger landowners free to dominate the lucrative free market in vegetables, fruits and meat; often prevented by the rotation from growing enough food to feed themselves, poor peasants were reduced to buying it from richer neighbors or merchants at high prices. Moreover, the effect of the system was to pull resources away from production of items of mass consumption toward that of foods for higher-income consumption. Access to subsidized inputs favored the well-off farmer: fertilizer was made available in proportion to the size of landholding and, in the early seventies, access to subsidized fodder was limited to larger owners in the lucrative cattle-raising sector. The neglect of the cooperatives also hurt the poor. Credit for machinery was now channeled to individuals rather than cooperatives and only the well off could raise the needed collateral; peasants thus became more dependent on renting tools and machinery from rich owners. The replacement of cooperative credit with banks operating on a commercial basis funneled long-term credits for improvement to bigger landowners. If it results in a general decline in the access of poorer peasants to credit, it will be a first big step in the reconcentration of land (Ibrahim, 1982: 198–217; NPUP 1978: 11–12, 18–34). Finally, corruption, though the result not of public policy but private actions by public officials, can nevertheless be seen as a regime bias which chiefly benefited the top bureaucratic elite and entrepreneurs at the expense of the average tax payer and the poor. A number of public programs did, however, appear to operate counter to this general tendency to favor the haves. First, in spite of efforts to shave the subsidization of low-income consumption goods, political dangers kept the program largely intact and it had a major welfare and even redistributory impact. The continued effort to maximize public employment was also a welfare measure, and the apparent government effort to raise the wages of the very lowest public employees and to periodically raise the minimum wage for all workers had some redistributory impact (al-Edel 1982: 160–2; Radwan 1981: 133).

Thus, market operations and public policy had conflicting effects on welfare and distribution. There is, unfortunately, little reliable or systematic data which would permit precise measurement of the outcome of these conflicting tendencies, and, in any case, their effect may well only be apparent in the longer run. There is, however, some scattered and fragmentary information on income distribution, consumption levels, employment, and social mobility which, when brought together, does give a rough tentative picture of developments.

Data on rural areas show conflicting forces at work. An equalizing tendency was the increase in real wages of agricultural workers, the lowest stratum of rural society, by more than 50% between 1974 and 1980. As a result the share of wages in agricultural GDP which had fallen from a high of 33% in the mid-sixties to 25% in 1970, had recovered to 26% in 1976 and probably continued to increase thereafter (Issawy 1982: 91–3; Radwan 1981: 113–15;

Waterbury 1982: 316–17). This tendency was due to labor scarcities created by migration from the village in certain areas; to the degree it is encouraging mechanization it may, however, be temporary. On the other hand, there is evidence of a fragmentation and modest reconcentration of landholding. The proportion of landless families probably increased (Radwan 1977: 22). Unviable micro-holdings also increased considerably, while larger (over 10 *feddan*) holdings increased their share of land at the expense of smaller ones, gaining 135,000 *feddans* from 1975 to 1978. The Gini Index of landholding inequality which had fallen from 0.64 in 1960 to 0.46 in 1974, reflective of two land reforms, was up again to 0.54 in 1979. Overall rural income inequality also increased from 0.35 in 1974 to 0.46 in 1977–8, most likely the result of land concentration, rent increases and the inequitable effects of the crop rotation system. Household expenditure surveys showed a similar increase in inequality. Thus, while the labor market was reducing inequality, that in land and commodities seemed to be increasing it (Zeitoun 1982: 279–95). Finally, Korayem's evidence indicates a worsening in the urban–rural income gap in the late seventies. While the ratio of rural to urban income increased in the sixties through the early seventies from 42% to 59.1%, by 1978 it was back to 44.5%. The high rates of extraction and lowered proportion of investment in agriculture must account for a good part of this change (Korayem 1981: 418).

Trends in urban income distribution are even less clear, partly a result of poor data, but perhaps also a reflection of conflicting forces at work. Consumption surveys show declining inequality from 1964 to 1974 (Issawy 1982: 96), but thereafter different indicators point in different directions. The picture for wages is especially ambivalent. Kanovsky's calculations show real wages falling 15% between 1973 and 1976 and because GNP per capita increased 14% in this period, he concludes that there must have been rapid growth in non-wage incomes and, thus, in inequality (Kanovsky 1981: 336). These data, however, largely pre-date the *Infitah* boom. By contrast, Radwan (1981: 134) reports data showing real income of workers in establishments of ten or more persons increasing around 30% from 1970 to 1977; these data may, however, reflect the relatively privileged position of workers in big, often public, firms. By the late seventies, nevertheless, labor scarcities in certain labor categories were driving up wage levels faster than inflation in the private sector; Mead calculated that before-inflation wages for skilled workers such as blacksmiths, plumbers, and tile fitters went up four to six times from 1970 to 1977 (Mead, 1979). On the other hand, the high level of disguised unemployment in the cities suggests that for the vast numbers of unskilled or irregularly employed persons outside public sector jobs after inflation income probably declined (Ikram 1980: 68; Radwan 1981: 140; *al-Talia*, June, August 1976). Data given by Radwan (1981: 133) also show that real incomes of educated middle-level government employees (i.e. the white-collar lower middle class) stagnated from 1970 to 1980. By contrast, there is indirect evidence of a disproportionate increase in the incomes of the top income strata. For example, under Nasir, incomes over £E10,000 were, theoretically, taxed away, though in practice evasion was significant. Under Sadat incomes far larger than this were reported. By 1974, 2000 families were reportedly receiving over £E35,000 and by 1976 this had increased to over 45,000. (Shukri 1978: 82; Waterbury 1976c: 311). In a study done by Muhi ad-Din in the late seventies, the top income bracket begins with £E130,000 (Radwan 1981: 135). In fact, it is widely accepted that a crop of new millionaires have emerged at the top of the stratification system (Mursi 1976; al-Talia, No. 12, 1975; Shukri 1978: 337–8). Finally, an indirect indicator of increasing overall income inequality are the changes in consumption of various types of goods. Thus, while between 1963 and 1976, the consumption of grain, an indicator of change in the living standards of the poor, increased by only 1.2% per year and that of cotton textiles and leather goods by modest amounts, the largely middle- and upper-class consumption of consumer durables increased at a steady significant clip from 1963 to 1973, and, thereafter, soared (Ikram 1980: 88).

Available data on change in social mobility and employment levels suggest a narrowing of opportunity since the sixties. The slight increase in official open unemployment from 2% in 1970 to 3.3% in 1978 probably indicates a wider growth in the incidence of underemployment (Ikram 1980: 68; Radwan 1981: 102). Ibrahim's study of social mobility found the sixties to be a period of high upward mobility for the lower and middle classes owing to combined economic expansion and redistributive policies, while the seventies were a time of sluggish mobility and virtual immobility for the lowest strata. While it seems likely that growing external opportunities and economic growth in the late seventies altered this picture, Ibrahim's 1979 survey did not register it; and the increase in unemployment suggests that migration was not enough, overall, to expand internal opportunities (Ibrahim 1982b).

In conclusion, it appears that the impact on Egyptians of the new economic order was very uneven. Higher-income groups benefited substantially from the liberation of the market and the bias of public policy. The old upper classes recovered and expanded their control over wealth-producing assets and their ability to use them; the state bourgeoisie enriched itself on commissions and corruption; and a multitude of middlemen, controlling the links to the Western market, were in a position to take their cut on every transaction. Middle-income groups were differentially affected. Those in the private sector, middle merchants, and rich peasants probably did well. But the publicly-employed middle class, disfavored by both the market and public policy, was hard put to stay even. The working classes were also differentially affected. Skilled workers and those who were able to emigrate had a chance to raise themselves up and those in the public sector were probably able to stay even. Many agricultural workers improved their lot. But the position of small-holding peasants seemed to be eroded. And high inflation, the decline of public services, the neglect of rural areas, and limited opportunities, translated into a worsening standard of living for many near the bottom.

On the whole, *Infitah*, allowing those with marketable assets and skills to advance themselves, had a strong differentiating effect which widened the gap between the top and bottom of the social pyramid. Yet certain scarcities on the labor market permitting elements of labor to move upward relative to the white-collar middle class, had a countervailing equalizing effect, and subsidization of basic commodities, kept the masses from slipping too far down into poverty. These equalizers had, however, high costs and perhaps limits beyond which they could not be sustained. On balance, the welfare and distributive performance of the *Infitah* regime was unimpressive and certainly inferior to the Nasirist record.

The cultural consequences of Infitah

The cultural consequences of *Infitah* need to be assessed because a sense of community and identity is an important value, *per se*, which has been affected by it. They must also be assessed because modernization is a function not just of capital and technology, but of motivation – to work hard, to put long-term benefits over short term ones, to postpone consumption, to accept responsibility – which appears rooted in a sense of self-worth and confidence inseparable from strong religious, ideological or national identity. The outside world may represent a challenge or stimulus for a culture, but a too-indiscriminate cultural opening is likely to result in a 'colonized consciousness' eroding the cultural bases of motivation.

Under Nasir, there was a strong drive to efface the debilitating Western cultural dependency and isolation from mass culture hitherto typical of the Westernized elite and to spread identification with a national culture throughout society. Education was nationalized, a renaissance in indigenous arts encouraged, and Egyptians brought to buy the local products hitherto scorned. Egyptian values and self-worth were reasserted, producing, in Hamamsy's words, a 'more culturally integrated and less schizophrenic society.' This revival had an economic dimension as well, namely, Egypt's effort to do and make everything itself 'from the needle to the rocket' (Hamamsy 1977). According to Amin, the economic growth of the 1956–64 period was a product of a 'remarkable psychological change' in which a 'feeling of national pride' replaced the earlier 'feeling of inferiority to the foreigner.' (Amin, 1981: 439).

Under *Infitah*, by contrast, there was an unmistakable reversion to the 'colonized consciousness,' led by a resurgence of cosmopolitanism among the elite. That indigenous culture was again de-valued and that of the colonizer admired and imitated in elite circles was apparent from Sadat's plea that Egypt be accepted in the West as a civilized outpost in the barbarous Middle East, and from Tewfik al-Hakim's denigration of the Arabs and embracing of 'civilized' Israel. There was an economic dimension to this, too. The view that everything Western was superior, everything *baladi* inferior returned – an attitude captured by the cartoonist Salah Jaheen who depicts two Egyptians marveling over the Great Pyramid: 'Fantastic, it must be imported!' Now Western money and technology could do everything for the Egyptians. Egypt would be rescued by a 'Carter Plan,' and the solution to any problem found by signing a contract with a Western firm. One typical consequence of this cultural climate, when combined with bureaucratic paralysis, was the tendency for officials to give up trying to get Egyptians to perform many tasks themselves and to contract them out to foreign firms. Thus a foreign firm was awarded a contract to run the railway passenger service, British teachers were imported to teach English, and a Western advertizing agency hired to conduct an expensive media campaign on birth control. Given a little will and organization, Egyptians were certainly competent to perform all these tasks. Such practices were not only expensive and inappropriate in a country with high underemployment, but if development means learning by doing things yourself, they were a step backward. Moreover, when foreign 'experts' were called in to do the jobs Egyptians should have been doing, the results were often curiously unsuited to local conditions. Thus, Egypt wasted millions on a foreign study of its traffic problems which recommended Cairo's manually operated traffic signals be replaced with automatic ones, a formula certain to worsen traffic chaos since what little order exists on Cairo's streets depends on the presence and judgment of the traffic policemen who man the signals (*al-Ahram* 19 Sept. 1979; MENA, 15 Mar. 1980).

It is questionable whether sound national development can take place in such a cultural climate. Once faith in national regeneration is lost, privatism, preoccupation with short-term particularistic gain, become the norm. To be sure, 'entrepreneurship' of a kind can flourish in such an environment, but, rather than the productive variety Egypt claims to want, it is likely to be of the *comprador* or 'parasitic' kind that seeks its fortune in middlemen operations, importation and black marketeering, and consumes its profits in high living or exports them to safe foreign banks.

Nor was the problem of the dilution and fragmentation of national identity exclusively a problem at the leadership level. On the one hand, colonial consciousness seeped downward in the spread of appetite for foreign goods; witness the welcome given by many common Egyptians to the Americans they believed would come bearing refrigerators and tape recorders. According to Ayubi (1982: 398) the corruption and wheeler-dealer mentality encouraged by *Infitah* was eroding honesty and the work ethic even among the mass public.

Galal Amin sees this as the chief danger of *Infitah*: 'Foreign capital may one day be nationalized, taxes made more progressive, and land redistributed. What can never be corrected however, if it is allowed to proceed too long, is cultural disintegration' (Amin 1981: 440). On the other hand, however, elite de-nationalization was far more advanced than that at the mass level; hence the elite–mass gap, bridged to an extent under Nasir, widened again under *Infitah* and, in turn, sparked a nativist, fundamentalist reaction. This cleavage threatened the unity of the national community without which a sound or stable pursuit of modernization was in jeopardy.

A 'soft' state in an open economy

It would be hard to argue, on the whole, that the combination of a 'soft' authoritarian–bureaucratic state with an open economy which emerged in Egypt under Sadat was, at least in the short run, a more successful model of development than the etatist–populist model it replaced. Egypt enjoyed an influx of new economic resources under this policy, but the capacity of the political system to manage them effectively proved quite limited. Its policy process was too vulnerable to the particularistic demands of the bourgeoisie and foreign interests on which it depended. It lacked the strong political institutions to mobilize public support behind a coherent policy, or to implement its policies efficiently. It could neither design nor implement a rational strategy for maximizing the benefits and minimizing the costs of *Infitah* or equitably distributing them.

To the extent that the goal was the development of Egypt's productive base, policy was inefficient and ill-designed. Corruption and the indiscriminate opening of the economy fueled speculative *comprador* activities and consumption at the expense of productive investment. Too few resources were channeled into Egypt's chief assets, her industrial base and hydraulic agriculture, and too many into tertiary activities. Because the regime lacked the will to rationalize the public sector, its viability was undermined under *Infitah* and parts of it threatened with 'de-nationalization.' This, plus uncontrolled foreign banking and exchange operations, threatened a harmful and unnecessary export of capital. The failure to limit private and public consumption resulted in growing indebtedness and another outflow of resources for debt service. Uncontrolled migration and an irrational education policy combined to produce scarcities of skilled manpower at the cost of development bottlenecks at home. Up to the end of the decade, the influx of foreign aid and worker remittances obscured the costs of these hemorrhages of capital and manpower, but when these inevitably decline, they are likely to be felt.

To the extent that the regime's goal was to create an extroverted, foreign-linked service economy, the regime's political weaknesses prevented it from pursuing the consistent policies of capitalist rationalization which would have created a compatible investment climate. Unplanned large-scale bureaucratic intervention for populist or other purposes continued, reflective of the regime's inability to make the shift in the burden of development to lower-income groups needed to guarantee high profits. Bureaucratic red-tape remained an intractable obstacle to entrepreneurship and, by the end of the seventies, organizational incapacity replaced capital scarcity as the biggest bottleneck in Egypt's development effort. Partly for these reasons, neither foreign nor local investment took on the dimensions anticipated by the regime. Whatever the basic goal of the regime, the bloated, often corrupt, unreformed bureaucracy with its scores of functionless ex-ministers and its thousands of functionless low-paid employees remained a parasitic drain on the economy.

Finally, *Infitah* translated into growing inequity and inequality. The corruption of the state and its colonization by the multitude of local and foreign interests spawned by *Infitah* discriminated against the have-nots and favored the haves. The public policies needed to get investment and the operations of the market basically also favored the haves. Yet, while the country paid a big price in inequality, it was far from clear that it was getting sound development in return.

In spite of the waste and costs of *Infitah*, it did have two immediate and one potential benefit for Egypt. First, the large influx of foreign resources did lift Egypt out of the stagnation of the post-1967 period and promised to endow her with durable and potentially productive assets, that is, a renovated infrastructure and an enlarged industrial base. Secondly, the volume of foreign aid permitted the continuing subsidization of necessities, and the export and growth of demand for labor drove up wages for some workers, thus adding a welfare dimension to *Infitah* which it would not otherwise have had. Finally, the mixed economy resulting from *Infitah* potentially endowed Egypt with three 'motors of development' – public, private and foreign. To be sure, the public sector was still unreformed and in danger of de-nationalization, the private sector too speculative and the foreign sector still too small to constitute a major center of dynamism. But it was possible that working in concert they might still set Egypt on the road to capitalist development. The critical question for the future of Egypt was how far, if at all, their contributions to productive advance would outweigh their costs. For better or worse, it may be that Brazil is the future of Egypt.

Chapter 10

The post-populist reshaping of Egypt

The vulnerabilities and systemic crisis of Nasirism

The analysis of post-populist change in Egypt must begin with the Nasir regime itself because its very strengths turned out to be vulnerabilities too, and because the regime helped stimulate the very environmental forces which generated a system-transforming crisis.

At the leadership level, where the Nasir regime was strongest, it also proved most vulnerable. Weber's (1964) concept of charismatic leadership provides the single most convincing key to understanding the regime. Nasir's revolution, a reaction to profound national and social crisis, embodied a challenge to the domestic and regional status quo, and it was basically from this challenge that his mass support flowed. It was charisma which enabled the regime to transcend its military origins and establish a strong authoritarian state capable of imposing its revolution from above. As Weber noted, however, charismatic authority is based squarely on the heroic performance of the leader: though he is less constrained than rulers whose power rests in institutions or custom, his authority is more conditional. The leader is thus driven to prove himself and to meet the expectations of his followers; much of the populism which constrained the regime's extractive capabilities was in part a product of Nasir's desire to meet the expectations of his broad cross-class constituency. The leader may also overextend himself: Nasir's need to sustain his role as Pan-Arab leader helped entangle him in costly and ultimately disastrous inter-state conflicts. Moreover, the concentrated personalized rule characteristic of charisma, while an asset in the imposition of radical change, retards the development of political institutions in which, Weber suggests, charismatic legitimacy must be routinized if it is to persist. The failure to institutionalize Nasirism in an ideological party which could replenish the elite from a popularly-recruited cadre, made the elite, once its victory over the old upper classes was consolidated, susceptible to the embourgeoisement foreseen by Mosca and Michels. Nasir built a huge authoritarian–bureaucratic state but without such a party it lacked an ideological–political motor to drive and control the statist economy, or to mobilize the sustained mass political activism needed to defend Nasirism

289

against its enemies. Without a viable party or parliament, the natural tendency of the authoritarian–bureaucratic state to patrimonialism and bureaucratic ossification could not ultimately be contained, undermining the regime's ability to manage the economy and defend itself from foreign enemies. In such a state, where charismatic authority is, at best, routinized in the position held by the leader, once the charismatic leader passes, it is very likely, as Weber suggests, to turn into patrimonial authority. So in Egypt: Nasir himself prepared the way for the presidential monarchy of his successor. The failure of Nasirism was therefore, to a great extent, as functionalists argue, a failure of institution-building.

Political leadership and institutions made Nasirism vulnerable to transformative pressures, but it was the environmental forces emphasized by Marxists which generated these pressures. The state achieved for a while considerable autonomy from the dominant class, the bourgeoisie in its various segments, but, though bourgeois interests were only partially and temporarily compatible with mature Nasirism, Nasir never decisively destroyed the formidable social power of this class. His etatist–populist course contained and curbed the bourgeoisie but in other ways fueled it; and his elite recruitment policies brought it into the very heart of the regime where it was poised to play a decisive role in reversing his course once he was gone. His effort to satisfy both the bourgeoisie and the masses made the regime vulnerable to a resource crisis and eroded its capacity to mobilize a surplus; his attempt to build 'socialism' with upper-middle-class managers instead of socialists deprived his experiment of the ideological commitment needed to sustain it. There was, in short, a major contradiction between the ideological superstructure of the regime and dominant elements of its social base. Short of a radical revolution destroying the class power of the bourgeoisie and mobilizing the masses, the political superstructure was bound, as Marxists argue, to give way before a resurgence of this power. Nasir judged, perhaps correctly, that the costs of such a revolution, even had he possessed the necessary political instruments (a radical party), would be excessive and incompatible with national unity, non-alignment and his centrist development strategy, the things he cared most about. To the end, his notion of the nation-building project, a product of his own middle-class origins, rested on the ideal of class unity, the reconciliation of differences between the bourgeoisie and the masses, and a middle course which spared both excessive burdens. In a sense Nasirism rested on a contradiction: to endure it had to radicalize, but if it did, it ceased to be Nasirism. In this lies the key to the inevitable transitional character of authoritarian–populist regimes: ultimately they must choose between capitalism and socialism, and the failure to choose the latter means to opt for the former.

Contradictions can, however, be reconciled, even overcome, for long periods of time and it is the essence of leadership to find ways of doing so. The regime probably could have muddled through with a centrist–populist strategy for a long time, juggling classes, perhaps finding a way to semi-institutionalize Nasirism in a center–left form of corporatism as in post-revolutionary Mexico. That this did not happen in Egypt cannot be separated from the intervention of external forces in the form of the 1967 war in which Israel, with American arms and connivance, struck a decisive blow at Nasirism. This event, a delayed reaction by forces associated with the dominant world order against a nationalist challenge to it, certainly fits the Marxist neo-imperialist scenario. This outcome was perhaps inevitable, for no authentic nationalist leadership in Egypt can avoid challenging imperialist control of the region; Nasirism, had it done otherwise, would not have been Nasirism. The defeat decisively undermined the charismatic authority of the regime; without the disillusionment and the ideological vacuum resulting from this event, subsequent developments are scarcely imaginable. The defeat exacerbated all the vulnerabilities of the regime, strengthened internal forces opposed to it, and threw the system into crisis. By the late sixties the conditions (system crisis), the forces (the bourgeoisie), and even the means (the authoritarian state) of major policy transformation existed. All that was required to set it in train was a mere change of leadership at the top, a new ruler prepared to lead it. Sadat was that man.

The forces of transformation under Sadat

The major impetus to change under Sadat flowed from an interaction between the regime's struggle to extricate itself from the twin-dimensioned crisis of economic stagnation and Israeli occupation, and that of the new leader to consolidate his power against rivals and build a dependable support base. These two struggles reinforced each other. Economic decline and national humiliation put mounting pressure on the regime to find a solution to the crisis; but the American–Israeli *combinazione* seemed unbeatable and the Soviet Union to offer no way out. Given this and the class interests of the elite, a leftwing solution was out of the question. On the other hand, a significant segment of the elite, aware that its interests would be served by a rightward turn, was easily convinced that Nasirism had reached a dead-end and that only an abandonment of nationalist militancy for accommodation with the US, and economic liberalization, could extricate Egypt from the Israeli grip and economic stagnation. The leader's values and drive to consolidate his power, interlocking with these forces, pulled in a similar direction. Sadat came to power already favorable, by virtue of his social ascent, personal connections to bourgeois circles and resentment of the other Free Officers, including Nasir, to a reversal of Nasirism. The transformation of Sadat, the rebel of humble origins into a pro-establishment conservative is certainly a classic case of Michel's embourgeoisement of leadership. But Sadat was also pushed and pulled 'right' by objective constraints and opportunities. He lacked the stature to pursue Nasir's centrist balancing act, and since his rivals were on the left and his potential support on the right, a rightward course allowing him to mobilize the bourgeoisie in the consolidation of his regime made, in the calculus of power, the most sense. Sadat also appears to have been rapidly convinced that he could not do without American help in extricating Egypt from its dilemmas. Thus he was led to a series of decisions which, step by step, committed Egypt deeper and deeper to a rightward course.

A series of foreign policy decisions led the march right. The decision to seek American diplomatic help partly precipitated the showdown with the Sabri faction and the destruction of the main elite group standing in the way of major change. This victory and the expulsion of the Soviet advisors won Sadat the support of most of the bourgeoisie, but also increasingly alienated the Soviets and narrowed alternatives to a Westward turn. The conservative Arab forces on which Egypt was becoming dependent, also pushed Sadat right. This all helped to shape the regime's strategy of limited war in 1973 and together with the outcome of the war, pushed Sadat to put all Egypt's eggs in the American basket in the 'first disengagement.' The first disengagement led to the second and so to the trip to Jerusalem, Camp David, and a separate peace. As he was ever-more deeply committed to an American-sponsored peace, Sadat's alternatives were further narrowed and his power and prestige increasingly at stake in a 'successful' conclusion; thus he had to accept what the Americans were prepared to offer and at the price they and the Israelis expected: an end to nationalist non-alignment, Egyptian commitment to an eventually separate peace even at the expense of Egypt's position in the Arab world, and an opening of Egypt to American and Israeli influence.

Infitah reinforced this systemic redirection. It responded to internal economic constraints and external opportunities, such as the rise of petro-power. It followed, as well, from foreign policy exigencies, that is, the need to stimulate and reinforce American interest in Egypt, to make her a suitable client. But it was also a concession to the bourgeoisie whose support the leader wanted. Once begun, internal and external interests combined to extend and consolidate it. *Infitah* and the 'peace process' fed each other, each deemed necessary to the success of the other. Once Egypt became economically dependent, the pressures of foreign donors and creditors, sometimes exercised directly on top elites, sometimes through local clients with a stake in the process, intensified. The expanding web of political, military and economic connections to the West which followed Sadat's policy changes, and the growth of local interests in the new course, gave it substantial roots in the regime's environment.

Though environmental forces were the major pressures behind system transformation, it was leadership skills and the authoritarian state inherited from Nasir which made it possible to launch and sustain Sadat's particular response to these pressures. At every major watershed in his rightward course Sadat faced opposition to the reversal of the Nasirite heritage from both established elites and elements of the mass public. Each time he defeated it. The traditions of politics in the authoritarian state go a long way to explain Sadat's success. These traditions largely excluded forces outside elite circles from the decision-making process. Neither elites nor masses possessed habits of open competitive politics and the state, while lacking the political institutions to aggregate wider opinion into the political process, was well equipped to muffle debate over the big issues unless it could orchestrate them and to repress the mobilization of public demands from below. Thus, those on the outside with a stake in Nasirism lacked the political resources to penetrate elite circles and those on the inside the will or means to mobilize them. Inside elite circles the Presidency was committed to change and Presidential dominance was decisive. This office proved to be the best institutionalized part of the political system, the segment in which Nasir's legitimacy had been most effectively routinized; all other institutions – party, press, even the military – proved impotent as bases from which to challenge it. In short, once the apex of the authoritarian state was captured by an embourgeoised elite, it became a formidable force for undoing the policies it was built to carry out. In addition, certain other political factors reinforced Sadat's power to steer 'right.' He proved to be a shrewd politician in the manipulation of this system. The failures of Nasirism and the legitimacy won by Sadat in the October War temporarily helped neutralize both elites and masses with a stake in the Nasirite tradition and gave Sadat a relatively free hand for the critical period of policy redirection (1974–6) which he used to eliminate the last vestiges of elite opposition and reconstruct a new elite firmly committed to change. And the support Sadat won in the establishment because of his promise that Presidential power would be used to serve rather than threaten established interests of the bourgeoisie, also counted for much. But even these factors – mass deference and the great weight carried by establishment forces – were partly artifacts of a political system lacking institutions of mass participation.

The outcome of system transformation

The outcome of Egypt's post-populist evolution was at least partially discernible by the end of the Sadat era. The clearest dimension of system change was in the purposes and social forces served by political power. It was now wielded, not for populist reform, but to defend and consolidate a new order most congenial to the dominant social force, the bourgeoisie, against radical challenges from below. This was clearest in the composition and ideology of the political elite, in the dominance of the political process by the bourgeoisie and in the content of public policy. As for the authoritarian state structure, it remained largely intact, but was altered, adapted to the more complex political arena in which it had to operate. This pattern of change and persistence can be seen on three levels of analysis, the elite, political structure and the impact of public policy.

Elite transformation

The clearest dimension of systemic change under Sadat was the transformation in the social composition and ideology of the elite. First, the middle-class military politicians who dominated the Nasirite state up to the end were gradually decimated, a process due in part to the de-politicization of the military establishment under external pressures and to Sadat's successful effort to rid himself of dangerous rivals. This opened the door to a civilianization and differentiation of the elite; into the places of the military, Sadat recruited elements of both the technocratic state bourgeoisie and the private bourgeoisie. This was partly an effort to construct an elite more supportive of and appropriate to the more complex society being created by *Infitah*. It was partly an effort to forge an elite which was both more deferent and yet, being representative of those who controlled the means of administration and production, able to consolidate the support of these strategic forces, long kept down by Nasir, for Sadat's regime. The growing web of ties between a state bourgeoisie using its power to acquire enhanced wealth and a private bourgeoisie made eligible by its wealth for new power, advanced the consolidation of the bourgeoisie as Egypt's ruling class.

This social transformation of the elite, combined with external pressures which appeared to render Nasirism unviable, produced a major transformation in elite political ideology, that is, in the elite's view of authority and the purposes it should serve. The charismatic impulse, legitimizing the concentration and use of power in the service of nationalism and revolution was, as Weber predicts, virtually exhausted. In its place, two partly competing, partly reinforcing tendencies emerged, a legal–rational one and a retraditionalizing or neo-patrimonial one. Rationalism was manifest in the emergence of technocrats at the top seeking to rule in the name of technical expertise and market efficiency unfettered by populism. A legal orientation, strengthened by the recruitment of lawyers and private sector elements, was manifest in pressures for the curbing of state intervention in the market and private life. A retraditionalizing tendency was apparent in the traditional legitimation and personalistic style of Sadat's rule, his glorification of traditional values, and the partial appropriation of the means of administration (i.e. corruption) on the part of elites. These two tendencies appeared to pull the regime in opposing directions, manifested in the continuing contradictions between personal and institutional authority, and in the effort to mix authoritarianism and liberalization. But this 'struggle' took the form less of manifest conflicts between well-defined elite factions than of a powerful ambivalence inside the mainstream elite. Moreover, the traditional and legal–rational orientations were not entirely incompatible. Both converged in a new conservative consensus on the limitation of political power. Thus, inspite of the persistence of muted elite conflict over specific policies, the elite seemed, by the end of the Sadat era, to be remarkably united in its conception of the forms and purposes of authority. This consensus included a gradual institutionalization of greater power-sharing among established elites and with the largely bourgeois constituency of the regime, a sufficient withdrawal of state intervention from the socio-economic sphere needed to give more scope to 'bourgeois freedoms' and reintegrate Egypt into the world capitalist market. But those authoritarian controls, legitimized by tradition and personal leadership, needed to prevent a challenge to this course from the mass political arena would be maintained. The effect of this orientation could at least partially be discerned in the adaptations of state structures and in the changes in public policy pursued by this transformed elite.

The adaptation of an authoritarian regime

The main lines of the authoritarian bureaucratic state forged under Nasir were clearly maintained under Sadat to help push through and then defend the new course on which he set Egypt. But the state was also adapted to the growing pluralization of its political environment, in an effort to accommodate the participatory demands of its constituency while containing the spread of opposition. This adaptation took both liberalizing and traditionalizing forms.

The dominance of the system by a personalized authoritarian Presidency clearly persisted undiminished and Sadat was no less determined to maintain it than Nasir. The position of the President atop the bureaucratic chain of command, his wide powers of appointment and dismissal and the substantial respect for legal legitimacy inside the elite allowed him to eliminate all intra-elite opposition and forge a deferent compliant elite. His legislative powers and dominance over parliament kept all major policy initiatives – in effect, the right to take the big decisions which set the bounds for all lesser ones – in his hands. Foreign policy decisions were virtually his personal domain. No effective institutional checks on Presidential power developed. The basic weakness and subordination of the political infrastructure to the authoritarian executive carried over from the Nasir period. Parliament, parties, press and judiciary were no more able to hold the executive accountable than heretofore. The ability of the President to change the rules of the political game almost at will was indicative of Egypt's continuing very modest level of political institutionalization. Even the informal intra-elite power balance, in which other major military-politicians had constrained Nasir, largely disappeared under Sadat. As such, the heart of the political process remained confined to elite circles, taking the form of intra-elite conflict for access to and influence over the President.

295

Access to the President was necessarily very limited: those in the established elite dominated access, and among these, those with close personal connections to the President enjoyed a great advantage in the political contest.

Yet, the change in the 'style' of rule under Sadat, that is, the evolution from charismatic dictatorship to Presidential monarchy, did make for a big difference in the scope and biases of Presidential power. The activist, interventionist style of the Nasir Presidency, frequently a response to the expectations of the leader's populist constituency, was curbed, and Presidential power used to stabilize and protect established interests; thus the scope of Presidential power was narrowed. The aloofness from and distrust of the elite, which limited Presidential responsiveness to the elite under Nasir was much diminished under Sadat who, by contrast, was linked to the elite by personal and clientage connections which became important avenues for influencing Presidential policy. The formerly tight Presidential control over the cabinet and political infrastructure was relaxed and a modicum of power seemed to flow downward to them from the Presidency. The cabinet did not become an autonomous power center but individual ministers enjoyed more autonomy in their own domains. The ruling party did not become an effective channel for the aggregation of political demands and supports, but, as it changed from an instrument for imposing a political consensus on a recalcitrant social elite to a framework for organizing 'the President's men,' it showed signs of developing into a recruitment channel, in particular for private sector elites. Parliament was given greater responsibility over lesser domestic policy matters, and became a more effective arena of interest articulation and, to a lesser extent, even aggregation, for the regime's bourgeois constituency. The mass media remained largely controlled, but portions of it enjoyed a brief autonomy, and the courts assumed a greater authority in defense of civil and property rights; in general there was a widened tolerance of political expression, chiefly at elite levels. Except in foreign policy, the President refrained from imposing detailed policy prescriptions in most issue areas. Intra-elite politics were thus more 'open' to the play of interests. Intra-elite conflicts over issues and bureaucratic rivalries became more overt under Sadat than Nasir. The relaxation of control over elites and widened opportunities for gain broadened the scope of the politics of spoils in the elite. In this process, the main sources of influence altered. Bureaucratic office and expertise remained important; revolutionary credentials dropped out and personal connections grew in importance, especially at the very top. And, increasingly, influence in the decision-making process also began to flow from a tacit 'representation' of societal interests by elites especially as greater access to the process was accorded those speaking for private interests outside the state. Thus, not only did ministers begin to lobby more openly for their bureaucratic domains, but parliamentary deputies and heads of associational interest groups started to speak with more authority for their constituents. In the recruitment process, traditional cooptation from the bureaucracy and academia on the basis of seniority, expertise or personal connections continued to dominate, but the representation of constituencies and influence in private society also began to count for something more in this cooptation. Lastly, private wealth, directly in 'corrupt' ways, or indirectly, through the prestige it conferred, began to influence both decision-making and recruitment. To be sure, these changes remained embryonic. Societal resources, whether wealth or support, still could not be overtly mobilized to challenge policies or claim power: the links between the elite and the mass political arenas remained tenuous, the solidarity of political bases precarious, and the Presidency still able to veto any demands from below. Private bases of influence independent of the state, leveled under Nasir, had yet to be reconstituted on a scale sufficient to compete with the state and its leader in an overt test of strength. But so long as state authority was not challenged, parts of society were accorded growing scope for the articulation of their interests in the policy process.

Even this limited liberalization was itself, however, largely confined to the establishment, that is, to elites and their privileged constituents. The institutionalization of broad public participation made no serious advances over the Nasir era, and indeed, no less than Nasir, Sadat's primary concern was to control the broader political arena, not to establish accountability to it. But his strategy of control was necessarily different. He lacked Nasir's overwhelming charismatic legitimacy, yet was committed to controversial policies which sparked opposition and polarized an expanding political arena. Yet his support depended on a relaxation of coercive controls. Sadat's strategy, in these conditions, took two quite different forms; on the one hand, he attempted a liberalizing adaptation of the political infrastructure to its more pluralized environment; on the other, he worked to enhance the traditional legitimacy of his personal rule.

The pluralization of the party system was the chief structural innovation designed to integrate the increasingly pluralized political forces into the regime. It had, however, only modest success. The ruling party, of modest ideological and organizational solidarity, constituted a tenuous patron–client link to mass society and some obstacle to the mobilization of opposition; but it was incapable of mobilizing active support for the regime, much less serving as a demand aggregation mechanism, and indeed it seemed more intent on mass de-mobilization. The opposition party experiment (and the simultaneous tacit tolerance of Islamic organizations) was chiefly designed to coopt and absorb the demands of political activists outside the regime's constituency: leftwing intellectuals, Islamic elements, and the still unreconciled segment of the old bourgeoisie. Sadat intended that the opposition would propose alternatives within the limits of broad Presidential policy and refrain from mobilizing support bases against the regime. To the extent opposition forces were accommodative to the regime, however, they failed to integrate significant elements of the public into the system, and to the degree they mobilized support, it was against the regime. The NPUP threatened to resurrect the ghost of Nasir. The New Wafd threatened to deprive the regime of support on the liberal–right of the political spectrum and the Labor party at the center; both, thus, challenged the regime's hold over its bourgeois constituency. The Islamic organizations threatened its legitimacy among significant elements of the mass public. The clear lesson of the party experiment was that to the degree the system was opened, opportunities widened for opposition forces to mobilize enough public support to threaten the legitimacy, if not the stability of the regime. Hence it had to retighten controls over the political arena. Yet the pluralization of the arena, advanced by the experiment, was not significantly reversed. A series of counter-elites persisted unabsorbed into legitimate political institutions and a set of ideological cleavages, based to a great extent on issues and broad social differentiations, including class, began to seep down to the level of the mass public.

If Sadat tried to satisfy political activists with limited liberalizing concessions, he sought acceptance among the more passive masses through the legitimacy of traditional personal rule. From the outset, he portrayed himself as a pious Islamic ruler and patriarchal leader. His image as a successful war leader added enormously to his personal authority after 1973. Sadat used this authority to promote mass de-politicization and deference. But after the mid-seventies, his pursuit of capitalist rationalization, accommodation with Israel and a Western alignment eroded his legitimacy on both national and religious grounds, and, as it declined, so did deference.

By the end of the decade, it appeared that the effectiveness of the regime's control strategy was waning: both liberal concession and traditional symbolism failed to stop the growth of opposition to policies which damaged the interests and offended the values of many Egyptians outside the establishment. The persistence of traditional deference, clientelism, mass illiteracy and economic dependence continued to limit the potential of active mass opposition to the regime. But under conditions of even limited liberalization, it found widened opportunity for expression, partly through the opposition parties and, to the extent the regime closed legitimate channels, in anti-system, even violent activity, the threat of which became a significant constraint on decision-makers. The mass public was thus not entirely powerless in Sadat's Egypt. But though such opposition was able to slow, even stall, aspects of the new policy, it had not, by the end of the Sadat period, proceeded beyond the capacity of the regime to contain. And, much opposition was largely a reaction to a *fait accompli*, for Sadat shrewdly embedded his policy in a web of local interests and external ties which made it extremely difficult and costly to reverse. Ultimately, when opposition became too threatening, repressive controls were successfully retightened. It appears, therefore, that authoritarianism persists in Egypt, not simply because of the lack of mass politicization, as in the neo-patrimonial model, but because such politicization has advanced far enough to pose a threat to the regime's policies but not far enough to burst the bounds of authoritarian containment. Ultimately modernization may generate levels of pluralization and politicization which, as in the functionalist model, will force the regime into a choice between full-scale liberalization and full-scale praetorianism or repression. For the foreseeable future however, limited liberalization and cycles of alteration between liberalization and repression seem sufficient to preserve regime stability.

Thus, the political system was remolded under Sadat, in at least two ways. In Weberian terms, the bases of authority shifted away from charismatic populism toward a hybrid system, in which patrimonial and legal–rational tendencies coexisted. Retraditionalization was most apparent in the conservative uses to which Sadat put presidential power, the intensely personal nature of his rule, the patrimonial practices which grew up around it, the traditional legitimation of authority and the efforts at mass de-politicization. Legal–rational liberalization was expressed in the narrowed scope of Presidential power and in the greater autonomy of elites and of the political infrastructure. Secondly, the class base of the state shifted decisively. The effacement of charismatic populism in favor of traditionalization and liberalization biased the political process in favor of the bourgeoisie. Patrimonial tendencies, corruption, and the use of personal connections in the political process favored those on the inside track. But, limited liberalization, because it opened access to the political process in such an unequal way, had a reinforcing rather than countervailing effect. A multitude of groups speaking for the haves now found access to the top, and liberalization of recruitment advanced the movement of bourgeois elements into the elite. Intra-regime channels available to the have-nots such as trade unions, carried no comparable weight and the regime largely prevented opposition forces from developing into legitimate channels for the expression of mass demands. Thus, the greater political freedom in Sadat's Egypt was chiefly freedom for the bourgeoisie to advance and defend its interests. This compared to the Nasir regime when no one social force enjoyed such an advantage because freedom and access were equally limited for all. And the replacement of Nasir, a leader who tried to stay above and balance off the classes and who frequently intervened to redress the balance on behalf of weaker forces, with Sadat, one who, dependent on the dominant social force, eschewed such intervention, could only be to the advantage of the haves. The adaptation of Egypt's institutional structures contributed, along with the change in elite composition, to turning the Sadat regime into a fairly clear form of bourgeois class rule. In the absence of a thorough social and political revolution, such a reassertion of the power of the dominant social force appears, as Marxists claim, to have been virtually inevitable.

From national–populism to Infitah

The transformation of public policy under Sadat was of a major order of magnitude, virtually reversing many of the priorities of the Nasir era. It put an end to Nasir's activist attempt to challenge the regional status quo, to balance the social classes, to intervene in society in the interest of equity and national-based development. The Sadat regime not only pulled back from these efforts to transform Egypt's environment, but deliberately promoted accommodation between the state and the dominant global and internal social forces.

On one level, this change can be seen as an 'adaptation' to the costs and failures of Nasirism, the resistance of Egypt's environment to its transforming efforts, that is, a concession to the limits of Egypt's national power and to the limited capacity of the bureaucratic state to promote economic development. But if Nasirism had its costs, so did Sadat's course, and the choice between costs cannot be explained without consideration of the political struggle. Briefly, the choice resulted from the recapture of political power by the bourgeoisie manifest in the change in elite composition and the opening of the state to this social force.

That public policy was the outcome of a political struggle can be seen in the gap between the policy of *Infitah* and its actual implementation; it resembled less a rational adaptation to new conditions which maximized Egypt's gains than the incoherent outcome of a tug-of-war between interests. The structure and operations of the political system was in good part responsible for this. Limited liberalization opened the door to the colonization of the decision-process, a race by the bourgeoisie to acquire new rights and privileges. An administrative system lacking strong leadership or well-institutionalized structures of decision-making and implementation was vulnerable to official corruption and incapable of overriding vested interests resistant to reform. A Westernized, economically dependent elite was susceptible to foreign pressures pulling it 'right.' Yet, its fear of popular reaction to a radical undoing of populism deterred it from a thorough capitalist rationalization of policy.

The outcome was a 'mixed' economic system which raised the costs and diminished the potential benefits of the *Infitah*. On the one hand, the regime failed to defend the achievements of the etatist era: thus, its failure to reform the public sector made it vulnerable to de-nationalization. On the other hand, the regime could not enforce a rigorous *laissez-faire* policy; bureaucratic obstacles to private initiative remained formidable and state intervention in the market significant. Egypt did gain massive new external financing which resulted in a new burst of growth, some durable new assets, and a revitalized private sector. But unrestricted *Infitah* could prevent neither the dissipation of large parts of the new wealth in conspicuous consumption, an influx of imports and investment damaging to national industry, nor hemorrhages of capital and skilled labor. Unrestricted *Infitah*, combined with official corruption, channeled private investment into speculative or *comprador* activities. And reliance on foreign financing translated into mounting debt and dependency. Thus, it was far from clear at the end of the Sadat era whether *Infitah* could support a sustained economic advance. Yet there is no doubt that *Infitah* gave the regime a new lease on life, and a direction – re-capitalization – which, short of revolution from below, is probably irreversible.

The distributory consequences of regime policy were equally ambivalent. The upper strata were the chief beneficiaries of the reactivation of the market and the liberalization of policy, while lesser strata paid most of its costs. The inegalitarian effects of the new course were diluted by the export of labor and the massive influx of aid and loans which produced a trickle-down effect and allowed the regime to maintain a social safety net of sorts. Should these external safety valves fail, however, the regime may yet be compelled to take more overt sides between social forces. But though *Infitah* may be preparing the way for an authoritarian–repressive model in which the masses are subjected to massive repression and made to bear the exclusive burden of capital accumulation to the benefit of the bourgeoisie and its international partners, this had not yet happened by the eighties: the regime had so far neither the need nor the will to make such a choice. In fact, the Sadat regime, was a 'softer' state than its predecessor; Nasir had the legitimacy to make, at various times, demands on all social forces; the Sadat regime, as the 1977 riots showed, had much less capacity to do so, and thus, did not.

The outcome of the regime's foreign policy was also two-sided. Peace and the return of the Sinai were major achievements. But the separate character of the peace had intangible but, nevertheless, very real costs. The weakening of Egypt's Arab role and her growing cultural and economic dependence on the West, risked alienation of national identity and a loss of independence. Egyptian policy bore the major responsibility for the fragmentation and opening of the Arab world to Israeli military power and American penetration in the seventies. This cut short the brief surge of Arab solidarity and power after 1973 from which a viable Arab regional system might have emerged and from which, as its hub, Egypt was bound to benefit. This outcome was partly a result of external constraints. But it was also a cost of the authoritarian and personalistic political system; had Sadat been accountable to the wider public, or even to other elites, especially the foreign policy professionals, Egypt would probably have played her cards better after 1973 and, just possibly, have won a comprehensive Middle East peace. Instead, the clock of national liberation in the Arab world, at least as measured by the conventional standards of Arab nationalism to which Egypt had long subscribed, was turned back at least a quarter of a century. It remained to be seen how seriously regime legitimacy, traditionally dependent on achievement or failure in the contest with foreign forces, had been damaged by this. For the time being, Egypt had entered one of its periodic phases of passivity and withdrawal from its Arab–Islamic environment.

Sadat's new Egypt after Sadat

Four years after Sadat's death the new order he founded remained intact. The global and internal forces which initially pushed Egypt down the road of change showed no signs of weakening. Egypt's dependency on American aid had, if anything, deepened with the leveling off of her own and Arab foreign exchange earnings which might have substituted for it. The growth of the private and joint-venture sectors had deepened the stake of the bourgeoisie in *Infitah*. The authoritarian–bureaucratic state appeared stable and cohesive. Mubarak's smooth succession was one sign of this; in contrast to Sadat's own succession, there was no major intra-elite split over power or policy and the established elite seemed firmly united against the threat from below. The rapid assumption of full powers by Mubarak was also a symptom of the institutionalization of Presidential office and the firm hold of legal legitimacy among the elite. The repressive apparatus proved reliable in dealing successfully with the Islamic groups prepared to challenge the regime violently. The new President did restore the limited liberalization suspended by Sadat in 1981. The opposition press was allowed to publish and even the NPUP and New Wafd were readmitted to the legitimate party system. This was an acknowledgment that the adaptation of the authoritarian state to its more pluralized environment could not be rolled back without risk of praetorianism; but it was also a sign of strength and flexibility. The corruption trials, an effort to purge the regime of some of the worst of the patrimonial practices which flourished under Sadat, probably restored some of the regime's tarnished legitimacy. This and the less personalistic and traditional style of the new President suggested that the elite was trying to adapt to a declining tolerance for patrimonial rule. Finally, continuity was apparent at the levels of domestic and foreign policy where there was some alteration in symbol but little in substance. There was talk of reforming *Infitah*, but not of scrapping it. Even the most vulnerable of Sadat's achievements, his separate peace with Israel, survived a major test, the Lebanon invasion. Although it was clear that the scale of Israel's attack was only possible because of the neutralization of her Egyptian front, Mubarak contented himself with the withdrawal of his ambassador from Israel, a passivity unthinkable under Nasir. On the whole, Sadat appeared to have institutionalized his work far more successfully than Nasir. The state Sadat passed on to his successor was erected on a sturdy and massive political structure, rooted in the dominant social forces and enmeshed in a web of interests and constraints which militated against any major intra-system change. If a significant reversal of the course

Sadat set was to come, it would almost certainly have to be through revolution from below, and that, in the immediate term, did not seem to be in the cards.

In the longer run, the regime's policies are bound to have a 'feedback' effect which can be expected to alter the political system, but because the consequences of policies pull in opposite directions it is hard to predict their effect. On the one hand, the decline of secular 'progressive' ideology, especially in the regime, and the end to statist activism, has reinforced a certain traditionalist revival in society, as manifested, for example in the strengthening of traditional pro-regime notables in village and quarter, and the spread of conservative religious influence throughout society. This is probably compatible with the persistence of a retraditionalized authoritarian state. Pulling in a contrary direction are forces pluralizing and mobilizing the political arena. The resurgence of the private bourgeoisie stimulated by the regime had not, by the end of the Sadat regime, reconstituted the large independent social bases of the pre-Nasir era needed for full-blown liberalism, and the massive bureaucratic state is sure to dominate Egyptian society for a long time; but the seeds of private countervailing power exercised on the state were apparent even under Sadat and the continuance of *Infitah* should broaden the bases of liberalization. On the other hand, the same policies also contribute to widening class divisions and the growth of opposition from below which, while deepening the pluralization of the political arena, reinforces the authoritarian proclivities of the regime. In the long-run, the regime will probably be forced into a choice between accommodating demands for participation and wholly repressing them, with all the risks attendant on such a course. But whether it moves toward liberalization or repression, the growth of class divisions in a regime with precarious nationalist credentials poses significant long-term threats of praetorianism or even revolution. The regime will try, as long as it can, to cope with these threats through a strategy which continues to mix doses of limited traditionalization, limited liberalization and limited repression. In that case, Egypt will be in a tradition which has become more typical than not in the post-populist Third World.

Notes

2 Egypt under Nasir

1 According to the theory of the hydraulic society a people which historically lived in a society dependent on a strong government for the maintenance of irrigation works, is likely to be habituated to obedience and submission to government. See Ayubi (1980: 77–136) for a discussion of the relevance of the concept to Egypt.

3 The making of Sadat's Egypt

1 One index of this was that in spite of apparent attempts by the left to manipulate the 1968 ASU elections, Sadat received 119 votes, not far behind Sabri's 134.
2 Moreover, kinship ties, emphasized so heavily by some writers, do not appear to have played an important role in the conflict. It is true that General Fawzi and Sami Sharif were so linked, but kinship ties also cut across the political factions. Mahmud Riad, who stood with Sadat, was so linked to elements in the losing faction and Sayyid Marei and Ali Sabri had kinship links. Robert Springborg (1975) notes these complications, but still insists on the importance of kinship in the calculus of power in Egypt.
3 In regard to Sadat's performance in the negotiations, Kissinger told the Israelis that Sadat had proved more yielding than his strategic position demanded. The Israelis, aware that they could not long maintain the mobilization needed to keep their foothold on the Canal West Bank, and convinced that control of the Canal, by ensuring Egypt's continuing involvement in the Arab–Israeli war, had been a mistake, would probably have been prepared to accept an agreement more favorable to Egypt (Fahmi 1983 70–5; Golan 1976: 146–54, 64).

4 The Presidency and the power elite

1 According to common Egyptian stereotypes, the *fahlawi* personality, found among the peasantry, is clever, adaptable, flattering to authority in its presence but contemptuous of it in its absence. The *saidi* of upper Egypt and supposedly of Bedouin blood, is supposed to be prideful, vengeful and straightforward.
2 Ghali Shukri (1978: 30–35) argues that Sadat was a supremely calculating player of the game of power, who always made sure to be on the winning side. He goes so far as to hold that Sadat was 'late' for the 1952 *coup* because he did not want to show his hand before he was sure it had succeeded.

3 The reader must be alerted to a problem of incomparability in the data on recruitment paths between the Nasir and Sadat periods. Dekmejian (1971), from whom the Nasir figures are taken, does not classify agronomists as engineers, evidently listing them according to the institution in which they were employed, chiefly the bureaucracy, possibly academia, while for the sake of consistency I have classified them according to profession, together with engineers. This incomparability understates the proportion of engineers in the Nasir era as compared to Sadat. It is also probably responsible for the apparent fall in bureaucrats from Nasir to Sadat and perhaps for part of the dip in academia. I try to take account of this problem in the analysis.

4 The process by which persons acquiring upward mobility through politics used power to get wealth and then increased it in private business can be illustrated through the cases of some well-known regime personalities. Mr X, a man of modest background, married high into the political elite during the Nasir regime. He managed to stay on good terms with Sadat who appointed him director of a joint Arab–Egyptian industrial firm. In this capacity he evidently paid himself and his cronies exorbitant salaries, and though ultimately dismissed on this account, accumulated the resources to subsequently go into private business, acquiring the local franchise of a Western company let into Egypt under *Infitah*. Dr Y began his career as an academic and served under Nasir and Sadat in several prominent public posts. In 1975 he was dismissed, amidst charges, never proved, that he was involved in commission-taking. Some years later, he put up £E250,000 as part of the capital of a joint venture business with a foreign firm of which he became director. Such cases are widely thought to be typical in Egypt today. For example, Adil Hussein counted among prominent businessmen in 1976 two ex-premiers, 22 ex-ministers, and dozens of ex-chairmen of public enterprises, under-secretaries of state and governors (Reported in Ayubi 1982: 354).

5 The analysis of elite 'implicit' ideology relies on three basic sources: Sadat's speeches, and to a lesser degree those of other members of the elite, the editorial commentary of the mainstream press, which, government controlled, is a good barometer of official opinion, and interviews with several leading regime elites, including two secretaries general of the ruling party and a member of its politburo.

5 Politics among elites

1 See the memoirs of General Mortegy (1975:23) commander of the land forces in 1967, in which the general tells Egyptians, 'Don't blame us; we were the victims of a bad regime and political leadership just like you.' See also statements by General Daghidi, put on trial for his performance as commander of the Eastern Air region in 1967 in *Middle East Intelligence Survey*, Vol. 1, No. 11, September 1–15, 1973.

2 *al-Ahali*, 22 Feb., 1978 charged that some managers were stealing the cadres and machines of the public sector to set up their own businesses under the names of relatives.

6 The political infrastructure

1 This analysis is based on semi-systematic interviews (24) with government party activists in 1978, and an ASPE document, 'A Project on the Main Lines of the Party's Program.'

2 This analysis of organization is based on interviews with party leaders including Mahmud Abu Wafia, Mansur Hassan and Fuad Muhi ad-Din; also public statements of leaders (*al-Ahram*, 16 Apr., 25 June, 14 Nov. 1979, 1 Jan. 1980; *al-Ahrar*, 8 Oct. 1979; MENA, 18 Nov., 2 Dec. 1979).

3 This analysis benefits from interviews with party leaders, especially Abd al-Fattah Shurbagi.

4 Among the strong candidates who lost were Mahmud Qadi, a prominent liberal independent; Shaikh Ashur Nasr, an Islamic populist; NPUP leader, Khalid Muhi ad-Din; and conservative ex-Free Officer, Kemal ad-Din Hussein.

5 The rule that 50% of the seats had to be filled by workers or peasants was largely circumvented. Well-off persons who would not by any conventional standard be considered workers or peasants, were so-classified, or high-status candidates ran in tandem with a lower-class client (in each electoral district there were two seats, one reserved for a worker or peasant).

6 The government rejected a broad-based parliamentary demand in early 1978 to break off the negotiations; in late 1978 one that the Arab Defense Pact be given priority over the peace treaty; in 1979 a resolution of the foreign affairs committee that normalization proceed only within the framework of a comprehensive settlement; and in 1980 that it be linked to West Bank autonomy.

7 Counter-elites and the pluralization of the political arena

1 This discussion of ideology draws basically on the party's published program, *Meshrūa al-Birnāmig al-Ām*, on issues of *al-Ahali*, the party newspaper, and on interviews with party leaders Khalid Muhi ad-Din and Rifat Sa'id.

2 This discussion of organization relies on interviews with party leaders, the organization report to the First National Congress, in *Qarrarat al-M'utamar al-Am al-Ula*, and from those of several branch congresses.

3 Of the vote, 8% translated into about 1% of the seats owing to the system of constituency voting; under proportional representation, the NPUP would have won about 20 seats. Reports claiming that the NPUP got only one percent of the vote confuse votes and seats. One percent of the vote (about 40,000 votes) would have been only one third of the party's membership at the time of the elections. Khalid Muhi ad-Din himself won about 22,000 votes and the NPUP elected three other deputies and stood 57 other candidates, some of whom made respectable showings.

4 Sadat denounced the NPUP for stirring up class hatred. Two leaders of the ruling party told the writer (Cairo, 1978) that the NPUP deputies were only the 'tip of the iceberg' and if controls were relaxed, Egypt could erupt in opposition.

5 Also, interviews with Ikhwan leaders Salah Ashmawi and Muhammed Abd al-Qadus, Cairo, 1979.

6 Data on New Wafd leaders are from interviews with the 35-man party high board. That on economic interests is, because of the habit of concealing wealth, probably understated. Data on Sadat ministers are from Chapter IV.

7 This analysis of ideology is based on (1) the party program, *Birnāmig Hizb al-Wafd al-Jadid* (Cairo, n.d.); (2) Interviews with party leaders Fuad Serag ad-Din (President), Hilmi Murad (Vice President) and Drs Numan Gomaa and Muhammed Nasr

(Assistant Secretaries); (3) Attitude questions included in a survey of party activists (see note 9).

8 Interviews with leaders of the Arab Socialist Party of Egypt, Cairo 1978.

9 The sample of New Wafd activists was obtained by questionnaires distributed to activists in two meetings held at the party's Cairo headquarters in early 1978. The sample is small (because police prevented the researcher from continuing the survey) and random sampling was impossible; as such the results can only be regarded as suggestive indicators. Since the survey was taken in Cairo, it probably underrepresents the party's rural membership. But if the past is any guide, the rural Wafdist was likely to be a prosperous landowner or professional not unlike his urban counterpart. Moreover, those found at party headquarters are likely to be most representative of the party's real hard-core activists.

10 Respondents were assigned to a class category according to reported economic interests (land, business), top positions (e.g. banker, hospital director, manager), and the relative status of their profession (doctor, lawyer, etc. being considered a 'large' professional, a teacher or journalist a 'small' one). Because of the room for error in this method and some incomplete data, the table represents a mere rough estimate.

8 The regime and the mass public

1 An article in *al-Ahram*, May 8, 1980, lamented the tendency of the people to hold the leader responsible for everything which goes wrong.

2 An attitude survey was given to 145 students at the American University in Cairo between 1977 and 1978. These students can be used as a surrogate for the Westernized bourgeoisie as a whole. AUC students are, by comparison to those of the 'national universities', disproportionately drawn from the highest stratum and most Westernized wing of the Egyptian bourgeoisie. Very unpoliticized, they appear to share their parents' opinions rather than expressing a student sub-culture. This method is not technically rigorous but in the absence of a research climate tolerant of opinion surveys, it was adopted as a plausible substitute; student responses, moreover, are probably more candid than would be those of their parents had the latter been surveyed. Unfortunately, it was not possible to do scientific sampling and in cases where statistical associations are reported, they were not statistically significant at the 0.05 level; hence the sample is not rigorously representative of the whole population under consideration. But responses seem congruent enough with what is known about the group studied to be taken as suggestive indicators of attitudes.

3 To test for biases in the attitude pattern owing to the somewhat disproportionate presence of families of Levantine and mixed European–Middle Eastern background and of Christians in the sample, all responses were carefully controlled for these social distinctions. Where they are associated with significant attitudinal variation, this is explicated in the analysis.

4 In this and subsequent ethnic breakdowns of the sample, the category 'European blood' refers to those with some European or Armenian ancestry. Of this category, 7.1% were pure Europeans, 71.4% mixed Egyptian and European, 14.3% Armenian, and 7.1% mixed Egyptian, European and some other nationality. The 'Arab' category refers to those with some Arab ancestry. Of these, 81% were pure Arab, while 19%

were mixed Egyptian and Arab. Those classified in the Turkish category, were 25% pure Turkish, 47% mixed Turkish and Egyptian, and 28% from families with Turkish fathers, but in which mothers had some Arab or European blood.

5 The low support for the Labor party is artificial as it had not been formed when part of the survey was given.

6 Scores were arrived at by giving each leader 5 points for each first ranking received, 4 for each second ranking, 3 for each third ranking, 2 for each fourth ranking, 1 for each fifth ranking, then subtracting from this total 5 points for each tenth ranking received, 4 for each ninth ranking, three for each eighth, 2 for each seventh and 1 for each sixth ranking received.

9 Public policy and the political economy of development under Sadat

1 Indicative of Sadat's lack of leadership in economic matters, are reports of the *Economist* (29 January, 1977) that he 'dozes off whenever the cabinet starts discussing economic matters,' and of *The Financial Times* (30 July, 1979) that 'he is not deeply interested in the economy.'

2 Ayubi (1979) cites statistical evidence from criminal records of a surge in corruption after *Infitah*.

3 The discussion of foreign investment under *Infitah* excludes the oil sector.

4 Dr K. Mustafa, in a report to the 4th Annual Symposium of Egyptian Economists, Cairo, May, 1979, showed that 66.8% of Egyptian families spend less than £E1 per day, at a time when a kilo of beans cost 35 piasters and a pack of cigarettes, 30 piasters (£E = 100 piasters).

Bibliography

Abd al-Fadil, Mahmoud. 1982. Educational expansion and income distribution in Egypt. In Abd al-Khalek and Tignor, 1982, pp. 351–74.

Abd al-Khalek, Gouda. 1977. The Open Door economic policy and economic growth in Egypt. In Gritli, 1977.

—. 1979. The Open Door economic policy in Egypt: a search for meaning, interpretation and implications. In *Studies in Egyptian Political Economy, Cairo Papers in Social Science*, Vol. 2, Monograph 3, pp. 74–97.

—. 1982. Foreign economic aid and income distribution in Egypt, 1952–1977. In Abd al-Khalek and Tignor, 1982, pp. 435–68.

— and Tignor, Robert. 1982. *The Political Economy of Income Distribution in Egypt*. London and New York: Holmes and Meier.

Abdel Malek, Anwar, 1968. *Egypt: Military Society*. New York: Vintage Books.

—. 1979. The occultation of Egypt. Arab Studies Quarterly, 1: 177–99.

Abu Talib, Sufi. 1978. The democratic socialist ideology of the May 1971 Revolution. *al-Ahram al-Iqtisadi*, 16 July (In Arabic).

Abul Ghar, Ibrahim. 1979. Public employee deviation: one picture of administrative corruption. Cairo: National Center for Social and Criminal Research (In Arabic).

Ahmad, Aijaz. 1975. The Arab stasis. *Monthly Review*, May, pp. 42–53.

Ajami, Fouad. 1981. *The Arab Predicament: Arab Political Thought and Practice Since 1967*. Cambridge: Cambridge University Press.

—. 1982. The Open Door economy: its roots and welfare consequences. In Abd al-Khalek and Tignor, 1982, pp. 469–516.

Akhavi, Shahrough. 1975. Egypt: Neo-Patrimonial Elite. In Frank Tachau, ed., *Political Elites and Political Development in the Middle East*. New York: John Wiley, pp. 69–113.

—. 1982. Egypt: Diffused elite in a bureaucratic society. In I. William Zartman, ed. *Political Elites in Arab North Africa*. New York: Longman, pp. 223–65.

Ali, Shafif Ahmad. 1977. Imaginary Ministers. *Ruz al-Yusuf*, 4 July.

Altman, Israel. 1979. Islamic Movements in Egypt. *The Jerusalem Quarterly*, 10: 87–105.

Amin, Galal. 1981. Some economic and cultural aspects of economic liberalization in Egypt. *Social Problems*, 28: 430–41.

Apter, David. 1965. *The Politics of Modernization*. Chicago: University of Chicago Press.

Aulus, Marie Christine. 1976. Sadat's Egypt. *New Left Review*, 98: 84–95.

Bibliography

Ayubi, Nizeh. 1979. Administrative corruption in Egypt: phenomenon, causes and costs. Cairo: National Center for Social and Criminal Research (In Arabic).

—. 1980. *Bureaucracy and Politics in Contemporary Egypt*. London: Ithaca Press.

—. 1982. Implementation capability and political feasibility of the open door policy in Egypt. In M. H. Kerr and E. S. Yassin, eds. *Rich and Poor States in the Middle East*. Boulder: Westview Press, pp. 349–413.

Aziz, Khayri. 1972. The national bourgeoisie. *al-Talia*, June.

Baker, Raymond. 1978. *Egypt's Uncertain Revolution under Nasir and Sadat*. Cambridge, Mass.: Harvard University Press.

—. 1981. Sadat's open door: opposition from within. *Social Problems*, 28: 378–84.

Beeri, Eliezer. 1966. Social class and family background of the Egyptian army officer class. *Asian and African Studies*, 2: 1–38.

Bentley, John. 1981. Social legislation and foreign investment in Egypt. Paper given at Conference on Law and Social Structure in the Middle East, Rabat.

Berger, Morroe. 1962. *The Arab World Today*. New York: Doubleday.

—. 1970. *Islam in Egypt Today*. Cambridge: Cambridge University Press.

Berque, Jacques. 1972. *Egypt: Imperialism and Revolution*. New York: Praeger.

Binder, Leonard. 1965. Egypt: the integrative revolution. In *Political Culture and Political Development*, eds. Lucian Pye and Sidney Verba, pp. 396–449. Princeton: Princeton University Press.

—. 1978. *In A Moment of Enthusiam: Political Power and the Second Stratum in Egypt*. Chicago: University of Chicago Press.

Birks, J. S. and Sinclair, C. A. 1979. Egypt: a frustrated labor exporter. *Middle East Journal*, 33: 228–303.

Bonander, Ann Marie. 1980. Implementing political decentralization: the role of AID in Egypt. Paper prepared for Seminar on Rural Politics in Egypt, AUC, Cairo.

Brown, William. 1980. *The Last Crusade: A Negotiator's Middle East Handbook*. Chicago: Aldine.

Buttner, Friedemann. 1979. Political stability without stable institutions: the re-traditionalization of Egypt's polity. *Orient*, 20: 53–67.

Cantori, Louis. 1975. The Wafd party and the Egyptian pre-independence struggle, 1918–24. Unpublished paper.

—. 1980. Egypt at peace. *Current History*, 78: 26–9.

— and Benedict, Peter. 1979. The semi-autonomous local political system: a study of an Egyptian urban community. Paper read at Conference on Local Development in the Middle East, University of Maryland, Baltimore.

Carr, David. 1979. *Foreign Investment and Development in Egypt*. New York: Praeger.

Cooper, Mark. 1979. Egyptian state capitalism in crisis: economic policy and political interests. *International Journal of Middle East Studies*, 10: 481–516.

Critchfield, Richard. 1978. *Shahhat: An Egyptian*. Syracuse: Syracuse University Press.

Deeb, Marius. 1979. *Party Politics in Egypt: The Wafd and Its Rivals, 1919–1939*. London: Ithaca Press.

Dekmejian, Hrair R. 1971. *Egypt Under Nasir*. Albany: State University of New York Press.

—. 1975. *Patterns of Political Leadership: Lebanon, Israel, Egypt*. Albany: State University of New York Press.

—. 1980. The anatomy of Islamic revival. *Middle East Journal*, 34: 1–12.

— and Dahry, Kamal. 1976. Elites and public policy: the Egyptian budgetary process. Paper read at 10th MESA Conference, Los Angeles.

Dessouki, Ali E. Hilal. 1978. The transformation of the party system in Egypt. In *Democracy in Egypt, Cairo Papers in Social Science*, Vol. 1, Monograph 2, pp. 7–24.

—. 1981. Policy-making in Egypt: a case study of the open door economic policy. *Social Problems*, 28: 410–16.

—. 1982a. The Islamic Resurgence: sources, dynamics, implications. In Ali Dessouki, ed. *Islamic Resurgence in the Arab World*. New York: Praeger, pp. 3–31.

—. 1982b The politics of income distribution in Egypt. In Abd al-Khalek and Tignor, 1982, pp. 55–87.

Dimbleby, Jonathan. 1977. Sadat's solitary hand. *New Statesman*, 15 August.

Edel, Reda al-. 1982. Impact of Taxation on income distribution: an exploratory attempt to estimate tax incidence in Egypt. In Abd al-Khalek and Tignor, 1982, pp. 132–64.

Egyptian Arab Socialist Organization. 1977. Project of basic organization. Cairo.

Entelis, John P. 1974. Nasir's Egypt: the failure of charismatic leadership. *Orbis*, 28: 451–64.

Fahmi, Ismail. 1983. *Negotiating for Peace in the Middle East*. Baltimore: Johns Hopkins University Press.

Farid, Salah. 1970. *Top Management in Egypt: Its Structure, Quality and Problems*. Santa Monica: Rand Corporation.

Fawzi, Hussein. 1969. *Sindbad Masri*. Cairo: Dar al-Ma'arif bi-Misr.

Fouad, Nemat. 1978. *Shakhsiyyat Misr*. Cairo: Hayyat al-Masri al-Am lil-Kitab.

—. 1979. The pyramid plateau project. In *Law and Social Change in Contemporary Egypt, Cairo Papers in Social Science*, eds. Cynthia Nelson and Klaus Koch, Vol. 2, Monograph 4, pp. 137–61.

Gami', Ahmad. 1979. The pyramid plateau project. In *Law and Social Change in Contemporary Egypt, Cairo Papers in Social Science*, eds. Cynthia Nelson and Klaus Koch, Vol. 2, Monograph 4, pp. 162–75.

Golan, Matti. 1976. *The Secret Conversations of Henry Kissinger*. New York: Quadrangle Books.

Gritli, Ali. 1977. *Twenty Five Years: An Analytical Study of Egypt's Economic Policies, 1952–77*. Cairo: Hayyat al-Masri al-Am lil-Kitab.

Guindi, Fadwa, al-. 1981. Veiling Infitah with Muslim ethic. *Social Problems*, 28: 465–83.

Hafiz, Hala. 1980. Land reclamation and tenure policies under Sadat. Paper prepared for Seminar on Rural Politics in Egypt, AUC, Cairo.

Halpern, Manfred. 1963. *The Politics of Social Change in the Middle East and North Africa*. Princeton: Princeton University Press.

Hamamsy, Laila Shukry. 1977. The assertion of Egyptian identity. In Saad Eddin Ibrahim and Nicholas Hopkins, eds. *Arab Society in Transition*. Cairo: American University in Cairo Press, pp. 49–78.

Hamid, Heba. 1980. Peasant attitudes in Abou Kebir. Paper prepared for seminar on Rural Politics in the Middle East, AUC, Cairo.

Hanafy, Asm. 1976. Where is the law?. *Ruz al-Yusuf*, 26 March.

Handoussa, Heba. 1979. Time for reform: Egypt's public sector industry. In *Studies in*

Egyptian Political Economy, Cairo Papers in Social Science, ed. Herbert M. Thompson, Vol. 2, Monograph 3, pp. 101–24.

Harik, Iliya. 1971. Opinion leaders and the mass media in rural Egypt. *American Political Science Review*, 65: 731–40.

—. 1972. Mobilization policy and rural change in Egypt. In Richard Antoun and Iliya Harik, eds. *Rural Politics and Social Change in the Middle East*. Bloomington: Indiana University Press, pp. 287–334.

—. 1973. The single party as a subordinate movement. *World Politics*, 26: 80–105.

—. 1974. *The Political Mobilization of Peasants*. Bloomington: Indiana University Press.

—. 1984. Continuity and change in local development policies in Egypt. *International Journal of Middle East Studies*, 16: 43–66.

Haykel, Muhammed Hassanein. 1975. *The Road to Ramadan*. New York: Reader's Digest Press.

Heaphy, James. 1965. The organization of Egypt: inadequacies of a non-political model of nation building. *World Politics*, 28: 177–93.

Hinnebusch, Raymond. 1981. The National Progressive Unionist Party: the nationalist left opposition in post populist Egypt. *Arab Studies Quarterly*, 3: 325–51.

Hizb al-Ahrar. 1977. *Birnamig al-Hizb*. Cairo.

Hizb al-Wafd al-Jadid. 1977. *al-Nizam al-Dakhili*. Cairo.

Humphreys, Steven. 1979. Islam and political values in Saudi Arabia, Egypt, and Syria. *Middle East Journal*, 33: 1–19.

Huntington, Samuel P. 1968. *Political Order in Changing Societies*. New Haven: Yale University Press.

Hussein, Mahmoud. 1973. *Class Conflict in Egypt*. New York: Monthly Review Press.

—. 1975. *L'Egypte, 1967–73*. Paris: Maspero.

Ibrahim, Ahmad. 1982. Impact of agricultural policies on income distribution. In Abd al-Khalek and Tignor, 1982, pp. 198–221.

Ibrahim, Saad Eddin. 1982a. Islamic militancy as a social movement: the case of two groups in Egypt. In Ali E. Hilal Dessouki, ed. *Islamic Resurgence in the Arab World*. New York: Praeger, pp. 117–37.

—. 1982b. Social mobility and income distribution in Egypt. In Abd al-Khalek and Tignor, 1982, pp. 375–434.

Ikram, Khalid. 1980. *Egypt: Economic Management in a Time of Transition*. Baltimore and London: Johns Hopkins University Press.

Issawy, Ibrahim Hasan. 1982. Interconnections between income distribution and economic growth in the context of Egypt's economic development. In Abd al-Khalek and Tignor, 1982, pp. 88–131.

Kanovsky, Eliyahu. 1978. Major trends in Middle East economic development. In Colin Legum, ed. *Middle East Contemporary Survey*. London and New York: Holmes and Meier, pp. 227–52.

—. 1981. Egypt's economy under Sadat. In Colin Legum and Haim Shaked, eds. *Middle East Contemporary Survey*. London and New York: Holmes and Meier, pp. 353–82.

Kerr, Malcolm. 1971. *The Arab Cold War: Gamal Abdul Nasir and His Rivals*. London and New York: Oxford University Press.

Korayem, Karima. 1981. The urban rural income gap in Egypt and biased agricultural pricing policy. *Social Problems*, 28: 417–29.

Lachine, Nadim. 1978. The open door policy of Anwar Sadat. Association of Arab American University Graduates, *Information Paper*, 21: 7–28.

Mabro, Robert. 1974. *The Egyptian Economy: 1952–72*. London: Oxford University Press.

Marei, Sayyid. 1978a. *Awrāq Siyāsiah* (Political Papers). Cairo: The New Egyptian Library.

—. 1978b. Political evolution of the one-party system to the multi-party system. In *Democracy in Egypt, Cairo Papers in Social Science*, ed. Ali E. Hilal Dessouki, Vol. 1, Monograph 2, pp. 38–41.

Mayfield, James. 1971. *Rural Politics in Nasser's Egypt*. Austin: University of Texas Press.

McLaurin, R. D., Mughisuddin, Muhammed. Wagner, Abraham R. 1977. *Foreign Policy-Making in the Middle East*. New York: Praeger.

Mead, Donald, 1979. The economics of Egypt. Lecture series, American University in Cairo.

Merriam, John G. 1982. Egypt after Sadat. *Current History*, 81: 5–8.

Messiha, Suzanne. 1980. *Export of Egyptian school teachers to Saudi Arabia and Kuwait: A Cost Benefit analysis. Cairo Papers in Social Science*, Vol. 3, No. 4.

Michels, Robert. 1962. *Political Parties*. New York: The Free Press.

Ministry of Economy, Economic Studies Unit. 1979. Study on Law 42 investment policies. Cairo.

Ministry of Information. 1974. *The October Working Paper*. Cairo

Mokhtar, Nermine. 1980. The Upper Economic Class in Egypt. Unpublished Masters Thesis, American University in Cairo.

Montasser, Essam. 1979. The open door policy. Lecture, American University in Cairo.

Moore, Clement Henry. 1974. Authoritarian politics in unincorporated society: the case of Nasser's Egypt. *Comparative Politics*, 6: 193–218.

—. 1980. *Images of Development: Egyptian Engineers in Search of Industry*. Cambridge, Mass.: MIT Press.

Mortegy, M. 1975. General Mortegy recalls facts. Cairo (In Arabic).

Mosca, Gaetano. 1939. *The Ruling Class*. New York: McGraw Hill.

Mursi, Fuad, 1976. This is the Infitah. Cairo: Dar al Thiqafa (In Arabic).

Nizar, Nazli. 1979. Socio-economic and political study of fruit gardens in Egypt. Paper presented to Seminar on Rural Politics in Egypt, AUC.

Nowaihi, Muhammed. 1979. Changing the law on personal status within a liberal interpretation of the *Sharia'*. In *Law and Social Change in Contemporary Egypt, Cairo Papers in Social Science*, eds. Cynthia Nelson and Klaus Koch, Vol. 2, No. 4, pp. 97–115.

NPUP. 1978. *What's happening in the Egyptian countryside?* Cairo (In Arabic).

Osman, Omar. 1980. The role of the agricultural cooperative in the Egyptian village, 1970–80. Paper presented to Seminar on Rural Politics in Egypt, AUC, Cairo.

Radwan, Samir. 1974. *Capital Formation in Egyptian Industry and Agriculture, 1882–1967*. London: Ithaca Press.

—. 1977. *Agrarian Reform and Rural Poverty: Egypt, 1952–72*. Geneva: ILO.

—. 1981. Trends in income distribution and poverty. Paper presented to Conference on Law and Social Structure in the Middle East, Rabat.

Rashid, Nihal. 1980. Changes in rural policy under Sadat. Paper given to Seminar on Rural Politics in Egypt, AUC, Cairo.

Riad, Mahmoud. 1982. *The Struggle for Peace in the Middle East*. London and New York: Quartet Books.

Rifat, Asam. 1978. The infitah of consumption. *al-Ahram al-Iqtisadi*, 15 May.

—. 1979. Public services for whom? *al-Ahram*, 21 December.

Rondot, Pierre. 1981. Anouar as-Sadat et l'Egypte (1970–80). *Défense Nationale*, January 1981, pp. 77–83.

Rubinstein, Alvin. 1972. Egypt since Nasser. *Current History*, 62: 6–13.

—. 1977. The Egypt of Anwar Sadat. *Current History*, 72: 19–21.

—. 1979. Egypt's Search for Stability. *Current History*, 76: 19–22.

Rugh, Andrea. 1979. *Coping With Poverty in a Cairo Community, Cairo Papers in Social Science*, Vol. 2, Monograph 1.

Sadat, Anwar. 1957. *Revolt on the Nile*. New York: John Day.

—. 1978. *In Search of Identity: An Autobiography*. New York: Harper and Row.

—. 1980. *Egypt and the New Arab Reality: A Working Paper by Anwar Sadat*. Cairo.

Sahib, Abd al-Qadir. 1976. The escapades of the fat merchants. *Ruz al-Yusuf*, 26 April.

Sa'id, Rifat, 1977. The Egyptian political parties: reality or illusion? *Al-Safir*, 27–9 October.

Salacuse, Jeswald. 1981. Foreign investment and legislative exemption in the Middle East: the new capitulations? Paper presented to Conference on Law and Social Structure, Rabat.

Sayed, Salah. 1978. *Workers' Participation in Management*. Cairo: AUC Press.

Serag ad-Din, Fuad. 1977. Why the new party? Cairo (In Arabic).

Shamir, Shimon and Gamma, Moshe. 1981. The Egyptian Israeli peace treaty. In Colin Legum and Haim Shaked, eds. *Middle East Contemporary Survey*. London and New York: Holmes and Meier, pp. 97–117.

Shazli, Saad. 1980. *The Crossing of the Suez*. San Francisco: American Mideast Research.

Sheehan, Edward. 1976. Step by step diplomacy in the Middle East. *Foreign Policy*, 22: 3–70.

Shukri, Ghali. 1978. *al-Thawra al-Mudāda fi-Misr*. Bayrut: Dar al-Talia.

Springborg, Robert. 1975. Patterns of association in the Egyptian political elite. In George Lenczowski, ed. *Political Elites in the Middle East*. Washington, DC: American Enterprise Institute, pp. 83–107.

—. 1978. Professional syndicates in Egyptian politics. *International Journal of Middle East Studies*, 9: 275–95.

—. 1979a. Patrimonialism and policy making in Egypt: Nasir and Sadat and the tenure policy for reclaimed lands. *Middle Eastern Studies*, 26: 49–69.

—. 1979b. Sayyid Bey Marei and political clientalism in Egypt. *Comparative Political Studies*, 12: 259–88.

Springer, Maria. 1980. The role of de-centralization in rural Egypt. Paper presented to Seminar on Rural Politics in Egypt, AUC, Cairo.

Stephens, Robert. 1974. *Nasser: A Political Biography*. New York: Simon and Schuster.

Vatikiotis, P. J. 1961. *The Egyptian Army in Politics*. Bloomington: Indiana University Press.

—. 1969. *The Modern History of Egypt*. New York: Praeger.

—. 1978. *Nasser and His Generation*. New York: St Martin's Press.

Waterbury, John. 1976a. Corruption, Political Stability and Development: Comparative Evidence from Egypt and Moroco. *Government and Opposition*, 11: 426–45.

—. 1976b. *Egypt: Burdens of the Past, Options for the Future*. Hanover: The American University Field Staff.

—. 1976c. Egypt: the wages of dependency. In L. Udovitch, ed. *The Middle East: Oil Politics and Hope*. Lexington, Mass: Lexington Books, pp. 291–351.

—. 1982. Patterns of urban growth and income distribution in Egypt. In Abd al-Khalek and Tignor, 1982, pp. 307–43.

Weber, Max. 1964. *The Theory of Social and Economic Organization*. New York: The Free Press.

Weinbaum, Marvin. 1983. Politics and development in foreign aid: US economic assistance to Egypt, 1975–82. *Middle East Journal*, 37 (4): 636–55.

Wheelock, Keith. 1975. *Nasser's New Egypt*. Westport, Conn.: Greenwood Press.

Ya'ari, Ehud. 1980. Sadat's pyramid of power. *The Jerusalem Quarterly*, 14: 110–21.

Yassin, Sayyid. 1978. Social Structure and Democratic Practice. In *Democracy in Egypt, Cairo Papers in Social Science*, ed. Ali E. Hilal Dessouki, Vol. 1, Monograph 2.

Zeitoun, Mohaya. 1982. Income distribution in Egyptian agriculture and its main determinants. In Abd al-Khalek and Tignor, 1982, pp. 268–306.

Index

Abdul Malek, Anwar, 3
Abdullah, Ismail Sabri, 133
Abu Ghazala, Abd al-Halim, 130
Abu Ismail, Ahmad, 104, 133–5
Abu Ismail, Shaikh Salah, 202
Abu al-Nur, Abd al-Muhsin, 41
Abu Talib, Sufi, 152
Abu Wafia, Mahmud, 88, 99, 106–7, 159–60, 162, 167–70
academics, 103, 152
agrarian relations law, 149, 177, 251
agricultural engineers 101–3, 142–3
agriculture: committee of parliament, 149; inequality in, 282–3; Nasir's policy, 26–7; policy conflicts, 142–4, 149–50; production, 27, 278; state marketing, 149; wages, 282–3
al-Ahali, 182, 194
Ahmad, Kamal, 175
al-Ahram, 60, 181–2
Ahrar Party, 133, 136, 145, 165–7, 170, 215–16
al-Ahrar, 182
Aib, Law of, 84, 90, 151, 174
Ajami, Fouad, 81
Akhavi, Shahrough, 5
al-Akhbar, 182
Ali, Kamal Hassan, 94, 103, 130
Amer, Marshal Abd al-Hakim, 16, 31, 32, 38
Amin, Ali, 60, 182
Amin, Mustafa, 139, 182
Anis, Muhammed, 217
Arab nationalist movement, 21–2
Arab World: Egyptian view of, 72, 75–6, 193–4, 226–7; grants to Egypt, 276; identification with, 116–17, 230–5, 240–1; Nasir's relations with, 21–2, 35–6; Sadat's relations with, 46–8, 54–7, 65–9, 74–6, 116–17, 301–2
Arab, Egyptians of descent, 230–41 *passim*
Arabs, *see* Arab World
Arab Socialism, 24
Arab Socialist Party of Egypt, *see* Misr Party

Arab Socialist Union, 19–20, 33; change under Sadat, 70, 158–65; in factory, 139; and NPUP, 188–90, 192; purge of, 49, 53; and succession struggle, 40–5 *passim*; in village, 250; *see also* government party
ASU, *see* Arab Socialist Union
Aswan High Dam, 22–3, 27
Atalla, Ibrahim, 140
authoritarian–bureaucratic state, 15–21, 44–6, 63, 64–5, 124–5, 295–9, 302
authoritarian–conservative regime, 2, 7–8
authoritarian–modernizing regime, 1
authoritarian–populist regime: features, 2; transformation, 3–7; Nasir's, 11–39
authoritarian–repressive regime, 8, 301

Badawi, Ahmad, 130
Badran, Osman, 143
Baghdadi, Abd al-Latif, 16, 32, 52
Bahgat, Ahmad, 174
baladi people, quarters, 33, 204–5, 247–9
balance of payments deficit, 34, 58, 277
banks, 24, 141, 274
Bank Misr, 141
bourgeoisie: agrarian, 149–50, 176–7; attitudes of, 229–43; elements of, 228–9; industrial, 148–9; and *Infitah*, 59; interest articulation of, 144–54; and Nasirism, 28–31, 290; and New Wafd, 209–11, 214–17, 220; in parliament, 176–7; recruitment into elite, 107–11; and Sadat, 50, 62, 65, 69–70, 89–90, 292; state, 28, 30–1, 59, *see also* businessmen, capitalism, private sector
budget deficits, 267
Bultiya, Abd al-Latif, 163
bureaucracy, 17–18, 27, 258–65; as elite–mass link, 227; obstacle to *Infitah*, 274–5; pathologies of, 18, 25, 32–3, 137, 260–3
bureaucratic feudalism, 45
bureaucratic politics, 16–17, 122–5, 258–65

317

bureaucrats, 27, 215, 246–7
businessmen, 104, 109–10, 144–9, 209, 215,
    239–40; *see also* bourgeoisie, private
    sector

cabinet, 122–5, 174–5
Camp David, 67, 74
capitalism, 22–3, 114–16; *see also*
    bourgeoisie, *Infitah*, private sector
Central Agency for Organization and
    Administration, 137, 140, 262–3
Chamber of Commerce, 144–8 *passim*
charismatic leadership, 6, 9; Nasir's 13–14,
    21, 34–5, 38, 289; routinization of, 6,
    45, 289
clientalism, *see* patron-clientalism
colonized consciousness, 82, 285
communists, 63, 234
construction industry 147–8, *see also* housing
Consultative Group for Aid to Egypt, 136,
    139
consumption, 25, 276–7
cooperatives, 26, 33–4, 250–1
Copts, 153–4
corruption, 25, 31–2, 88–9, 247, 260–3
counter-elites, 186–222
courts, 183–5
cultural dependency, 82, 285–7

Dakruri, Muhammed Ibrahim, 136
al-Dawa, 182, 201–6 *passim*
decision-making, 122–5, 155–7
Dekmejian, Hrair R., 6
democracy, 13, 85–6, 117–19, 191, 212
democratic socialism, 74, 113, 115–16
de-Nasirization, 61–4
Dhahabi, Muhammed, 203
distribution: under *Infitah*, 279–85, 301;
    under Nasir, 27–8; populist, 2; and
    public finance, 265–7

economic liberalization, *see Infitah*
economic performance: under Nasir, 26–7;
    under Sadat, 277–8
economic policy: attitudes of bourgeoisie to,
    238–40; and foreign policy, 59–60, 292;
    under Nasir, 22–6, 37–8; under Sadat,
    57–60, 64, 131–44, 257–88; *see also*
    Infitah
economists: in elite, 100, 103, 110
Economy, Ministry of, 99, 123, 136
education: under Nasir, 24, 26; policy, 243,
    267–9; politics of 152–3
elections: parliamentary, 70–1, 75, 159,
    171–4, 195–6; trade union, 196–7,
    245–6; in village, 250–2

elite–mass linkage, 18–21, 45, 163–4, 225–8,
    245–8, 250–52
elite theory, 6–7, 10, 291
elites
    under Nasir: composition, 15–16; core,
        96; conflict among, 16–17, 31–2;
        middle, 17
    under Sadat, 78–121; class makeup,
        108–9; composition, 91–112; core,
        94–100; de-militarization of, 109–10;
        education of, 100–1; embourgeoisement
        of, 6, 8, 30–1, 108–9, 111, 289–91;
        gubernatorial, 107–8; ideology of,
        112–21; levels of, 91–2; ministerial,
        100–5; occupation, 101–6; party, 105–7;
        politics among, 122–57; presidential
        control of, 86–90; recruitment of, 92–3,
        101–5; rotation of, 88; transformation,
        109–12, 294–5; Wafd and regime,
        210–11
embourgeoisement, *see under* elites
employment, 24, 26, 137–8, 267–9, 284
engineers, 30, 100–3, 108, 110, 150–1
etatism, 14–15, 24, 114–16, 119–20, 133
European, Egyptians of descent, 229–43
    passim

Fahmi, General Muhammed Ali, 74, 130
Fahmi, Ismail, 52, 73
Fa'iq, Muhammed, 41
Farag, Ibrahim, 215
Fawzi, General Muhammed, 41, 44, 126–7
Fawzi, Mahmud, 41–2, 49
food riots of 1977, 71–2, 135, 184; and
    NPUP, 192, 197–8; and urban mass,
    248–9
foreign assistance, 276
foreign debt, 58, 277
foreign exchange, 36, 38, 273, 276, 280
foreign policy
    of Egyptian parties: of Ahrar, 166; of New
        Wafd, 213–14; of NDP, 161; of NPUP,
        190–1; of SLP, 168–9
    Mubarak's, 302
    under Nasir, 21–3, 35–6, 46–7
    under Sadat: attitudes towards, 232–5;
        ideology of, 116–17; in 1971–3, 46–9; in
        1974–6, 54–7; in 1977–81, 65–9;
        outcome, 291–2, 301–2
foreign trade, 273, 275–6
Fouad, Nemat, 167, 184–5
Free Officers, 92–7, 124; under Nasir,
    12–13, 15–17, 31–3, 38; in NPUP,
    188–9; and Sadat, 40–4, 49, 52, 61, 82,
    87–8, 96, 99
functionalism, 4–5, 9–10, 299

Gallal, Sayyid, 168, 200, 248
Gama'at al-Islamiyya, 202–3, 205
Gamasi, General Abd al-Ghani, 72, 74, 88, 99, 129–30
government employees, 28; *see also* white-collar employees
government party 160–65; *see also* ASU, Misr Party, NDP
governors, 107–8
Guma, Sha'rawi 41, 43
al-Gumhuriyya, 189

al-Hakim, Tawfiq, 116
Halpern, Manfred, 4
Hamid, Salah, 135
Hariri, Abd al-Aziz, 175
Hassan, Abd al-Fattah, 214–15
Hassan, Mansur, 94, 99, 106–7, 110, 145, 161, 180
Hatim, Abd al-Qadir, 41, 49, 99
Haykel, Muhammed Hassanein, 41, 49, 52, 60–1, 181
Higazi, Abd al-Aziz, 61, 64, 134
Hilal, Izz ad-Din, 94, 99, 142
housing, 147–8, 270–1; parliamentary committee, 147; Ministry, 148, 271, *see also* construction industry
Hussein, Kemal ad-Din, 16, 32, 52, 173, 175
Hussein, Mahmoud, 3
hydraulic society, 14, 21, 87, 223, 304n1

Ibrahim, Saad ad-Din, 205, 281, 284
ideology: of Islamic opposition, 200–4; under Nasir, 14–15, 31–2; of New Wafd, 211–14; of NDP, 161–2; of NPUP, 190–2; under Sadat, 112–21; 294–5
al-Ikhwan, 21, 50, 76, 201–2, 204–6, 236; *see also* Islamic opposition
illiteracy, 26, 267–8
Iman, Shaikh, 202
IMF, 64, 134–5
imperialism, 3, 11–12, 14, 21, 116, 190, 291
incivisme, 37, 263
industrialists, 148–9
industrial policy, 22–5, 138–42, 148–9, 269–70
industrialization, 22, 26, 34, 278
Industry, Federation of, 145, 148
Industry, Ministry of, 123, 137–41 *passim* 156
inequality, 11, 15, 23, 27–8, 114–15, 204, 238–40, 279–85, 228, 301
Infitah, 57–9, 112, 114–16, 133–57 *passim*, 272–88; conflict over, 61–2, 133–8; and housing and public services, 270–1; and parties, 161–2, 165–6, 168–9, 191,

212–14; and public sector, 138–42, 269–70; and system change, 292, 300–1; views of bourgeoisie, 238–42; *see also* economic policy
inflation, 62, 267, 277, 281
institutionalization, *see under* political institutions
intelligence agencies, 88
interest articulation and aggregation, 124–5, 164–5; *see also* interest groups
interest groups, 20, 144–57; trade unions as, 245–6
investment: authority, 123, 139, 141; law, 133–4, 136, 272; under *Infitah*, 134–6, 272–5, 277–8; under Nasir, 23–6, 34, 36
Islam, 21; establishment, 153–4; and NPUP, 196; and regime, 16, 113–14, 206–8; *see also* Islamic legislation, Islamic opposition, *al-Ikhwan*, religion
Islamic fundamentalism: see *al-Ikhwan*, Islamic opposition, Muslim Brotherhood
Islamic legislation, 114, 153–4, 176 see also *sharia'*
Islamic Liberation Party, 63, 203
Islamic opposition, 29, 63, 71–2, 76–7, 198–208, 225, 227, 244, 249, *see also* *al-Ikhwan*, Islamic Liberation Party
Ismail, Hafiz, 61
Ismail, Marshal Ahmad, 94, 99, 128–9
Ismail, Nabawi, 94, 99, 106, 120
Israel: and 1967 war, 35–7; and 1973 war, 46–8; Egyptian policy toward, 55–7, 65–8; Egyptian views of, 116–17, 151, 168, 190–1, 202, 232–5, 240; normalized relations with 68, 75–6; Sadat trip to, 66–7, 72–3; treaty with, 68, 74–5

journalists, 51, 75, 151, 180–2, 189
judiciary, 20, 183–5

Kamel, Ahmad, 41
Kamil, Muhammed Ibrahim, 74
Khalil, Mustafa, 52, 75, 94, 99, 107, 150, 170
Khuli, Hassan Sabri, 49
Kishk, Shaikh Abd al-Hamid, 202
Kissinger, Henry, 55–6, 80

labor, *see* workers, *also under* syndicates
labor, export of, 276, 279
landowners, 28, 106–7, 109, 142–3, 172, 177, 209–11, 249, 252–3, 281–3
land reclamation, 27, 142–4
land reform, 13, 22, 24, 26–7, 149–50
law: of personal status, 154, 174, 200; rule of, 118, 183–5

Index

lawyers: in elite 101–4, 110; in Wafd, 209–11
Lawyers' Syndicate, 51, 151–2, 219–20
left: attitudes toward, 236; on campus,
243–4; and Sadat, 51–3, 62–3, 71–2,
113; in trade unions, 245–6 *see also*
NPUP
legitimacy: Nasir's 13, 17, 38; Sadat's, 41,
43, 87, 117, 183, 226–7, 244, 255, 299
liberalization: economic, *see Infitah*; political,
117–19, 158, 171, 181, 297–9, *see also*
under political institutions
liberal transformation, 5, 8–9
Libya, 47, 67, 127, 129–30, 203
local government, 251–2

Maghrabi, Abd al-Azim, 193
Mahgub, Rifa'at, 159
Mahmud, Muhammed Hamid, 94, 99,
106–7, 120, 143
managers, 25, 138–42, 269
manbar (manāber, pl) 159–60, 192
manpower policy, 267–9
Marei, Sayyid, 41, 42, 49, 51, 53, 61, 82–3,
88, 97–8, 118, 120, 123, 138, 142–3,
158–9, 169–70, 244
Marxism: popular view of, 194; and Sadat,
113–14; theory and Egypt, 3–4, 9–10,
290–1, 299
Marxists, 19, 187
mass media, 20, 180–2
mass public, 223–56, 263–4
medical care, 272
Medical Syndicate, 151
Mehalla al-Kubra, uprising, 245
Michels, Robert, 6, 291
middle class: counter-elite, 12; under Nasir,
27–8, 30, 108; salaried, 4, 11–12, 16, 23;
see also white-collar employees
military
under Nasir: conflict with civilians, 13, 17;
coup d'etat of, 2, 12; as political cadre,
15–16; professionals, 35, 38;
reconstruction of, 35; rule by, 12–13, 21
under Sadat: anti-Sovietism, 43; de-
politicization of, 45, 87, 109–10,
125–31; de-radicalization of, 125–6,
129–31; in the elite, 99–111 *passim*; and
Muslim opposition, 205; in NPUP,
188–9; politics of, 60–1, 74, 125–31; in
succession struggle, 43–5; unrest in,
51–2, 130; *see also* Free Officers
Misr al-Fatat, 167–70 *passim*
Misr Party, 160; *see also* government
party
Moore, Clement Henry, 5
Mosca, Gaetano, 6

Mubarak, Husni, 61, 75, 88, 98, 129–30,
161; regime of, 302–3
Muhi ad-Din, Fuad, 99, 107
Muhi ad-Din, Khalid, 187, 192, 193, 196
Muhi ad-Din, Zakaria, 52
Murad, Hilmi, 143, 211, 212, 214
Murad, Mustafa Kamil, 133, 136, 165–6
Mursi, Fuad, 133
Muslim Brotherhood, 12–13; *see also*
Ikhwan, Islamic opposition
Mustafa, Shukri, 203, 204

Nasir, Gamal Abdul: attitudes toward, 61–3,
162, 190–1, 212, 236–7; Egypt under,
11–39, 289–91; and Free Officers,
16–17, 31–2; leadership, 13–14, 15,
16–17, 38; and Sadat, 80, 82
Nasirism: 112–13; decline, 29–39; failure to
institutionalize, 19, 33–4, 290; roots of,
11–12
Nasirites: in NPUP, 188–90
Nasr, Shaikh Ashur, 73, 175, 202, 217, 218
Nasser, Mumtaz, 173, 179
Nassif, Muhammed Leithy, 44
National Coalition, 76
National Council on Production, 141, 145
National Democratic Party, 74, 160, 163–4,
173; *see also* government party
national democratic revolution, 3, 190
National Progressive Unionist Party, 71–4
passim, 160, 187–98; and workers, 245
nationalism, 14–15, 81–2, 116
nationalist: foreign policy, 21–2, struggle, 3,
11; victories, 13–14, 21–2
nationalizations, 23–4; of Suez canal, 13, 23
Nazir, Gamal, 140
NDP, *see* National Democratic Party
Neo-Patrimonial, 5, 8, 265, 294, 299
New Wafd, 73–4, 160, 208–20
NPUP, *see* National Progressive Unionist
Party

October Paper, 54, 112, 114, 116
Open Door Policy, *see Infitah*
Osman, Osman Ahmad, 74, 97, 143, 145,
147, 150, 179
oversight, governmental, 177–9

Palestinians, 51, 67, 68, 161, 168, 190, 214,
232–5
parliament, 19, 43, 75, 164, 174–80, 248, 252
participation, political: elite view of, 118–19;
mass propensity for, 53, 223–5, 254–6,
298–9; under Nasir, 16–17, 20–1;
pressures for, 70, 220–2; in succession
crisis, 45–6; under Sadat, 53

320

parties of pressure, 170–1, 220–1
party system; dominant, 170; elite of, 105–7,
    111; pluralization of, 70–1, 158–60,
    170–1, 220–2, 297–8; single, 19–20
patrimonialization, 32–3, 84, 91, 112, 265,
    290, 294, 299 *see also* traditionalization
patron-clientalism, 32, 45, 53, 65, 172–4,
    224, 227, 246, 247, 248, 252, 255
peasants, 11, 249–53; and Free Officers, 12,
    29; and land reform, 27, 149, 177; in
    NDP, 164; in NPUP, 193, 197; in
    Wafd, 217
pharaonic identity, 117, 230–1
planning, 25, 259, 269
PLO, 56–7, 66, 67, *see also* Palestinians
pluralism, 8, 20
pluralization, 27, 37, 70–1, 156–7, 158–60,
    186, 220–2, 249, 297, 302–3, *see also
    under* political institutions
police, 32, 183
political alignments, 28–9, 234–7, 253–4
political arena, 228–56, 297–9
political culture, 223–4, 249
political identity, 230–3
political infrastructure, 158–85; *see also*
    political institutions
political institutions: as elite–mass linkage,
    227, 255–6; in functionalist theory, 4–6;
    liberalization of, 117–19, 158–85, 208,
    220–2, 295–9 (*see also* pluralization);
    under Nasir, 18–21, 32–4; Sadat view
    of, 84–6; semi-institutionalization of,
    44–6, 112, 131, 293, 295–7; in
    succession crisis, 42, 44–6; weakness of,
    287
political rights, *see* rights
Pope Shenouda, 154
populist coalition, 28–9, 34, 37
populist policies, 23, 28, 77, 114–16
post populist regime, 1–9; in Egypt, 289–303
praetorianism, 5, 9, 45, 256
Presidency: conflict over, 41–2, 44–5; control
    over elite, 86–90; and decision-making,
    122–5; and democracy, 85–6;
    legitimation of, 45, 293; and parliament,
    174–6; and parties, 160; powers, 43,
    78–9, 86–90, 293, 295–7, 299; Sadat
    style of, 83–6; traditionalization of, 84,
    90–1; under Nasir, 15
presidential monarchy, 7, 90–1, 296
press, 20, 151, 180–2, *see also*
    journalists
prime ministers, 98–9, 122–3
private sector, 24, 25, 29–30, 104, 107, 111,
    114–15, 119, 144–53, 211, 237–40, 275,
    see also capitalism, bourgeoisie

professionals, 103–8, 150–3, 163, 167, 189,
    209–11, 215–17
public finance, 265–7
public policy, 257–88, 300–2;
    implementation of, 258–65; making of,
    122–5; under Nasir, 21–8, 31–2, 34, 38
public sector, 24–6, 58, 114, 137, 138–42,
    269–70
public services, 270–2
Pyramid Plateau scandal, 73, 90, 147, 157,
    167, 178–9, 184–5

Qaddafi, Muammar, 47, 60, 127, 235–6
Qadi, Mahmud, 134, 217
Qaysuni, Abd al-Munim, 95, 99, 123, 135,
    137

Ratib, Aisha, 154
recruitment, leadership, 16, 17, 19, 92–3,
    100–12, 163, 180
religion: elites, 153–4; and politics, 201,
    207–8; revival of, 199–200; *see also*
    Islam, Islamic opposition
rent control, 24, 148, 270–1
repression, 77, 221–2, 227–8, 255–6
resource crisis, 23, 34–5, *see also* savings gap
revolution: from above, 21–8; of 1952, 1, 12;
    symbolism of, 113
Riad, Mahmud, 41, 49
Rifa'at, Kemal ad-Din, 16, 187–9, 192
Rifaat, Waheed, 215
rights, 20, 84, 118–19, 183–5
routinization, 6, 90, 289, 293
Rushdi, Rashad, 174
Ruz al-Yusuf, 181–2, 189

Sabai, Yusuf, 67, 151
Sabri, Ali, 16, 40–5 *passim*, 123, 126, 132,
    190
al-Sada, Ibrahim, 138, 182
Sadat: attitudes to west, 81–2; background,
    80–3; and bourgeoisie; 229, 236, 240–3;
    concept of democracy, 85–6, 118–19;
    death, 77; and elite, 86–90; goals, 82,
    84–6; and law of personal status, 154;
    legitimacy, 49–50, 54, 62, 63–4, 87,
    226–7; life style, 84; nationalism, 81–2;
    and opposition, 50–3, 60–5, 69–77,
    85–6, 118–19, 169–70, 197–8, 206–7,
    218–20; personality, 80–5; personal
    political orientation, 47, 80–3; relations
    with Nasir, 32, 82–3; socio-economic
    ideas, 59, 72, 113–15; struggle to
    survive, 40–53; style of leadership, 66,
    83–6, 122–25, 259; succession crisis,
    40–6; traditionalism, 80, 84; and US,

68–9; and USSR, 48, 56, 68–9, 80; wife of, 83, 226
Sadiq, Muhammed, 43, 44, 49, 52–3, 127–8
Sa'id, Rifat, 189
Salim, Mamduh, 44, 49, 64, 98, 106, 123, 128, 134, 135, 160
Saudi Arabia, 36, 47, 48, 74, 199, 202, 206
savings gap, 25, 34, 277
Sayyid, Hamdi, 151
Sayyih, Hamid, 99, 123, 135
Serag ad-Din, Fuad, 208–19 *passim*
al-Sha'b, 168, 182
Shabab Muhammed, 203
Shafa'i, Hussein, 41, 49, 52, 61
Shafa'i, Zaki, 134
Shaikh al-Azhar, 72, 153, 227
Shalkani, Ahmad, 136
sharia', 200–7 *passim*
Sharif, Sami, 41, 44
Shazli, Saad ad-Din, 60, 127, 128–9
Shindi, Wagih, 137, 140
Shinnawi, Abd al-Khalek, 150
Shurbagi, Abd al-Fattah, 165
Shukri, Ibrahim, 120, 167–70
Sidqi, Aziz, 41, 49, 52, 53, 98, 120, 123, 133, 158
Sinai I, 54–7
Sinai II, 54–7, 65–6
Sinai occupation, 35, 46–8
Siriya, Salih, 203
SLP, *see* Socialist Labour Party
Socialist Labour Party, 74, 76–7, 146, 160, 167–70
social mobility, 28, 284
Springborg, Robert, 5
students, 51–2, 63, 197, 202–3, 205, 243–4
subsidies, 24, 25, 28, 71, 134–5, 137, 266, 282
succession crisis, 40–6
Suez Canal, 13, 42, 46, 57
Sulaiman, Lufti, 195
syndicates: labor, 20, 245–6; professional, 20, 144, 150–2
Syria, 42, 48, 57, 66–7

Taha, Ahmad, 134, 173, 211
Takfir wal-Hijra, 72, 203, 205
Takla, Layla, 168–9
al-Talia, 181–2, 189

taxation, 24, 28, 115, 138, 140–1, 145–6, 265–7, 272–3, 281, 284
technocrats, 15–16, 43, 131–2
Tawfiq, Hassan, 140
Tilmisani, Omar, 201, 207
trade unionists: in NPUP, 189, 196–7; *see also* syndicates
traditionalization, 5, 6, 7–8, 84, 90–1, 113–14, 294–5, 299, 303
transportation, 271–2
Tuhami, Hassan, 49, 94, 99
Turkish, Egyptians of ancestry, 230–41 *passim*

Ubayd, Fikri, Makram, 99, 104, 106–7, 146, 160–1, 163, 180
ulama, 200, *see also* religion, elite
umdeh(umad), 92, 250, 252
US: and *Infitah*, 60, 135–6; Nasir policy toward, 36, 46; public attitudes toward, 51, 190, 213, 232–5, 240–1; and Sadat, 42, 46–7, 48, 54–7, 65–9, 81–2, 84, 116–17, 127, 128, 130
USSR: and Nasir, 24, 35–6, 46; public attitudes toward, 213, 232–5; and Sadat regime, 42–4, 47–8, 52–3, 56, 68–9, 80, 126–8
Utaifi, Gamal, 179

Vatikiotis, P. J., 4

Wakid, Lutfi, 189
war: of attrition, 35–6, 42; of 1967, 35–6, 199, 291; of 1973, 46, 48, 55, 199
Weber, Max, 6, 8–9, 289–90, 294, 299
welfare, 28, 279–85
West Bank (of Jordan River), 56, 67–8
white-collar employees, 246–7, *see also* government employees, middle-class
workers: and employers, 146–7; industrial, 244–6; under Nasir, 13, 28–9; and NPUP, 189–90, 195–7; strikes, 51, 63, 118; unemployment of, 23, 62, 284; wages of, 27–8, 146–7, 245–6, 283

Yemen, 22, 32
Yunis, Mahmud, 211

Zuhayri, Kamal, 151

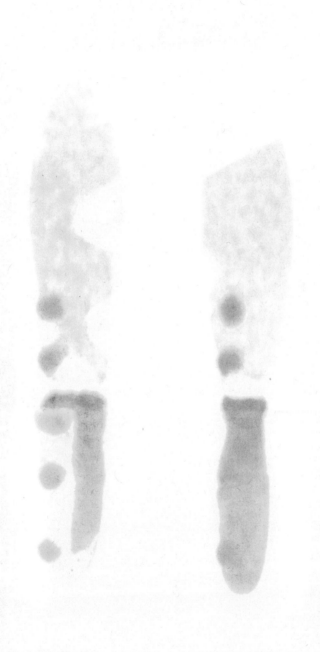

DT 107.85 .H56 1985

Hinnebusch, Raymond A.

Egyptian politics under
  Sadat

Clackamas Community College
Library